econoguide®
'00

Walt Disney World, Universal Studios Florida, SeaWorld,

and other major Central Florida attractions

Corey Sandler

CB
CONTEMPORARY BOOKS

To Willie and Tessa
May their lives always be a magical theme park

Published by Contemporary Books
A division of NTC/Contemporary Publishing Group, Inc.
4255 West Touhy Avenue, Lincolnwood (Chicago), Illinois 60712-1975 U.S.A.
Copyright © 2000 by Word Association, Inc.
Printed in the United States of America
International Standard Serial Number: 1521-9267
International Standard Book Number: 0-8092-2649-9

00 01 02 03 04 05 LB 18 17 16 15 14 13 12 11 10 9 8 7 6 5 4 3 2 1

Contents

(Gallery of Arts and History) / France (*Impressions de France*, Plume et Palette, La Signature, La Maison du Vin, Galerie des Halles) / United Kingdom (The Toy Soldier, Lords and Ladies, Pringle of Scotland, The Queen's Table, The Magic of Wales, The Tea Caddy) / Canada (*O Canada!*, Northwest Mercantile, La Boutique des Provinces)

and Chocolate Shop / Downtown Disney Restaurants (Rainforest Café, Cap'n Jack's Oyster Bar, Wolfgang Puck Express, Ronald's Fun House)

Should You Take Your Kids Out of School? / Disney Seminars and Camps (Wonders of Walt Disney World, Camp Disney, Hands-On Programs for 11- to 15-Year-Olds, Disney Adult Discoveries) / The Disney Institute

Disney Cruise Line / Disneyland Paris / Tokyo Disneyland

The Universal Story / Universal Studios Escape Tickets / A Place to Spend the Night

Back to the Future . . . The Ride / Woody Woodpecker's Kidzone / E.T. Adventure / Animal Actors Stage / Woody Woodpecker's Nuthouse Coaster / Curious George Goes to Town / Fievel's Playland / A Day in the Park with Barney

Earthquake—The Big One / Amity Games / Jaws / Dynamite Nights Stunt Spectacular / Wild, Wild, Wild West Stunt Show

Twister / Kongfrontation / Beetlejuice's Graveyard Revue / The Blues Brothers in Chicago Bound / Arcades

Hercules and Xena: Wizards of the Screen / Hitchcock's 3-D Theatre / The Funtastic World of Hanna-Barbera / The Boneyard / Nickelodeon Studios

Terminator 2 3-D / Lucy: A Tribute / The Gory, Gruesome & Grotesque Horror Make-Up Show / AT&T at the Movies

Acknowledgments

Dozens of hard-working and creative people helped move my words from the keyboard to the place where you read this book now.

Among the many to thank are Editorial Director Linda Gray and Editor Adam Miller of Contemporary Books for working with me as we expand the *Econoguide* series.

Julia Anderson of Contemporary Books managed the editorial and production processes with professionalism and good humor.

Our appreciation extends to Walt Disney World, Universal Studios Florida, Sea World Orlando, and Busch Gardens Tampa for their assistance. Among those who have gone out of their way to help us are Kena Williams Christian, Craig Dezern, Amy Foley, Michael Goldstein, Nick Gollatscheck, Michael McLane, Rhonda Murphy, Ed Stone, and many others.

Thanks to the hotels, restaurants, and attractions who offered discount coupons to our readers.

Special thanks go to Janice Keefe, who worked long and hard in the Word Association offices to collect and process the discount coupons. Thanks to Amy James and Joan Manring Hull, who helped wrestle a million details into proper order. Val Elmore worried my words into grammatical sense.

And finally, thanks to you for buying this book. We all hope you find it of value; please let us know how we can improve the book in future editions. (Please enclose a stamped envelope if you'd like a reply; no phone calls, please.)

You can send me E-mail at: csandler@econoguide.com

And you can check out information about all of the books in the Econoguide travel book series on our Web page, at http://www.econoguide.com

Corey Sandler
Econoguide Travel Books
P.O. Box 2779
Nantucket, MA 02584

Introduction to the 2000 Edition

Orlando began celebrating the new Millennium almost a year ahead of the rest of the world. Then again, they had a lot to cheer about: the greatest amount of change and expansion ever.

In 1999, Universal Studios opened its second theme park, the technological and storytelling marvel known as Islands of Adventure, which includes Spider-Man, the most advanced theme park ride yet, as well as a pair of roller coasters (The Hulk and Dueling Dragons) that seem several steps beyond the laws of physics. Nearby, an exciting new world of entertainment and dining, Universal CityWalk, welcomed its first visitors. At the still-impressive Universal Studios Florida, construction began on a techno-thriller for 2000 based on the quirky "Men in Black" blockbuster movie.

At Walt Disney World, new attractions were popping up in every corner of the sprawling empire: the wild GM Test Track at Epcot, the fabulous Fantasmic show and the thrilling Rock 'n' Roller Coaster at Disney-MGM Studios, new wonders at Disney's Animal Kingdom, and a state-of-the-art return to The Many Adventures of Winnie the Pooh at the Magic Kingdom.

At Downtown Disney, the weird and wonderful Cirque du Soleil took up

The Econoguide Best of Orlando and Central Florida

Walt Disney World	Universal Studios Escape	Other Attractions
Magic Kingdom	Universal Studios Florida	SeaWorld Orlando
Disney's Animal Kingdom	Universal Studios Islands of Adventure	Kennedy Space Center Visitor Center
Epcot Center	Universal CityWalk Orlando	Wet 'n Wild
Disney-MGM Studios		Gatorland
Downtown Disney		Busch Gardens Tampa Bay
Cirque du Soleil		
Blizzard Beach		
Typhoon Lagoon		

residence in a permanent circus tent. Across the way, the Disney Quest indoor virtual reality theme park opened its doors for real.

SeaWorld Orlando broke ground on a wicked roller coaster dubbed Kraken, which it promises will be higher, faster, and longer than anything else in town. At the same time, work also began on a completely new theme park across the road, a first-of-its-kind marine park that will be limited to just a thousand well-heeled visitors per day.

But wait: the Kennedy Space Center Visitor Complex opened an impressive peek into the construction of the International Space Station. In Tampa, Busch Gardens debuted a blast from the past—a double wooden roller coaster. New shopping theme parks opened or expanded on International Drive and nearly everywhere else in town.

And politicans and the business community are making plans for a light rail system to connect the airport to downtown, with a stop at Universal Studios. Oh, and speaking of Universal Studios, they made a purchase of 2,000 acres on the other side of I-4, which would allow them to put a few more theme parks and other entertainments there. That's no problem for Disney, which has room for a few more parks within the boundaries of Walt Disney World.

How in the world can you keep track of everything going on in Central Florida? Here's a humble suggestion: Welcome to the 2000 edition of *Econoguide '00: Walt Disney World, Universal Studios Florida, SeaWorld, and Other Major Central Florida Attractions.*

An Insider's Guide

I'm a huge fan of Orlando. I've been there enough times that I'm on a first-name basis with flight attendants, car rental clerks, and hotel check-in staff. And I swear that the ghoul in charge of the Tower of Terror saves me the front row in the soon-to-be-out-of-control elevator.

I don't know of many other places with so much to do, so many interesting places to visit . . . and so many ways to spend hard-earned dollars.

My goal in the Econoguide series is to help you get the most for your money and make the best use of your time. This is not a guide for cheapskates; you will, though, learn how to travel well—better than the folks in front and behind you in line. (Oh, and I'll offer some tips on how to reduce the chances of finding long lines.)

I've gone back and walked every mile of every major park and attraction and looked everywhere for changes and new features.

And, of course, you'll also find a new selection of money-saving coupons. Pardon me for saying so, but buying this book is a no-brainer: you'll save many times the cover price by using just a few of the coupons, including ticket discounts at Universal Studios, travel agencies, hotels, and much more.

About Walt Disney World and Orlando

Walt Disney World is a magical kingdom of fantastic delights for children of all ages; I recommend it highly.

I also love Universal Studios Florida, SeaWorld, and dozens of other excellent attractions and recreational opportunities in the Orlando and Central Florida region.

But let's get something straight here: as wonderful an entertainment opportunity as they are, Walt Disney World, Universal Studios Escape, SeaWorld, and all the rest are basically gigantic vacuum cleaners aimed at your wallet.

Disney's greatest accomplishment in Orlando was the creation of an entire world of entertainment: four theme parks, three water parks, half a dozen golf courses, a baseball stadium, a world-class automobile racetrack, a collection of dozens of hotels, hundreds of restaurants, and thousands of little diversions from horseback riding to boating to bicycling to tennis to cooking lessons. There's a whole island of restaurants and nightclubs, a gigantic movie theater complex, and a permanent circus. For many people, a week's visit to Orlando could be spent entirely within the boundaries of the Walt Disney World resort.

As 1999 comes to an end, though, Disney has company for the first time. As I've noted, Universal Studios now has two parks on its property, the Wet and Wild water park nearby, a huge rock and roll club, its own island of restaurants and clubs, and the first of five planned hotel complexes.

Not Too Cute

After visits that have totaled up to months at Walt Disney World, Disneyland, Disneyland Paris, and Tokyo Disneyland, I've come up with my All-Purpose Disney Attraction Classification Guide. I've decided that Disney attractions can be divided into "Disney Cute," "Disney Smart," and "Disney Wow."

Disney Cute is Mickey Mouse, Winnie the Pooh, Aladdin, It's a Small World, Tiki Birds, Snow White, Cinderella, and Dumbo. That's where they set the hook with young children and their parents.

Disney Smart is Disney's Animal Kingdom, Epcot's Future World, Epcot's World Showcase, Epcot's Innoventions, the Hall of Presidents, the Carousel of Progress, and the Special Effects and Production Tour. Here's where Disney magic helps us learn.

Disney Wow is GM Test Track, Rock 'n' Roller Coaster, Countdown to Extinction, Space Mountain, Twilight Zone Tower of Terror, Star Tours, The Great Movie Ride, Thunder Mountain Railroad, and Splash Mountain. These are the things that make us say, "Ooh."

One of the reasons for Disney's success is that they have learned to mix Cute, Smart, and Wow. It's the reason children come back as adolescents and then as parents; it's the reason adults can have a good time accompanying their youngsters.

Add to this Disney's impressive devotion to expanding its attraction to adults with things such as water parks, golf courses, tennis courts, nightclubs, and spectacularly sybaritic hotels, and it's only just begun: Disney's Wide World of Sports, the spring training home of the Atlanta Braves, the national headquarters of the Amateur Athletic Union, and much more. Then there is the Disney Institute, a graduate course in fun. Call those "Disney for Adults,"

Theme Park Top 10. According to the trade magazine "Amusement Business," Walt Disney World included four of the top six theme parks in North America in 1998. Universal Studios Florida, SeaWorld Florida, and Busch Gardens Tampa are also in the Top 10. Here are the magazine's estimates:
1. The Magic Kingdom at Walt Disney World, 15.6 million visitors.
2. Disneyland, Anaheim, Calif., 13.7 million.
3. Epcot at Walt Disney World, 10.6 million.
4. Disney-MGM Studios at Walt Disney World, 9.5 million.
5. Universal Studios Florida, 8.9 million.
6. Disney's Animal Kingdom at Walt Disney World, 6 million.
7. Universal Studios Hollywood, 5.1 million.
8. SeaWorld Florida, 4.9 million.
9. Busch Gardens Tampa, 4.2 million.
10. SeaWorld California, 3.7 million.

and they will be the reason Disney will continue to be a lure for us all once we are too jaded for Cute, too educated for Smart, and (alas) too old for Wow.

Why This Book?

Now, don't get me wrong: Walt Disney World and Universal Studios Escape may be the best-designed, best-run and most overall satisfying tourist attractions on this planet. But you also have the right to spend your time and money as carefully as possible. That's what this book is all about.

This book is designed to help you get the very most from your time and money as you travel to Orlando and visit the parks and myriad other attractions there.

About Independence

That other book about Walt Disney World, the one with "The Official Guide" stamped on its cover, is an impressive collection of material. But, in my humble opinion, it suffers from a fatal closeness to its subject: it is prepared with the Walt Disney Company (and published by a Disney company). I suspect that explains why it finds very little that is anything less than wonderful within the boundaries of Walt Disney World, and why it almost ignores the world outside.

In that official book, there is hardly a mention of Universal Studios Escape, SeaWorld, or Busch Gardens, for example. This is not because they are unworthy of mention, or that visitors to Walt Disney World don't visit those attractions and others. The reason for their absence is the fact that the Walt Disney Company does not profit from them.

So, let me state again our independence: the author and publisher of this book have no connection with Walt Disney World, Universal Studios Escape, SeaWorld, Busch Gardens, or any of the other attractions written about here. Similarly, there is no financial interest in any of the discount coupons published within the book.

Our profit comes from you, the readers of this book, and it is you we hope to serve as best we can.

About the Author

Corey Sandler is a former newsman and editor for the Associated Press, Gannett Newspapers, IDG, and Ziff-Davis Publishing. He has written more than 125 books on travel, video game, and computer topics; his titles have been translated into French, Spanish, German, Italian, Portuguese, Polish, and Chinese. When he's not traveling, he lives with his wife and two children on Nantucket island, 30 miles off the coast of Massachusetts.

We hope you'll look for these other *Econoguide* titles by Corey Sandler, also from Contemporary Books: *Econoguide '00: Las Vegas, Reno, Laughlin, Lake Tahoe*; *Econoguide '00: Disneyland, Universal Studios Hollywood, and Other Major Southern California Attractions*; *Econoguide '00: Washington D.C., Williamsburg, Busch Gardens, Richmond, and Other Area Attractions*; *Econoguide '00: London: with Day Trips to Bath, Brighton, Oxford, Windsor, and Other Popular Destinations*; *Econoguide '99–00: Golf Resorts and Courses USA*; *Econoguide '99–00: Ski and Snowboard America: the Best Resorts in the United States and Canada*; and *Econoguide '99–'00: Cruises: Cruising the Caribbean, Mexico, Hawaii, New England, and Alaska*.

Part I
On the Road to Orlando

Chapter 1
A Central Florida Vacation Calendar

Here are two hypothetical days spent on a trip to Orlando:

July 4. It wasn't exactly the flight you wanted. However, you're grateful for the privilege of forking over $840 for a coach seat in the jammed cabin of the jet. All of the rooms inside the park—at $240 per night—are sold out, but you were lucky enough to pay just $150 for a very ordinary hotel room that is a 20-minute bumper-to-bumper drive from the parking lots.

According to the tram driver, you are parked near the Magic Kingdom, although you're not certain you're in the same county. When you get to the ticket booths, there's a 30-minute wait just to get on the monorail to the entrance. Once inside, you sprint to Tomorrowland to find that the line for Space Mountain includes what seems to be the occupants of every car you passed on the long, long ride through the gigantic parking lot.

Or perhaps you've set as your goal the thrilling new GM Test Track at Epcot. In your mind's eye you imagine zipping around the 50-degree curves at 65 mph; when you get there you find a traffic jam with people in line all the way back to the airport.

And you'd better plan on showing up for lunch at 10:45 A.M. and dinner at 4:30 P.M. if you hope to find a table at the lowliest overpriced burger stop. But there are always the cooling thrills at Blizzard Beach, right? True, but the line for Florida's only ski resort stretches back to Philadelphia.

March 20. It seems like it's just your family and a crew of flight attendants, stretched out at 30,000 feet. Even nicer, you were able to grab a deep-discount excursion fare ticket for $298. Your hotel room outside the parks cost $29.95, and the road to the kingdom is empty.

The monorail stands empty and waiting for you at the transportation center. Your leisurely walk to Space Mountain puts you into a 10-minute queue; later in the day you drop into a rocket car without breaking stride. At Epcot, your private vehicle waits your arrival at the GM Test Track.

Take your pick of restaurants, and feel free to take a break in the afternoon

1

and run over to Typhoon Lagoon; temperatures often reach 80 degrees, and the lagoon is like the beach on a semi-private tropical island.

Do I have to point out which trip is likely to be more enjoyable?

Our Guiding Rule

The basic *Econoguide* strategy to getting the most out of your trip is this: *Go when most people don't; stay home when everyone else is standing in line.*

Specifically, we suggest you try to come to Florida when school is in session and in the weeks between holidays: between Labor Day and Thanksgiving, between Thanksgiving and Christmas, between New Year's Day and Presidents' Week, between Presidents' Week and Spring Break/Easter, between Easter and Memorial Day.

We're not just talking about the crowds at Walt Disney World, Universal Studios Escape, SeaWorld, and elsewhere in Central Florida. We're also talking about the availability of discount airline tickets, off-season motel rates, and restaurant specials.

You'll find lower prices when business is needed, not when the "No Vacancy" lamp is lit. The best deals can be found in low-season or what travel agents call the shoulder-season, midway between the slowest and busiest times.

This doesn't mean you can't have a good time if your schedule (or your children's) requires you to visit at high-season. We'll show you ways to save money and time, any time of the year.

A Central Florida Vacation Calendar

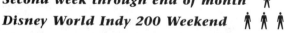

KEY: 🯇 = Semi-private   🯇 🯇 = Moderate crowds

🯇 🯇 🯇 = Heavy crowds   🯇 🯇 🯇 🯇 = Elbow-to-elbow

January

New Year's Day 🯇 🯇 🯇

Second week through end of month 🯇

Disney World Indy 200 Weekend 🯇 🯇 🯇

(Semi-private, except for Indy 200 Weekend.
Warmer than most anywhere else.
Room rates at low-season level, except during special events.)

New Year's Day and a few days afterward are the crowded aftermath of the Christmas rush. But when the kids go back to school and most of the adults return to work after the Christmas–New Year's holiday, attendance drops off sharply. The second week of January through the first week of February is usually the second least crowded period of the year, with attendance averaging about 25,000 visitors per day at Walt Disney World. Watch out, though, for the late-January weekend when an Indy 200 race is held at the track near the Magic Kingdom; the race draws as many as 50,000 visitors and many of them spill over to the parks after the race. The Walt Disney World Marathon is held in mid-January, drawing more than 10,000 participants and their supporters.

During this time. the parks close early and do not offer nighttime parades or fireworks, but you'll be able to walk right onto most major rides and attractions; room rates are at their lowest level.

February

First ten days 👤 👤

(Moderate crowds. Warm but not hot.
Room rates at shoulder-season level.)
Early February is a period of average attendance, reaching 30,000 to 35,000 visitors daily. The parks generally close early except for weekends, and there are no nighttime parades or fireworks.

February

Presidents' week holiday period 👤 👤 👤

Late February 👤 👤

(Heavy crowds for holiday week. Room rates at high-season level.)
Presidents' Week (celebrated in many school districts in and around the period from February 12 to February 22) is a time of fairly heavy attendance, up to about 45,000 visitors daily. Watch out for Race Week in Daytona, too. The parks are open late, with nightly parades and fireworks.

March

Entire month 👤 👤

(Back to moderate attendance. Thermometer nudges into the 80s.
Room rates at shoulder-season level.)
Attendance falls off to moderate from the end of February through the first week of April, averaging about 35,000 visitors. There are days in early March when you will have the parks to yourself, but at other times you will join thousands of college kids on early Spring Break or baseball fans drawn south for Spring Training. Nevertheless, this is not a bad time to come to Florida—with luck you will run into 80-degree water park weather. The parks generally close early and there are no nighttime parades or fireworks in the first half of the month; during Spring Break the parks are open later.

April

Second and third week 👤 👤 👤

(The Easter Parade can get pretty thick. Consistent
80-degree weather. Room rates at high-season.)
The second and third weeks of April are among the most crowded times of

the year, as Easter visitors and Spring Break students clog the turnstiles at rates of up to 60,000 per day. The parks are open late, with parades and fireworks.

First and fourth week 🚶 🚶

(A lovely time, with moderate attendance and room rates at shoulder- or creeping into high-season rates.)

Sneak in before or after the Spring Break rush. The parks generally close early, and there are no nighttime parades or fireworks.

May

Entire month 🚶 🚶

(Moderate attendance, swimming weather, and shoulder-season rates.)

Another relatively quiet period, from the end of April through the first week of June. Expect average attendance of 30,000 to 35,000 per day. The parks generally close early, and there are no nighttime parades or fireworks.

June to August

The crazy days of summer 🚶 🚶 🚶

(Lots and lots of company. Hot sun and high-season rates.)

Just after Memorial Day the throngs of people come. And stay. Crowds of about 60,000 per day can be expected from the first week of June through the third week of August. Room rates are at high-season for the entire summer. Temperatures average in the 90s; and you can expect a few heavy downpours or steady rains. Parks are open late, with nighttime parades and fireworks scheduled.

And just to make things even more crowded, sometimes it seems as if half of Brazil comes north for warm weather in August.

September to Mid-November

The post-summer doldrums 🚶

(Theme park heaven: no lines, no crowds, low, low rates. Watch out for Golf Classic weekend, though. Temperatures still high.)

Where have all the tourists gone? On the day after Labor Day, the turnstiles slow to a crawl, averaging about 20,000 visitors per day. Room rates reach bottom, too. The weather is quite good, although the occasional tropical storm or hurricane can dampen a few days here and there. The parks generally close at 6 P.M. or 7 P.M., but the lack of lines should allow you to see everything you want. There are some late hours on weekends, with parades or fireworks.

In recent years, the Golf Classic has occupied a weekend in late October, bringing thousands of PGA fans to hotels and the parks.

November

Thanksgiving for what? 🚶 🚶 🚶

(Merchants give thanks for the huge crowds at Thanksgiving. Rates at high-season level.)

The one-week period around Thanksgiving brings a brief return to "No Vacancy" at motels and in attraction lines. Average attendance is about 55,000 visitors. The parks generally close early, except for the holiday week and weekends surrounding it.

December

First through third weeks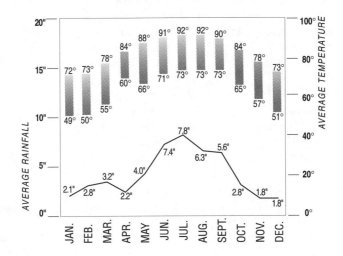

(Mickey can get lonely at times like these, and hotels will almost pay you to come and stay.)

This is it: the secret season. From after Thanksgiving until the day Christmas vacation starts is the quietest time of the year for a visit. Attendance levels average 15,000 to 20,000 per day, and lines are rare. Room rates are rock-bottom, too. The parks generally close early, and there are no nighttime parades or fireworks, except for weekends.

Christmas Holiday

(Your sisters and cousins and aunts will all be in line, in front of you. You may need a loan for the super-high-season room rates.)

The Christmas–New Year's holiday is the most crowded, least time-efficient time to visit Central Florida. You'll be shoulder to shoulder with an average of 75,000 to 80,000 other visitors each day at Walt Disney World, with large crowds and long lines at Universal Studios, SeaWorld, and other area attractions. Parks are open late, with nighttime parades and fireworks.

The crowds can become so large that some of the parks actually close the gates by mid-morning. Don't feel too bad if you're shut out. It could be worse: you could be inside. In line.

You cannot count on temperatures warm enough for swimming, either. Room rates are at their highest levels, too. It's a festive, happy time, but

CENTRAL FLORIDA WEATHER AVERAGES

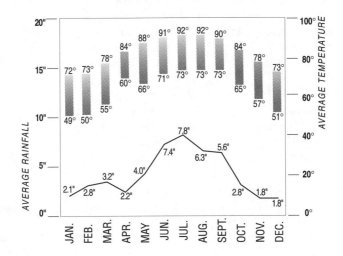

SPECIAL EVENTS
Late January–Early Late January. Disney World Indy 200.
February. Chinese New Year at Epcot.
Mid-February. Pleasure Island Mardi Gras.
Mid-March. St. Patrick's Day Celebration at Pleasure Island.
Walt Disney World Easter Parade. Magic Kingdom.
Spring (Mid-April through early June). Epcot International Flower & Garden Festival.
Memorial Day Weekend. Special late-night entertainment and late hours at all parks.
Late October. Walt Disney World Golf Classic.

frankly, we'd rather be alone or close to it. If you must go, be sure to arrive at the park early and follow the Power Trip plan for your best chance.

Holiday Special Events

The "Walt Disney World Happy Easter Parade," televised nationally, marches down Main Street on Easter Sunday; check with Disney reservations in advance to see if the parade may be videotaped a few days ahead of Easter itself; it usually is.

The annual Epcot International Flower & Garden Festival takes place on the grounds of the park from mid-April through June 1.

Just how powerful is Disney? How's this: The Magic Kingdom predicts a 100 percent chance of snow flurries in balmy central Florida for Mickey's Very Merry Christmas Party each year.

Of course, this is Disney and it's not really snow. But then again, that's not really a mouse wearing those size 48 shoes, either. (Sorry to disillusion you.) Instead, there's a phalanx of artificial snow machines set up behind Main Street U.S.A. to blanket the crowds at the end of the nightly "Mickey's Very Merry Christmas Parade." And there are also special stage shows and holiday fireworks.

The Christmas party requires a separate admission ticket; in recent years the park was cleared at the end of each day and then reopened at 8 P.M., remaining open until 1 A.M. Certain length-of-stay ticket packages included the extra night's admission.

At the Disney-MGM Studios in recent years, the park has looked like a hardware store gone crazy with the "Osborne Family Light Extravaganza." And Epcot celebrates "Holidays Around the World" and World Showcase pavillions.

At Universal Studios Florida, big annual events include a monstrous Halloween party and an extended Mardi Gras celebration in late winter.

The Best Day to Go to the Park

When Mommy, Daddy, Willie, and Tessa arrive in Orlando on Sunday (the most common arrival date) for a week's visit (the most common length of vacation) the first place they will go is the Magic Kingdom on Monday. Epcot comes next, then the Disney-MGM Studios. The remainder of the week is usually given over to other area parks and attractions.

But, we feel the best plan for your visit is to adopt what we call a Contrarian View. In other words, go against the common logic that says, "We came here for the Magic Kingdom and that's where we'll go first."

Disney's Animal Kingdom, which opened in the spring of 1998, will be the first stop for many visitors because it is the newest park at Walt Disney World.

Analysts expect Disney's Animal Kingdom will draw somewhere in the neighborhood of 20,000 visitors per day at slow times to 40,000 in peak periods, for an annual attendance of about 11 million. These numbers are similar to those of Epcot, which is in second place behind the Magic Kingdom among theme parks at Walt Disney World.

Universal's Islands of Adventure will be a major draw for years to come; you can expect long lines there during holiday periods and much of the rest of the year as well. The good news is that the new park may reduce the crowds a bit at the neighboring Universal Studios Florida.

	GO	DON'T GO
Magic Kingdom	Sunday	Monday
	Thursday	Tuesday
	Friday	Wednesday
		Saturday
Disney's Animal Kingdom	Sunday	Monday
	Thursday	Tuesday
	Friday	Wednesday
		Saturday
Epcot	Sunday	Tuesday
	Monday	Wednesday
	Thursday	Saturday
	Friday	
Disney-MGM Studios	Sunday	Tuesday
	Monday	Wednesday
	Friday	Thursday
	Saturday	
Universal Studios Florida, Universal Studios Islands of Adventure and other area attractions	Sunday	Wednesday
	Monday	Thursday
	Tuesday	Saturday
	Friday	

Herewith is one schedule you might want to consider if you are visiting Central Florida during one of the busy times of the year. It starts, you might note, with arrival on Saturday, which is a bit against the tide; if you get to Orlando early enough you may be able to visit a water park or other attraction (other than the Magic Kingdom) that night.

By the way, it should be obvious that seven days is not enough time to come close to sampling all that Orlando and Central Florida has to offer; if time and money is no object, we'd suggest a two-week visit with about half of the time devoted to Disney World and the other days for Universal Studios, SeaWorld, Busch Gardens, and all of the other attractions of the area.

The Econoguide Contrarian Schedule

SATURDAY
Arrive in Orlando. Visit water
parks, smaller attractions, dinner
theaters, Pleasure Island, or
Church Street Station

SUNDAY
Magic Kingdom, Animal Kingdom,
Disney-MGM Studios,
Universal Studios Florida, or
Universal's Islands of Adventures

MONDAY
Universal's Islands of Adventure
or Disney-MGM Studios

TUESDAY
SeaWorld, beach, golf, water parks, or
other attractions

WEDNESDAY
Busch Gardens, Space Center,
Cypress Gardens, or
Splendid China

THURSDAY
Epcot Center

FRIDAY
Magic Kingdom,
Animal Kingdom

SATURDAY
A second chance at the park of
your choice (avoid Magic Kingdom and
Animal Kingdom)

Come the Millennium

Disney is a company that certainly knows how to party—witness the 25th
anniversary celebration at the Magic Kingdom that began in 1996 and lasted

FLORIDA HIGHWAYS

more than a year, featuring a makeover of Cinderella's Castle as a giant birthday cake.

But if you thought that was a blowout, wait until the millennium. Disney insiders say there will be a coast-to-coast celebration that will begin in Orlando in 1999 and run straight through the opening in early 2001 of Disney's California Adventure, a new theme park at Disneyland in Anaheim.

In Florida, Epcot will be the center of the celebration, with a redecoration of Spaceship Earth, a new pavillion saluting cultures and peoples around the world, a fantastic new daily procession, and a nightly sound, light, and fireworks extravaganza.

And, of course, Universal Studios Escape will not let the millennium pass unnoticed. Expect special events

A sideways glance from The Hulk Coaster
© *1999 Universal Studios Escape*

centering on the new Islands of Adventure park, Universal CityWalk, and the original Universal Studios Florida.

In California, Disney's California Adventure at Disneyland is officially expected to open in early to mid-2001. For more details about the new park, see *Econoguide '00: Disneyland, Universal Studios Hollywood and other major Southern California Attractions*, available at major bookstores.

By the way, your chances of getting a room at Walt Disney World around December 31, 1999, are about as good as Minnie winning a speed-typing contest (check out those fingers!). Rooms at the park have been sold out since 1997. But that doesn't mean you can't find a room somewhere in Orlando or Kissimmee or thereabouts—expect to pay a premium, though, and you can depend upon lots of company at the parks.

MAJOR ROADS NEAR WALT DISNEY WORLD

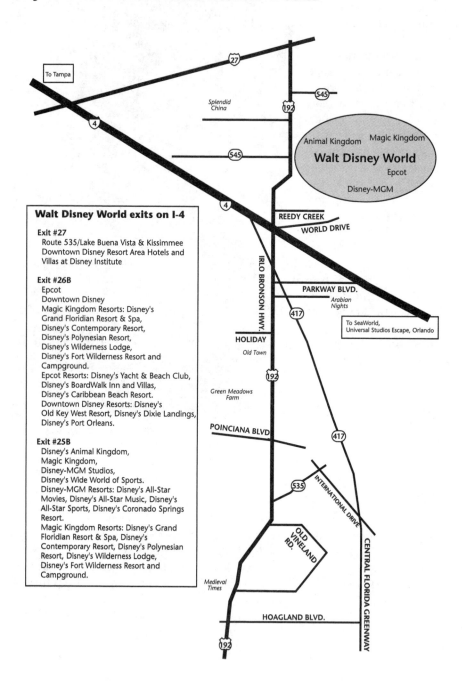

To Tampa

27

Splendid China

545

192

Walt Disney World
Animal Kingdom   Magic Kingdom
Epcot
Disney-MGM

4

545

4

REEDY CREEK
WORLD DRIVE

IRLO BRONSON HWY.

Walt Disney World exits on I-4

Exit #27
Route 535/Lake Buena Vista & Kissimmee
Downtown Disney Resort Area Hotels and
Villas at Disney Institute

Exit #26B
Epcot
Downtown Disney
Magic Kingdom Resorts: Disney's
Grand Floridian Resort & Spa,
Disney's Contemporary Resort,
Disney's Polynesian Resort,
Disney's Wilderness Lodge,
Disney's Fort Wilderness Resort and
Campground.
Epcot Resorts: Disney's Yacht & Beach Club,
Disney's BoardWalk Inn and Villas,
Disney's Caribbean Beach Resort.
Downtown Disney Resorts: Disney's
Old Key West Resort, Disney's Dixie Landings,
Disney's Port Orleans.

Exit #25B
Disney's Animal Kingdom,
Magic Kingdom,
Disney-MGM Studios,
Disney's Wide World of Sports.
Disney-MGM Resorts: Disney's All-Star
Movies, Disney's All-Star Music, Disney's
All-Star Sports, Disney's Coronado Springs
Resort.
Magic Kingdom Resorts: Disney's Grand
Floridian Resort & Spa, Disney's
Contemporary Resort, Disney's Polynesian
Resort, Disney's Wilderness Lodge,
Disney's Fort Wilderness Resort and
Campground.

PARKWAY BLVD.
Arabian Nights

417

To SeaWorld,
Universal Studios Escape, Orlando

HOLIDAY
Old Town

192

Green Meadows Farm

POINCIANA BLVD

417

INTERNATIONAL DRIVE

535

OLD VINELAND RD.

CENTRAL FLORIDA GREENWAY

Medieval Times

HOAGLAND BLVD.

192

Chapter 2
Planes, Trains, and Automobiles

The way I figure it, one major airline is pretty much like any other. Sure, one company may offer a larger plastic bag of peanuts while the other promises its flight attendants have more accommodating smiles. Me, I'm much more interested in other things:

1. Safety
2. The most convenient schedule
3. The lowest price

Sometimes I'm willing to trade price for convenience, but I'll never risk my neck for a few dollars.

That doesn't mean I don't try my darnedest to get the very best price on airline tickets. I watch the newspapers for seasonal sales and price wars, clip coupons from the usual and not-so-usual sources, consult the burgeoning world of Internet travel agencies, and happily play one airline against the other.

Alice in Airlineland

There are three golden rules to saving hundreds of dollars on travel: be flexible, be flexible, and be flexible.

• Be flexible about when you choose to travel. Go during the off-season or low-season when airfares, hotel rooms, and other attractions offer substantial discounts.

• Be flexible about the day of the week you travel. In many cases, you can save hundreds of dollars by changing your departure date one or two days in either direction. Ask your travel agent or airline reservationist for current fare rules and restrictions.

The lightest air travel days are generally midweek, Saturday afternoons, and Sunday mornings. The busiest days are Sunday evenings, Monday mornings, and Friday afternoons and evenings.

In general, you will receive the lowest possible fare if you include a Saturday in your trip, buying what is called an *excursion fare*. Airlines use this as a

Checking in again.
Having a boarding pass
issued by a travel agent
is not the same as
checking in at the
airport; you'll still need
to show your ticket at
the counter so that the
agent knows you're
there.

way to exclude business travelers from the cheapest fares, assuming that businesspeople will want to be home by Friday night.

• Be flexible on the hour of your departure. There is generally lower demand—and, therefore, lower prices—for flights that leave in the middle of the day or very late at night.

• Be flexible on the route you will take, or your willingness to put up with a change of plane or stopover. Once again, you are putting the law of supply and demand in your favor. A direct flight from Philadelphia to Orlando for a family of four may cost hundreds more than a flight from Philadelphia that includes a change of planes in Raleigh-Durham or Atlanta before proceeding to Orlando.

Don't overlook the possibility of flying out of a different airport, either. For example, metropolitan New Yorkers can find domestic flights from La Guardia, Newark, or White Plains. Suburbanites of Boston might want to consider flights from Worcester or Providence as possibly cheaper alternatives to Logan Airport. In the Los Angeles area there are planes going in and out of LAX, Orange County, Burbank, and Palm Springs, to name a few airports. Look for airports where there is greater competition: try Birmingham instead of Atlanta, or Louisville instead of Cincinnati, for example.

• Plan way ahead of time and purchase the most deeply discounted advance tickets, which usually are noncancelable. Most carriers limit the number of discount tickets on any particular flight; although there may be plenty of seats left on the day you want to travel, they may be offered at higher rates.

In a significant change during the past few years, most airlines have modified "nonrefundable" fares to become "noncancelable." What this means is that if your plans change or you are forced to cancel your trip, your tickets retain their value and can be applied against another trip, usually for a fee of about $50 to $75 per ticket.

• Conversely, you can take a big chance and wait for the last possible moment, keeping in contact with charter tour operators and accepting a bargain price on a "leftover seat" and hotel reservation. You *may* also find that some airlines will reduce the prices on leftover seats within a few weeks of departure date; don't be afraid to check regularly with the airline, or ask your travel agent to do it for you. Some travel agencies have automated computer programs that keep a constant electronic eagle eye on available seats and fares.

• Take advantage of special discount programs such as senior citizens' clubs, military discounts, or offerings from organizations to which you may belong. If you are in the over-60 category, you may not even have to belong to a group such as AARP; simply ask the airline reservationist if there is a discount available. You may have to prove your age when you pick up your ticket or boarding pass.

• It may even make a difference what day of the week you buy your tickets. In recent years, airlines have tested out higher fares over the relatively quiet weekends. They're looking to see if their competitors will match their higher rates; if the other carriers don't bite, the fares often float back down by Monday morning. Shop during the week.

Other Money-Saving Strategies

Airlines are forever weeping and gnashing their teeth about huge losses due to cutthroat competition. And then they regularly turn around and drop their prices radically with major sales.

Double indemnity. Your homeowner's or renter's insurance policy may include coverage for theft of your possessions while you travel, making it unnecessary to purchase a special policy. Check with your insurance agent.

I don't waste time worrying about the bottom line of the airlines; it's my own wallet I want to keep full. Therefore, the savvy traveler keeps an eye out for airline fare wars all the time. Read the ads in daily newspapers and keep an ear open to news broadcasts that cover the outbreak of price drops. If you have a good relationship with a travel agent, you can ask to be notified of any fare sales.

The most common times for airfare wars are in the weeks leading up to the quietest seasons for carriers, including the periods from mid-May to mid-June (except the Memorial Day weekend), between Labor Day and Thanksgiving, and again in the winter, with the exception of Christmas, New Year's, and Presidents' Day holiday periods.

Don't be afraid to ask for a refund on previously purchased tickets if fares go down for the period of your travel. The airline may refund the difference, or you may be able to reticket your itinerary at the new fare, paying a $50 penalty for cashing in the old tickets. Be persistent—if the difference in fare is significant, it may be worthwhile making a visit to the airport to meet with a supervisor at the ticket counter.

Study the fine print on discount coupons distributed directly by the airlines, or through third parties such as supermarkets, catalog companies, and direct marketers. A typical coupon offers $50 to $100 off full fare or certain types of discount fares. It has been my experience that these coupons are often less valuable than they seem. Read the fine print carefully, and be sure to ask the reservationist if the price quoted with the coupon is higher than another fare for which you qualify.

If you are traveling to a convention, you may be able to get in on an airline discount negotiated by the group. In fact, you may not need any affiliation at all with a convention group to take advantage of special rates, if offered. All the airline will ask is the name or number of the discount plan for the convention; the reservationist is almost certainly not going to ask to see your union card or funny hat. Ask about discounts at convention and visitors bureaus.

Finding a bucket shop. Look for ads for ticket brokers and bucket shops in places such as the classified ads in *USA Today*, the "Mart" section of the *Wall Street Journal* or in specialty magazines such as *Frequent Flyer*.

Consider doing business with discounters, known in the industry as consolidators or, less flatteringly, as "bucket shops." Look for their ads in the classified sections of many Sunday newspaper travel sections. These companies buy the airlines' slow-to-sell tickets in volume and resell them to consumers at rock-bottom prices.

Some travel agencies can also offer you consolidator tickets. Just be sure to weigh the savings on the ticket price against any restrictions attached to the tickets; for example, they may not be changeable, and they usually do not accrue frequent flyer mileage.

Beating the Airlines at Their Own Game

As far as I am concerned, the airlines deserve all the headaches we travelers can give them because of the illogical pricing schemes they throw at us—things such as a fare of $350 to fly 90 miles between two cities where they hold a monopoly, and $198 bargain fares to travel 3,000 miles across the nation. Or round-trip fares of $300 if you leave on a Thursday and return on a Monday versus $1,200 if you leave on a Monday and return the next Thursday.

A creative traveler can find ways to work around most of these roadblocks. Nothing I'm going to suggest here is against the law; some of the tips, though, are against the rules of some airlines. Here are a couple of strategies:

- *Nested tickets*. This scheme generally works in either of two situations— where regular fares are more than twice as high as excursion fares that include a Saturday night stay over, or in situations where you plan to fly between two locations twice in less than a year.

  Let's say you want to fly from Boston to Orlando. Buy two sets of tickets in your name, one from Boston to Orlando and back to Boston. This set has the return date for when you want to come back from your second trip. The other set of tickets would be from Orlando to Boston and back to Orlando; this time making the first leg of the ticket for the date you want to come back from the first trip, and the second leg of the trip the date you want to depart for the second trip.

  If this sounds complicated, that's because it is. It will be your responsibility to keep your tickets straight when traveling.

  Several major airlines announced they would crack down on such practices by searching their computer databases for multiple reservations. And travel agencies have been threatened with loss of ticketing privileges for assisting their clients in this way.

  But that doesn't mean you can't buy such tickets. Check with a travel agent for advice. One solution: buy one set of tickets on one airline and the other set on another carrier.

- *Split tickets*. Fare wars sometimes result in supercheap fares through a connecting city. For example, an airline seeking to boost traffic through a hub in Atlanta might set up a situation in which it is less expensive to get from Chicago to Orlando by buying a round-trip ticket from Chicago to Atlanta, and then a separate round-trip ticket from Atlanta to Orlando.

  Be sure to book a schedule that allows enough time between flights; if you miss your connection you could end up losing time and money.

Standing Up for Standing By

One of the little-known secrets of air travel on most airlines and most types of tickets is the fact that travelers who have valid tickets are allowed to stand by for flights other than the ones for which they have reservations on the same day of travel; if there are empty seats on the flight, standby ticket holders are permitted to board.

Here's what I do know: if I cannot get the exact flight I want for a trip, I make the closest acceptable reservations available and then show up early at the airport and head for the check-in counter for the flight I really want to take. Unless you are seeking to travel during an impossibly overbooked holiday period or arrive on a bad weather day when flights have been canceled, your chances of successfully standing by for a flight are usually pretty good.

Call the airline the day before the flight and check on the availability of seats for the flight you want to try for.

Overbooking

Overbooking is a polite industry term that refers to the legal business practice of selling more than an airline can deliver. It all stems, alas, from the unfortunate habit of many travelers who neglect to cancel flight reservations that will not be used. Airlines study the patterns on various flights and city pairs and apply a formula that allows them to sell more tickets than there are seats on the plane, in the expectation that a certain percentage will not show up at the airport.

But what happens if all passengers holding reservations do show up? Obviously, the result will be more passengers than seats, and some will have to be left behind.

The involuntary bump list will begin with the names of passengers who are late to check in. Airlines must ask for volunteers before bumping any passengers who have followed the rules on check-in. Now, assuming that no one is willing to give up their seat just for the fun of it, the airline will offer some sort of compensation—either a free ticket or cash, or both. It is up to the passenger and the airline to negotiate an acceptable deal.

The U.S. Department of Transportation's consumer protection regulations set some minimum levels of compensation for passengers who are bumped from a flight as a result of overbooking.

It is not considered "bumping" if a flight is canceled because of weather, equipment problems, or the lack of a flight crew. You are also not eligible for compensation if the airline substitutes a smaller aircraft for operational or safety reasons, or if the flight involves an aircraft with 60 seats or less.

How to Get Bumped

Why in the world would you *want* to be bumped? Well, perhaps you'd like to look at missing your plane as an opportunity to earn a little money for your time instead of an annoyance. Is a two-hour delay worth $100 an hour to you?

How about $800 for a family of four to wait a few hours on the way home—that could pay for a week's stay at a motel plus a meal at the airport.

If you're not in a tremendous rush to get to your destination—or to get back home—you might want to volunteer to be bumped. I wouldn't recommend doing this on the busiest travel days of the year, or if you are booked on the last flight of the day, unless you are also looking forward to a free night in an airport motel.

My very best haul: on a flight home from London, my family of four received a free night's stay in a luxury hotel, $1,000 each in tickets, and an upgrade on our flight home the next day.

Bad Weather, Bad Planes, Strikes, and Other Headaches

You don't want pilots to fly into weather they consider unsafe, of course. You also wouldn't want them to take up a plane with a mechanical problem. No matter how you feel about unions, you probably don't want to cross a picket line to board a plane piloted by strikebreakers. And so, you should accept an airline's cancellation of a flight for one of these legitimate reasons.

Here's the bad news, though: if a flight is canceled for an "Act of God" or a labor dispute, the airline is not required to do anything for you except give your money back. In practice, carriers will usually make a good effort to find another way to get you to your destination more or less on time. This could mean rebooking on another flight on the same airline, or on a different carrier. It could mean a significant delay in the worst situations, such as a major snowstorm.

Here is a summary of your rather limited rights as an air passenger:
- An airline is required to compensate you above the cost of your ticket only if you are bumped from an oversold flight against your will.
- If you volunteer to be bumped, you can negotiate for the best deal with the ticket agent or a supervisor; generally, for your inconvenience, you can expect to be offered a free round-trip ticket on the airline.
- If your scheduled flight is unable to deliver you directly to the destination on your ticket, and alternate transportation such as a bus or limousine is provided, the airline is required to pay you twice the amount of your one-way fare if your arrival will be more than two hours later than the original ticket promised.
- If you purchase your ticket with a credit card—strongly recommended in any case—the airline must credit your account within seven days of receiving an application for a refund.

All that said, in many cases you will be able to convince an agent or a supervisor to go beyond the letter of the law. I've found that the very best strategy is to politely but firmly stand your ground. Ask the ticket clerk to put you on another flight, or for a free night in a hotel and a flight in the morning, or for any reasonable accommodation. Don't take no for an answer, but stay polite and don't move. Ask for a supervisor; stay polite and start over again. Sooner or later, they'll do something to get you out of the way.

And then there are labor problems like those that faced American Airlines in 1997 and again in 1999. Your best defense against a strike is to anticipate it before it happens; keep your ears open for labor problems when you make a reservation. Then keep in touch with your travel agent or the airline in the days leading up to a strike deadline. It is often easier to make alternate plans or seek a refund in the days immediately before a strike; wait until the last minute and you're going to be joining a very long and upset line.

In the face of a strike, a major airline is likely to attempt to reroute you on another airline if possible; if you buy your own ticket on another carrier you are unlikely to be reimbursed. If your flight is canceled, you will certainly be able to claim a full refund of your fare or obtain a voucher in its value without paying any penalties.

Airline Safety

There are no guarantees in life, but in general, flying on an airplane is considerably safer than driving to the airport. All of the major air carriers have very good safety records; some are better than others. I pay attention to news reports about FAA inspections and rulings and make adjustments as necessary. And though I love to squeeze George Washington till he yelps, I avoid start-up and super cut-rate airlines because I have my doubts about how much money they can afford to devote to maintenance.

Among major airlines, the fatal accident rate during the last 25 years stands somewhere between .3 and .7 incidents per million flights. Southwest Airlines and America West Airlines have (as of mid-1999) never suffered a fatal accident; smaller airlines that have perfect records include Reno Air and Midwest Airlines.

The very low numbers, experts say, make them poor predictors of future incidents. Instead, you should pay more attention to FAA or NTSB rulings on maintenance and training problems.

Not included in these listings are small commuter airlines (except for those that are affiliated with major carriers).

The best policy. Consider buying trip cancelation insurance from a travel agency, tour operator, or directly from an insurance company (ask your insurance agent for advice). The policies are intended to reimburse you for any lost deposits or prepayments if you must cancel a trip because you or certain members of your family become ill. Read the policy carefully to understand the circumstances under which the company will pay.

Take care not to purchase more coverage than you need; if your tour package costs $5,000 but you would lose only $1,000 in the event of a cancelation, then the amount of insurance required is just $1,000. Some policies will cover you for health and accident benefits while on vacation, excluding any pre-existing conditions.

Be sure you understand your contract with your airline; you may be able to reschedule a flight or even receive a refund after payment of a service charge; some airlines give full refunds or free rescheduling if you can prove a medical reason for the change.

Don't wait to drop a card. Keep in touch with your travel agent or tour operator. In many cases they can anticipate major changes before departure time and will let you know. And many operators will try hard to keep you from demanding a refund if you find a major change unacceptable. They may offer a discount or upgrade on a substitute trip or adjust the price of the changed tour.

About Travel Agencies

Here's my advice about travel agents in a nutshell: get a good one, or go it alone.

Good travel agent are those who remember who they work for: you. There is, though, a built-in conflict of interest here, because the agent is in most cases paid by someone else. Agents receive a commission on airline tickets, hotel reservations, car rentals, and many other services they sell you. The more they sell (or the higher the price), the more they earn.

I would recommend you start the planning for any trip by calling the airlines and a few hotels and finding the best package you can put together for yourself. *Then* call your travel agent and ask them to do better.

If your agent contributes knowledge or experience, comes up with dollar-saving alternatives to your own package, or offers some other kind of convenience, then go ahead and book through the agency. If, as I often find, you know a lot more about your destination and are willing to spend a lot more time to save money than will the agent, do it yourself.

There is one special type of travel agency worth considering. A number of large agencies offer rebates on part of their commissions to travelers. Some of these companies cater only to frequent flyers who will bring in a lot of business; other rebate agencies offer only limited services to clients.

I use an agency that sends me a check after each trip equal to 5 percent of all reservations booked through them. I have never set foot in their offices, and I conduct all of my business over the phone; tickets arrive by mail or by overnight courier when necessary.

You can find discount travel agencies through many major credit card companies (Citibank and American Express among them) or through associations and clubs. Some warehouse shopping clubs have rebate travel agencies.

And if you establish a regular relationship with your local travel agency and bring them enough business to make them glad to see you walk through their door, don't be afraid to ask for a discount equal to a few percentage points.

Another important new tool for travelers is the Internet. Here you'll find computerized travel agencies that offer airline, hotel, car, cruise, and package reservations. You won't receive personalized assistance, but you will be able to make as many price checks and itinerary routings as you'd like without apology.

Several of the Internet services feature special deals, including companion fares and rebates you won't find elsewhere. Some of the best Internet agencies include:

Atevo	www.atevo.com/
Flifo	www.flifo.com/
1Travel	www.1travel.com
Microsoft Expedia	www.expedia.msn.com

Tour Packages and Charter Flights

Tour packages and flights sold by tour operators or travel agents may look similar, but the consumer may end up with significantly different rights.

It all depends whether the flight is a scheduled or nonscheduled flight. A scheduled flight is one that is listed in the *Official Airline Guide* and available to the general public through a travel agent or from the airline. This doesn't mean that a scheduled flight will necessarily be on a major carrier or that you will be flying on a 747 jumbo jet; it could just as easily be the propeller-driven pride of Hayseed Airlines. In any case, though, a scheduled flight does have to meet stringent federal government certification requirements.

In the event of delays, cancellations, or other problems with a scheduled flight, your recourse is with the airline.

A nonscheduled flight is also known as a charter flight. The term *charter* is sometimes also applied to a package that includes a nonscheduled flight, hotel accommodations, ground transportation, and other elements.

Charter flights are generally a creation of a tour operator who will purchase all of the seats on a specific flight to a specific destination or rent an airplane and crew from an air carrier.

Tour cancelations are rare. Most tour operators, if forced to cancel, will offer another package or other incentives as a goodwill gesture. If a charter flight or charter tour is canceled, the tour operator must refund your money within 14 days.

Charter flights and charter tours are regulated by the federal government, but your rights as a consumer are much more limited than those afforded to scheduled flight customers.

Written Contracts

You wouldn't buy a hamburger without knowing the price and specifications (two all-beef patties on a sesame seed bun, etc.).

Why, then, would you spend hundreds or even thousands of dollars on a tour and not understand the contract that underlies the transaction?

When you purchase a charter flight or a tour package, you should review and sign a contract that spells out your rights. This contract is sometimes referred to as the "Operator Participant Contract" or the "Terms and Conditions." Look for this contract in the brochure that describes the packages; ask for it if one is not offered. The

Lug-it-yourself. If you are using a scheduled airline to connect with a charter flight, or the other way around, your baggage will not be automatically transferred. You must make the transfer yourself.

Charter and tour flights operate independently of other flights. If you are on a trip that combines scheduled and nonscheduled flights, or two unrelated charter flights, you may end up losing your money and flight because of delays.

It may make sense to avoid such combinations for that reason, or to leave extra hours or even days between connections. Some tour operators offer travel delay insurance that pays for accommodations or alternative travel arrangements necessitated by certain types of delays.

proper procedure for a travel agent or tour operator requires they wait until the customer has read and signed the contract before any money is accepted.

Remember that the contract is designed mostly to benefit the tour operator, and each contract may be different from others you may have agreed to in the past. The basic rule here is: **if you don't understand it, don't sign it.**

Orlando International Airport

Orlando's airport has grown from a backwater Florida strip to one of the busiest—and most efficiently operated—terminals in the country. Located about 30 minutes west of Walt Disney World and other Orlando and Kissimmee attractions, it is served by several major highways as well as bus and limousine service.

There are three main clusters of gates at the airport; each cluster is connected to the single ticketing and baggage claim area by an automated monorail; you won't be the first to observe that the first semi-thrill ride of your vacation is at the airport.

Here are the gate assignments as they existed in mid-1999; be sure to check with your airline on arrival for any changes:

Gates 1–29 "A" Side of Terminal

Air Canada	Canada 3000
Air Jamaica	Canadian Airlines
American	Continental
American Eagle	Lacsa
American Trans Air	TWA
Bahamasair	

Gates 30–59 "B" Side of Terminal

AirTran Airlines	Spirit
All Nippon Airways	United
Northwest	US Airways

Gates 60–99 "B" Side of Terminal

America West	Martinair Holland
British Airways	Saudia
Comair	TransBrasil
Delta	Varig
Icelandair	Virgin Atlantic
LTU	

Area Transportation Information

Orlando International Airport Visitor Information. (407) 825-2352.

I-Ride. A bus service along International Drive, connecting hotels, attractions, and restaurants. The trolley-like bus runs from SeaWorld to Belz Factory Outlet seven days a week from 7 A.M. to midnight, about 15 minutes apart, making more than 50 stops between SeaWorld Orlando and the Belz Factory Outlet World.

In its first full year of operation, the service carried more than 1.2 million passengers. A single adult fare is 75 cents; children 12 and younger ride free when accompanied by a paying adult. One-day passes are $2; multi-day passes are also available. For information, call (407) 248-9590. www.Iridetrolley.com

Both Church Street Station and the Mercado have their own shuttle services that take patrons to and from International Drive hotels.

LYNX/Tri-County Regional Transportation Authority. Public transportation in Orlando and adjoining areas. (407) 841-8240. www.golnx.com

Amtrak. Operates daily train service to Orlando from New York, Tampa, and Miami. Area stops include downtown Orlando, Winter Park, and Sanford. The Auto Train transports passengers and their cars from Lorton, Virginia, each day, departing in the afternoon and arriving about 9 A.M. of the next day in Sanford, 25 miles northeast of downtown Orlando. (407) 843-7611. (800) 872-7245.

Greyhound Bus Lines. The Kissimmee station is located at 16 N. Orlando Ave. Shuttle vans and taxis are available from the station. (407) 292-3424.

Mears Transportation. Shuttle van, town car, and limousine service from Orlando International Airport to hotels and attractions. (407) 423-5566

The Virgin Connection. Virgin Atlantic Airways has made Orlando its largest gateway in the United States, with more than 20 per week. Guests heading for a Virgin Atlantic flight can check their bags at a facility alongside the Virgin Megastore in Downtown Disney and spend the day at Walt Disney World before their night flight to London or Manchester.

Drive?, He Said

Everyone's conception of the perfect vacation is different, but for me, I draw a distinction between getting there and being there. I want the getting part to be as quick and simple as possible, and the being there part to be as long as I can manage and afford. Therefore, I fly to most any destination more than a few hundred miles from my home. The cost of driving, hotels, meals en route, and general physical and mental wear and tear rarely equals a deeply discounted excursion fare.

If you do drive, though, you can save a few dollars by using the services of the AAA or another major automobile club. And before you head out, make certain your vehicle is in traveling shape: a tune-up and fully inflated, fully inspected tires will certainly save gas, money, and headaches.

If you plan to travel by bus or train, be aware that the national carriers generally have the same sort of peak and off-peak pricing as the airlines. The cheapest time to buy tickets is when the fewest people want them.

Renting a Car for a Florida Trip

If you are planning to stay at a hotel within Walt Disney World you may be able to do without renting a car, although you will not be able to get to attractions

Fast food. One advantage to bringing a car to the park is the chance to save a bit of money and get a more relaxed, better meal by ducking out of the park at lunch and visiting a decent buffet or menu restaurant; come back to the park for some evening rides and the fireworks. (Be sure to get your hand stamped when you leave the park *and* hold on to your ticket stub—both are needed for readmission on the same day. Your parking receipt is also valid for reentry to any of the parking lots.)

and restaurants outside the Disney boundaries without calling a cab or car service. If you are staying at a hotel outside Walt Disney World, you may be able to use a shuttle bus to the parks; but again, you will find yourself with limited options.

You should therefore consider renting a car. The good news is that Orlando is perhaps the most competitive rental market in the country. Except during peak periods, you may be able to rent a small car for about $100 to $150 per week, or a luxury car for twice that amount.

Your travel agent may be of assistance in finding the best rates; you can make a few phone calls by yourself, too. Rental rates generally follow the same low-shoulder-high-season structure. I have obtained rates as low as $59 a week for a tiny subcompact (a convertible, no less) in low-season.

Every major car rental agency, and many not-so-major, have operations in Orlando. Shop on the basis of price and convenience.

Consider the value of your time in choosing among rental companies with locations at the Orlando airport, including Hertz, Avis, and National, and those who conduct their business a few miles away. The lowest rates are generally offered by companies that put you on a bus and take you to their lot; you'll have to wait for a bus in both directions, adding as much as 30 minutes to each end of your transactions. Alamo, perhaps the biggest operator in Orlando, is one of the farthest away and often features one of the slowest counters; on one recent trip, in the relatively slow month of May, I lost a full hour in line at Alamo. They earned this special mention.

Car Rental Gotchas

Car rental companies will try—with varying levels of pressure—to convince you to purchase special insurance coverage. They'll tell you it's "only" $7 or $9 per day. What a deal! That works out to about $2,500 or $3,330 per year for a set of rental wheels. The coverage is intended primarily to protect the rental company, not you.

Check with your insurance agent before you travel to determine how well your personal automobile policy covers a rental car and its contents. We strongly recommend you use a credit card that offers rental car insurance; such insurance usually covers the deductible below your personal policy. The extra auto insurance by itself is usually worth an upgrade to a "gold card" or other extra-service credit card.

The only sticky area comes for those visitors who have a driver's license but no car, and therefore no insurance. Again, consult your credit card company and your insurance agent to see what kind of coverage you have, or need.

Although it is theoretically possible to rent a car without a credit card, you will find it to be a rather inconvenient process. If they cannot hold your credit card account hostage, most agencies will require a large cash deposit—perhaps as much as several thousand dollars—before they will give you the keys.

> **Extra miles.** Don't let it force you to pay too much for a rental car, but all things being equal, use a rental agency that awards frequent flyer mileage in a program you use.

Pay attention, too, when the rental agent explains the gas tank policy. The most common plan says you must return the car with a full tank; if the agency must refill the tank, you will be billed a service charge plus what is usually a very high per-gallon rate.

Other optional plans include one where the rental agency sells you a full tank when you first drive away and takes no note of how much gas remains when you return the car. Unless you somehow manage to return the car with the engine running on fumes, you are in effect making a gift to the agency with every gallon you bring back.

I prefer the first option, refilling the tank on the way to the airport on getaway day.

Super Rental Deals

If you can figure out a way to get to Florida inexpensively in the spring, you can take advantage of the glut of rental cars that agencies wish were elsewhere—mostly up north.

Companies including Avis, Budget, Hertz, and National offer cars for as little as $6 a day, provided you drop off the car in one of a few dozen northeast cities. Under most plans you can hold on to the car for as long as two weeks.

The situation is reversed in the fall, when car agencies want to send vehicles down south for the snowbirds.

A Guide to Highway 192

A new road sign system helps demark a 12-mile stretch of the confusing U.S. Highway 192, also known as Irlo Bronson Highway.

In the initial project, markers are numbered from 4 at the western end near Splendid China and the entrance to Walt Disney World, to 15 at the eastern end of the Kissimmee tourist area just short of Hoagland Boulevard.

Here are a few landmarks:

4	Splendid China
5–6	A World of Orchids
6–7	Walt Disney World main gate
7–8	Disney's Wide World of Sports
	I-4 to SeaWorld, Universal Studios Florida,
	Orlando, Church Street Station
	Disney's Celebration
8–9	Arabian Nights, Water Mania
9–10	Old Town, Pirate's Cove

10–11	Movie Rider, Wild Bill's, Poinciana Boulevard crosses U.S. 192, Green Meadows Farm
11–12	Capone's Vineland Road intersection
12–13	Congo River Golf
13–14	Manufacturer's Outlet Mall
14–15	Medieval Times, Jungleland, River Adventure Golf Hoagland Boulevard intersection

Interstate 4 Exits in Kissimmee/Orlando Area

25A	US 192 East. Motel strip toward downtown Kissimmee. Water Mania, Old Town, Medieval Times.
25B	US 192 West. Main gate of Walt Disney World. Motel strip, Splendid China.
26A/B	Epcot Center, Disney-MGM Studios, Typhoon Lagoon, Epcot Resorts, Disney Village, Pleasure Island.
27	SR 535 to Kissimmee and Lake Buena Vista. Hotel Plaza Resorts, Disney Village Resorts, Fort Wilderness, River Country.
27A	SeaWorld. Central Florida Parkway Eastbound (toward Orlando) only.
28	528 East (Beeline) to SeaWorld, Orlando International Airport and Kennedy Space Center. (Toll road.)
29	SR 482 (Sand Lake Road) to Orlando, Orlando International Airport, and International Drive.
30A/B	Highway 435 (Kirkman Road). Universal Studios.
31	Florida Turnpike south to Miami or north to Wildwood.
33A	Hwy. 441, 17-92 (South Orange Blossom Trail).
38	Anderson Street, Orlando. Church Street Station.

Accident and Sickness Insurance

The idea of falling ill or suffering an injury while hundreds of miles away from home and your family doctor can be a terrifying thought.

But before you sign on the bottom line for an Accident and Sickness insurance policy, be sure to consult with your own insurance agent or your company's personnel office to see how far your personal medical insurance policy will reach. Does the policy cover vacation trips and exclude business travel? Can you purchase a "rider" or extension to your personal policy?

The only reason to purchase an Accident and Sickness policy is to fill in any gaps in coverage you already have. If you don't have health insurance of any kind, a travel policy is certainly valuable, but perhaps you should consider whether you should spend the money on a year-round policy instead of taking a vacation.

Also be aware that nearly every kind of health insurance has an exclusionary period for preexisting conditions. If you are sick before you set out on a trip, you may find the policy will not pay for treating the problem.

Chapter 3
Sleeping and Eating for Less

Everybody's got to sleep and eat. But no two people seem to place the same value on a bed and a meal.

When I travel, I tend to spend as little time as possible in my room—I collapse into bed much too late to visit the pool or stroll the lobby, and I'm off on my next adventure at sunrise. So I'm looking for something quiet, clean, safe, and convenient to my next day's plans. Others, though, get all wrought up about glass elevators, room service, retail shops, and the number of channels on the television set in the room.

Econoguide to Best Food at Walt Disney World
Best Steak Dinner: Yachtsman Steakhouse at Disney's Yacht Club Resort, or Concourse Steakhouse at Disney's Contemporary Resort.
Best Seafood: Fulton's Crab House at Downtown Disney. Close seconds: California Grill at Disney's Contemporary Resort and Flying Fish Café at Disney's BoardWalk.
Best Theme Eatery: Rainforest Café at Disney's Animal Kingdom. Close second: House of Blues at Downtown Disney.
Best Sushi: California Grill at Disney's Contemporary Resort. Close seconds: Kimono's at Walt Disney World Swan, and Matsu No Ma Lounge in Japan at the Epcot World Showcase.
Best Vegetarian Fare: Spoodles at Disney's BoardWalk resort.
Best Milkshakes: Mom's specials at the 50's Prime Time Cafe at Disney-MGM Studios, or Beaches and Cream Soda Shop at Disney's Beach Club Resort.
Best High Tea: Rose & Crown Pub & Dining Room at United Kingdom in Epcot World Showcase, and Garden View Lounge at Disney's Grand Floridian Resort & Spa.
Best Wine Cellar: Victoria & Albert's at Disney's Grand Floridian Resort & Spa. Close seconds include California Grill at Disney's Contemporary Resort, Spoodles at Disney's BoardWalk resort, and Artist Point at Disney's Wilderness Lodge.
Best Beer Selection: Big River Grille and Brewing Works at Disney's BoardWalk resort. Close second: ESPN Club at Disney's BoardWalk.

Econoguide to Best Food at Universal Studios Escape
Emeril's Restaurant Orlando. CityWalk
Latin Quarter. CityWalk
Pat O'Brien's. CityWalk
Bob Marley–A Tribute to Freedom. CityWalk
Mythos. Universal Studios Islands of Adventure

On the other hand, when I travel to a Disney theme park, my gustatory goal is to find a place to eat where there are cloth napkins and the butter does not come in the shape of mouse ears. For some of you, that's exactly the goal.

In this chapter, we'll take an Econoguide tour through the many options for sleeping and eating in and around Walt Disney World. I'll begin with the hotels and restaurants within the boundaries of the park. By the beginning of 1999, there were more than 25,000 rooms under Disney ownership in some 27 resorts.

(Our coverage of restaurants within the theme parks themselves can be found within the chapters on the Magic Kingdom, Epcot, Disney-MGM Studios, Universal Studios Florida, SeaWorld, and Busch Gardens Tampa.)

Negotiating for a Room

Notice the title of this section: it's *not* called "buying" a room. The fact of the matter is that hotel rooms, like almost everything else, can be be negotiated by the savvy traveler.

Here is how to pay the highest possible price for a hotel room: walk up to the front desk without a reservation and say, "I'd like a room." Unless the No Vacancy sign is lit, you may be charged the "rack rate," which is the published maximum nightly charge.

Here are a few ways to pay the lowest possible price:

1. Before you head for your vacation, spend an hour on the phone and call directly to a half dozen hotels that seem to be in the price range you'd like to spend. (We recommend membership in AAA and use of their annual tour books as starting points for your research.)

Start by asking for the room rate. Then ask them for their *best* rate. Does that sound like an unnecessary second request? Trust me, it's not: I can't begin to count the number of times the rates have dropped substantially when I have asked again.

[True story: I once called the reservation desk of a major hotel chain and asked for the rates for a night at a Chicago location. "That will be $149 per night," I was told. "Ouch," I said. "Oh, would you like to spend less?" the reservationist answered. I admitted that I would, and she punched a few keys on her keyboard. "They have a special promotion going on. How about $109 per night?" she asked.

Not bad for a city hotel, I reasoned, but still I hadn't asked the big question. "What is your best rate?" I asked. "Oh, our best rate? That would be $79," said the agent.

But, wait: "OK, I'll take it. I'm a triple A member, by the way." Another pause.

"That's fine, Mr. Sandler. The nightly room rate will be $71.10. Have a nice day."]

When you feel you've negotiated the best deal you can obtain over the phone, make a reservation at the hotel of your choice. Be sure to go over the dates and prices one more time, and obtain the name of the person you spoke with and get a confirmation number if available.

2. But wait: when you show up at your hotel on the first night, stop and look at the marquee outside and see if the hotel is advertising a discount rate. Most of the hotels in the Walt Disney World area adjust their prices based on attendance levels at the park. It is not uncommon to see prices change by $10 or more over the course of a day.

Here's where you need to be bold. Walk up to the desk as if you *did not* have a reservation, and ask the clerk: "What is your best room rate for tonight?" If the rate they quote you is less than the rate in your reservation, you are now properly armed to ask for a reduction in your room rate.

Similarly, if the room rate advertised out front on the marquee drops during your stay, don't be shy about asking that your charges be reduced. Just be sure to ask for the reduction *before* you spend another night at the old rate, and obtain the name of the clerk who promises a change. If the hotel tries a lame excuse, such as "That's only for new check-ins," you can offer to check out and then check back in again. That will usually work; you can always check out and go to the hotel across the road that will usually match the rates of its competitor.

3. And here is the way to make the most flexible choice, in the low-season only. Come down without a reservation, and then cruise one of the motel strips such as I-192 (Bronson) or International Drive. Check the outdoor marquees for discount prices and make notes. Find a phone, and make a few calls to the ones you found attractive. Once again, be sure to ask for the best price. The later in the day you search for a room, the more likely you are to find a hotel ready to make a deal.

Wrong numbers. Be sure you understand the telephone billing policy at the motel. Some establishments allow free local calls, while others charge as much as 75 cents for such calls. (We're especially unhappy with service charges for 800 numbers.) Be sure to examine your bill carefully at checkout and make sure it is correct. We strongly suggest you obtain a telephone credit card and use it when you travel; nearly all motels tack high service charges on long distance calls and there is no reason to pay it.

Here's my card. Membership in AAA brings some important benefits for the traveler, although you may not be able to apply the club's usual 10 percent discount on top of whatever hotel rate you negotiate. (It doesn't hurt to ask, though.) Be sure to request a tour book as well as Florida and Orlando maps from AAA, even if you plan to fly to Florida; they are much better than the maps given by car rental agencies.

Safety first. The small safes available in some hotels can be valuable to the traveler; be sure to inquire whether there is a service charge for their use. We've been in hotels that apply the charge regardless of whether we used the safe or not; look over your bill at checkout and object to any charges that are not proper. In any case, we'd suggest that any objects that are so valuable you feel it necessary to lock them up should probably be left home.

Weekly, not weakly. Are you planning to stay for a full week? Ask for the weekly rate. If the room clerk says there is no such rate, ask to speak to the manager: he or she may be willing to shave a few dollars per day off the rate for a long-term stay.

Dialing for Dollars

As I cited in my "True Story," you must be aggressive in representing your checkbook in negotiations with a reservation agent. Sometimes, you will also need to be persistent.

The fact is that a single room may be offered at four different prices by four different agents: you may find the lowest price by calling directly to the hotel; in some cases, a chain's toll-free central reservations service may have some special deals. Occasionally, travel agents are offered special promotional rates.

If you're doing your own booking, call the central reservations number for a chain establishment and follow up with a direct call to the hotel. If you use a travel agent, request that the agent verify the lowest rate indicated on the agency's computer with a direct call to the hotel.

Think of it this way: if you can save $20 a night on a week's stay, your first few meals are on the house.

Where Should You Stay?

Except for the busiest times of the year—Christmas through New Year's, Spring Break, and the Fourth of July through mid-August, among them—you're not going to have *any* trouble locating a place to stay in the Orlando-Kissimmee area. In fact, the biggest problem is choosing among the various options.

In this chapter, I'll offer a tour of the main hotel areas in and around Walt Disney World.

How should you choose a place to stay? I'd suggest you start by deciding on a price range you'd be willing to pay. Then decide what sort of accommodations fit your needs—in the Kissimmee-Orlando area you can find single rooms and spacious suites in nearly every price range. At the extremes—the least expensive and the most expensive—the difference in quality can be substantial. In the middle price ranges, the difference among rooms is often mostly related to location.

If you're traveling with a family, do you want a multi-bedroom suite or connecting single rooms? Is a kitchen or refrigerator necessary? (You can easily save $20 a day for a family of four by eating breakfast in your room; but if a room with a refrigerator costs $25 more per day, it's no deal at all.)

Are you willing to drive 15 minutes in the morning and at the end of the day to save some money or obtain a better room for the same price? Few would argue with the statement that some of the most exciting and most convenient hotels are to be found within the Walt Disney World park boundaries, but they come at a not insignificant premium.

Following are ranges for low-season rooms; high-season rates can be as much as double:

$25 to $60 per night. East and west of I-4 on I-192, also known as Irlo Bronson Highway. The farther east or west you go on Bronson, up to about eight miles from I-4, the lower the prices.

You'll also find budget motels in the South Orange Blossom Trail area, and in some downtown Orlando districts, about 20 to 30 minutes away from Walt Disney World.

$50 to $100 per night. Walt Disney World budget hotels, including the All-Star Sports, Music, and Movies Resorts.

Other moderately priced establishments can be found on International Drive; resort motels are found on I-192 and the Apopka-Vineland Road area. About half an hour away, rooms in this range can also be found in downtown Orlando and near Orlando International Airport.

$100 to $300 per night. Walt Disney World premium hotels, first-class hotels in Lake Buena Vista, and better establishments along International Drive.

Quick tickets. Guests in hotels within Walt Disney World can purchase tickets—at regular prices—at guest services desks within their hotels, saving a few minutes of waiting at the park.

Babysitter club. Guests at hotels at Walt Disney World can hire an in-room babysitter by consulting with Guest Services or the In-Room KinderCare Learning Center.

Clearing the air. If you don't indulge, ask for a nonsmoking room at check-in. With luck, the air will be somewhat cleaner and furniture somewhat fresher.

As you can see, the room rates are pretty self-selecting for location and, to a large extent, the quality of the room. Next you can make decisions on extras, including special recreational facilities.

Hotels Within Walt Disney World

Within Walt Disney World are five clusters of hotels and resorts. Reservations can be made through travel agencies or through the Disney central travel desk at (407) 934-7639. For information via the Internet, connect to www.disney-world.com/vacation.html

Hotels accept American Express, MasterCard, Visa, and the Disney Credit Card. In most cases, reservations must be cancelled more than 72 hours prior to the arrival date; check-in time is 3 P.M. and checkout 11 A.M.

Disney World Resorts Price Ranges

Rates are per night, vary by season, and are subject to change. Hotels within the resort start at the Budget level; lower-priced accommodations are available outside the Disney border.

$$ Budget ($74 to $104)
 Disney's All-Star Sports Resort
 Disney's All-Star Music Resort
 Disney's All-Star Movies Resort

$$$ Moderate ($119 to $164)
Disney's Caribbean Beach Resort
Disney's Dixie Landings Resort
Disney's Port Orleans Resort
Disney's Coronado Springs Resort

$$$$ Deluxe
Disney's Beach Club Resort $264 to $540
Disney's Contemporary Resort $214 to $410
Disney's Wilderness Lodge $175 to $390
Disney's Polynesian Resort $274 to $530
Disney's BoardWalk Inn $254 to $580
Disney's Yacht and Beach Club Resort $264 to $540
Disney's Grand Floridian Resort & Spa $299 to $645
Dolphin and Swan Resorts $265 to $410; suites $610 to $2,850
Disney's Old Key West Resort $229 to $300

Housekeeping Villas
Disney's Old Key West Resort $305 to $1,050
Disney's Fort Wilderness Homes $179 to $254
  Cabins $204 to $275
  Camp sites $35 to $74
Disney's BoardWalk Villas $254 to $1,540
Villas at Disney Institute $204 to $510

Children under 18 stay free in rooms with their parents; an additional charge of $8 to $15 per adult is added for more than two adults in a room.

Disney hotels have two to four "seasons" for room prices. Super Value rates are generally in effect in January and September. Value rates are offered in early February, post-Easter to early June, the end of August, and from October 1 through mid-December. Regular rates are generally in effect from mid-February through mid-April, and from mid-June through mid-August. The highest Holiday rates are charged from mid-December through New Year's Eve.

Magic Kingdom Resort Area

★★★**Disney's Wilderness Lodge $$$$.** 901 Timberline Drive, Lake Buena Vista. (407) 824-3200. A rustic, 728-room lodge patterned after the famed "Old Faithful Inn" at Yellowstone National Park. The lodge includes massive log columns, totem poles, and stone fireplaces—just the sort of thing you'd expect in Central Florida, right? But wait: there's also a 12-story geyser, a waterfall, and a rocky swimming pool that begins in the lobby as a hot spring and works its way outside. The resort, located between the Contemporary Resort and Fort Wilderness, offers a view of the Electrical Water Pageant, with launch service to the parks.

The **Cub's Den** offers a supervised dining and Western-theme entertainment club for children from ages 4 to 12, including movies, live animal shows from Discovery Island, and video games. The club is open from 5 P.M. to midnight, at a charge of $6 per hour.

Artist Point ($$$) celebrates the flavors of the Pacific Northwest with items such as maple-glazed king salmon, elk sausage, and pan-seared rainbow trout at dinner, served from 5:30 to 10 P.M. The gourmet eatery is transformed in

Disney Hotels and Restaurants
★★   Better hotels
★★★   Superior hotels
★★★★ Econoguide Best
$ Budget room rates
$$ Moderate room
        rates
$$$ Deluxe room rates
$$$$ Premium room
        rates

Hotel Restaurant Price Ranges
Entrée prices at dinner.
Prices are approximate
and subject to change.
$ $10 and less
$$ $10 to $19
$$$ $20 to $34
$$$$ $35 and more

the early morning from 7:30 to 11:15 A.M. as the site of a character breakfast with Pocahontas, John Smith, Meeko, and more.

The Whispering Canyon Café ($$) features all-you-can-eat buffets for breakfast and dinner and a family-style cookout each evening. At lunchtime, an à la carte menu includes sandwiches, burgers, and chili.

Roaring Forks ($) offers counter-service burgers, sandwiches, salads, and other basic fare.

Transportation to the Magic Kingdom includes boat service from the hotel dock, and buses to the other theme parks and elsewhere in Walt Disney World.

★★Disney Contemporary Resort $$$$. 4600 North World Drive, Lake Buena Vista. (407) 824-1000. Is it a hotel with a monorail running through the middle, or a monorail station with a hotel surrounding it? Either way, it's a most unusual setting and just a mouse trot from the main gate of Walt Disney World. It's a great place to view the nightly Electrical Water Pageant in season, especially if your room faces the lagoon. The resort includes 1,052 rooms, a health club, and a marina. Note that not all of the rooms are in the 15-story, A-shaped main building with the monorail station but may be located in the more ordinary annex buildings along the lake. There are suites on the hotel's 14th floor that include private concierge and special services.

The **Concourse Steakhouse** has trellised ceilings that allow peeks through to the 90-foot-high atrium lobby and the monorail trains passing through. Breakfast, lunch, and dinner are offered from 7 A.M. through 10 P.M., with dinner entrees from about $15. Specialties include charbroiled steak, oven-roasted chicken, pasta dishes, and seafood.

The **Contemporary Café** offers a breakfast and dinner buffet.

High above it all, on the 15th floor, is by most accounts Disney's best (and among the priciest) gourmet eatery. The **California Grill** ($$$) has offerings ranging from sushi and lemon grass soup to spicy braised lamb shank with Thai red curried lentils, Atlantic salmon baked under a black-olive crust with grilled vegetable ratatouille, and pan-seared yellowfin tuna with black beans. Offerings change with the seasons. Dinner is served from 5:30 to 10 P.M. You can watch specialties being prepared within the exhibition kitchen, or catch a view of the fireworks or water parade from the windows.

Chef Mickey's Restaurant ($$) features a breakfast or dinner with the majordomo mouse himself. Dinner selections include shrimp, prime rib, carved meats, and a salad bar. Breakfast is served from 7:30 to 11:30 A.M., priced at $13.95 for adults and $7.95 for children ages 3–11. Dinner is available from 5 to 9:30 P.M., priced at $17.95 for adults and $7.95 for children ages 3–11.

Recreational facilities include a white sand beach, six clay tennis courts, two heated outdoor swimming pools with a water slide, and the Olympiad fitness center. Guests can rent Water Sprites from the hotel's marina, or they can hire a waterskiing boat that comes with driver and skis.

The **Mouseketeer Clubhouse** is open from 4:30 P.M. to midnight for children from 4 to 12 years old; rates are about $4 per hour for the first child and $2 per hour for each additional youngster. For information and reservations call (407) 824-3038. Two different movies (Disney titles, of course) are shown each night in the theater at the **Fiesta Fun Center**, which is also the home of a large collection of video arcade machines.

Transportation to the parks is by monorail, water taxi, and bus. You can also catch a water taxi to Discovery Island.

★★★★**Disney's Grand Floridian Resort & Spa $$$$.** 4401 Grand Floridian Way, Lake Buena Vista. (407) 824-3000. An opulent resort along the shores of Seven Seas Lagoon with its own monorail station. A mixture of Victorian elegance and modernity in white and coral trim; in typical Disney fashion, it is much prettier than the real thing probably ever was. The hotel drew its design from some of the grand old hotels of Palm Beach at the turn of the century, including the Royal Poinciana.

The spectacular five-story Grand Lobby is topped by stained-glass skylights and lit in the evening by grand chandeliers. A Big Band entertains nightly. Some of the rooms include quirky dormers and turrets, as well as balconies that offer close-up views of the Magic Kingdom.

Special rooms include 15 honeymoon suites and other suites with as many as three bedrooms.

The resort includes 901 rooms, a health club, tennis courts, a marina with Water Sprites and sailboats, and a white sand beach on Seven Seas Lagoon.

The **Mouseketeer Club** for children from 4 to 12 years old is open from 4:30 P.M. to midnight. Rates are $4 per hour, with a four-hour maximum. Call (407) 824-2985 for reservations.

The prime restaurant is **Victoria and Albert's** ($$$$), with just 65 seats and a most refined atmosphere where you'll be attended by a butler and maid in Victorian dress. The prix-fixe menu, which usually includes meat, fish, and poultry offerings, is priced at about $80 per person before orders from the extensive and expensive wine list. Some samples: salmon sautéed in olive oil with olives, capers, and tomato; roasted rack of lamb with Madeira almond sauce; and Bailey's Irish Cream soufflé. The restaurant is one of the few in Walt Disney World that require men to wear jackets. Depending on the season, there may be just one or two seatings per evening; reservations are a must. And for the ultimate in up-close dining, you can attempt to reserve The Chef's Table, located right in the kitchen; you and your guests can watch and interact with the chef and his team as they prepare a dinner based on your preferences. The Chef's table seats up to six and is often booked up to six months in advance.

Citricos ($$$), a posh eatery featuring Mediterranean, Caribbean, Italian, and South Florida cuisine, is a mix of New and Old World design and menu with an "on-stage" kitchen. Specialties include Florida lobster rataouille with lamb loin, and a citrus souffle. Most dishes are prepared without butter or cream sauces, emphasizing oils infused with herbs and spices. Decadent desserts include chocolate ravioli with licorice ice cream.

Other changes at the Grand Floridian Resort & Spa include expanded concierge services and the addition of a 44-foot yacht available for private parties on the lake right outside its doors.

1900 Park Fare ($$) offers buffet breakfasts and dinners in an attractive room that features carousel horses, a 100-year-old band organ named Big Bertha, and Disney characters. The breakfast buffet with Mary Poppins and friends from 7:30 to 11:30 A.M. is priced at $15.95 for adults and $9.95 for children ages 3 to 11 and includes Mickey Mouse waffles, pancakes, French toast, eggs, and more. At dinner with Mickey and Minnie from 5:30 to 9 P.M., the adult price is $21.95, and offerings include grilled chicken, baked fish, and salads.

The showplace seafood and steak eatery is **Narcoossee's** ($$$), with diners surrounding an open kitchen in a building that is built out into Seven Seas Lagoon. Open for lunch from 11:30 A.M. to 3 P.M., and dinner from 5 to 10 P.M.; entrees start at about $15 and climb sharply. The chef calls the menu "Floribbean" with specialties such as oven-roasted Caicos baby conch and roasted grouper with crabmeat crust. *Narcoosee*, by the way, is a Native American word meaning "little bear."

Afternoon tea and light fare is served at the **Garden View Lounge** ($$). The **Grand Floridian Café** ($$) offers a coffee-shop menu all day, including Pasta Havana with garlic, cilantro, white wine, lemon juice, and cream sauce served with your choice of vegetables, chicken, or shrimp; mango chicken; and filet mignon. Informal meals, including pizza, burgers, and sandwiches, are available at **Gasparilla Grill and Games** ($).

There are two clay tennis courts and a heated swimming pool; the marina at the white sand beach offers watercraft for rent.

Transportation to the parks is by monorail, water taxi, and bus. The parking lot is across the road; at the end of a long day, it can feel like the next county.

★★★**Disney's Polynesian Resort $$$$.** 1600 Seven Seas Drive, Lake Buena Vista. (407) 824-2000. A Disneyfied version of Hawaiian Island architecture and landscaping, including palm-lined, torch-lit walkways, tropical gardens, two exotic swimming pools (one with a slide built into a volcano), and a station on the monorail. Oh, and did I mention the indoor waterfall in the lobby? This place is especially magical at night.

Dancers perform at the nightly **Polynesian Revue** dinner show; there are four other restaurants in the complex. The resort includes 855 rooms in two- and three-story island-style longhouses, plus a marina, pools, and a kid's club. You can rent Water Sprites, sailboats, and other watercraft at the marina.

Every room has a patio, with most offering a view of the lagoon or one of the swimming pools. Special suites that include King Kamehameha concierge services are on the lagoon side of several of the longhouses.

The **'Ohana Feast** ($$$), served nightly from 5 to 10 P.M., includes fire-grilled meats, fowl, and shrimp, and stir-fried vegetables and noodles. A character breakfast ($$) is served from 7:30 to 11 A.M., hosted by Minnie and friends.

New in 1999 at the Polynesian Resort is **Kona Café**, an energetic casual restaurant that mixes Pacific Rim spices and American classics for breakfast, lunch, and dinner. Pots of Kona coffee are ground to order all day.

Every afternoon at 4:30 P.M., **Mickey's Tropical Revue** (The Legend of Minnie-Lani and Koa-Mickey) is presented under a canopy at Luau Cove. The kiddie show includes cameos by Minnie, Pluto, Goofy, Chip 'n' Dale, and, of course, Mickey. The family-style dinner ($$$) includes specialty drinks. Reservations are advised.

In the evening, Luau Cove is home to a **Polynesian Luau** ($$$), including hula and fire dancers. In most seasons there are seatings at 6:45 and 9 P.M.

Kids have their own club at **Neverland**, for children from ages 4 to 12. Open from 5 P.M. to midnight, with a three-hour minimum at $8 per hour; there's even a special buffet for the kids served from 6 to 8 P.M. Call for reservations at (407) 824-2170.

The resort includes two heated outdoor swimming pools, a sand volleyball court, and a white sand beach. Watercraft are available for rent at the marina.

Transportation to the parks is by monorail, water taxi, and bus. You can also see the nightly Electrical Water Pageant from the resort.

Fort Wilderness Resort and Campground $$–$$$$. 4510 North Fort Wilderness Trail, Lake Buena Vista. (407) 824-2900. Park your camper, pitch a tent, or rent one of Disney's Fleetwood Trailer Homes, complete with air-conditioning, television, telephone, kitchen, and daily housekeeping service. All of the 784 campsites at the secluded 780-acre site include electrical hookups, water, and a charcoal grill; most have sanitary hookups. The sites are intended for tent or trailer campers up to 65 feet. Comfort stations, a trading post, and shower and laundry facilities are nearby.

Pay attention to the campsite number you are assigned; a knowledgeable visitor (like all of the readers of this book) may be able to improve on the location. Low numbers from 100 to 599 are near the beach and Pioneer Hall. The high numbers, from 1,500, are quiet and remote.

Inside one of the 408 wilderness homes, you'll probably have a hard time remembering you are within the woods; the one-bedroom units include a double or bunk bed, and a double Murphy bed in the sitting area. The air-conditioned homes feature a full kitchen and daily maid service.

Disney's Fort Wilderness Resort and Campground also offers **wilderness cabins**. Yes, they're cabins, but they also feature daily maid service, cable television, and air conditioning with sleeping accommodations for six and a full kitchen and outdoor grill.

Nightly rental rates range from $199 to $234 per night. The 130 cabins are slowly replacing Wilderness Homes, which are manufactured houses, at the campground.

The Tri-Circle D Petting Farm is located between Pioneer Hall and Horse Barn, open to children of all ages, for free. Kids weighing under 80 pounds can also ride a pony at the farm.

The resort includes horseback riding, fishing, canoeing, and biking. There are two heated swimming pools and a large beach on Bay Lake. Nearby are the

Osprey Ridge and Eagle Pines golf courses, the **River Country** water park, and **Discovery Island**. There's a nightly campfire gathering near the **Meadow Trading Post**, including free Disney movies and sing-alongs with Chip 'n' Dale. Fort Wilderness is also a good place to watch the nightly Electrical Water Pageant.

In the center of the resort is **Pioneer Hall**, which includes the **Hoop-Dee-Doo Musical Revue** ($$$), an all-you-can-eat hoedown dinner show presented three times a night in peak season and featuring fried chicken, spare ribs, corn on the cob, and strawberry shortcake. Reservations are essential most nights.

Crockett's Tavern ($) is open for dinner only, from 4 to 11 P.M., featuring snacks and fast food.

The **Trail's End Buffet** ($), which features a dramatic high-beamed ceiling, offers meals all day. Breakfast is offered from 7:30 to 11 A.M., lunch from 11:30 A.M. to 3:30 P.M., and dinner from 4 to 10 P.M. The dish du jour becomes pizza from 9:30 to 11 P.M. nightly.

You can purchase groceries at the **Crossroads of Lake Buena Vista** shopping center just outside of the Walt Disney World park or bring them with you in your own vehicle.

Transportation to the parks is by bus, tram, and water taxi.

A limited number of tents are available for rent if you don't want to bring your own equipment.

Shades of Green on Walt Disney Resort—U.S. Armed Forces Recreation Center. The former Disney Inn, situated between two PGA tour golf courses (probably the only ones in the world with sand traps shaped like Mickey Mouse), this 288-room rustic resort is offered to vacationing servicemen and women from all branches of the armed forces, as well as civilian employees of the Department of Defense and certain other present and former employees and spouses of military branches; reservations are made through the central accommodations office.

Epcot and Disney-MGM Resort Area

★★★**Disney's Yacht and Beach Club Resorts $$$$.** 1800 Epcot Resorts Boulevard, Lake Buena Vista. (407) 934-8000. A pair of attractive resorts nearby to Epcot Center and the Disney-MGM Studios Theme Park and set around their own lake. The Yacht Club is the more formal of the two, made to appear like a New England grand hotel with its own small lighthouse. Both hotels share **Stormalong Bay**, a fantasy lagoon filled with pools and water activities, including water slides, bubble jets, and a whirlpool. A fleet of boats is available for rent, too.

The Yacht Club includes 635 rooms and the Beach Club an additional 580; it also has a health club, tennis courts, a marina, a beach, and a pool. The **Sandcastle Club** is for kids ages 4 to 12, open from 5 P.M. to midnight with a charge of about $4 per hour for the first child and $2 per hour for additional kids. Dinner is available for an additional charge. Call (407) 934-6290 for information.

The **Cape May Café** ($$) features a nightly indoor New England–style clambake with clams, mussels, chicken, chowders, and more, served buffet style from 5:30 to 9:30 P.M. There's also a breakfast buffet from 7:30 to 11 A.M. starring Goofy, Chip 'n' Dale, and a special guest for $12.95 and $7.95.

At the Yacht Club, there's the **Yachtsman Steakhouse** ($$$) from 5:30 to 10 P.M., where you can dine on Chateaubriand, steak, prime rib, fish, or poultry.

The **Yacht Club Galley** ($) features a buffet breakfast and menu items all day, including pot roast, barbecue pork ribs, Pasta Primavera, and Seafood Sunrise, which is a dish of shrimp, scallops, crab cake and rice pilaf with saffron dijon and spicy tomato sauce.

Down by the beach shared by both clubs is **Hurricane Hanna's Grill** ($), open for lunch and dinner for burgers and dogs, and **Beaches and Cream** ($), serving all-American hot dogs and ice cream.

The resorts are within walking or quick tram distance of the International Gateway entrance to Epcot Center; you can also catch a water taxi to the Disney-MGM Studios or a bus to the Magic Kingdom.

★★★**Walt Disney World Dolphin $$$$.** 1500 Epcot Resorts Boulevard, Lake Buena Vista. (407) 934-3000. ★★★**Walt Disney World Swan $$$$.** 1200 Epcot Resorts Boulevard, Lake Buena Vista. (407) 934-4000. Why not have a gigantic triangular hotel with a huge dolphin's head on top, or a rounded building graced by a pair of tremendous swans? This is Walt Disney World, after all. Two of the most distinctive hotels of the park face each other across a large grotto pool that has a waterfall and whirlpools.

The Dolphin, operated by Sheraton, offers 1,509 rooms and includes several interesting eateries. **Harry's Safari Bar & Grille** ($$$) offers seafood, beef, and yards of ale. **Juan & Only's Cantina** ($$) is known for its Mexican specialties, including a fajita bar. **Palio** ($$) is a casual Italian bistro that features strolling musicians and a wood-fired oven.

Next door at the Swan (operated by Westin Hotels and Resorts) you will find the **Garden Grove Cafe** ($$) in a greenhouse, and **Kimono's** ($$), an Oriental lounge and sushi bar. At night, the Garden Grove becomes **Gulliver's** ($$$), serving prime rib and fresh seafood in a fanciful setting. The room is also used for character breakfasts and dinners.

The resorts include a health club, tennis courts, a marina, a beach, and **Camp Dolphin** and **Camp Swan** for kids from ages 4 to 12; the camps are generally open evenings from about 4 P.M. to midnight; call to check hours and make reservations.

Disney's Fantasia Gardens and **Fantasia Fairways Miniature Golf** are located across the road from the Swan and Dolphin.

Both hotels are within walking distance of, or a short tram ride to the International Gateway entrance of Epcot near the France Pavilion. Water taxis run to Disney-MGM Studios. Buses head to the Magic Kingdom and other parts of Walt Disney World.

★★**Disney's Caribbean Beach Resort $$$.** 900 Cayman Way, Lake Buena Vista. (407) 934-3400. One of the best bargains within the park, the sprawling 2,112-room resort spreads across five "villages" named after Caribbean islands (Aruba, Barbados, Jamaica, Martinique, and Trinidad). Each colorful village has its own pool and beach, with rooms in two-story buildings.

In addition, the five communities are linked to the **Old Port Royale** ($) food court along **Barefoot Bay**. You'll find a wide range of fast-food choices, including **Wok Shop** (for basic Chinese fare), **Cinnamon Bay Bakery**, **Montego's Deli**, **Port Royale Hamburger Shop**, **Bridgetown Broiler** (grilled chicken and fajitas), and **Royale Pizza & Pasta Shop**; outside is a large swimming pool that includes a fort with water slides and water cannon.

The **Captain's Tavern** ($$) includes Aruba scallops blackened with herbs, Cayman Paella, Trinidad Chicken, pork chops, and rib eye steak.

Guests can also rent a bike or boat at the marina, and there is a lovely 1.5-mile walking or jogging path around the lake at the resort. And there is **Parrot Cay**, a children's playground on a small island.

Transportation to the parks is by bus.

Disney's All-Star Sports Resort $$. 1701 West Buena Vista Drive, Lake Buena Vista. (407) 939-5000. Together with the All-Star Music and All-Star Movies resorts, this is Disney's "economy" zone; the hotels are spiffed-up motels with comparatively small rooms. The 246-acre site is just southwest of the Disney-MGM Studios and near the **Blizzard Beach** water park. Transportation to the theme parks is by bus.

The 1,920-room All-Star Sports Resort focuses on five sports themes: football, baseball, basketball, tennis, and surfing. All around are unusual sports scenes, including palm trees arranged to look like a basketball team at tip-off, an interior courtyard that resembles a football field, a quiet pool in the shape of a baseball infield, and wild sports icons.

At the **Surf's Up** building, bold colors glisten on 38-foot-tall surfboards and nearly a thousand colorful fish appear to be swimming along a wavy balcony; two giant shark fins encircle a free-form pool surrounded by swaying palms. At the **Hoops Hotel**, huge pennants from favorite college teams cover the roof line, and five-foot basketballs hang from the railings. The baseball-theme **Home Run Hotel** features stadium lights, scoreboards, and an outfield fence. Footballs and helmets big enough for Godzilla welcome guests to the **Touchdown Hotel**. And stairwells shaped like cans of tennis balls decorate the **Center Court** hotel.

The central check-in is at **Stadium Hall**, which features red, white, and blue seats, caged basketball court lighting, and red lockers. At the **End Zone** ($) food court, open from 6 A.M. to 11 P.M., giant sports figures perch atop brightly colored dining booths.

The scheme carries over to the guest rooms, too, which offer sports bedspreads, megaphone light fixtures, and bold artwork.

Disney's All-Star Music Resort $$. 1801 West Buena Vista Drive, Lake Buena Vista. (407) 939-6000. The 1,920-room All-Star Music Resort features country, rock, Broadway, calypso, and jazz themes.

Check-in for the music-theme hotel is in **Melody Hall**, where you'll also find the **Intermission** food court ($), open from 6 A.M. to 11 P.M.

Disney's All-Star Movies Resort $$. The third installment in the All-Star group features giant icons from favorite Disney movies, including *101 Dalmatians*, *Toy Story*, *Fantasia*, *The Mighty Ducks*, *Fantasia 2000,* and *The Love*

Bug. There are 1,920 more rooms plus a hockey-rink swimming pool and a Fantasia pool where Sorceror Mickey directs a liquid symphony.

Pongo and Perdita from "101 Dalmatians" and Buzz Lightyear from "Toy Story" tower more than 35 feet tall. Giant sorceror's hats, spell books, brooms and buckets decorate the Fantasia area, and the Mighty Ducks section scores points with giant hockey sticks, goalie nets, and duck-shaped hockey masks.

Also at the resort is a segment from *Fantasia 2000* named "The Steadfast Tin Soldier", with larger-than-life icons that include a ballerina, a jack-in-the-box, and tin soldiers.

★★★★**Disney's BoardWalk Inn $$$$** and ★★★★**Disney's BoardWalk Villas $$$$.** 2101 Epcot Resorts Boulevard, Lake Buena Vista. (407) 939-1500. Way back before there was such a thing as a Disney theme park (yes, kids, there was such a time) our forebears ventured to the beach to grand "boardwalk" resorts, including famed Coney Island in New York, and others along the Jersey Shore. It's a place of striped awnings and balconies like those of oceanfront inns of the 1930s.

Flash forward to Disney's BoardWalk resort, which re-creates some of the old-time fun with 378 hotel rooms and 532 Vacation Club time-share units in a 45-acre area along Crescent Lake near Epcot, across the water from Disney's Yacht and Beach Club Resorts with views of Crescent Lake or gardens. Guests can walk around the lake on the boardwalk to Epcot, take a boat to Epcot or the Disney-MGM Studios, or take a bus to the Magic Kingdom and other destinations within Walt Disney World.

This is one of the loveliest spots at Walt Disney World, with hardly a mouse in sight. Take the time to explore some of the eateries and stores around the lake; there is a fascinating collection of old photos and pageant tickets from beach towns like Atlantic City.

Among the guest rooms are 14 two-story **Garden Suites**, luxury accommodations made to look like New England homes that have white picket fences and gardens. The foremost place to stay is the 2,000-square-foot **Steeplechase Suite** at the **Innkeeper's Club**.

The **Little Toots** child care facility is open from 4 P.M. to midnight for youngsters ages 4 to 12, at a rate of $4 per hour. Also offered is the **Keister Coaster Club**, a day program that offers tours of Walt Disney World Resort properties and other outdoor activities, priced at $55 per child. For information and reservations call (407) 939-6301.

The **ESPN Club** sports bar is an athletic supporter's heaven, with more television monitors and big screens than your average appliance store; they display a wide range of sporting events. The menu offers a range of bar food and drink including Bloody Mary Chili. Specialties include Tailgate BBQ Pork, Mighty Duck "Chick Trick," penne pasta, and the Slider Burger.

Jellyrolls offers dueling pianos (and piano players) and snacks.

At the **Big River Grille & Brewing Works** ($), the brewmaster crafts five specialty beers, served along with pub pies, sausages, and gourmet burgers, and more substantial entrees, including yellowfin tuna marinated in teriyaki sauce, breast of chicken with shiitake mushrooms in Rocket Red Ale sauce, and

House calls. House Med, an in-room health care service, can dispatch a medical technician to your hotel room between 8 A.M. and 11 P.M.; the technician can consult with a physician to obtain certain prescription medicines if necessary. Call 648-9234 for assistance.

You can also find many walk-in medical clinics listed in the Orlando or Kissimmee phone book.

"tilted" veal loaf, from 10 A.M. to 2 A.M. The three flagship beers brewed on the premises are the aggressive Rocket Red Ale, Title Pale Ale, and Wowzer's Wheat, the lightest in body and flavor, featuring orange peel added during the brewing.

Atlantic Dance is a "big band" lounge. The libations of choice include 25 signature martinis; you can also indulge in a hand-rolled cigar. Admission is about $3 during the week and $5 on weekends; you must be 21 or older to enter. Open 8 P.M. to 2 A.M. nightly. Atlantic Dance made the transition from "big band" to pop music in 1998.

Also at the resort is **Spoodles** ($$), featuring Mediterranean cuisine from France, Spain, Italy, Greece, and North Africa for breakfast, lunch, and dinner, from 7 A.M. to 10 P.M. A breakfast buffet offers traditional and unusual baked and stir-fried offerings. Lunch and dinner offerings include tapas: Spanish Lamb Pinchos, barbecued Moroccan beef skewers, oak-grilled vegetable antipasto platter with balsamic syrup, and wood-oven-roasted half chicken or snapper.

The **Flying Fish Café** ($$$) offers seafood and steaks each evening from 5 to 10 P.M. and later on the weekends. Specialties include a "fritto misto" of rock shrimp, squid, and the catch of the day served with braised cranberry beans and lemon pepper aioli; oak-wood-grilled center-cut pork chop; spicy barbecue glazed salmon filet with corn pudding and sugar snap peas; and potato-wrapped striped bass with leek fondue and cabernet sauvignon reduction.

The original concept for this resort seemed to imply that Disney would add a rock-'em, roll-'em wooden coaster; as built, the coaster is a water slide that enters into the Luna Park swimming pool, including a 200-foot roller-coaster water slide and water-spouting elephants.

Outside the **BoardWalk Inn**, one of the vacation resorts, is a fully operational miniature carousel dating from the 1920s from famed carousel-maker Marcus Illions.

Admission and parking is free for the boardwalk, shops, and restaurants; valet parking is also available. An admission charge is levied for Jellyrolls and Atlantic Dance, and you must be 21 or older.

★★★**Disney's Coronado Springs Resort $$$.** 1000 West Buena Vista Drive, Lake Buena Vista. (407) 939-1000. A moderately priced convention hotel, an attractive 1,967-room spread that pays homage to Francisco de Coronado's explorations from Mexico to the American Southwest. It is also the only place in the world where Mexico and Santa Fe face Polynesia across a lake.

Located on 136 acres on the west side of World Drive, near Blizzard Beach and the Disney-MGM Studios Theme Park, the resort's haciendas lie in the shade of palm trees, nearby to a white sand beach on 15-acre Lago Dorado and four themed pools, including one large water hole with a slide. The resort appears as a series of three- and four-story *palacios* tinted in shades of desert sand, sunset pink, and tropical green. There are also two-story cabanas on the northern shore of the lake.

At the edge of the lagoon, the five-story Mayan pyramid is the splashy centerpiece of an oversized family fun pool, complete with twisting waterslide.

Guests stay in one of three major areas: the Casitas, representing urban centers such as Santa Fe; the Ranchos, villas landscaped with sagebrush and cactus; and the Cabanas, inspired by the beachside resorts along the Gulf Coast.

The lobby and reception area is built around La Fuente de las Palomas, a fountain that bubbles up from a Spanish urn under a domed ceiling painted with images of white clouds and doves against a perfect blue sky.

The resort features a 95,000-square-foot convention center and the largest hotel ballroom in the Southeast. Oh yes, there are also colorful plazas, palm trees, and a rocky shoreline along a lake; a 50-foot-tall Mayan pyramid lords over the pool and water play area.

The **Maya Grill** ($$$), along the lake, is open for breakfast from 7 to 11:30 A.M. and for dinner from 5 to 10 P.M. The restaurant is operated by one of the premier restaurateur families of Mexico and features a wood-fired grill where cooks braise meats and fish over an open fire. The relatively small restaurant is a hidden gem at Walt Disney World.

The **Pepper Market Food Court** ($) features Southwest, Mexican, and American dishes for all meals. You'll pick up your food from various serving stations and have your dinner card punched; a cashier translates the punch into a bill when you are ready to leave.

Francisco's ($) is a bright outdoor café-style eatery featuring lighter fare.

Recreational facilities include a sand volleyball court at the "Dig Site" pool area. Bicycles and watercraft are available for rent at **La Marina**.

Disney Village Resort Area

★★**Disney's Port Orleans Resort $$$.** 2201 Orleans Drive, Lake Buena Vista. (407) 934-5000. A re-creation of the French Quarter of New Orleans, packed with G-rated Disney detail. The resort's swimming pool is located at **Doubloon Lagoon** and includes a sea-serpent water slide: down the tongue and into the water.

Restaurants at **Port Orleans Square** include some of the more unusual offerings in the park. At the **Sassagoula Floatworks & Food Factory** ($), decorated with Mardi Gras props, check out the **King Creole Broiler**, with creole specialties; **Basin Street Burgers and Chicken; Preservation Pizza Company**, and **Jacques Beignet's Bakery**, featuring New Orleans beignets (fried dough fritters).

Bonfamille's Café ($$) offers steaks, seafood, and other dishes with a creole flair served in an attractive courtyard setting, with dinner entrees priced from about $5 to $20 and served from 5 to 10 P.M.; entrees include jambalaya, blackened sea scallops, chicken and sausage creole, and steak dishes. Breakfast is also served from 7 to 11:30 A.M., and you can expand your horizons to include eggs with andouille sausage and crawfish in creole sauce, New Orleans beignets, and turkey breast with broccoli and cheddar cheese topped with hollandaise; if you insist, you can also order pancakes.

The resort includes 1,008 rooms in seven three-story buildings, a marina, and a pool. Transportation to the parks is by water taxi or bus.

★★**Disney's Dixie Landings Resort $$$.** 1251 Dixie Drive, Lake Buena Vista. (407) 934-6000. A bit of the old South, this is another of Disney's moderately priced resorts. The huge 2,048-room resort, divided into "parishes," includes a marina and five pools; the buildings are styled after plantation mansions and low bayou homes. The Mansion rooms are a bit more formal, evoking memories of grand staircases and columns; the bayou rooms in tin-roofed structures look as if they would fit in well with the swamp.

There's a stocked fishing hole and a country-style water slide at **Old Man Island** at the center of the resort. Boats and bicycles are available for rent at **Dixie Levee**.

The real Old Town. Orlando was established as a campground for soldiers during the Seminole Indian War of 1835 to 1842, and it then continued as a trading post. The war resulted in removal of most Native Americans in Florida to reservations in Oklahoma.

The Orlando Metropolitan Area was the seventh-fastest growing area in the country, according to the 1990 Census. Its population grew 53 percent between 1980 and 1990, to 1,072,748. The city itself includes 54 lakes.

A food court is offered at a central marketplace named **Colonel's Cotton Mill** ($) and includes the **Acadian Pizza 'n' Pasta**, **Bleu Bayou Burgers and Chicken**, **Cajun Broiler**, **Riverside Market and Deli**, and the **Southern Trace Bakery**.

Boatwright's Dining Hall ($$) offers a Cajun and American menu in a reproduction of a shipbuilding shed overlooking the Sassagoula River. Specialties include gumbo, grilled catfish Bayou Teche, roasted chicken, and prime rib, with dinner entrees from about $5 to $20, served from 5 to 10 P.M.; breakfast is also served from 7 to 11:30 A.M.

Transportation to the parks is by water taxi and bus.

★★**Disney's Village Resort $$$$.** Magnolia Way, Lake Buena Vista. (407) 827-1100. A collection of light and open townhouses, "treehouses," and multilevel villas in the woods near the Disney-MGM Studios Theme Park and Epcot Center.

For some families, renting one of these villa rooms may be less expensive or more convenient than taking two small hotel rooms. Most of the smaller one-bedroom Club Suites include refrigerators, and one- and two-bedroom Vacation Villas include fully equipped kitchens.

Nearby are the **Lake Buena Vista Golf Course**, five lighted pools, tennis courts, and a marina. The resort includes 585 units and a health club. Villas range from one- and two-bedroom villas to the fancier Fairway and Treehouse Villas. You can also rent one of four Grand Vista Suites, fully furnished homes originally intended as model homes for a residential or time-sharing resort.

Some of the best bass fishing in Walt Disney World is in the canals right outside the door of many of the villas.

The resort is across the lagoon from **Pleasure Island** and next to the **Disney Village Marketplace** shops and restaurants. Groceries for the villas are available at the **Gourmet Pantry** within the resort, or you can take a short drive outside the park to the **Crossroads of Lake Buena Vista** shopping center (outside the park, it is nevertheless on Disney property . . . don't want to let any of those dollars leak out of the company's hands, do we?)

The restaurant at the resort is the **Lake Buena Vista Club** ($), a family eatery in the clubhouse on Club Lake Drive. Open all day; specialties include Key West Caesar Salad, burgers, and chicken.

Transportation to the parks is by bus.

★★**Disney's Old Key West Resort $$$$.** 1510 North Cove Road, Lake Buena Vista. (407) 827-7000. Deluxe studios and one- to three-bedroom vacation homes with whirlpool tubs. Shared facilities include a video library, four pools, tennis courts, and a marina.

Olivia's Cafe ($$) is open all day with outdoor and indoor seating for Key West specialties that include conch egg rolls, conch chowder, Mangrove Snapper wrapped in a banana leaf and steamed with herb butter, Florida Paella, and Mojo Chicken drizzled with fresh lime vinaigrette. A character breakfast with Winnie the Pooh and Tigger too is offered Sundays and Wednesdays.

★★★**Disney's Vacation Club Resort $$$$.** 1510 North Cove Road, Lake Buena Vista. (407) 827-7700. Located on the **Lake Buena Vista Golf Course**, units range from studios that sleep four to one-, two-, and three-bedroom units and Grand Villas with beds for as many as 12.

I could write a book about real estate—until I do, here's my best advice about buying a time-share at Walt Disney World or anywhere else: don't do it on an impulse. Talk to your accountant or a financial adviser or someone else who is not in the business of selling you something other than advice.

In any case, you don't have to buy a time-share to stay at the resort; unsold rooms, or rooms turned back to Disney for resale by owners, are available for rent.

The restaurant at the club is **Olivia's**, which specializes in Key West dishes from conch fritters to Key lime pie, with entrees priced from about $5 to $20.

★★★**The Villas at The Disney Institute $$$$.** 1901 Buena Vista Drive, Lake Buena Vista. (407) 827-1100. In the woods near Disney's adult-learning complex, each home away from home can accommodate from four to eight people.

At the **Seasons Dining Room**, with the change of the calendar comes new choices on the menu, featuring dishes from California to the Mediterranean and beyond.

The Villas are also within walking distance of restaurants at Pleasure Island and the Disney Village Marketplace.

Disney Hotel Plaza

Best Western Lake Buena Vista Resort Hotel	$89 to $199
Hotel Royal Plaza	$89 to $195
Courtyard by Marriott	$99 to $179
Grosvenor Resort	$117 to $183

Wyndham Palace Resort & Spa	$149 to $229
Doubletree Guest Suites Resort	$152 to $299
The Hilton Resort	$210 to $325

Seven hotels built and operated by major (non-Disney) hotel companies are clustered near the Disney Village Marketplace and Pleasure Island. Guests can drive or use Disney buses to get to the park. These are high-quality hotels without the fanciful touch of Disney-owned properties.

★★**Wyndham Palace Resort & Spa.** Formerly the Buena Vista Palace, a 27-story lakeside tower with views of much of Walt Disney World and nine restaurants and a **Recreation Island** with three pools. The resort includes more than 1,014 rooms and suites, a health club, tennis courts, and pools. Restaurants include the top-of-the-tower haute cuisine **Arthur's 27** and **The Top of the Palace Lounge.** There's also the less-formal **Outback** restaurant with seafood and steaks. **Summer Kids' Klub** is a program for children from ages 4 to 12. (407) 827-2727 or (800) 327-2990. www.wyndham.com

★★**Courtyard by Marriott.** A family-oriented hotel with a 14-story central atrium and 323 rooms. This was originally the Howard Johnson Resort Hotel, until it was converted lock, stock, and towels to a Marriott. Phone (407) 828-8888 or (800) 223-9930.

★★**Doubletree Guest Suites Resort.** Each one- or two-bedroom suite includes a microwave, refrigerator, and small wet bar, and the 229-room hotel offers a pool and tennis courts. The restaurant is the **Streamers Restaurant.** This hotel had previously been the Guest Quarters Suite Resort. (407) 934-1000 or (800) 222-8733.

★★★**Grosvenor Resort.** A lakeside tower with 625 rooms that includes a large recreation facility featuring tennis and handball courts, a children's playground, and heated swimming pools. **Baskerville's,** a British-theme restaurant, is modeled after Sherlock Holmes' 221B Baker Street home in London; next door is **Moriarty's,** a pub named after the great detective's archnemesis. (407) 828-4444 or (800) 624-4109.

★★★**The Hilton at Walt Disney World Village.** A large resort and conference center directly across from the Disney Village Marketplace. In 1999, a top-to-bottom renovation was underway with a Main Street Disney theme. It includes nine restaurants and lounges, among them **Covington Mill** and a **Benihana** Japanese steak house. Also featured is an outdoor spa. The **Vacation Station Kid's Hotel** caters to kids from 4 to 12 years old; guests at the hotel can park their kids for two hours for as little as $2.25, with additional charges for more hours. (407) 827-4000 or (800) 782-4414.

★★**Hotel Royal Plaza.** This 396-room hotel includes two restaurants and lounges with nightly entertainment, a pool, and tennis courts. The **Verandah Café** is open until midnight. (407) 828-2828 or (800) 248-7890.

★★**Best Western Lake Buena Vista Resort Hotel.** A lakeside hotel with a Caribbean flavor and a rooftop nightclub known as **Toppers** that offers a spectacular view of Walt Disney World. The **Traders** restaurant offers breakfast and dinner, and the **Parakeet Café** has pizza and snacks. (407) 828-2424 or (800) 348-3765.

Why Stay at a Hotel Within Walt Disney World?

The hotels within Walt Disney World are among the most attractive, most imaginative places to stay at any major tourist area we know of. They offer all sorts of extras not available outside the park, and quite a few conveniences.

However, all of this comes at a price. The lowest rates at Walt Disney–owned or –operated hotels, or those operated by major chains on the park property, generally start at around $70 per night in low-season, which is the high end of most standard off-site hotels. It is up to you to decide what value to place on the extras that come with your higher room rates; you should also consider the possibility of obtaining similar special treatment outside the park. (I heard of one family that booked perfectly nice rooms a few miles outside of the park and used just some of the money they saved to engage limousine service to and from the park.)

Insider advantages to guests who stay at Walt Disney World Resorts include:

Free parking within Walt Disney World for the length of their stay.

Complimentary use of the Walt Disney World transportation system, including monorail, bus, ferryboat, and launch transportation to the parks, avoiding crowded parking lots.

Sleepover camp. Sometime in 2001 the creatures in Animal Kingdom will have a bit of company. The 1,300-room Disney's Animal Kingdom Lodge, nearby the park, will have its own savannah and animal features.

Advance reservations for dining, Disney Dinner Shows, and Disney Character Breakfasts. Guests can make reservations as soon as they receive confirmation of hotel reservations.

Preferred access to tee times on all five championship golf courses. Also available are horseback riding, swimming, tennis, health clubs, and other facilities. (Golf, horses, tennis, and other activities, though, are not free.)

Hotels Outside the Park

I-192/Irlo Bronson Memorial Highway/Vine Street Kissimmee

Katella Avenue, which fronts on the main entrance to Disneyland in California, turned out to be one of Walt Disney's worst nightmares. When Disneyland was first built, it was surrounded by lush green orange groves. But with the success of the park, the environs became an unending stretch of unattractive strip motels, gift shops, miniature golf courses, and fast-food restaurants.

When Disney began secretly buying up tens of thousands of acres of Central Florida swamp and cypress groves in the 1960s, it was with the intention of shielding his new park deep within a green barrier. There was to be no Katella Avenue at Walt Disney World.

And, in fact, Disney was successful. The Magic Kingdom, Epcot Center, Disney-MGM Studios Theme Park, Disney's Animal Kingdom, and all of the other attractions within the park seem to exist in a world unto themselves. There are tens of thousands of hotel rooms within the park as well as places to eat for all guests and day visitors, but the sheer size of the park swallows them up and hides them from sight of each other.

But, of course, the Walt Disney Company cannot own every square mile of Florida, even though they probably would if they could.

There are two principal places where Disney meets the real world: at Apopka-Vineland Road (S.R. 535) and at I-192. And then there is the rest of the Orlando-Kissimmee area.

Most of the hotels and attractions on I-192 can be found between I-4 and I-441 (Main Street/South Orange Blossom Trail) in Kissimmee. I-4 at I-192 actually lies within the southern end of the huge Walt Disney World property.

West of I-4, toward I-27, is the less popular side of I-192, although a number of newer hotels have been built in the area. Room rates at low-season range from as low as $29 at I-27 to about $75 per night closer to the park. Hotels in this area often include "Main Gate" or "West Gate" in their name.

The busier side of I-192 runs about 10 miles from I-4 east to Main Street in Kissimmee. The area closest to I-4 is often called "Main Gate East." Near I-4 you will find attractions including Arabian Nights, Old Town, and Water Mania.

Bunkhouse logic. The far distant reaches of I-192 and the backroads outside the obvious tourist areas are the homes of the lowest rung on the ladder—I have seen rates as low as $19.99 for the night. Be sure to read the fine print; some prices are for single guests only, with an additional $5 or $10 for a second person. Several hotels advertise a low price and then add a "service charge" to the nightly bill.

And don't be afraid to ask to see the room you are being offered *before* you sign the register. If the room is dirty or otherwise unacceptable, you can walk away; if they refuse to show you a room when you ask, run away.

Between the intersection of S.R. 535 and Kissimmee are Medieval Times, Fun 'n Wheels, and the Kissimmee Municipal Airport. A few miles past South Orange Blossom Trail and just short of the intersection with the Florida Turnpike is the Osceola County Stadium, the Spring Training home of the Houston Astros.

Lake Buena Vista, Apopka-Vineland Road, Crossroads, World Center

The "back door" to Walt Disney World can be found off S.R. 535: Apopka-Vineland Road. Here Hotel Plaza Boulevard leads into the Disney Hotel Plaza area, Disney Village, and Pleasure Island. Farther along the road are the entranceways to the Magic Kingdom, Epcot, Disney-MGM Studios, and the other attractions within the park.

Some of the property in this area is actually owned and controlled by the Walt Disney Company, although it is not technically within the park. Many of the area hotels offer free transportation to Walt Disney World, and some may be on the route for transportation companies that pick up passengers at Orlando International Airport; inquire when you call for information.

I-192 is a many-named splendor. I-192 bears several different names in its traverse from I-27 west of the park to and through downtown Kissimmee. For much of its length near the park, it is known as Irlo Bronson Memorial Highway. (Bronson was a prominent local politician and developer.) Near Kissimmee, it is called Vine Street; past Kissimmee toward St. Cloud, it is named 13th Street. Some segments are also known as Space Coast Highway. *You can call it 192 anywhere and people will know what you mean.*

★★**Embassy Suites Resort Lake Buena Vista.** 8100 Lake Avenue. An all-suite hotel in Lake Buena Vista, with bedroom, living room, dining, and kitchen areas, refrigerator, and microwave. (407) 239-1144 or (800) 257-8483. $$$-$$$$

★★**Holiday Inn Sunspree–Lake Buena Vista.** 13351 S.R. 535. A family resort just outside the Disney Village Marketplace area on S.R. 535. All of the 507 rooms include a refrigerator and microwave; some offer KidSuites, a mini-room for the youngsters within the parents' suite. There's also a free activity program for children from ages 3 to 12 from 8 A.M. to midnight. Restaurants include **Maxine's**, with breakfast and dinner buffets.

Max's Funtime Parlor has breakfast and dinner buffets with Character Shows, featuring the Kidsuite Gang: Max, Maxine, Paully Wog, Grahammie Bear, Mollee Mouse, and Mattie Mole.(407) 239-4500 or (800) 366-6299. $$–$$$. *Discount coupon for character breakfast or dinner buffet in this book.*

★★**Howard Johnson Park Square Inn.** 8501 Palm Parkway. A family-oriented resort with 308 rooms; suites include a refrigerator and microwave. The **Courtyard Cafe** offers a breakfast buffet and dinner from a menu. (407) 239-6900 or (800) 635-8684. $$–$$$

★★**Hyatt Regency Grand Cypress.** Near the Disney Village Hotel Plaza. A 750-room tower plus 146 villas in and around 45 holes of golf, 12 tennis courts, and a huge pool with waterfalls and a 45-foot water slide. Phone the Hyatt Regency Grand Cypress at (407) 239-1234 or (800) 233-1234 or the Villas of Grand Cypress at (407) 239-4700 or (800) 835-7377. $$$$

★★★**Marriott's Orlando World Center.** S.R. 536 and I-4. The complex sprawls across 200 landscaped acres and includes 1,501 rooms and suites, an 18-hole golf course, several large pools, and tennis courts. There are five restaurants, including **Mikado's**, a Japanese steak house. There's a children's "lounge" for ages 4 to 12, open from 8 A.M. to 11 P.M.. The **Orlando World Center** is often used for large conventions, offering Disney and other entertainment for spouses and children while business goes on within its meeting rooms. (407) 239-4200 or (800) 228-9290. $$–$$$$

★★**Radisson Inn Lake Buena Vista.** 8686 Palm Parkway. Offering 200 rooms and a pool with water slide. (407) 239-8400 or (800) 333-3333. $$–$$$

International Drive (SeaWorld to Universal Studios Escape)

The next major stop on our tour is the International Drive area, a five-mile uninterrupted stretch of every national hotel and restaurant chain you've ever heard of, and some you probably haven't. This road serves no purpose other than for the tourist; it's a convenient midway location for the visitor looking to explore in all directions. Room rates run from about $50 to $100 in low-season at motels; a few fancy hotels have rooms at about double those prices.

One end of International Drive begins south of the Beeline Expressway at the entrance to SeaWorld. From there, it wanders more or less northerly to pass by the Orange County Convention and Civic Center, the Mercado shopping area, across Sand Lake Road (S.R. 482), in front of Wet 'n Wild and then heads east across Kirkman Road near the main entrance to Universal Studios Escape.

International Drive is, then, just minutes from SeaWorld, Universal Studios, Wet 'n Wild, and half a dozen other smaller attractions. There are restaurants of all descriptions on the road, as well. The road is about a 15-minute drive south to Walt Disney World or north to Orlando.

North of the Beeline, International Drive includes several exotically named hotel circles, including Hawaiian Court, Samoan Court, Austrian Court, and Jamaican Court.

North of Sand Lake Road, you will be across the road from Wet 'n Wild. Just before Kirkman Road, look for American Way on the left side.

Nearby to Universal Studios are Kirkman Road, Turkey Lake Road, and Republic Drive (renamed as Universal Boulevard in 1998).

Along the way, we have skipped over the hotel that may be the queen of International Drive, the elegant and somewhat unusual **Peabody Orlando**. The first-class hotel, with rooms that range from about $300 to $390, and suites that climb to $1,450, includes concierge services, an Olympic-sized swimming pool, a health club, and extensive meeting and convention facilities. (There are special rates for seniors and special promotions through the year.)

Restaurants include the gourmet eatery **Dux**, a Northern Italian trattoria known as **Capriccio**, and the **B-Line Diner**, which is reminiscent of a 1954 burger-and-milk-shake diner. But, we have skipped over the most unusual feature of the Peabody; while Disney has its mouse, SeaWorld has its whale, and Universal Studios has its shark, the Peabody has its trained ducks. Every day at 11 A.M., five somewhat trained mallards march down a red carpet to the lobby fountain, accompanied by the official duck master, to the tune of John Philip Sousa's "King Cotton" march. At 5 P.M., the procession goes the other way and the ducks return to their Royal Duck Palace. The show is free and open to visitors as well as guests. The hotel's shuttle to the theme parks, by the way, is known as the Double Ducker.

Orlando International Airport Area

The airport is located about 30 minutes away from Walt Disney World. If your plane arrives late, or if you are preparing for an early-morning departure, you might want to consider staying near the airport. Room rates for "name" hotels are higher than those in the tourist areas of Kissimmee; expect to pay $60 to $125 per night in low-season and from $70 to $150 per night in high-season.

The closest hotel to your airline's arrival gate doesn't even require you to leave the airport. The Hyatt Regency Airport hotel is within the main airport building; you might want to consider one night's stay there if your plane arrives very late or leaves very early. Rates at the Hyatt range from about $119 to $220, depending on the season.

Other hotels close to the airport can be found along Semoran Boulevard (S.R. 436), which leads into Frontage Road and McCoy Road, two service roads that run parallel to the Beeline Expressway (Route 528). Also in the neighborhood are T. G. Lee Boulevard and Augusta National Drive.

Moving west from the airport you are heading for the South Orange Blossom Trail area.

South Orange Blossom Trail/Sand Lake Road/ Florida Mall Area

Near the intersection of the Beeline Expressway and the combined Route 17-92 and 441—which is better known as the South Orange Blossom Trail— you will find a collection of more than a dozen brand-name motels. The farther north you travel, toward Orlando, the more likely you are to find lower-priced locally owned motels. (You'll also find some "adult" bookstores and strip joints.)

Rumor has it that there once was grass in the neighborhood. This is strictly a place to sleep, with the exception of the intersection of South Orange Blossom Trail with Sand Lake Road (S.R. 482). Here you will find the Florida Mall, with shopping, movie theaters, and chain restaurants. Sand Lake connects to the east with McCoy Road and runs directly into the airport.

Nightly rates in this area range from about $40 to $100 in off-season and $50 to $150 per night in high-season.

A Guide to Area Motels (Outside the Walt Disney World Resort)

$	Economy: $25 to $45 low-season; $45 to $65 high-season
$$	Budget: $45 to $75 low-season; $65 to $90 high-season
$$$	Moderate: $75 to $125 low-season; $100 to $200 high-season
$$$$	Deluxe: $125 to $200 low-season; $200 to $400 high-season
★★	Better
★★★	Superior
★★★★	Econoguide Best

(Bronson = Irlo Bronson Highway, also known as U.S. Highway 192)

Kissimmee (1 to 10 miles from Disney)

Adventure Motel. 4501 West Bronson. (407) 396-0808. $

Ambassador Motel. 4107 West Vine Street. (407) 847-7171. $

★★★**Best Western–Eastgate.** 5565 West Bronson. (800) 223-5361, (407) 396-0707. $–$$

★★★**Best Western–Maingate.** 8600 West Bronson. (800) 327-9151, (407) 396-0100. $$-$$$

★★★**Best Western Suites.** 4786 West Bronson. (800) 468-3027, (407) 396-2056. $$$

Budget Inn East. 307 East Vine Street. (407) 847-8010. $

Budget Inn–West. 4686 West Bronson. (407) 396-2322. $$

Casa Rosa Inn. 4600 West Highway 192. (800) 432-0665, (407) 396-2020. $

Central Motel. 4698 West Bronson. (407) 396-2333. $

Chateau Motel. 3518 West Vine Street. (407) 847-3477. $

Kiss me, you bull. Kissimmee has been among Florida's premier cattle raising areas, best known for its Brahma cattle way before the mice arrived.

Comfort Inn-Maingate West. 9330 West Bronson. (800) 440-4473, (941) 424-8420. $

Comfort Inn–Maingate. 7571 West Bronson. (800) 223-1628, (407) 396-7500. $$

Condo Lodge. 3187 West Vine Street. (800) 866-2660, (407) 931-2383. $$

Continental Motel. 4650 West Bronson. (800) 432-1030, (407) 396-1030. $

★★★**Courtyard by Marriott Orlando Maingate.** 7675 West Bronson. (800) 568-3352, (407) 396-4000. $$–$$$

Crown Motel. 3834 West Highway 192. (407) 933-4666. $

Days Inn East of Magic Kingdom. 5840 West Bronson. (800) 327-9126, (407) 396-7969. $$

Days Inn Eastgate. 5245 West Bronson. (800) 423-3864, (407) 396-7000. $–$$

Days Inn Kissimmee East. 2095 East Bronson. (800) FLA-2192, (407) 846-7136. $$

Days Inn Maingate West of Walt Disney World. 7980 West Bronson. (800) 327-9173, (407) 396-1000. $$-$$$

Days Inn–South Kissimmee. 4104 West Vine Street. (800) 874-5557, (407) 846-4714. $$

Days Suites East of Magic Kingdom. 5820 West Bronson. (800) 327-9126, (407) 396-7900. $$

★★★**Doubletree Guest Suites Resort Orlando Maingate.** 4787 West Bronson. (407) 397-0555. $$$

Econolodge. 4669 West Bronson. (800) 523-8729, (407) 396-1890. $

Econolodge Hawaiian Resort. 7514 West Bronson. (800) 365-6935, (407) 396-2000. $$

Economy Inns of America–Kissimmee. 5367 West Bronson. (800) 826-0778, (407) 396-4020. $

Enterprise Motel. 4121 West Vine Street. (800) 833-2655, (407) 933-1383. $

Flamingo Inn. 801 East Vine Street. (800) 780-7617, (407) 846-1935. $

Fountain Park Resort Hotel. 5150 West Bronson. (800) 327-9179, (407) 396-1111. Lakeside. $$

Four Points Sheraton. 4018 West Vine Street. (407) 870-2000. Suites. $$$

Four Winds Motel. 4596 West Bronson. (800) 826-5830, (407) 396-4011. $

Golden Link Motel. 4914 West Bronson. (800) 654-3957, (407) 396-0555. On Lake Cecile. $

★★★**Hampton Inn–Maingate.** 3104 Parkway Drive. (800) 426-7866, (407) 396-8484. $$

★★★**HoJo Inn–Maingate East.** 6051 West Bronson. (800) 288-4678, (407) 396-1748. $$

★★★**Holiday Inn Express Kissimmee East.** 2145 East Bronson. (407) 846-4646. $$

★★★**Holiday Inn Hotel & Suites Maingate East.** 5678 West Bronson. (800) 366-5437, (407) 396-4488. $$–$$$

Holiday Inn Kissimmee Downtown. 2009 West Vine Street. (800) 624-5905, (407) 846-2713. $–$$

Holiday Inn Maingate West. 7601 Black Lake Road. (800) 365-6935, (407) 396-1100. $$

★★★**Holiday Inn Nikki Bird Resort.** 7300 West Bronson. (407) 396-7300. Resort. $$–$$$

★★★**Homewood Suites Hotel.** 3100 Parkway Boulevard. (800) 255-4543, (407) 396-2229. $$$–$$$$

Howard Johnson. 4543 West Bronson. (407) 396-1340. $

Howard Johnson Maingate Central. 4985 West Bronson. (888) 753-4343, (407) 396-4343. $

Howard Johnson Hotel Maingate West. 8660 West Bronson. (800) 638-7829, (407) 396-4500. $–$$

Howard Johnson Inn Maingate East. 6051 West Bronson. (800) 288-4678, (407) 396-1748. $–$$$

Howard Johnson Inn & Suites Lakefront Park. 4836 West Bronson. (800) 952-5464, (407) 396-4762. $–$$

Howard Johnson Kissimmee Hotel. 2323 East Bronson. (800) 521-4656, (407) 846-4900. $

★★★**Hyatt Orlando.** 6375 West Bronson. (800) 233-1234, (407) 396-1234. Resort. $$–$$$

★★★**Doubletree Resort & Conference Center.** 3011 Maingate Lane. (800) 239-6478, (407) 396-1400. $$$

Key Motel. 4810 West Bronson. (407) 396-6200. Lakefront. $

Knight's Inn–Maingate. 7475 West Bronson. (407) 396-4200. $–$$

Knight's Inn–Maingate East. 2880 Poinciana Boulevard. (800) 843-5644, (407) 396-8186. $$

Lambert Inn. 410 West Vine Street. (407) 846-2015. $

Larson's Inn–Main Gate. 6075 West Bronson. (800) 841-2837, (407) 396-6100. $$

Magic Tree Resort. 2795 North Old Lake Wilson Road. (407) 396-2300. Suites. $–$$

Maple Leaf Motel. 4647 West Bronson. (800) 333-5477, (407) 396-0300. $

Masters Inns. 2945 Entry Point Boulevard. (800) 826-0778, (407) 396-7743. $

Motel 6–Maingate West. 7455 West Bronson. (407) 396-6422. $

Motel 6–Orlando East. 5731 West Bronson. (407) 396-6333. $

Palm Motel. 4519 West Bronson. (407) 396-0744. $–$$

Park Inn International Kissimmee. 4960 West Bronson. (800) 327-0072, (407) 396-1376. $$

Parkway Motel. 4529 West Bronson. (407) 396-2042. $

Quality Inn–Lake Cecile. 4944 West Bronson. (800) 864-4855, (407) 396-4455. Lakeside. $$

Quality Suites Maingate East. 5876 West Bronson. (800) 848-4148, (407) 396-8040. $$–$$$$

Quality Inn Maingate West. 7785 West Bronson. (800) 634-5525, (407) 396-1828. $–$$$

★★**Radisson Resort Parkway.** 2900 Parkway Boulevard. (800) 634-4774, (407) 396-7000. $$–$$$$

Ramada Inn. 4559 West Bronson. (800) 544-5712, (407) 396-1212. $

Ramada Limited. 5055 West Bronson. (800) 446-5669, (407) 396-2212. $–$$

★★★**Ramada Plaza Hotel Gateway.** 7470 West Bronson. (800) 327-9170, (407) 396-4400. $$–$$$

Ramada Resort Maingate. 2950 Reedy Creek Boulevard. (800) 365-6935, (407) 396-4466. $$–$$$

Record Motel. 4651 West Bronson. (800) 874-4555, (407) 396-8400. $

Red Carpet Inn East. 4700 West Bronson. (800) 462-6063, (407) 396-1133. $

★★★**Red Roof Inn Resort at Maingate.** 7491 West Bronson. (800) 669-6753, (407) 396-6000. $$–$$$

Red Roof Inn #204. 4970 Kyngs Heath Road. (800) 843-7663, (407) 396-0065. $–$$$

Regency Inn. 2050 East Bronson. (800) 955-4683, (407) 846-4545. $–$$

Resort Suites. 4694 West Bronson. (800) 432-0695, (407) 396-1780. $–$$$

Riviera Motel. 2248 East Bronson. (800) 226-8010, (407) 847-9494. $

Sevilla Inn. 4640 West Bronson. (800) 367-1363, (407) 396-4135. $

★★★**Sheraton Lakeside Village.** 7769 West Bronson. (800) 848-0801, (407) 396-2222. $$–$$$

Shoney's Inn Orlando/Kissimmee Maingate. 4156 Vine Street. (800) 222-2222, (407) 870-7374. $–$$

Sleep Inn Maingate. 8536 West Bronson. (800) 225-0086, (407) 396-1600. $–$$

Stadium Inn & Suites. 2039 East Bronson. (800) 785-7567, (407) 846-7814. $–$$

★★**Star Island Resort & Country Club.** 2800 North Poinciana Boulevard. (800) 423-8604, (407) 396-8100. $$$$

Sun Motel. 5020 West Bronson. (407) 396-2673. $

Super 8 Motel Lakeside. 4880 West Bronson. (800) 325-4872, (407) 396-1144. $–$$

Super 8 Motel Maingate. 5875 West Bronson. (407) 396-8883. $–$$

Thriftlodge East Gate. 4624 West Bronson. (800) 648-4148, (407) 396-2151. $–$$

Thrifty Inn. 1620 West Vine Street. (407) 847-7224. $

Traveler's Inn on Lake Cecile. 4900 West Bronson. (800) 643-8657, (407) 396-1668. $–$$

★★★**Travelodge Hotel Maingate East.** 5711 West Bronson. (800) 327-1128, (407) 396-4222. $$–$$$

Travelodge Suites–East Gate Orange. 5399 West Bronson. (407) 396-7666. $–$$$

★★★**Westgate Towers.** 7600 West Bronson. (888) 808-7410, (407) 396-2500. $$–$$$$

Kissimmee (10 to 15 miles from Disney)

Best Western–Kissimmee. 2261 East Bronson. (800) 547-3278, (407) 846-2221. $

★★**Caribbean Villas.** 2003 Trinidad Court. (800) 327-4730, (407) 846-4405. $$

Colonial Motor Lodge. 1815 West Vine Street. (800) 325-4348, (407) 847-6121. $$

Days Inn Downtown. 4104 West Bronson. (800) 647-0010, (407) 846-4714. $$

Lake Buena Vista (1 to 10 Miles from Disney)

Comfort Inn. 8442 Palm Parkway. (800) 999-7300. $–$$

Days Inn Lake Buena Vista. 12799 Apopka-Vineland Road. (800) 224-5058. (407) 239-4441. $$

Days Inn Lake Buena Vista Village. 12490 Apopka-Vineland Road. (800) 521-3297, (407) 239-4646. $$

★★**Embassy Suites Resort Lake Buena Vista.** 8100 Lake Avenue. (407) 239-1144. Suites. $$$–$$$$

★★★**Holiday Inn Sunspree Resort Lake Buena Vista.** 13351 State Road. 535. (800) 366-6299, (407) 239-4500. $$–$$$

Howard Johnson Park Square Inn and Suites. 8501 Palm Parkway. (800) 635-8684, (407) 239-6900. $$

★★★**Hyatt Regency Grand Cypress.** One Grand Cypress Boulevard. (800) 233-1234, (407) 239-1234. $$$$

Lake Buena Vista Resort & Suites. 12205 Apopka-Vineland Road. (800) 423-3297, (407) 239-0444. $$

★★★★**Orlando World Center Marriott.** One World Center Drive. (800) 621-0638, (407) 239-4200. $$$$

★★**Radisson Inn Lake Buena Vista.** 8686 Palm Parkway. (407) 239-8400. $$$

★★**Residence Inn By Marriott Lake Buena Vista.** 8800 Meadow Creek Drive. (800) 331-3131, (407) 239-7700. $$$

★★**The Villas of Grand Cypress.** One North Jacaranda. (800) 835-7377, (407) 239-4700. $$$$

Wyndham Garden Hotel Lake Buena Vista. 8688 Palm Parkway. (800) 996-3426, (407) 239-8500. $$–$$$

International Drive and Convention Center Area (10 miles from Disney, 1 to 5 miles from SeaWorld and Universal Studios)

(Note: Republic Drive from the Convention Center to Universal Studios Escape was renamed as Universal Boulevard in 1998.)

★★★**Arnold Palmer's Bay Hill Club.** 9000 Bay Hill Boulevard, Orlando. (800) 523-5999, (407) 876-2429. $$$–$$$$

★★★**Best Western Plaza International.** 8738 International Drive, Orlando. (800) 654-7160, (407) 345-8195. $$–$$$

Buena Vista Suites. 14450 International Drive. (800) 537-7737, (407) 239-8588. $$$

★★★**Caribe Royale Resort Suites.** 14300 International Drive, Lake Buena Vista. (800) 823-8300, (407) 238-8000. $$$

The Castle Hotel–Holiday Inn. 8620 Universal Boulevard, Orlando. (800) 952-2785, (407) 345-1511. $$$

★★★**Clarion Plaza Hotel Orlando.** 9700 International Drive, Orlando. (800) 627-8258, (407) 352-9700. $$–$$$

★★**Comfort Suites Orlando.** 9350 Turkey Lake Road. (800) 277-8483, (407) 351-5050. $$

Country Hearth Inn. 9861 International Drive. (800) 447-1890, (407) 352-0008. $$

★★**Courtyard By Marriott International Drive.** 8600 Austrian Court, Orlando. (800) 321-2211, (407) 351-2244. $$

Cypress Pointe Resort. 8651 Treasure Cay Lane, Lake Buena Vista. (800) 824-5790, (407) 238-1225. $$$

Days Inn Convention Center/SeaWorld. 9990 International Drive, Orlando. (800) 224-5055, (407) 352-8700. $$

Days Inn East of Universal Studios. 5827 Caravan Court. (800) 327-2111, (407) 351-3800. $$

Days Inn International Drive. 7200 International Drive. (800) 224-5057, (407) 351-1200. $$

Days Inn Lakeside. 7335 Sand Lake Road. (800) 777-3297, (407) 351-1900. Lakeside. $$

★★★**Delta Orlando Resort.** 5715 Major Boulevard. (800) 634-4763, (407) 351-3340. $$$

★★**The Doubletree Castle Hotel.** 8629 International Drive, Orlando. (800) 952-2785, (407) 345-1511. $$$

★★**Embassy Suites on the Jamaican Court.** 8250 Jamaican Court. (800) 327-9797, (407) 345-8250. $$$

★★**Embassy Suites Orlando South.** 8978 International Drive. (800) 433-7275, (407) 352-1400. $$$

★★**Enclave Suites at Orlando.** 6165 Carrier Drive. (800) 457-0077, (407) 351-1155. $$$

★★**Fairfield Inn International Drive by Marriott.** 8342 Jamaican Court. (800) 228-2800, (407) 363-1944. $$

The Floridian Hotel of Orlando. 7299 Universal Blvd. (800) 445-7299, (407) 351-5009. $$

Gateway Inn. 7050 Kirkman Road. (800) 327-3808, (407) 351-2000. $$

★★**Hampton Inn.** 6101 Sandlake Road. (800) 763-1100, (407) 363-7886. $$

★★**Hampton Inn at Universal Studios.** 5621 Windhover Drive. (800) 231-8395, (407) 351-6716. $$

★★**Hampton Inn South of Universal Studios.** 7110 South Kirkman Road. (800) 763-1100, (407) 345-1112. $$

★★**Hawthorn Suites Hotel.** 6435 Westwood Boulevard. (800) 527-1133, (407) 351-6600. $$–$$$

Holiday Inn Express International Drive. 6323 International Drive. (800) 365-6935, (407) 351-4430. $$

Holiday Inn International Drive Resort. 6515 International Drive. (800) 286-2747, (407) 351-3500. $$

Holiday Inn Universal Studios. 5905 Kirkman Road. (800) 327-1364, (407) 351-3333. $$

Howard Johnson Lodge International Drive North. 6603 International Drive. (800) 722-2900, (407) 351-2900. $$

Howard Johnson South International. 9956 Hawaiian Court. (800) 826-4847, (407) 351-5100. $$

Inns of America. 8222 Jamaican Court. (800) 826-0778, (407) 345-1172. $–$$

★★**La Quinta at International Drive.** 8300 Jamaican Court. (800) 531-5900, (407) 351-1660. $$

Las Palmas Hotel. 6233 International Drive. (800) 327-2114, (407) 351-3900. $$

MIC Lakefront Inn. 6500 International Drive. (407) 345-5340. Lakeside. $$

★★★**Omni Rosen.** 9840 International Drive. (800) 800-9840, (407) 354-9000. $$$$

★★**Orlando Marriott.** 8001 International Drive. (407) 351-2420. $$$

★★**Parc Corniche Condominium Suite Hotel.** 6300 Parc Corniche Drive. (800) 446-2721, (407) 239-7100. $$$

★★★★**The Peabody Orlando Hotel.** 9801 International Drive. (800) 732-2639, (407) 352-4000. $$$$

Quality Inn International. 7600 International Drive. (800) 825-7600. $–$$

Quality Inn Plaza. 9000 International Drive. (800) 999-8585, (407) 345-8585. $$

★★**Quality Suites International Drive Area.** 7400 Canada Avenue. (800) 228-2027, (407) 363-0332. $$

★★**Radisson Barcelo Hotel.** 8444 International Drive. (800) 304-8000, (407) 345-0505. $$

★★Radisson Twin Towers Hotel. 5780 Major Boulevard. (800) 843-8693, (407) 351-1000. $$

Ramada Limited. 5625 Major Boulevard. (800) 200-8117, (407) 354-3996. $–$$

Ramada Resort & Conference Center. 7400 International Drive. (800) 327-1363, (407) 351-4600. $$

Ramada Suites by SeaWorld. 6800 Villa de Costa Drive. (800) 663-1405, (407) 239-0707. $$$

Red Roof Inn #200. 9922 Hawaiian Court. (800) 843-7663, (407) 352-1507. $$

★★★Renaissance Orlando Resort. 6677 Sea Harbor Drive. (800) 327-6677, (407) 351-5555. $$$$

★★Residence Inn by Marriott—Orlando International Drive. 7975 Canada Avenue. (800) 227-3978, (407) 345-0117. $$$

Rodeway Inn. 6327 International Drive. (800) 999-6327. $–$$

★★Sheraton World Resort. 10100 International Drive. (800) 327-0363, (407) 352-1100. $$$

★★Summerfield Suites Hotel. 8480 International Drive. (800) 839-4964, (407) 352-2400. $$$

★★Summerfield Suites Hotel. 8751 Suiteside Drive. (800) 833-4353, (407) 238-0777. $$$

Super 8 Motel. 5900 American Way, Orlando. (407) 352-8383. $

Travelodge Orlando Flags. 5858 International Drive. (800) 722-7462, (407) 351-4410. $

Universal Tower Resort Motel. 5905 International Drive. (800) 327-1366, (407) 351-2100. $$

★★Wellesley Inn Orlando. 5635 Windhover Drive. (800) 444-8888, (407) 345-0026. $$

Westgate Lakes Resort. 10000 Turkey Lake Road. (800) 424-0708, (407) 345-0000. $$$

★★Wynfield Inn Westwood. 6263 Westwood Boulevard. (800) 346-1551, (407) 345-8000. $$

Orlando International Airport and Southeast Orlando (10 to 20 miles from Disney)

Budgetel Inn. 2051 Consulate Drive, Orlando. (800) 428-3438, (407) 240-0500. $$

★★Comfort Inn Florida Mall. 8421 South Orange Blossom Trail, Orlando. (800) 327-9742, (407) 855-6060. $$

Days Inn. 3300 South Orange Blossom Trail, Orlando. (407) 422-4521. $$

Days Inn/Lodge–Florida Mall. 1851 West LandStreet Road. (800) 331-3954, (407) 859-7700. $

★★Doubletree Guest Suites Orlando International Airport. 7550 Augusta National Drive. (407) 240-5555. $$

Hampton Inn–Airport. 5767 T. G. Lee Boulevard. (407) 888-2995. $$

★★**Holiday Inn Orlando Florida Mall at Central Park.** 7900 South Orange Blossom Trail. (407) 859-7900. $$

Holiday Inn Orlando International Airport. 5750 T. G. Lee Boulevard. (407) 851-6400. $$

Howard Johnson Hotel. 8700 South Orange Blossom Trail. (800) 327-7460, (407) 851-2330. $

Howard Johnson Plaza Hotel Orlando Airport. 3835 McCoy Road. (407) 859-2711. $$

★★**Hyatt Regency Orlando International Airport.** Main Terminal. (800) 233-1234, (407) 825-1234. $$$

★★**Orlando Airport Marriott.** 7499 Augusta National Drive. (800) 766-6752, (407) 851-9000. $$$

Quality Inn & Suites. 4855 South Orange Blossom Trail. (800) 444-3001, (407) 851-3000. $$

Radisson Hotel Orlando Airport. 5555 Hazeltine National Drive. (800) 333-3333, (407) 856-0100. $$–$$$

Renaissance Hotel Orlando. 5445 Forbes Place. (800) 762-6222, (407) 240-1000. $$$

Rodeway Inn–Florida Mall. 8601 South Orange Blossom Trail. (407) 859-4100. $–$$

★★**Sheraton Plaza Hotel at the Florida Mall.** 1500 Sand Lake Road. (800) 231-7883, (407) 859-1500. $$$

Travelodge Orlando Central Park. 7101 South Orange Blossom Trail. (800) 578-7878, (407) 851-4300. $

West Orlando, Downtown Orlando, East Orlando (10 to 20 miles from Disney)

Best Western Orlando West. 2014 West Colonial Drive. (800) 645-6386, (407) 841-8600. $$

Harley Hotel of Orlando. 151 East Washington Street. (800) 321-2323, (407) 841-3220. $$

Holiday Inn at the Orlando Arena. 304 West Colonial Drive. (800) 523-3405, (407) 843-8700. $$

Holiday Inn Express. 3330 West Colonial Drive. (407) 299-6710. $

Omni Marriott Downtown. 400 West Livingston Street. (800) 421-8001, (407) 843-6664. $$–$$$

Ramada Orlando Central. 3200 West Colonial Drive. (800) 828-5270, (407) 295-5270. $$

Altamonte Springs, Winter Park (25 to 30 miles from Disney)

Days Inn Altamonte/Orlando North. 235 South Wymore Road. (800) 224-5059, (407) 862-2800. $

Days Inn Orlando/Winter Park. 901 North Orlando Avenue. (800) 611-6575, (407) 644-8000. $$

Holiday Inn Orlando-Altamonte Springs. 230 West Highway 436. (800) 226-4544, (407) 862-4455. $$

Holiday Inn Orlando North at Winter Park. 626 Lee Road. (407) 645-5600. $$

Langford Resort Hotel. 300 East New England Avenue, Winter Park. (407) 644-3400. $$

Sheraton Orlando North Hotel. 600 North Lake Destiny Drive. (800) 628-6660, (407) 660-9000. $$$

Travelodge. 450 Douglas Avenue, Altamonte Springs. (800) 327-2221, (407) 862-7111. $

Davenport (10 miles from Disney)

Comfort Inn–Maingate South. 5510 U.S. Highway 27 North (800) 255-4386, (941) 424-2811. $$

Days Inn South of Disney. I-4 and U.S. 27. (800) 424-4999, (813) 424-2596. $$

Holiday Inn Express. I-4 and U.S. 27, Baseball City. (800) 225-3351, (941) 424-2120. $$

Campgrounds and RV Parks

Disney's Fort Wilderness Resort. Lake Buena Vista. (407) 934-7639. Within Walt Disney World in 740 acres of woods. Campsites and cabins. $$–$$$$

Fort Summit Camping Resort. I-4 and U.S. 27, Baseball City. (800) 424-1880, (941) 424-1880. 300 sites. $

Kissimmee/Orlando KOA. 4771 West Bronson, Kissimmee. (800) 331-1453, (407) 396-2400. $

Sherwood Forest Mobile Home Estate & RV Resort. 530 West Bronson. (407) 396-0999. $

Eating for Less

As a tourist magnet, the Orlando area offers just about every type of restaurant from fancy to ordinary, from American to European to Asian. (One of the most eclectic gatherings of foreign restaurants can be found within the World Showcase pavilions of Epcot Center.) But the emphasis seems to be on "family" restaurants. If there is a single major franchise fast-food restaurant in America that is not represented in the Orlando area, I don't know about it.

The biggest collections of fast-food restaurants can be found on I-192 (Bronson) and International Drive. If you're really into deep-fried grease, you can probably find seven different McDonald's or Burger Kings or Pizza Huts, one for every night of a week's stay.

Somewhat unique to the South are the all-you-can-eat buffets, which usually offer breakfasts in the range of $2 to $5, lunches from $4 to $8, and dinners from $6 to $12. Chains include Ponderosa Steak House, Sizzler, Shoney's, and Gilligan's. Be aware that quality can vary from one buffet to the next; in my opinion, Sizzler offers the best quality in the area. By the way, don't hesitate to ask to inspect the buffet before buying your way into the buffet line.

You may also want to check out several Chinese buffets along I-92 east and west of Walt Disney World. And an interesting new entrant in the market is the Magic Bull Steakland at the intersection of I-92 and S.R. 535, which offers an Argentinian steak house menu and buffet.

Babysitting

In addition to the various kids' clubs at Walt Disney World resorts, you can engage a private babysitter from agencies such as Kinder-Care, at (407) 827-5444. Be sure to follow the same precautions on vacation as you would at home.

Chapter 4
Walt Disney World:
You've Got to Have a Ticket

As if you don't already face enough decisions—dates, airlines, hotels, and more—there is also the matter of those little pieces of cardboard called admission tickets. Actually, they are not all that little: a family of four including two children under 10 years of age visiting Walt Disney World for five days could easily spend (are you ready for this?) nearly $700 for daily tickets. If the kids are over the age of 10, they (or rather, you) pay full fare; four five-day tickets will set you back more than $800. Add in a day at Universal Studios and a day at Sea World, and the cost crosses $1,000.

But, like everything else we write about in this *Econoguide,* there are various ways to analyze the available options. The very best thing you can do is to sit down with a piece of paper and make a plan *before* you leave for Florida. Don't wait until you are standing at the ticket counter with a hundred people eyeing your back, your children tugging at your sleeves, and tears in your eyes to decide on your ticket strategy.

Instead, fit your plans to one of the available ticket packages. And don't overlook the money-saving strategies we discuss here—or the discount coupons for Universal Studios, Sea World, and other attractions you'll find in the back of this book.

Home delivery. Tickets can be purchased by mail by sending a check, made payable to the Walt Disney World Company, to Box 10030, Lake Buena Vista, FL 32830-0030. Mark the envelope "Attention: Ticket Mail Order," and include an additional $2 for the privilege. Allow as much as six weeks for processing. We'd advise calling Walt Disney World first to check if ticket prices have changed: (407) 824-4321.

You can purchase tickets by phone using credit cards by calling the same number.

And, you can also purchase tickets at Disney Stores in many malls around the country.

First the Bad News

Remember what we said about Walt Disney World being a gigantic vacuum aimed at your wallet? Well, the great sucking sound begins at the ticket counter.

Walt Disney World Tickets

Prices were in effect in the summer of 1999, and do not include 6 percent Florida sales tax. All prices are subject to change without notice; in recent years, Disney has raised prices each spring. You may also find other ticket plans over the course of the year.

Tickets can be purchased at Walt Disney World, through some travel agents, through Disney's web page, and by calling (407) 560-7277.

	Adult (Ages 10+)	Child (3–9)
1-day, 1-park ticket	$44.00	$35.00

(Magic Kingdom, Epcot, Disney's Animal Kingdom, or Disney-MGM Studios)

Park-Hopper Pass 4-day	$167.00	$134.00

(Unlimited admission to Magic Kingdom, Epcot, Disney's Animal Kingdom, and Disney-MGM Studios, including multiple parks on one day. Unused days never expire.) 5-Day Park-Hopper Passes are also available.

Park-Hopper Plus Pass 5-day	$229.00	$183.00

(Unlimited admission to Magic Kingdom, Epcot, Disney's Animal Kingdom, and Disney-MGM Studios, including multiple parks on one day. Also includes two, three, or four single admissions to Blizzard Beach, Typhoon Lagoon, River Country, Pleasure Island, or Disney's Wide World of Sports for the number of days on your pass. Unused days never expire.) 6- and 7-Day Park-Hopper Plus Passes are also available.

Disney Quest	$25.00	$20.00
Cirque du Soleil	$56.50	$45.20
River Country	$15.95	$12.50
Blizzard Beach	$26.95	$21.50
Typhoon Lagoon	$26.95	$21.50
Pleasure Island (18 and older)	$18.86	—
Disney's Wide World of Sports	$8.00	$6.75

Annual Passes

Theme Park Annual Pass	$309.00	$259.00

(Unlimited admission to Magic Kingdom, Epcot, Disney's Animal Kingdom, and Disney-MGM Studios for one year, plus free parking and savings on selected hotels and special events.)

Premium Annual Pass	$415.00	$355.00

(Unlimited admission to Magic Kingdom, Epcot, Disney's Animal Kingdom, and Disney-MGM Studios, plus Blizzard Beach, Typhoon Lagoon, River Country, Disney's Wide World of Sports, and Pleasure Island for one year, plus free parking and savings on selected hotels and special events.)

Pleasure Island Annual Pass (18 and older)	$49.95	—

Length-of-Stay Pass

Offered only to guests at Walt Disney World resorts; the pass includes unlimited admission to the Magic Kingdom, Disney's Animal Kingdom, Epcot, Disney-MGM Studios, Blizzard Beach, Typhoon Lagoon, River Country, Pleasure Island, and Disney's Wide World of Sports. Passes are good from the moment of check-in until the end of the day of departure.

Prices are only slightly lower than an equivalent All-in-One Hopper Pass sold at the gate, but the passes are available in a wider range of day options.

If one of the Disney ticket plans matches your schedule exactly, you're in luck and you'll save some money. But if the plans are not exactly what you need, you *could* end up wasting money instead of saving.

All ticket prices and limitations listed here were in effect in mid-1999 and are subject to change. In recent years, Disney has adjusted prices in early spring; the "adjustments" have almost always been upward.

As in the past, tickets have no expiration date; if you have leftover days on a pass, you can take it with you and use it the next time you visit the park. And because park ticket prices seem to be on an inexorable march upward, you may end up with a small return on your investment when you return in later seasons. (However, in past years, Disney has not allowed old tickets to be used at parks that have opened since the tickets were sold.)

In recent years, Disney has made it difficult to use one money-saving trick. The tickets have always been "non-transferable," but Disney had no way to enforce that rule. It used to be that you could give your unused tickets to a friend or other family member, or sell your unused entrance passes to one of the many "gray market" ticket booths in the vicinity of the park. The gray marketeers would buy and sell extra tickets at a discount.

In recent years, Disney has tried various methods to make it difficult to transfer ownership of a ticket from one person to another. Methods have included printing a picture of the owner on the ticket and even a high-tech device that measured the dimensions of your hand and compared it with a record on file.

The latest wrinkle: a credit card–like medium with information stored in a magnetic stripe on the back. When you use the ticket, the data is updated by Disney's computer; it is very difficult or impossible for an individual to know the remaining value on a ticket.

This doesn't mean that gray marketeers won't try to buy and sell Disney tickets outside the park. What it does mean is that the buyer should beware even more than usual. If it were my money, I would be very leery of buying any of the credit-card media and would only consider buying a standard cardboard ticket *without* a photograph of some stranger and only after I examined the ticket very carefully for signs of alteration or fraud. And then I would pay for the tickets only with a credit card so that I could challenge payment if necessary. Finally, I would consider this sort of arrangement only if the amount of money involved were small enough to lose without causing major pain. With all of those caveats in mind, you might as well buy the tickets from Disney or one of its authorized resellers, including AAA.

Walt Disney World Ticket Plans

One-Day/One-Park Ticket. Good in one park only. You will be allowed to exit and return to the park on the same day—be sure to have your hand stamped—but you cannot go to another park or ride the monorail or bus system to another park.

Park-Hopper Pass. Good in all four parks for four or five days. You can go from one park to another on the same day—be sure to have your hand stamped. The four passes do not have to be used consecutively, and they are valid forever. Includes unlimited use of Walt Disney World transportation system.

Park-Hopper Plus. Good in all four parks. You can go from one park to another on the same day—be sure to have your hand stamped. The passes do not have to be used consecutively and are valid forever. Five-day passes are also valid for two admissions to Disney's Wide World of Sports, Typhoon Lagoon, River Country, or Pleasure Island. (Six- and seven-day passes include three and four admissions to the secondary parks respectively.)

Annual Passport. Valid for unlimited admission to all four parks during regular operating hours, for one year from the issue date. The pass also includes free parking and special advance reservation privileges for restaurants and shows.

Premium Annual Passport. The gold ticket at Walt Disney World, this pass adds Pleasure Island and all of the water parks for a year's time; also included is free parking and some special privileges for reservations.

Resort Guest Special Tickets. Guests at Disney-owned or -operated hotels within the park can purchase special **Length of Stay** passes based on hotel reservations, and good from the moment you arrive until midnight of the day you check out. These plans, priced slightly lower than those offered to visitors, include various combinations of access to theme parks and other attractions; the plans change over the course of the year, depending on current marketing efforts. They don't always make economic sense: be sure to compare the package price to individual tickets or other packages that might better fit your plans. And be sure to compare any pass for a lengthy stay against the cost of an Annual Passport. And remember that a length-of-stay pass at Walt Disney World does not include tickets to attractions outside of the park, such as Universal Studios Florida, Sea World, and Busch Gardens. If you leave the confines of Disney for one of those locations you may end up paying for a Disney admission that you won't use.

An Econoguide to Disney Tickets

Which of the three types of tickets should you buy? There is no one answer because no two families follow the same schedule on a trip to Central Florida.

Obviously, if your plans call for a full week's stay and you plan to visit every corner of the park—from the Magic Kingdom to Epcot to MGM Studios to Pleasure Island at night, and Blizzard Beach, Typhoon Lagoon, and River Country on hot afternoons, then the Park-Hopper Plus Pass makes the most sense. You can visit multiple parks on the same day with a multi-day pass; with the five-day pass you can also make two visits to the water parks, Pleasure Island, or Disney's Wide World of Sports.

If you are in town for a weekend and plan only a two-day visit, you'll probably want to buy just single admission tickets.

Now, here's a more complex decision: suppose you plan to visit Disney theme parks for four days and also want to go to Blizzard Beach, Typhoon

Lagoon, Pleasure Island, or River Country or all of them during your stay. It *may* make more sense to buy a five-day pass. Add up the value of admission to the secondary parks you will visit and subtract them from the cost of the pass. Then you'll have to decide what to do with the unused ticket.

What do you do if your child graduates to adult ticket status while you still have days left on your non-expiring multi-day ticket? Go to Guest Services where you can apply the value of the ticket against a new adult ticket. Or, tell your 11-year-old to look like a 9-year-old at the ticket turnstile.

And then, here's another interesting plan. We call it the Annual Pass 11-month Year: Suppose you know that a yearly visit to Walt Disney World is in the cards for the next several years. Here's a way to save hundreds of dollars over a one-year period: purchase an Annual Pass and then schedule two trips within 365 days. For example, visit Orlando in March of one year and February of the next.

How much money could you save with an 11-month year? Let's say you visit Walt Disney World for six days at the theme and water parks, buying an All-in-One Hopper Pass for six days. At 1998 prices, this visit would cost $896 plus tax for a family of two adults and two children. Come back again in 1999, and you'll pay at least $896 more for another set of passes: total ticket cost is about $1,792 for the two visits.

Now consider Premium annual passes, good for one year from the date of first use. Passes for two adults and two children at 1998 rates would cost $1,476.

Your potential savings under this example: $316, which will buy a few free meals. In fact, the savings can be even higher if you include the value of free parking, included in the price of the Annual Passes.

But your savings turn into a significant loss if you don't return to Walt Disney World within a year.

Buying Discount Tickets

Yes, you can get Disney tickets for wholesale. But it takes a bit of doing. There are two routes to discounts: an unofficial, unauthorized path and an official path.

First the **official** ways:

1. Book an all-inclusive hotel and park admission package from the Walt Disney Company. Packages include the top-of-the-line "World Adventure," "Grand Plan," and "Admiral Plan" packages, which offer rooms, tickets, use of recreational facilities, and breakfast, lunch, and dinner every day at the hotel or within the parks. Other plans that include some or all meals are "Family Vacation Fun," "Festival Magic," "Resort Romance," and "Camping Adventure."

Be sure to figure the true value of the package. Ask for the regular room rate, and then add in the value—to you—of recreation and meals to determine if there is a real discount.

2. Book a hotel and admission package from one of the hotels outside of the park. Again, find out the regular hotel charge to determine if your admission tickets are being offered at a discount.

3. Use an admission pass discount such as the **Magic Kingdom Club**, described later.

4. Look for very occasional promotions by the Walt Disney Company through some of the official tourist agencies in the Orlando area. One place to check is the Orlando/Orange County Convention & Visitors Bureau, which operates an office at 8445 International Drive. Write to the bureau at P.O. Box 690355, Orlando, FL 32869.

5. Buy tickets through AAA or other travel associations or through credit card companies that may offer slightly discounted tickets.

Unofficially Yours

Now, a few unofficial ways.

1. Buy your tickets from one of the official tourist and convention offices. They may have discount tickets directly from Walt Disney World, or they may have some tickets that have come through the gray market, such as extra supplies from hotel packages.

2. Buy your tickets from one of the ticket brokers along tourist roads described above. You'll likely be offered passes at 10 percent to 20 percent off the list price. Their sources include hotel packages as well as any tickets they may have bought from visitors. Be sure to examine the tickets carefully to make sure they are valid. We'd advise against trying to use one of the "picture" tickets that is not yours; but you may find some older and still valid tickets without the photos. The safest way to pay for anything is with a credit card, next safest is with a personal check, and the least safe is with cash.

A mark, a yen, a buck, or a pound. Ticket booths at Walt Disney World accept American Express, MasterCard, Visa, traveler's checks, personal checks with ID, cash, pennies, children . . . just kidding about the kids.

Lines at ticket booths are usually within reasonable limits within half an hour before and after opening time; lines will build at mid-morning as much as 15 minutes. You can save time by purchasing tickets at all Disney-owned or -operated hotels and many large area resorts.

Joining the Club

Think of the Magic Kingdom Club as the Mickey Mouse Club for adults and seniors.

The **Magic Kingdom Club Gold Card** offers a small discount of a few dollars each day on admission tickets to Disneyland, Walt Disney World, Disneyland Paris, and Tokyo Disneyland. There are also discounts to Walt Disney World attractions including Pleasure Island, River Country, Typhoon Lagoon, and Blizzard Beach. There are also some discounts from regular prices at the more expensive restaurants in the Magic Kingdom, Epcot, and Disney-MGM Studios resorts.

Other benefits include discounts on selected Disney Resort hotels, at The Disney Store, at Disney Village Marketplace and Pleasure Island shops, and special rates with National Car Rental.

In 1999, a two-year membership sold for $65 for a family, reduced to $50 for Disney stockholders and senior citizens. It all sounds very good—and it might be—for a family that is serious about all things Disney. We'd estimate the card makes sense if you spend $500 or more over a two-year period on flights, rooms, and meals that are covered by the card. Note that you may end up spending more money on a Disney room than you would outside one of the parks. And discounted rooms are limited in supply.

To join the Magic Kingdom Club, call (800) 413-4763.

As with any "deal," be sure to compare prices you could obtain by yourself. For example, the airfare discount generally applies to full ticket price, and excursion fares may be cheaper; the hotel discounts may still be more costly than a direct booking at a lower-priced hotel, even another Disney property.

Tickets for Other Attractions

The other attractions in the Orlando area are much more willing to strike a deal. You can usually purchase slightly discounted tickets for Universal Studios, SeaWorld, many dinner theaters, and other entertainment from brokers in hotels and on tourist strips. Shop around before you buy, and examine the tickets carefully.

And be sure to check out the many discount coupons from attractions that you will find in the back of this book.

Free Tickets!

Two Disney Tickets for $5! Free Universal Studios Passes!

Impossible? Not at all.

Completely free? Well . . .

You can't help but notice the come-ons as you travel in the prime tourist areas of Irlo Bronson Highway (Highway 192) in Kissimmee and International Drive in Orlando. And in many hotels, you'll be assaulted in the lobby.

We've already discussed the discount ticket deals, available from brokers who have tickets available for a few dollars off the list price for dinner theaters and some of the theme parks other than at Walt Disney World. (You can also use the discount coupons in the back of this book for Universal Studios, SeaWorld, Busch Gardens, Splendid China, Cypress Gardens, and a host of other attractions.) No, here we are talking about those seemingly impossible offers of free or near-free tickets.

The pitch works something like this: "All you've got to do is go to this wonderful resort, eat a free breakfast, and listen to our two-hour presentation about our time-sharing/interval ownership/vacation club. Even if you don't buy, we'll give you two free tickets to Walt Disney World. There's no pressure."

Well, it's all true, except for the "no pressure" part.

You'll start by filling out a simple form at the ticket counter. There are usually a few qualifying questions to see if you have sufficient income to make a timesharing purchase—the threshold is usually pretty low, around $30,000 per year in annual income. And then you'll likely be asked to make a "deposit" of about $20 to hold your place at the presentation. The deposit will be returned along with your "free" tickets. (There are two reasons for the deposit: the deposit is the commission earned by the ticket broker for delivering you

Mickey'll take Manhattan. The Magic Kingdom opened on October 1, 1971. Walt Disney World includes 28,000 acres or some 43 square miles of land, making it about the size of San Francisco or twice the size of Manhattan.

The Magic Kingdom takes up about 107 acres; its parking lot is even bigger, at 125 acres. (By way of comparison, Disneyland occupies just 80 acres in California.)

Here are a few more measurements of the elements of Walt Disney World: Epcot Center, 300 acres including a 40-acre lake; Disney-MGM Studios Theme Park, 154 acres; Ft. Wilderness, 600 acres; Dixie Landings/ Port Orleans, 325 acres; Disney Wilderness Preserve, 8,500 acres.

And the Disney's Animal Kingdom sprawls over some 500 acres, which is nice if you're a rhino.

to the sales group, as well as an inducement to make sure you show up for your appointment.)

I've sat through a few of the presentations and have earned my free tickets and the return of my deposit, just as promised. I've also had to fight off some pretty insistent sales pitches. Sometimes the two or nearly three hours of my time have been worth the $75 value of a pair of tickets; sometimes I've felt like it would be worth $100 to pay the salespeople to let me escape before the time was up.

The typical pitch tries to compare the amount of money you have spent on your hotel room to the annual cost of a mortgage for a timeshare. The operations typically sell a specific week, or period of weeks. The rate ranges from about $10,000 to $25,000; there are also additional charges for maintenance, owner's groups, and other expenses.

Should you consider buying a timeshare? Most hard-nosed financial experts consider them to be less-than-wonderful investments. They talk about the fact that you may be locked into a location or time period that may not always work with your changing lifestyle. They worry about unexpected expenses—if the elevator fails or the swimming pool leaks or other major expenses occur, the bill will come to the homeowners. And finally, there is not a very good history of increasing monetary value for timeshare purchases.

One way to check on the value of timeshares is to go to the resale market. There are several agencies in and around Orlando that specialize in unloading timeshares from private parties. If there is a big disparity between buying from the developer and buying from a reseller, or if the reseller has an unexpectedly large inventory of shares for sale, you should be very suspicious.

In any case, make sure you consult your accountant or attorney before signing anything.

Chapter 5
Walt Disney World (and Universal Studios Escape) with Children

Doesn't the title of this section sound ridiculously obvious? Well, yes and no: the fact is that for many kids a visit to Walt Disney World or Universal Studios Escape is the biggest thing that has ever happened to them—and although it almost always will be a most wonderful vacation, there are also special concerns for youngsters and their parents.

Here are 10 suggestions to make a trip with young children go well.

1. Involve the children in the planning. Obtain maps and brochures and study them at the dinner table; read sections of this book together. Work together on a schedule for the places you want to visit on each day.

2. Draw up the "rules" for the visit and make sure each child understands them and agrees with them. The basic rule in our family is that our young children always have to be within an arm's length of mom or dad.

3. Study and understand the height and age minimums for some of the more active rides at the parks. Don't build up expectations of your 41-inch-tall child for a ride that requires you to be 42 inches in height. (Did we hear someone say something about lift pads in shoes? Just remember that the rules are there to protect children from injury.)

4. Come to a family agreement on financial matters. Few parents can afford to buy everything a child demands; even if you could, you probably wouldn't want to. Consider giving your children a special allowance they can spend at the park; encourage them to wait a day or two into the trip so they don't hit bottom before they find the souvenir they really want to take home.

5. When you arrive at the park—and as you move through various areas—always pick a place to meet if you become separated. Landmarks include Cinderella's Castle or the carrousel in the Magic Kingdom, Spaceship Earth in Epcot, a particular vantage point for the Tree of Life at Disney's Animal Kingdom, the Chinese Theater in Disney-MGM Studios, the Back to the Future steam locomotive or the Gak fountain at Universal Studios Florida, or One Fish, Two Fish, Red Fish, Blue Fish in Seuss Landing at Universal Studios Islands of Adventure. You should also have a backup plan—instruct your children to find

a uniformed park attendant if they are lost and plan on checking with attendants yourself if you have misplaced a child.

You might want to attach a name tag to youngsters (available at Guest Services in the parks if you don't have your own) or put a piece of paper with your name and hotel in your child's pockets. Some parents even issue their kids walkie-talkie radios and keep one in their own pockets!

6. For much of the year, the sun in Central Florida is quite strong. Keep your kids (and yourself) under hats and be sure to use a sunscreen, especially at midday. You may want to bring bottles of water for the entire family—it's a lot cheaper than soda at the snack bars, and better, too.

7. You are not supposed to bring food into the park. Then again, we've never seen a paying guest searched for hidden sandwiches inside the park. You may choose to leave lunch in your car and come out for a break—this is easier at Epcot or Disney-MGM Studios because of the proximity of the parking lot to the park. There are lockers outside the gates at the other parks.

8. A good strategy with youngsters, especially if you are staying inside the park or nearby, is to arrive early and then leave at lunchtime for a quick nap or a swim; return at dusk to enjoy the evening at the park. You'll miss the hottest and most crowded part of the day and probably enjoy yourself much more. Be sure to have your hands stamped when you leave the park and hold onto your tickets (including your parking pass) if you intend to return.

9. Although you can bring your own stroller, it is also easy to rent one for the day at the parks. Park the stroller near the *exit* to the attraction so that it is waiting when you come out. Don't leave any valuables with the stroller. If you move from one Disney park to another during a single day, show your receipt at the new park to obtain a stroller when you arrive.

10. Most restrooms (male and female) include changing tables. You can also purchase diapers and even formula at most theme parks; ask at Guest Services. There are also places set aside for nursing mothers.

Dad, I Promise . . .

One of the best things about going to Walt Disney World or Universal Studios with kids is that a resourceful parent should be able to milk a few weeks of "If you don't behave right now, I'm not taking you to Florida" threats.

My resourceful son Willie went even further and came up with his own contract. Call it:

The Ten Theme Park Commandments

I. Thou shalt not leave thy parents' sight.

II. Thou shalt not go on twister rides after a meal.

III. Thou shalt not complain about the lines.

IV. Thou shalt not fight with thy sister or brother.

V. Thou shalt not ask to buy something at the shops
that costs more than the admission ticket.

VI. Thou shall enjoy any of the boring things
that Mom and Dad want to see.

VII. Thou shall stand still so Dad can take at least one picture.

VIII. Thou shalt not pester the characters to talk.
IX. Thou shalt not sing, "It's a Small World After All"
more than 16 times in a row.
X. Thou shall go on at least one educational ride, even if it has a long line.

A Kid's Eye View of the Best of Walt Disney World and Universal Studios Escape

What are the best attractions for youngsters (3 to 10 years old)? Well, you know your particular child's interests and fears better than anyone else, but here are some favorites and a few warnings. *(Key appears on next page.)*

Magic Kingdom

Dumbo, the Flying Elephant
Cinderella's Golden Carrousel
It's a Small World
Jungle Cruise
Pirates of the Caribbean ①
Peter Pan's Flight
Mad Tea Party ②
Ariel's Grotto

The Many Adventures of Winnie the Pooh
Mickey's Toontown Fair
The Barnstormer
Country Bear Jamboree
Tom Sawyer's Island
Tomorrowland Speedway ③
Enchanted Tiki Room
Splash Mountain ③

Epcot

Journey Into Imagination
Honey I Shrunk the Audience
Food Rocks (The Land) ①
Universe of Energy ①

Wonders of Life ④
The Living Seas
River of Time (Mexico)
GM Test Track ④

Disney's Animal Kingdom

Kilimanjaro Safaris
Kali River Rapids ④
Festival of the Lion King
Journey Into Jungle Book

It's Tough to be a Bug!
Countdown to Extinction ④
Affection Section
Gorilla Falls Exploration Trail

Disney-MGM Studios

Fantasmic! ①
Doug Live!
Jim Henson's Muppet*Vision ~~3D~~ 4D ①
Honey, I Shrunk the Kids Movie Set Adventure

Voyage of the Little Mermaid ①
The Great Movie Ride ①
Beauty and the Beast Live on Stage
Sounds Dangerous ①

Universal Studios Florida

Woody Woodpecker's KidZone
Animal Actors Stage
Fievel's Playground
Funtastic World of Hanna-Barbera ②
E.T. Adventure

Earthquake—The Big One ①/ ③
Twister ①
Jaws ①/ ④
Wild, Wild, Wild West Stunt Show ①
Back to the Future ④

Universal Studios Islands of Adventure

The Cat in the Hat

Caro-Seuss-el

One Fish Two Fish Red Fish Blue Fish

If I Ran the Zoo

Dudley Do-Right's Ripsaw Falls ②

Me Ship, The Olive

The Eighth Voyage of Sinbad ①

Jurassic Park River Adventure ① / ②

Pteranadon Flyers ②

Camp Jurassic

Notes:

① Loud noises and special effects (pirates, skeletons, beasts) may startle unprepared children.

② Can make some children dizzy.

③ Adult must accompany small children.

④ DISNEY-MGM STUDIOS: Star Wars may be a bit rough for youngsters. EPCOT: Body Wars, Cranium Command, and GM Test Track may be too intense for very young. Parental guidance advised for "The Making of Me." UNIVERSAL STUDIOS: Back to the Future is too intense for some children; use your judgment based on your knowledge of your own child. Jaws, Twister, and Earthquake have some wild effects but most children find them fun. MAGIC KINGDOM: Splash Mountain is charming, but it does include one drop over a waterfall; it's not as scary as it looks, but some children may not be ready. DISNEY'S ANIMAL KINGDOM: Countdown to Extinction is a wild ride through Animatronic dinosaurs and exploding meteors. Some youngsters may be scared, but most will beg for a second and third and fourth trip. Kali River Rapids is a relatively wild river raft ride that may frighten some youngsters.

Babysitting

Guests at resorts within Walt Disney World can hire in-room babysitters from KinderCare Guest Services, at (407) 827-5444. The service may also be able to provide sitters for guests at major hotels outside of the park.

An interesting option for parents with children from ages 2 through 10 is **Kids Time,** which operates a supervised play area with toys, sports, video games, and art activities seven days a week from early morning through late evening. Snacks and meals are available. Kids Time is located in the West Colonial Oaks Shopping Center at 7230 West Colonial Drive, near Universal Studios and International Drive. Call (407) 298-5437 for information.

Part II
Walt Disney World

Chapter 6
The Keys to the Kingdom . . . and the Rest of Walt Disney World

So, you want to go to Disney World. Great! Which Walt Disney World do you have in mind?

- The world of Mickey and Minnie and Dumbo and 1,000 live elephants, okapi, giraffe, kangaroos, two-toed sloth, gorillas, and black rhinos?[1]
- The only place on the planet where China touches Norway, Santa Fe overlooks Polynesia, and where you can drive among the dinosaurs?[2]
- The home of R2D2, Humphrey Bogart, the Alien, Kermit the Frog, and an elevator guaranteed to fail hundreds of times a day?[3]
- The stately adult pleasure dome of Merriweather A. Pleasure, where you can boogey (almost) all night?[4]
- Florida's only ski resort and Santa's elves' summer golf course?[5]
- The terrifying plunge of Humunga Kowabunga or the splashdown at Whoop 'n Holler Hollow?[6]
- The campfire sing-along at the trading post?[7]
- The place where you can hitch a ride in hard rock group Aerosmith's speedy luxury limo?[8]
- A place with five championship-level golf courses?[9]
- The home port of the largest private flotilla in the world, bigger than many navies?[10]
- A place where guests volunteer as Crash Test Dummies?[11]
- A dinner table in a rainforest or parked at a drive-in movie?[12]
- A spectacular old-style ballpark, home to the Spring Training camp of a major-league team?[13]
- Or a world-class Indy-style auto race course?[14]

Oh, *that* Disney World.

---

[1]The Magic Kingdom and Disney's Animal Kingdom
[2]Epcot Center and Disney's Coronado Springs
[3]Disney-MGM Studios
[4]Pleasure Island
[5]Blizzard Beach and Winter Summerland
[6]Typhoon Lagoon and River Country
[7]Fort Wilderness

[8]Rock 'n Roller Coaster at Disney-MGM Studios
[9]The Magic Linkdom
[10]The Walt Disney World marinas
[11]GM Test Track at Epcot
[12]Rainforest Café or Sci-Fi Dine-in Theater
[13]Disney's Wide World of Sports
[14]Walt Disney World Speedway

Pets. Never leave your cat, dog, mouse, or other pet in your car; heat can build up tremendously in a parked vehicle, and animals can die. If you must bring a pet with you, bring proof of vaccination and use one of the Pet Care Kennels at Magic Kingdom Park Transportation and Ticket Center, at the entrance to Epcot, at the entrance to the Disney-MGM Studios, Disney's Animal Kingdom, and near the entrance to Disney's Fort Wilderness Resort and Campground. The kennels are intended for dogs and cats, but the animal lovers there will also care for birds, ferrets, small rodents, and non-venomous snakes in their own carriers. The kennels are not set up to house exotic animals. Rates are $6 per day per pet. Walt Disney World Resort Guests may board pets overnight for $9 per night, and guests staying off-property may board pets overnight for $11 per night.

Let's start with an important definition:

Walt Disney World is the huge entertainment complex that includes within it the **Magic Kingdom, Epcot Center, Disney's Animal Kingdom**, and the **Disney-MGM Studios Theme Park** as well as **Blizzard Beach, Typhoon Lagoon, River Country**, the six Disney golf courses, **Disney Downtown** (including **Pleasure Island, Disney Village**, and **Disney's West Side** encompassing **DisneyQuest and Cirque du Soleil**), **Disney's Wide World of Sports**, and the hundreds of Disney-operated and Disney-licensed hotels and restaurants within the property lines of the World.

Covering 47 square miles, Walt Disney World is about the size of San Francisco, or twice the size of Manhattan. Of more than 30,000 acres, only about one-fourth has been developed, with another quarter designated as a wilderness preserve.

My goal in this, the largest section of the book, is twofold: first, to break down the huge World into smaller and more understandable pieces and, second, to put them back together in a way that shows how to get the most out of it.

There are nine chapters in this section:
- The Keys to the Kingdom
- The Magic Kingdom
- Epcot Center
- Disney-MGM Studios
- Disney's Animal Kingdom
- Disney Water Parks
- Downtown Disney
- Educational Opportunities at Walt Disney World
- Inside the World of Disney, an exploration of various other things Disney.

Later on in the book, we'll return to Walt Disney World to discuss dinner theaters, sports, recreation, and educational opportunities.

Each of the theme park chapters begins with a list of Econoguide "Must-see" attractions and the exclusive "Power Trip" tour. We hope you'll take the time to read the chapters before you go and once again when you're in Florida.

A Few Ways Around the Waiting Lines

The good news about Walt Disney World is that things are getting better and better all the time. There's a rockin' new coaster at Disney-MGM Studios; there are amazing animal encounters at Disney's Animal Kingdom, and a wild automobile test facility at Epcot Center.

The not-so-good news: thousands of people on line ahead of you, especially during the busy summer season and holiday periods.

But there may be hope: Disney's **FASTPASS** system, introduced in the summer of 1999.

When guests arrive at an attraction offering FASTPASS, they have the choice of waiting in line or making a reservation to come back later.

To use the system, visitors insert their regular theme park admission ticket into a card reader to receive a FASTPASS with a scheduled return time. At the appointed hour, they can walk right into the preshow area without waiting in line.

The first park to offer the system was Disney's Animal Kingdom, at Kilimanjaro Safaris, Countdown to Extinction, and Kali River Rapids. The system was due to be installed at Disney-MGM Studios at Rock 'n' Roller Coaster, and at the Magic Kingdom at Space Mountain and Splash Mountain.

FASTPASS may also arrive at Epcot Center, at the GM Test Track.

Here's the fine print: you can only register for one FASTPASS appointment at a time. If you have a reservation for a 2 P.M. coaster ride, you cannot use your ticket to reserve a river rapids expedition until after the appointed time.

Another way around waiting lines is to take advantage of **Magic Kingdom E-Ride Nights**, offered on certain evenings at the Magic Kingdom and available to guests at Walt Disney World hotel guests who purchase multi-day tickets. The park is open "after hours", usually between 10 P.M. and 1 A.M., with several of the more popular attractions open for special guests.

Guests at Disney World hotels can also enter selected parks 90 minutes earlier than other visitors on **Surprise Mornings**. In 1999, the early-bird perk was offered at Disney-MGM Studios on Sunday and Wednesday, Magic Kingdom on Monday, Thursday, and Saturday, and at Epcot Center on Tuesday and Friday.

Getting to the Magic Kingdom

The idea behind the Walt Disney World transportation system was a good one: getting to the Magic Kingdom *should* be a magical experience. When you leave your car you *should* be in an entirely different world.

"We'll have visitors park way on the other side of a large lagoon and then let them take an exciting monorail ride or a soothing ferryboat to the main gate," the planners said. "By the time they're in the park, they'll completely forget about the outside world."

So far, so good, but let's consider how it works out more than 30 years after the planners made their drawings.

First you park way out in East Overshoe, practically the next county. Then you must walk to the central aisle of the parking lot and wait for a gigantic snake-like tram to take you to the Transportation and Ticket Center (TTC). You'll have to show your ticket there and then choose between a monorail or a ferryboat ride around or across the Seven Seas Lagoon to the main gates.

Back of the bus. Can you park at a Disney hotel lot and ride a monorail, boat, or bus directly to one of the parks? The answer is yes . . . and no. In theory, you must have a guest ID card to ride one of the internal modes of transport. However, cards are rarely asked for, and Disney encourages guests at Walt Disney World to sample the restaurants and shops at its hotels. Disney also quietly sells a daily transportation ticket for $2.50.

Total time from parking to your first step onto Main Street is about 30 minutes at the start of the day and as much as an hour at peak periods from about 10 A.M. to noon when there are long lines at the monorail or ferryboat.

At the end of the day, you'll have to reverse the process. And you *did* remember where you parked your car, right?

For most visitors to the Magic Kingdom staying outside of the park, there's no easy way around the process, except to follow one of our general rules: arrive early. If you're staying within Walt Disney World, consider taking the monorail, water taxi, or bus right from your hotel.

The situation is very different at Epcot Center, Disney-MGM Studios, and Disney's Animal Kingdom, where you can park and walk or take a single short tram ride to the gates.

If you're driving, four low-power radio signals on three AM frequencies keep visitors abreast of information at the resort. Guests can tune to 1030 (driving toward the Magic Kingdom), 900 (exiting the Magic Kingdom), 810 (entering Epcot), and 900 (exiting Epcot).

From Within Walt Disney World

One of the advantages of staying at a hotel within Walt Disney World is the availability of Disney's own bus, monorail, and boat fleet.

The buses go directly to the entrance of the Magic Kingdom, Disney's Animal Kingdom, Epcot, and Disney-MGM Studios. Similarly, the boat services from some Disney hotels go directly to the Magic Kingdom or to the back door International Gateway entrance to Epcot. Visitors staying at a Disney hotel with a monorail stop have direct service only to the Magic Kingdom; you'll have to transfer at the TTC to an Epcot train or a Disney-MGM Studios bus if either is your destination.

The principal transportation system at the Magic Kingdom—and one of the most famous—is the Mark IV Monorail system, which links the Magic Kingdom and the TTC, and a second route that runs from the TTC to Epcot Center. A local version of the Magic Kingdom loop stops at several of the major hotels within the park.

Everything You Always Wanted to Know about the Monorail

Well, almost everything. The current models have eight 113-horsepower motors in various cars of the train; the train can't be split up into smaller units.

The monorails run on 600-volt DC power drawn from Disney's own power plant north of the Contemporary Resort, across the road from the monorail maintenance shop.

There is a total of 13.6 miles of rail, including spur lines and maintenance areas. More than half, 7.6 miles, is the Epcot "beam"; the Lagoon beam to hotels and the Exterior beam to the Magic Kingdom are each about 2.6 miles.

By the way, There is one row of seats in the front cab with the driver of the monorail. Ask one of the attendants to place you there for an interesting and different perspective; you may have to let a train pass by if there are many people waiting in line.

Five if by Monorail, Seven if by Ferry

Another component of the transportation system at the Magic Kingdom is decidedly low-tech: Disney's fleet of ferryboats that cross the lagoon from the TTC to the gates of the park. At most times, there are two boats in constant operation with a third available for peak periods.

The scaled-down versions of the famous Staten Island Ferries in New York are double-ended vessels, meaning they don't need to turn around at either end of their trip. You walk on at one end and walk off at the other. By the way, the ferries are free-floating; unlike the riverboat at the Magic Kingdom, there is no rail beneath the water.

The ferries are a very pleasant way to travel, especially on a pretty evening at the end of a long day.

Commuting from Epcot. If your plan for the day calls for a start at the Magic Kingdom and ends with a special dinner at Epcot, you might try this strategy: arrive early at Epcot and park there. Ride the monorail to the transfer point at the Transportation and Ticket Center and pick up the monorail to the Magic Kingdom. Then reverse that route in the afternoon and you will be able to stay as late as you want at Epcot and pick up your car there. The alternate plan works, too, on nights when the Magic Kingdom is open later than Epcot; park at the Magic Kingdom, and ride the monorail to Epcot to begin your day.

Although the monorail may look speedy, in truth it is only about a minute or two faster than the ferryboat in getting from the TTC to the Magic Kingdom. And the two ferryboats can carry about three times as many passengers as one monorail train. So, if the line for the monorail is lengthy, go by sea.

WALT DISNEY WORLD ROADWAYS

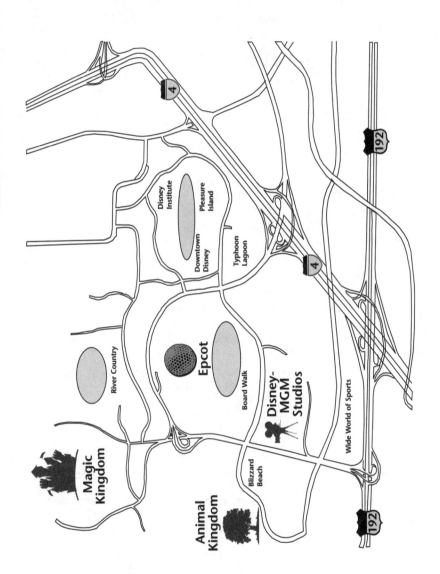

Chapter 7
The Magic Kingdom

Once upon a mouse, back in 1928, Walter Elias Disney created a short cartoon named "Steamboat Willie." Its star was a mouse, Willie, who soon thereafter underwent a name change and achieved stardom as Mickey Mouse.

Everything else since then has been built upon the slender shoulders of the cute little rodent, along with his gal, Minnie, and buddies Donald, Daisy, Snow White, as well as a cast of thousands of other cartoon and movie favorites.

Disney's film studio began to grow rapidly; Walt set up a little park alongside his first movie studios to entertain visitors, exhibiting his collection of scale model trains among other things. When he moved into television in the early 1950s, Disney struck a deal with ABC Television to help fund the construction of the Disneyland park in California, which opened in a former orange grove in 1955. Although much has changed in the nearly 50 years since Disneyland was first planned, the basic structure of that park, and all that have followed, is the same. Here's a how-de-doo: In 1995, Disney bought the entire ABC network.

Today, breathes there a man, woman, girl, boy, or mouse who has not dreamed of visiting the Magic Kingdom? The entertainment vision of Walt Disney—along with the incredible marketing skills of the company he left behind—has made Disney's parks and symbols probably the world's best-known popular icons. You can see Mickey Mouse T-shirts on the streets of Moscow, Epcot towels on the beaches of the Caribbean, Minnie dresses on the boulevards of Paris, and Roger Rabbit hats in the alleys of Tokyo.

In 1992, Disneyland Paris joined the three other parks—Disneyland, Walt Disney World, and Tokyo Disneyland—on the global map.

In Florida, by far the largest of all the Disney parks, the empire sprawls across miles of land and includes four major theme parks and dozens of other attractions. However, it is still The Magic Kingdom—home of Fantasyland, Adventureland, Frontierland, and Tomorrowland—that is what visitors think of when they first set out for Orlando.

MAGIC KINGDOM MUST-SEES

Space Mountain
(Tomorrowland)

Splash Mountain
(Frontierland)

The Haunted Mansion
(Liberty Square)

Pirates of the Caribbean
(Adventureland)

Jungle Cruise
(Adventureland)

Big Thunder Mountain Railroad
(Frontierland)

Buzz Lightyear's Space Ranger Spin
(Tomorrowland)

The Timekeeper
(Tomorrowland)

It's a Small World
(Fantasyland)

Mickey's Country House
(Mickey's Toontown Fair, adults excused)

The Many Adventures of Winnie the Pooh
(State-of-the-art Fantasyland dark ride)

Tom Sawyer Island
(Frontierland)

In this section, I'll offer the Ultimate Unauthorized Tour of the Magic Kingdom, area by area. I'll tell you which rides are "must-sees" and which ones are not worth crossing the road for.

Power Trip #1

Adults and Adventurous Kids:
Space Mountain/Buzz Lightyear Plan
The arrival of Buzz Lightyear adds to the enduring magnetic attraction of Space Mountain in Tomorrowland.

To ride one or both, get to the park before opening and wait at the rope barrier at the right side of the top of Main Street, as close to Tomorrowland as you can get. Join the gate-opening sprint to **Space Mountain** in Tomorrowland for an eye-opening start to your day. When you're back on Earth, take a ride on **Buzz Lightyear's Space Ranger Spin**. Or go first to Buzz Lightyear and then ride Space Mountain.

While you're in the neighborhood, you might want to visit the ExtraTERRORestrial at **Alien Encounter.** Or not.

If there is not much of a waiting line, hop onto the **Skyway** for a lift to the far end of Fantasyland. Check the hours of operation first.

Walk to **Splash Mountain** and **Big Thunder Mountain Railroad** and ride both. By now, alas, the lines for major attractions are probably starting to grow.

Backtrack to the **Haunted Mansion** in Liberty Square for a howl. You have now completed five of the most exciting and most crowd-drawing attractions for older visitors. Take an early lunch and then walk across the top of Frontierland and into Adventureland to join the line for **Pirates of the Caribbean.**

At this point, we'd suggest changing direction and walking in a clockwise direction back toward Tomorrowland; visit any other ride that appeals to you as you go. Check out *The Timekeeper* for jazzy fun. If you have the time, come back for a ride after dark on **Splash**

Mountain or **Big Thunder Mountain Railroad.** Or, take another trip on **Space Mountain**; try the opposite set of tracks from the one you took the first time.

And though this Power Trip is intended for older visitors, I still recommend a visit to the new **Many Adventures of Winnie the Pooh,** the state-of-the-art in dark rides.

Power Trip #2
Adults and Adventurous Kids:
Splash Mountain Plan

Get to the park before opening and wait at the lefthand rope barrier at the top of Main Street near the Crystal Palace. Join the gate-opening sprint to **Splash Mountain** in Adventureland.

Or, here's an interesting alternate: enter the park before the opening, and go up to the Disney World Railroad immediately; there will be a train waiting there that will depart at the moment the park officially opens. Ride to the Splash Mountain exit and get off the train and into line; you should be able to beat most of the thundering horde racing across the park on foot.

When your feet are back on dry land, sprint over to **Big Thunder Mountain Railroad** for a tour.

Head across the park to Liberty Square and enter the **Haunted Mansion** for a howl. Continue into Fantasyland and, if there is not much of a waiting line, hop onto the **Skyway** for a lift to the far end of Tomorrowland. Blast off on **Space Mountain.** Then visit Buzz Lightyear's new digs.

We'd grab lunch now and work our way back across the park to the last remaining big draw, **Pirates of the Caribbean** in Adventureland.

And again, I recommend the new **Many Adventures of Winnie the Pooh** for children of all ages. Go there late in the day when the kiddies are through.

For the rest of the day, visit any other ride that appeals to you as you go. If you have the time, come back for a ride after dark on both **Splash Mountain** and **Big Thunder Mountain Railroad**—it's a whole new experience after the sun goes down.

Power Trip #3
Children (and Parents Under Their Control)

Head left from Main Street and enter Adventureland. Ride **Pirates of the Caribbean** and the **Jungle Cruise.** (You can also take the Disney World Railroad from the top of Main Street to the Adventureland stop.)

Depending on how adventurous your children are, you may want to go early to Splash Mountain, which is an utterly charming ride that also includes a few

Closing time. Closing time varies according to the season, and is sometimes adjusted from day to day based on attendance patterns; it can be as early as 6 P.M. or as late as midnight. Check at the park for details. The announced closing time is actually a relative thing, usually meaning the time when the last person is allowed to join a ride line. The parks themselves are cleared out about an hour or so after then, and the final bus or other transportation to parking lots or hotels leaves about 90 minutes after closing time.

Lockers. Store extra clothing and other items at one of the coin-operated lockers beneath the Main Street Railroad Station and at the Transportation and Ticket Center. It costs $5 to rent a locker for the day; you'll receive $2 back when you return the key. Your one-day rental can be transferred to Epcot or Disney-MGM Studios; consult the attendant.

seconds' drop over a waterfall—it looks a lot more scary than it really is.

The newest attraction in Fantasyland is the bouncy **Many Adventures of Winnie the Pooh**, sure to draw lines; lucky parents get to go with their kids. Other youngsters will want to head first for **Buzz Lightyear's Space Ranger Spin**, a combination of a dark ride with a shooting gallery.

Walk into Frontierland and (depending on the ages and inclinations of the children) ride **Splash Mountain** and **Big Thunder Mountain Railroad**. Resist the temptation to take the raft to Tom Sawyer Island at this time.

Enter Liberty Square. Ride **The Haunted Mansion** if your children don't mind a few hundred Disney spooks.

At Fantasyland, visit **It's a Small World** and (if absolutely necessary) ride **Dumbo, the Flying Elephant**. The lines for the **Tomorrowland Speedway** will probably have built up to 30 or more minutes by now; we'd suggest coming back some other morning or in the evening.

Escape to Tomorrowland, bypassing Mickey's Toontown Fair for the moment. Ride the **Astro Orbiter** and (if the children are up to it, and if the lines are of a reasonable length) **Space Mountain**. Parental Guidance: we would recommend against taking young children into **Alien Encounter**.

Now you are free to reverse direction and explore the less-crowded rides. We recommend families next visit **Mickey's House** in Mickey's Toontown Fair, **Cinderella's Golden Carrousel** in Fantasyland, the raft ride to **Tom Sawyer Island** in Frontierland, and **The Hall of Presidents** in Liberty Square for children studying American history.

The Opening Dash

The Magic Kingdom usually opens at 9 A.M., although it may open at 8 A.M. at extremely busy times of the year. Guests at Walt Disney Resorts are allowed an hour's head start to certain areas of the park on some days.

The first part of the park that officially opens is Main Street; you can visit some of the shops or grab a bite to eat before your day really begins. Visitors are stopped at gates at the top of Main Street—one to the left near the Crystal Palace, one in the center heading toward Cinderella Castle, and one to the right just short of Tomorrowland.

The first rule of the Power Trip called for you to get to the park early; the second rule is to get yourself a good position at one of the three gates. Go to the left if your first goal is Splash Mountain, Big Thunder Mountain, or another attraction in Adventureland or Frontierland. Line up at the rightmost gate if you want to go to Space Mountain, Alien Encounter, Tomorrowland Speedway, or another Tomorrowland ride. And head up the center to go to Fantasyland.

Just before the gates open for the masses, you'll hear a bit of music and an announcement that quotes Walt Disney's dedication of the park; then the speaker will conclude by asking visitors to walk slowly and carefully into the park; of course, the crowds will stampede wildly instead.

Whether you walk or run, if you are anywhere near the front of the waiting line when the gates open, you should be able to get onto any ride in the park with no more than a 15-minute wait, which is about as good as it gets.

A general rule for any part of Walt Disney World is to head immediately for the ride or rides you expect will have the longest lines and get them out of the way early. Then go on to as many other major attractions as you can before the lines become too long. Spend the afternoon visiting lesser attractions, and then go back to major draws at the end of the day as the crowds lessen and the parades and fireworks pull people out of line.

Attractions at the Magic Kingdom
Main Street, U.S.A.

Somewhere, someplace, at some time, there was an America like this. It's a place of small stores with friendly proprietors, where the streets are clean and the landscape neat, and where a scrap of paper never lingers on the ground.

At the start of your visit to the Magic Kingdom, think of Main Street, U.S.A. as an interesting place to walk through on the way to somewhere else. Come back later to browse, shop, or eat; if you are following our advice, you will have arrived early at the park with a specific destination in mind.

But when you do come back, marvel at the attention to detail of the storefronts and interior decorations of the shops. Most of the names on the second story windows are those of former and present Disney employees responsible for creation or maintenance of the park.

Main Street is also the place to be if you are a serious parade fan; the entertainment moves toward the railroad station just inside the gates—that may be the best seat in the house to watch the parade. You can, though, also see the parades near Cinderella Castle and on the streets of Frontierland, both of which are nearer the major attractions of the park.

The famous Disney parades change every few years, and in high-season there may be as many as three parades a day—an afternoon Disney character parade and two evening electrical events. Pick up an Entertainment Show Schedule at the entrance to the park or at City Hall.

Return of the Main Street Electrical Parade. The spectacular Main Street Electrical Parade was brought out of mothballs on Memorial Day 1999 for a one-year nostalgia tour; the popular show may be extended if the reception is as strong as expected by some Disney executives.

The updated parade features 575,000 lights in a 26-float procession of Disney fantasy themes that include Peter Pan, Dumbo, Alice in Wonderland, Pete's Dragon, and Cinderella's Pumpkin Coach. Grand Marshal of the parade is the Blue Fairy from *Pinocchio,* aglitter in a winged gown of more than 10,000 blue, amber, and crystal lights.

Disney phone numbers. Walt Disney World dining reservations: (407) 939-3463 Disney resort hotel reservations: (407) 934-7639 Golf tee times: (407) 824-2270 Pleasure Island: (407) 934-7781

Meeting places. Try not to select the front of Cinderella Castle as a meeting place for groups that go their own way within the park. This location can become quite crowded during the daily parades and other events. Instead, choose the back side of the castle near the carrousel or a landmark off the parade route.

According to Disney Imagineers, the Main Street Electrical Parade was based on the Walt Disney World Electrical Water Pageant, which takes place nightly on Bay Lake. The first version of the parade was presented at Disneyland. A version of the parade arrived at Walt Disney World in 1977; that spectacular was packed up and moved to Disneyland Paris. The revived parade is an update of Disneyland's show.

The music for the parade is Baroque Hoedown, a Disney composition that is interwovem with classic Disney musical themes.

A secret spot, slightly less crowded, from which to watch parades is near the exit from Pirates of the Caribbean and the entrance to Splash Mountain near the Pecos Bill Café. A pathway under the railroad is the start or end of most parades.

One place worth stopping before you begin your exploration is **City Hall** in Town Square. Step up to the counter to obtain entertainment and Disney Character schedules; maps in English, French, German, Spanish, or braille; written show descriptions for visitors with special needs; and other information. By the way, City Hall opens when the ticket gates open (up to half an hour or so before the rope is dropped at the top of Main Street), allowing you to make a quick stop there before you join the dash to Space Mountain or Splash Mountain or Dumbo or whatever's your immediate pleasure.

Walt Disney Railroad. A pleasant way to tour the park (our favorite way to end a day), these real steam engines take passengers on a 1½-mile, 15-minute circuit of the park.

Walt Disney was a railroad nut, even running a small-scale system in his own backyard. The four engines that are part of the Magic Kingdom's rolling stock were built in the United States but spent much of their working lives in Mexico's Yucatan peninsula hauling sugar cane. The wheels, side rods, and other major parts of the engines are original, although the boilers and cabs have been rebuilt. Originally constructed to burn coal or wood and later converted to oil, the steam engines are now powered by diesel fuel.

The "Lilly Belle," named for Disney's wife, was built in 1928, coincidentally the same year Mickey Mouse made his screen debut. Also on the tracks is the "Roy O. Disney," named for the boss's brother, the "Walter E. Disney," named for the man himself, and the less-often seen "Roger Broggie," christened after a long-time Disney employee and friend.

The recorded spiel of the conductor has become politically correct in recent years, removing references to marauding Indians and instead extolling the friendly Native Americans waiting to greet visitors.

Main Street Vehicles. Old-fashioned cars, a horse-drawn trolley, and fire engines move slowly down Main Street to Cinderella Castle. (Following not far behind the horses are uniformed sanitation engineers with shovels.)

Cinderella Castle. The hallmark of the Magic Kingdom, it is, of course, every child's mind's-eye image of the way a castle really should be. It sits at the focal center of the park marking both the top of Main Street, U.S.A. and the entranceway to Fantasyland.

Walt Disney World's castle is loosely based on Sleeping Beauty's castle as described in the fairy tale and the Disney movie that brought it to life. It is constructed of fiberglass over steel beams; there's not a single brick in the castle. Way up top is a small apartment originally intended for Walt Disney and his family, but never used.

Disney insiders say there had been consideration of creating a place to stay within the castle as part of the park's 25th anniversary celebration; among the problems was how to deal with the fact that at night guests would have been within the park when it was officially closed. The proposed solution was to assign a personal escort for all guests, which wouldn't have been too big of a deal, because room rates were expected to be several thousand dollars per night. In any case, it didn't happen, and the rooms within remain unfinished.

You can, though, go halfway up the tower to **Cinderella's Royal Table** for a theme park theme meal. And be sure to check out the elaborate mosaics in the entranceway; they tell the familiar story of the girl with the glass slipper in Italian glass, real silver, and gold.

> **Tall tale.** Cinderella Castle is 189 feet tall—nine feet higher than Spaceship Earth in Epcot. (The castle at Disneyland in California, by the way, is named Sleeping Beauty Castle and is much smaller, with towers just 71 feet tall.)

> **Family matters.** The Coat of Arms above the castle on the north wall (facing Fantasyland) is that of the Disney family. Outside the entrance to King Stefan's Banquet Hall are plaques for other Disney executives. There's no word on whether Michael Eisner has commissioned a family portrait for the public portion of the park.

Tomorrowland

When Tomorrowland was originally conceived, it was as a showcase of the future. Ironically, the world of tomorrow at the Magic Kingdom eventually became the most dated and tired part of the park.

In 1995, Tomorrowland underwent the most complete remake of an original area at any Disney park. Today's Tomorrowland looks forward and backward at the same time: the setting is straight out of Buck Rogers's science fiction movies of the 1920s and 1930s.

Only in the world of Disney could a place begin way out in the future, fall way behind the times, and then be remade at a cost of millions so that it appears to be a 1930s view of the year 2000. The concept was first tried out at Disneyland Paris; a similar remake was undertaken at Disneyland in California.

Tomorrowland has been recast as an Interplanetary Convention Center. **Space Mountain** is now the headquarters for the Intergalactic Tracking Network. **Alien Encounter** is the setting for a trade fair for products that are a few hundred years away from your neighborhood Kmart. Overhead is the **Tomorrowland Transit Authority** and you'll be able to visit the **Metropolis Science Center** for an extraordinary experiment in time travel.

Tomorrowland is once again a must stop on your visit to Walt Disney World. Only now the lines are going to be at least as long as anywhere in the park; head here early or at the end of the day to avoid the lines.

WOW **Space Mountain.** Every Disney visitor with a bit of spunk—and his or her mom and dad—has got to visit Tomorrowland at least once to catch a rocketship to Ryca 1.

Space Mountain is the big enchilada, the highmost high, the place where hundreds of Magic Kingdom visitors have dropped their eyeglasses, cameras, and hairpieces. It is also one of the most popular of all of the attractions at Walt Disney World (as is the similar—but not identical—ride at Disneyland; another version, named Discovery Mountain and based on Jules Verne's book, *From the Earth to the Moon,* is at Disneyland Paris).

Space Mountain is a masterpiece of Disney Imagineering, merging a relatively small and slow (top speed of about 28 mph) roller coaster with an outer space theme. The small cars zoom around indoors in near-total darkness, the only light coming from the projected images of stars and planets on the ceiling. The ride is a triumph of scene-setting, the amusement park equivalent of a big-budget movie's special effects.

The cars feel like they are moving much faster than they are because you have no point of reference in the dark. And no, the cars don't turn upside down.

As you enter the building, you'll see a chart of the FX-1 Intergalactic Tracking Network, representing some of the launches and satellites of a future civilization. When you reach the loading area for the ride—the final queue that can give you 20 more minutes of exquisite teasing torture before you are loaded into your spaceship—check out the video monitors hung from the ceiling.

The televisions bring you continuous reports from PNN—the Planetary News Network. You'll hear from the Hubble Traffic scanner on traffic congestion on Route 4066 in the outer galaxy. Wendy Beryllium's weather report calls for 620 degrees on Mercury and a chilly negative 360 degrees on Neptune. The extended forecast for the planet Earth calls for partly cloudy skies, rising oceans, and a giant comet smashing into the planet sometime in the next hundred million years.

There's a report on the construction of the Mall of Mars. And if you hang on long enough, you will get to see an episode in the lifestyles of the rich and alien.

And be sure to catch the wild ads from Crazy Larry, the used spaceship dealer. What a deal: free floor mats with any intergalactic cruiser!

Overhead, a projector paints the pictures of huge rolling asteroids; you will not be the first to observe that they look like close-ups of chocolate chip cookies. Disney has never revealed its recipe.

Finally, you'll reach the busy launching pad packed with technicians and engineers loading spacecraft.

There are two tracks within the building and the ride is slightly different on each; the left side has more sharp turns, while the right side has more sharp dips. The waiting line splits into left and right queues as you enter the loading area. Each train seats six persons, one behind the other.

Professional Space Mountain riders—and there are tens of thousands of them—will argue over which seat affords the best ride. The last seat seems to benefit from a "whip" effect as the cars make sharp turns; we prefer the very front chair, where you don't have the back of someone else's head to mar the illusion of space travel and there is a terrific blast of on-rushing air as you move on the track. At busy times, you probably will not be able to cajole an attendant into allowing you to select the seat of your choice; late at night or on the occasional slow day you might be in luck.

Do keep a hand on your personal belongings; wrap camera and purse straps around your feet and make sure that children are properly placed beneath the restraining bar. (Disney launch technicians will double-check the safety arrangements, too.)

And then it's over. The ride is about 2 minutes and 40 seconds in length, and nowhere near as fast or as wild as a major roller coaster such as the new Rock 'n' Roller Coaster at Disney-MGM Studios, or The Hulk and Dueling Dragons at Universal Studios Islands of Adventure, but Space Mountain has that certain Disney touch that will keep you coming back again and again to wait in line for your next space voyage.

Now, speaking of waiting lines: they can easily extend to 90 minutes or more on a busy afternoon. The general rule to avoid long lines at the Magic Kingdom especially applies here. Get to the ride when the gates first open and you may be able to stroll right on board, or come back to the ride at the end of the day. Another somewhat quiet time is during the dinner hour, from about 6 to 7 P.M.

If both tracks are operating, a crowd backed up to the front door means a wait of about an hour; sometimes, though, attendants will build up the line outside while the inside queues clear out. This is often done at the end of the day to discourage huge crowds as closing hour approaches.

Children under three cannot ride Space Mountain, and those under seven must be accompanied by an adult; all riders must be at least 44 inches tall, and pregnant women and others with back or health problems are advised against riding.

Space Mountain, along with other major rides such as Big Thunder Mountain Railroad and Splash Mountain, offers a "switch off" arrangement if not

Lost and found. A family of four touring Walt Disney World for four days and not losing at least one backpack, two sets of sunglasses, and three hats is unlike any we know. On the day of a loss, check at City Hall in the Magic Kingdom or Guest Services at Epcot, Animal Kingdom, or the Disney-MGM Studios. After a day, items are taken to a central lost and found at the Transportation and Ticket Center.

all of the people in your party want to ride the coaster, or if you are traveling with a child too young or too small to ride. Inform the attendant at the turnstile at the launching area that you want to switch off; one parent or adult can ride Space Mountain and change places with another at the exit so everyone can take a turn.

To the left of the entrance to Space Mountain, **Cool Scanner** offers a refreshing water mist on hot days.

WOW Buzz Lightyear's Space Ranger Spin. It's *Toy Story* live, in a new ride that combines a zippy dark ride with a shooting gallery.

You'll be teamed with astro-superhero Buzz Lightyear on a daring mission to rescue the universe's crystollic fusion cell supply (better known as batteries) from the clutches of the evil Emperor Zurg.

You'll be assigned to your personal two-seater XP-37 Space Cruiser, spinning through ten scenes of toys, asteroids and meteors, and strange and wondrous aliens in the Gamma Quadrant. Each car includes a joystick to spin the car and a pair of infrared laser guns to knock down all manner of threats by Zurg—basically, shoot any and all of the orange Emperor Zurg insignias scattered throughout the ride. When your laser hits a target it triggers animation, sound and light effects and your score—which varies according to the complexity of the shot—is tallied on an LED screen on the cruiser's dashboard.

The final scene takes you through a tunnel of energy, a fun holdover from the Take Flight attraction, which was the former occupant of the building.

At a Disney press event, I rode through the Gamma Quadrant with Buzz Aldrin, the famed NASA astronaut; does the name Buzz Lightyear ring a bell here? Aldrin scored pretty well on the ride, by the way, reaching the Planetary Explorer level, which only seemed right.

Alien Encounter: The ExtraTERRORestrial. We've come a long, long way from Mickey Mouse to an up-close and personal meeting with the ExtraTERRORestrial. The attraction was the subject of some of the most intensive hype of any new project at the Magic Kingdom; visitors were promised they would be participants in a terrifying "sensory thriller." But when the show opened in January of 1995, it lasted only a few weeks before the powers that be ordered it shut down and reworked to make it scarier.

Alas, I still find the encounter to be a lot more hype than horror. The show is not as technologically impressive as "Honey, I Shrunk the Audience" at Epcot nor as stomach-turning as the Twilight Zone Tower of Terror at the Disney-MGM Studios. It's worth a visit, but I'd recommend against joining a lengthy line for the privilege.

As you stroll through Tomorrowland, you'll see billboards from the Tomorrowland Chamber of Commerce inviting you to visit the "Tomorrowland Interplanetary Convention Center" for an exhibit by X-S Tech, a mysterious company promoting a mysterious new technology. When you enter the convention center, you will see displays on some of their strange businesses, including Electro Robotics, Cryo Cybernetics, and more. There are also some clever billboards advertising such attractions as "Lunar Disneyland—The Happiest Place Off Earth" and an invitation to the "Tomorrowland Swap Meet" where the offerings include a collection of previously owned robots.

Once you're in the preshow area you will meet L. C. Clench, the otherworldly spokesman for X-S Tech . . . there's something not quite right about this guy, er . . . alien. His slogan: "If something can't be done with X-S, it shouldn't be done at all."

When you enter into the display area, you'll meet the robotic host T.O.M. 2000 (Technobotic Oratorical Mechanism, Series 2000) who is there to demonstrate the X-S Series 1000 Teleportation System. He's going to show the use of teleportation using the aid of his cute little alien friend, Skippy. Hmm . . . teleportation, as in *The Fly*? You don't suppose there's a chance of something going wrong with the device, do you?

When you are escorted into the demonstration area and locked into your seat by an overhead harness (locked into your seat!), the audience will be scanned for a suitable subject.

Of course, something goes wrong. A wild alien is loose among the audience . . . which is locked into its seats!

Much of the show consists of very loud sound effects, bright flashes, and a whole lot of screaming coming from all around you. It took a moment before we realized that most of the screaming was on the soundtrack.

Alien Encounter replaced the hopelessly outdated *Mission to Mars* show (so old, it was originally called *Voyage to the Moon*). There are two theaters, each seating 134 persons; visitors must be at least 48 inches tall.

Under foot. Among the most amazing wonders of the Magic Kingdom is one that most visitors never see. Below your feet are nine acres of underground "utilidor" corridors hiding the sewers, water pipes, air conditioning, electrical cables, communications links, and garbage collection facilities. There is also an extensive system of tunnels that allow employees to come and go within the park virtually unseen; have you ever wondered why you have never seen Mickey walking to work, or seen a Mike Fink keelboat captain strolling through Tomorrowland?

Actually, the tunnels are the first level of the Magic Kingdom. Because of the high water table of much of Florida, the tunnels were put in place first and then covered over with dirt, much of it from the excavation of the lagoon.

About that trash: as you might expect in a Magic Kingdom, Disney does not use an ordinary garbage truck. Refuse is sucked to a central collection point through a huge network of pneumatic tubes.

WOW *The Timekeeper.* Jules Verne, H. G. Wells, and a few modern-day stars lead us on a stunning multimedia exploration of time and space, presented in Circle-Vision 360 and including an appearance by English actor Jeremy Irons and wildman Robin Williams as the voice of Timekeeper.

The adventure begins with a preshow in which you are introduced to Timekeeper and his robotic assistant "9-Eyes," who has guess-how-many cameras. The amusing introduction includes a newsreel about the development and testing of 9-Eyes, including a test trip of Niagara Falls.

Listen carefully as Robin Williams, err, the Timekeeper lets loose with a stream of quick jokes, some of the funniest in the Magic Kingdom. "No longer are we limited to traveling from place to place and losing our bags beforehand," he tells us.

Anyway, it seems that Timekeeper has perfected the long-sought-after art of time travel and is about to embark on a journey back in time to visit some of the great visionaries of all time, including Jules Verne and H. G. Wells. Many of Frenchman Verne's predictions, including space travel, subways, and submarines have come true; Englishman Wells was a great visionary but few of his dreams, including time travel and alien invasions, have (thus far) come true.

Timekeeper sets out on a voyage back in time to the Universal Scientific Exposition of Paris in 1900. There he meets Verne and Wells who are in the midst of an argument about their beliefs. Verne accuses Wells of being a hopeless dreamer and scoffs at his idea of time travel.

9-Eyes comes into the middle of it all when it is spotted by Verne, who grabs hold of the strange device and suddenly becomes dragged along on a fantastic voyage that includes the high-speed TGV train in modern France, downtown Parisian traffic, an undersea trip, and a stop at the madhouse of New York City ("home of 10 million dreams and one parking space").

After a few more spectacular visits, including a glimpse of the higher-tech future of the year 2189 in Paris (note that the Eiffel tower has a 300th anniversary banner on it, and watch for Jules Verne and H. G. Wells flying by in a time machine), the entourage is deposited back at the site of the science exposition of Paris.

The film may be a bit over the heads of young children—literally and figuratively, since there are no seats in the theater—but for all others *The Timekeeper* is sure to be an instant Disney classic.

The Transportarium show debuted at Le Visionarium at Disneyland Paris. In the European version of the film, French superstar Gérard Depardieu made a cameo appearance as an airport baggage handler in a sequence involving the Concorde at Orly Airport near Paris. And if you watch very carefully, it is apparent that most of the actors spoke French with English overdubbed later.

The theater is large and at most times of the day you should be able to get into the 20-minute show with no more than a 20-minute wait; if the line extends out the door, you may want to come back at another time in the day.

Galaxy Palace Theater at Rockettower Plaza. An outdoor theater located between the Transportarium and the Carousel of Progress, used for live shows.

Tomorrowland Transit Authority. The former **WEDway People-Mover,** reworked a bit as part of the remake of Tomorrowland. The new loading station is **Rockettower Plaza.** Trains of 20-passenger cars of the Tomorrowland Transit Authority Metroliner Blueline circle slowly above Tomorrowland, taking a quick peek into a part of Space Mountain (a good way for the faint of heart to get some idea of what the excitement is about).

The PeopleMover is a pet project of the Magic Kingdom, demonstrating an unusual means of propulsion—the linear induction motor. The track and the car form a motor together, as magnetic pulses pull the car down a flat coil.

There is rarely a significant line for this 10-minute ride, which we still found to be about seven minutes too long. Still, it's a seat and a bit of a view.

Astro Orbiter. A basic amusement park ride with rotating rockets and an up/down lever, but in typical Disney fashion it seems like much more.

Nowhere near as threatening (to some) as Space Mountain, it nevertheless is not for people with a fear of heights.

As part of the overall remake of Tomorrowland, the ride was rebuilt and is now one of the most recognizable features of that section of the park, with the Jules Verne theme of rotating planets and moons. It is especially impressive at night. If you think about it, Astro Orbiter is a slightly faster and somewhat higher version of Dumbo, the Flying Elephant.

Tomorrowland Arcade. The fanciful power station for the world of the future, located at the exit from Space Mountain, also contains a fabulous video arcade. Disney designers again looked backward to the rounded, streamlined architecture of the art deco 1930s for their presentation of the future.

Carousel of Progress. The future ain't what it used to be. That was very evident as the Carousel of Progress grew further and further out of date in the 1980s. Its concept of the future had moved into the past.

This ride, originally presented at the 1964–65 World's Fair in New York, tells the story of the march of technology in American homes. It was interesting in 1964 and amusing in 1984, but hopelessly outdated in the 1990s; in 1994, Disney opened a slightly updated version of the show featuring the voice of raconteur Jean Shepherd.

The basic concept of the Carousel remains unchanged; the theater seats revolve around a stationary central core populated by Audio-Animatronic robots. The show takes about 22 minutes.

The first few scenes of the show are unchanged from the earlier version, with a new narration by Jean Shepherd and the return of the original theme song. The show starts at the turn of the century as electricity was first making its appearance in the home; the second scene takes place

Left, right, up, down. Check out the world of transportation at the right corner of the Space Mountain building near the Carousel of Progress. In one spot you can see the Disney steam train, the modern monorail, and the electric Tomorrowland Transit Authority cars. To your left is the aerial skyride and the earthbound Tomorrowland Speedway. Above it all are the Astro Orbiters. And then think of the rocket ships on rails within the mountain.

Robo-stars. Disney claims that the Carousel of Progress has had more performances than any other stage show in the history of America; of course, it's not really a stage show because all of the actors have electric motors inside them.

His, hers, and its. The little signs over the restrooms in Tomorrowland depict male and female robots.

at the time of Lindbergh in the 1920s, and then we move on to the promising 1940s. (Many adults will be amused to see a working model of the vibrating belt exercise machines that were the rage into the early 1950s.)

The fourth stage setting takes us a few years beyond the current day. A young boy loans his grandmother his virtual reality game, which she takes over. When grandma calls out her score of 550, the voice-actuated oven burns the turkey.

Even with the small amount of updating, it is still worth noting that the Carousel is an all-white, middle-class world and not all that thrilling, and also one in which dad is still pretty much the indisputable king of the castle.

The best seat is down front in the center of the auditorium. Note the eyes on the various robot dogs in each scene—the dog is the best actor in the troupe.

By the way, longtime fans of Jean Shepherd, one of the great cynics of our time as well as a great storyteller, may be a bit disconcerted to hear him end the show by saying "Have a great big beautiful tomorrow."

Skyway. Entrance to the aerial tramway that runs to Fantasyland. Passengers must exit at Fantasyland, although it is a simple matter to go down the stairs and back up again to return to Tomorrowland if you desire. For most of the day, lines for the five-minute ride are rarely longer than a few minutes; however, when a parade or show lets out, a sudden influx of visitors can cause buildups of half an hour or more; at those times we'd suggest walking instead. The trip is especially dramatic in the evening. The Skyway is regularly closed when it is windy or during very quiet times of the year.

Tomorrowland Speedway. Every kid we know dreams of getting behind the wheel of Daddy's car; most adults we know dream of taking a spin around a Grand Prix racecourse. Perhaps that is why this attraction, which doesn't have much to do with Tomorrowland that we can think of, is such a popular destination. Adults, alas, will probably find the trip rather boring; children will often beg for another go around the course.

There are four parallel tracks of about a half-mile each, and the little race cars have real gasoline engines that will propel them forward at up to a zippy seven mph. The steering gear works, too, allowing the driver to move the car left and right down the course, although there is a center rail that will keep the car from completely leaving the track.

Children must be at least 52 inches tall to ride in one of the cars alone; otherwise their feet won't reach the gas pedal. Mom or Dad, though, can sit alongside and press the pedal while junior happily steers.

Waiting lines can reach to nearly an hour on the most crowded days; visit the track early or late to make the best use of your time. A circuit takes about four minutes.

Merchants of Venus. Outfit yourself for intergalactic travel with unusual clothing and souvenirs. The unusual feature here is the robotic T-shirt painting machine that creates customized outfits. And be sure to check out the color hologram outside the store, facing the Astro Orbiters.

Fantasyland

This is the stuff of young dreams: Dumbo, Peter Pan, Alice in Wonderland, Snow White, and the toy riot of It's a Small World. Fantasyland is a bright and cheerful place, decorated in splashes of color and sprinkled with snippets of song. Over it all is Cinderella Castle (described already in the section about Main Street, U.S.A.).

Dumbo, the Flying Elephant. Disney has taken a very ordinary amusement park ride and made it something special, at least for little visitors. Riders sit within fiberglass flying elephants that can move up and down as they circle around a mirrored ball and a statue of Timothy Mouse, the little guy who becomes Dumbo's manager in the classic Disney animated movie.

A set of 16 Dumbos circle a golden crown with a set of gears and huge pinwheels, which all look like a kid's drawing of a machine. This ride has always held a tremendous draw for young children, with lines of up to an hour for the 90-second ride. The new design should cut those lines by almost half, but still, if your kids insist on an elephant-back ride, head for Dumbo early or late in the day. One of the rites of passage for youngsters, we suspect, is the day they announce they're willing to skip the lines for Dumbo in favor of a second pass at Space Mountain.

Ariel's Grotto. A watery world in the shadow of Dumbo where fans of *The Little Mermaid* can meet Ariel herself. On hot days, visitors young and old may want to dance in the fountains.

Cinderella's Golden Carrousel. One of the few mostly "real" things in this world of fantasy, the carousel dates back to 1917 and was used by generations of kids in New Jersey. Many of the horses are hand-carved originals, although the herd has been augmented with some fiberglass replicas and the overhead canopy has been Disneyfied with images from the company's films. No two of the horses are identical. The musical organ, which plays selections from Disney hit movies, is an Italian original.

The lines for the two-minute ride ebb and flow; we'd suggest you wait for the times when you can walk right on board.

WOW It's a Small World. Every little girl's wildest dream: a world of beautiful dancing dolls from all over the world. There is nothing to get your heart beating here, but even the most cynical—including little boys and adults—will probably find something to smile about in this upbeat boat ride. We especially enjoy the Audio-Animatronic cancan dancers.

This 11-minute ride was originally designed for the 1964–65 World's Fair in New York, but unlike the Carousel of Progress, the Small World ride has timeless appeal. The sound system was updated and improved in recent years.

The boats are large and the lines move pretty quickly (if two queues are being formed, the line to the left moves a bit faster), but we'd advise coming to this attraction early or late in the day. Children who like this ride will probably also enjoy the shorter Rivers of Time ride at the Mexican pavilion of Epcot.

Peter Pan's Flight. A mellow excursion into some of the scenes from Disney's version of the story of the little boy who doesn't want to grow up. Riders sit in a small pirate ship that suspends them a foot or so off the floor.

Everyone's favorite scene is the overhead view of London by night, which does a pretty good job of simulating Peter's flight. Strictly for kids.

At Disneyland Paris, a jazzed-up version of this ride is one of the more popular attractions; not so at the Magic Kingdom, although lines can still reach to 45 minutes or more on busy days.

Mad Tea Party. A Disney version of a rather common amusement park ride in which circular cars move around a track and also spin around on platforms. If it sounds dizzying, that's because it is: the very young and others with sensitive stomachs or ears might prefer the carrousel across the way. However, the riders have some control over how fast the cups spin; grab hold of the wheel in the center of the cup and don't let go for the least movement.

The ride is covered over with a tent-like structure, taking the cups and most of the waiting line out of the elements. The ride has been designed like a scene from Disney's classic 1951 film, *Alice in Wonderland*. Our favorite part is the drunken mouse who pops out of the teapot in the center.

The ride itself is only about 90 seconds long; the wait can be much more than that. I'd recommend hopping on board only if lines are short.

Fantasyland Character Festival. Here's your chance to press the fantasy flesh of many favorite Disney characters in an unusual setting in the former home of 20,000 Leagues Under the Sea. That venerable ride was shut in 1995 with rumors of a reworking, but its future may lie entirely in the past. One Disney executive did tell me in 1999 that it's most likely any future use of the area will make use of the lagoon in some way.

WOW! The Many Adventures of Winnie the Pooh. Oh, bother! It's a Blustery Day and the pages of our favorite book are blowing out of the building and into Fantasyland.

Welcome to a lovingly detailed step into the pages of one of the best-known children's books. Our giant honey pot vehicles carry up to six people into the pages of the book. We begin in Chapter 1, in which Pooh begins his search for honey in a very enchanted place.

"Happy Winds-day," says Gopher. "Maybe for you," replies Piglet. Pooh announces, "I'm in the mood for food," but Eeyore doubts the bear will reach the tree.

We move on to Rabbit's Garden, where Kanga holds onto Roo, flying like a kite in the wind, and into Owl's House. And then we enter the dramatic darkness of the Blustery Night, where we meet Tigger for the first time. "Come bounce with me," he invites, and so we do. Ever sat in a bouncing giant honey pot before?

One of the more dramatic scenes is Pooh's Dream, a view into his nightmare. What could he possibly fear? Why Heffalump and Woozle honey thieves, of course. Watch for the jack in the boxes.

And then Pooh wakes up in the Floody Place, and here Disney Imagineers pull out all the stops. There's water all about, and we seem to float through the room. The only one who isn't upset about the flooding is Pooh, happy to find that the rising water allows him to float to a honey bonanza high up in a tree.

All in all, this is one hunny of a ride, and great step forward in the venerable history of Disney dark rides. Pooh takes about three-and-a-half minutes, and 16 to 18 cars are on the track at any one time. I'd suggest coming early or late to avoid the crowds sure to come to this happy new place.

Pooh replaced an old favorite in the park, Mr. Toad's Wild Ride based on one of Disney's more obscure films, *The Adventures of Ichabod and Mr. Toad*, which was in turn loosely based on the book *The Wind in the Willows*. As good as that ride was, this one is much better.

By the way, the catchy music for the Pooh ride is by the composer of the score for *Mary Poppins* and the It's a Small World attraction.

Snow White's Scary Adventures. The word "scary" has returned to the doorway of this attraction, a tipoff to the fact that in some small ways this ride emphasizes the grimmer parts of the Brothers Grimm fairy tale, as presented in Disney's 1938 animated movie. The ride can't hold a fading candle to the spooks in the Haunted Mansion across the way in Liberty Square, but there are a few more skeletons and witches than very young children might expect.

A remake a few years ago created a kinder, gentler Snow White removing some of the darker elements of the ride, making the Florida version more like its California, Paris, and Tokyo cousins.

Parents be warned: it's still a bit scary at the start with some ghoulish ghouls and wicked witches, but happier at the end. The new version uses about half of the old "sets," but now Snow White herself appears for the first time in Florida. In fact, she's there in five scenes: at the wishing well in the courtyard of the castle, in the scary forest, at the dwarf's cottage, with the Prince when he kisses her to break the Witch's spell, and (of course) riding off with the Prince to live happily ever after.

The revision of the show was accompanied by a 50 percent increase in capacity for the vehicles; cars now carry six passengers instead of four.

The Legend of The Lion King. A sophisticated live actor and puppet show with special effects, music, and animation based on Disney's *Lion King* cartoon feature. Presented in the Fantasyland Theater (the former Magic Journeys location), the show puts the audience into the shadow of huge puppets on a 125-foot-wide stage.

The eight-minute standing preshow opens with a (small) live actor dressed as Rafiki, introducing the story of *The Lion King* and including the "Circle of Life" song from the movie.

Once you enter the theater itself, you will be asked to move all the way across the row to the far side of the auditorium. If you want to try to claim the best view in the middle, hold back until about 25 people have entered a row.

The puppets—some of which require as many as four puppeteers beneath the stage to operate—speak and sing with the recorded voices of some of the humans who gave words to the film characters, including Jeremy Irons as Scar, James Earl Jones as Mufasa, Whoopi Goldberg as Shenzi, and Cheech Marin as Banzai. The theater uses fantastic lighting, wind machines, and curtains of water as part of its effects. Jets of steam erupt from the floor, and lightning

Child under tow. On a crowded day, it is possible to lose sight of your children from time to time. Discuss with them beforehand a place to meet if you get separated; you can also obtain name tags to place on your children at City Hall or the Baby Center next to the Crystal Palace. Disney employees are well trained on how to deal with a lost child; track one down for assistance.

The Baby Center is specially designed to assist in nursing or changing infants; most other rest rooms throughout the parks have some accommodation for these needs. The Baby Center also offers for sale emergency rations of formula, replacement pacifiers, bottles, and diapers. Strollers are available for rent beneath the railroad overpass at the entrance to the Magic Kingdom.

crashes from above. Mountains and grasslands rise from below. Some young children may find the sound a bit loud, but the familiar story of *The Lion King* will entrance all.

Lines for the 28-minute show will build during the middle of the day; come early or late or during a parade. If the waiting line extends outside from under the canopy you will not make it into the next show, which means your waiting line will be at least an hour.

Skyway. The Fantasyland entrance to the aerial tramway, which returns to Tomorrowland; it's a great way to get a glimpse of the north end of the park. Passengers must exit at Tomorrowland, although it is a simple matter to go down the stairs and back up again to return to Fantasyland if you desire. The trip is especially dramatic in the evening; time your voyage properly and catch an aerial view of the nightly parade.

Mickey's Toontown Fair

Walt Disney World, Disneyland, and the entire Disney empire were built from the ears of the most famous rodent of all, but until 1989 Mickey didn't have a place of his own. That year, Disney honored the mouse's 60th (!) birthday with the first new area at Walt Disney World since its opening. Mickey's Starland became one of the most popular areas of the park for the youngest visitors. As part of the 25th Anniversary celebration at Walt Disney World, Starland received a major makeover, reopening as Mickey's Toontown Fair.

There are no outerspace roller coasters or multimillion dollar water slides here; instead we have the sort of giddy happiness that has sustained the mouse's popularity for all of these years. Disney also uses the area to present and promote some of its newer cartoon stars, including Goof Troop, Dark Wing Duck, Rescue Rangers, Tale Spin, and DuckTales. Lines to meet and greet Mickey, Minnie, and the other local stars can become quite lengthy in the middle of the day; come early or late if you can.

WOW Mickey's Country House. If you have kids, or ever were one, then there's not a whole lot of doubt about this: you've got to visit Mickey Mouse's house. It's a walk-through tour of the Mickster's private digs. Out back, in the **Judge's Tent**, the man . . . err, the mouse . . . himself appears to sign autographs.

WOW Minnie's Country House. Ms. Minnie is even more sociable than her friend across the street; here you can explore the house—be sure to press the buttons on the answering machine by the telephone. Minnie awaits in the gazebo in her garden from time to time.

Toontown Hall of Fame. A shrine to the greatest Disney cartoon characters of all time, with regular appearances by many local celebrities. Parents be warned: there is also a large gift shop within.

The Barnstormer at Goofy's Wiseacre Farm. A kid-sized roller coaster with kid-size thrills. Riders sit in cars that look like old biplanes. The tracks include a wide turn that flies through a barn where kids are waiting their turn to ride. Similar to Gadget's Go-Coaster at Mickey's Toontown at Disneyland, it is about twice as long. In the distance over the top of the coaster is the real thing, at least as far as the Magic Kingdom: Space Mountain.

Donald's Boat. The Miss Daisy, which has seen better days and sprouts leaks from all over. It's a great place to cool off on a hot day. Disney Imagineers have created a dry lake to surround the boat—here's your chance to walk on pseudo-water. Alas, Grandma Duck's Petting Farm was removed to make room.

Toontown Farmer's Market. An outdoor stand where you can make your own strawberry shortcake for about $3.

Walt Disney World Railroad. The vintage railroad that circles the Magic Kingdom has a station at the back of Toontown Fair. The next stop is Main Street, and the third stop is in Frontierland.

Liberty Square

A peaceful laid-back corner of America, home of the presidents (robotically assisted), a festive riverboat (which runs on underwater tracks), and a haunted mansion (which is too creepy to pass by without a tour). The square is also home to a massive live oak tree festooned with 13 lanterns—one for each of the 13 original colonies—like the Liberty Trees used as political statements in pre-Revolutionary times.

WOW The Haunted Mansion. Scare yourself silly in this masterpiece of an attraction with some of the most sophisticated special effects at Walt Disney World. During the years there have been hundreds of creepy and decrepit little improvements. If it's been a while since you last visited, you should be sure to go back; be sure to bring your death certificate.

World's fair fare. Disney was involved in four major pavilions at the 1964–65 New York World's Fair, including Pepsi's "It's a Small World—A Salute to UNICEF" ride, General Electric's "Carousel of Progress," the Illinois pavilion's "Great Moments with Mr. Lincoln," and Ford's "Magic Skyway" ride.

The first three World's Fair exhibits were later recycled for use at Disney parks: "It's a Small World" was moved to Disneyland and became the model for very similar and popular rides at Walt Disney World, Tokyo Disneyland, and Disneyland Paris. The GE "Carousel" was moved to Walt Disney World; it was updated a bit in 1994 but remains essentially unchanged. And "Great Moments with Mr. Lincoln" was Disney's first big success with Audio-Animatronics and was moved to Disneyland's Main Street, where it played for many years.

The ride is something of a rite of passage for kids, moving from Mickey and Minnie to the (humorous) dark side of Disney.

The experience begins in the graveyard waiting line; before you let the tombstones make you feel too creepy, stop and read some of the inscriptions. They're a howl!

The attendants, dressed as morticians, are among the best actors in the park, almost always staying in character. They will tell you to "fill in the dead space" in the line. When the elevator at the start of the ride fills up they may announce "No more bodies." They play their roles well—we've tried our best over the course of years to make them crack a smile, without any success.

Once you are admitted to the mansion itself, you will be ushered into a strange room that has an interesting visual trick—is the ceiling going up or the floor going down? Either way, the portraits on the wall are a real scream. (Don't read this if you don't want to know. OK, you have been warned: at Walt Disney World, the ceiling moves up and the floor stays where it is; at Disneyland, the floor moves down and the walls are stationary. The stretching room was put into place in California as a way to get visitors to the loading level which is on the other side of the railroad tracks. When the Florida house was built, there was no need to go down a level, but Imagineers wanted to keep the same illusion even if it was accomplished in a different way.)

The experience is accompanied throughout by a decidedly strange sound-track that is among the more literate writing found at Walt Disney World—that is, if you are able to hear it in the rather fuzzy sound system.

Here's part of the introduction from the stretching room:

> *When hinges creak in doorless chambers and strange and frightening sounds echo through the halls, whenever candlelights flicker where the air is deathly still, that is the time when ghosts are present, practicing their terror with ghoulish delight.*
>
> *Your cadaverous pallor betrays an aura of foreboding, almost as though you sense a disquieting metamorphosis. Is this haunted room actually stretching? Or is it your imagination? And consider this dismaying observation: this chamber has no windows, and no doors.*
>
> *Which offers you this chilling challenge: to find a way out! Of course, there's always my way.*

You'll enter onto a moving set of chairs and settle in for a tour through a house that is in the control of the largest collection of spooks this side of the CIA.

Says your Ghost Host: "We find it delightfully unlivable here in this ghostly retreat. Every room has wall-to-wall creeps and hot and cold running chills."

We've ridden the ride many times and see something different each time. Among the best effects are the dancing ghouls at the dinner party, the moving door knockers, and the face within the crystal ball.

This ride is probably the single best combination of Disney Audio-Animatronics, moviemaking, and scene setting at the Magic Kingdom. There are all sorts of delightful details on the ride, enough to make it worth several rides if you have the time. Here are a few you might want to look for: the needlepoint that reads "Tomb Sweet Tomb"; the legs sticking out from under the banquet table in the ghostly wedding reception; the skull-shaped notes rising out of the top of the organ at the reception.

You'll meet Madame Leota, a disembodied guide who will help you attempt to make contact with the spirits within the mansion.

Rap on a table, it's time to respond, send us a message from somewhere beyond. Goblins and ghoulies from last Halloween, awaken the spirits with your tambourine. Wizards and witches wherever you dwell, give us a hint by ringing a bell.

The best special effect of the ride is the wedding party scene, where guests move from mortal coil to diaphanous spirit and back. After the party, you'll meet the famous Grim Grinning Ghosts, captured within luminous globes. Through dozens of rides at the Magic Kingdom, Disneyland, and Disneyland Paris we were completely unable to figure out what they were saying until recently. Here's part of their song:

When the crypt doors creak and the tombstones quake, spooks come out for a swinging wake. Happy haunts materialize and begin to vocalize; grim grinning ghosts come out to socialize.

Now don't close your eyes and don't try to hide, or a silly spook may sit by your side. Shrouded in a daft disguise, they pretend to terrorize; grim grinning ghosts come out to socialize.

Tomb with a view. Our favorite Haunted Mansion tombstones include: "Dear departed brother Dave. He chased a bear into a cave"; "Here rests Wathel R. Bender. He rode to glory on a fender"; and "Here lies good old Fred. A great big rock fell on his head." And there is, "Rest in peace cousin Huet. We all know you didn't do it."

More favorites, from the cemetery at the exit of the ride: Bluebeard's tomb reads, "Here lyeth his loving wives. Seven winsome wives, some fat some thin. Six of them were faithful, but the seventh did him in." Other pun-full names on the wall include Paul Tergyst, Clare Voince, Metta Fisiks, and Manny Festation.

Many of the names are drawn from the Imagineers who designed the original ride.

As the ride comes to an end, Madam Leota will urge you to hurry back. Make final arrangements now.

During the past year, Disney has been subtly increasing the realism of the ride, perhaps in reaction to the overall explicitness of our society. The skeletons are just a bit more real, the ghosts are just a bit more ghoulish. Most noticeable is a new ending, where your vehicle will travel through a graveyard full of ghostly trees, among the tombs.

Some very young children may become a bit scared, although most kids of all ages can see the humor among the horrors. And speaking of humor, stop to read the inscriptions on the tombs at the exit.

Lines for this show vary greatly; the best times to visit are early or late in the day. Try not to join the crowds streaming toward the mansion's door each time the Hall of Presidents lets out or the riverboat arrives. The ride lasts about nine minutes, including a two-minute preshow.

Car talk. One of the announcements you may hear if the Haunted Mansion ride stops to load a passenger in a wheelchair is: "Please remain seated in your doom buggy."

The original Haunted Mansion was at Disneyland in California. Because it was to be built near the New Orleans area of Frontierland, the idea was to make it look like an early 1800s Southern mansion; however, it actually ended up looking more like an old home in Baltimore. Walt Disney himself vetoed one design that made the house appear to be derelict (Disney's first falling-down house would come some 30 years later with the construction of the Twilight Zone Tower of Terror at Disney-MGM Studios.)

The original plans also called for a walk-through tour, with groups of about 40 visitors escorted through the house by a butler or maid who would tell the story. The first story line was quite different, too, and not at all sugar-coated: it told of a wealthy sea merchant who built a fabulous mansion for his new bride, but then killed her in a rage after she learned he was really a bloody pirate. Her ghost came back to haunt him and tormented him so much that he finally hung himself from the rafters, giving the mansion two unhappy spirits.

About all that is left of the gruesome story is the brief glimpse of a hanging body above the stretching room, the weathervane in the shape of a sailing ship on the top of the cupola of the mansion, and some of the paintings that have a seafaring theme.

The Hall of Presidents. A living history lesson that features some of Disney's best Audio-Animatronic robots. The show is derived from the Illinois pavilion at the 1964–65 New York World's Fair, which startled fairgoers when a seated Abe Lincoln wearily came to life to address the audience. In the Magic Kingdom version of the show, all 42 American presidents are represented on stage.

The only two speaking parts in the Hall of Presidents are Lincoln and Bill Clinton. In 1994, President Clinton became the first sitting president to have a speaking role in the pageant, with a speech recorded in the Oval Office in which he pays tribute to America as "a symbol of freedom and an inspiration to people around the world." Clinton's speech includes the theme that "there is nothing wrong with America that cannot be cured by what is right with America."

As Clinton speaks, watch the small gestures and movements of the other presidents. Abe Lincoln sneaks a peek at his notes every once in a while; some of the others appear to make little comments to each other or fidget a bit.

The shows at the Hall of Presidents start on the hour and on the half hour. The first part of the show involves a series of detailed paintings projected on the large center screen; then the curtains pull back to reveal the assembled presidents.

The first part of the show features a new narration by poet Maya Angelou, who thrilled the audience at Clinton's inauguration with a poem. Angelou, one of our great minds and great voices, is also one of the few women and African Americans given individual recognition in the park. Her presentation includes a brief but relatively frank discussion of slavery.

The flag-waving show and a spectacular film that precedes the robotics may have particular appeal to school children studying American history. Others may enjoy the technical artistry of the robots, and some may enjoy studying the details of the costumes on each of the chief executives.

The show takes about 22 minutes; the 700-seat auditorium quickly eats up waiting lines and the maximum wait should be no more than two shows, or about 40 minutes.

By the way, there is a show at the American pavilion at Epcot, the American Experience, that is somewhat similar but considerably flashier, concentrating on other great figures from the history of our nation.

Liberty Belle Riverboat. A brand-new golden oldie took to the waters in 1997 with the launching of the *Liberty Belle*, a steam-powered sternwheeler that replaced the older replicas, the *Adm. Joe Fowler* and the *Richard F. Irvine*; they were retired after carrying some 90 million people during the past years. The boat circles the half-mile Rivers of America attached to an underwater rail. The ride itself is no great shakes, but it is a pleasant reprieve on a hot day.

Your narrator is pilot Sam Clemens. The ride takes about 20 minutes; lines rarely extend beyond a full boat load.

Mike Fink Keelboats. Small riverboats that follow the same circuit as the Riverboat, a bit faster and a bit more personal with your own guide. Mike Fink, by the way, was a riverboat captain of legend who had an adventure with Davy Crockett. The small boats here, the *Bertha Mae* and the *Gullywhumper*, take about 10 minutes for a circuit. Because of the small capacity of the boats, we'd advise you avoid joining a long line if there is one; we'd also suggest against duplicating a trip on the keelboats and one on the riverboat. The keelboats run only during the day, and may not run during the off-season.

Adventureland

Ahoy, mateys: welcome to a most unusual corner of Central Florida, where you will find a Caribbean island, an African veldt, a South Pacific bird tree, and more. Adventureland includes some of the most dramatic landscaping touches in the Magic Kingdom and the most popular band of pirates since Penzance.

WOW Pirates of the Caribbean. Yo, ho, ho . . . one of Disney's very best. After an approach through a dank dungeon waiting area (and past a parrot wearing an eye patch!), you'll settle into a broad-beamed boat for a cruise into the middle of a pirate raid on a Caribbean island town.

You'll love the moonlit battle scene as your boat passes beneath the guns of two warring ships; cannonballs will land all around you in the cool water. Pay attention, too, to the jail scene where a group of pirates tries to entice a mangy dog to bring them the key. The ride includes a wondrous collection of Audio-Animatronic humans and animals, including robotic chickens and pigs.

Some young children may be scared by the simulated cannon fire and the skulls and bones that are fairly liberally strewn about in some of the caves of Pirates of the Caribbean. And some adults may find bones of their own to pick—things such as the depiction of women as objects for sale at auction.

However, the ride just might offer an opportunity to discuss such unhappy elements of history with youngsters.

The ride begins with a little bit of a watery drop; your boat is dropping below the Disney World Railroad tracks overhead to the ride area, which (like Splash Mountain and Space Mountain) actually lies mostly outside the boundaries of the park.

In any case, Pirates of the Caribbean is a masterpiece of Disney artistry. You don't want to miss this one!

And not content to leave a good thing alone, Disney has introduced a much improved audio system to the ride. I was thrilled to finally be able to understand the background warning at the entrance to the lagoon: "Dead men tell no lies." And a bit further into the ride you'll also be able to hear some of the boasts and taunts of the pirates as they go about their good-natured dastardly deeds.

And finally, listen for the parrot in the treasure trove at the end of the ride: he's singing, "Yo ho, yo ho, a pirate's life for me."

Lines can become quite long at midday; head for this popular trip when the park first opens or in late afternoon. As you enter the queue, keep to your left to save a few minutes in line. The waiting area is mostly under cover, which makes it a good place to be in the rain or on a very hot day. The ride itself takes about seven minutes.

Swiss Family Treehouse. This is one of those "no accounting for taste" attractions—you'll either love it or hate it, probably depending upon how deeply the story of the *Swiss Family Robinson* is engraved upon your memory. Actually, this attraction is a remembrance of the 1960 Disney movie version of the classic novel *Swiss Family Robinson*, written by Johann David Wyss and completed by his son Johann Rudolf Wyss in 1813.

The treehouse winds up and across a Disney simulation of a banyan tree (constructed of sculpted concrete and steel). There are a lot of stairs to climb and a few ropewalk bridges; on a busy day, your view may be mostly the backside of the tourist in front of you. It takes five to ten minutes to walk up, through, and down the tree; incredibly, there can sometimes be lengthy lines for the privilege; if there's a line and you're determined to climb this tree, come back late in the day.

The "tree" received a remake at the end of 1997, with new and improved details added to this old house.

WOW! Jungle Cruise. Another Disney classic, this is an escorted boat tour through a simulated wild kingdom that somehow stretches from the African veldt to the Amazon rain forest to the Nile valley and the jungles of southeast Asia.

You'll see some of Disney's most famous special effects, like the automated hippos who lurk just below the water's top and the cavorting elephants who will spray water from their trunks. The shores are lined with robotic zebras, lions, and giraffes. The best part of the ride is the hokey but still entertaining patter of the tour guides in pith helmets. ("Be sure to tell all your friends about Jungle Cruise," our guide told us. "It cuts down the lines." As we were readying to board our boats, we were advised to guard against confusion in loading. "Note that there is one dock to the left, and one to the right: it's a paradox." Ouch. As we passed into a section of Egypt's famous river, we were told, "If you don't believe me, you're in da Nile."

And another guide told us, "Don't worry about looking stupid—I'm doing that for you." But my favorite bad joke involved horticultural commentary: "I'd like to point out my favorite plants in the jungle. I like that one, and that one, and that one."

Amateur gardeners may be thrilled by the amazing collection of plants, flowers, and trees—most of them real—that Disney groundskeepers manage to keep alive. One of the tricks is a network of gas heaters that warms the occasionally chilly air of Florida in the winter.

The ride is just short of 10 minutes; the line to get on board, alas, can sometimes wind around and around the corral for more than an hour. Go early or late on busy days. It is actually most dramatic by night, and especially silly.

Sources say that Jungle Cruise is due for an update and expansion; one possibility is that some of the Audio-Animatronic figures from the former World of Motion ride at Epcot will move to the Magic Kingdom.

Enchanted Tiki Room Under New Management. Tropical Serenade is among the strangest of all of the attractions at the Magic Kingdom, and you've got to be in exactly the right frame of mind to enjoy the show. In 1998, the birds returned after a short hiatus to present a new version of the venerable, corny show.

The Tiki Room is the home of the **Enchanted Tiki Birds**, a collection of more than 200 wisecracking, wing-flapping, automated winged creatures, along with a collection of singing flowers, totem poles, and statues. Your hosts are José, Michael, Pierre, and Fritz.

The waiting area for the show includes a stop in front of a waterfall that features volcano flames. Here we're introduced to Iago (from *Aladdin* and voiced once again by the professionally annoying Gilbert Gottfried) as the booking agent for the entertainer who complains about everything, including the fact that the birds are late for the show. "Maybe they hit traffic," his companion suggests. "Don't say that!" says Iago.

The interior of the theater is as tacky as ever, and the exceedingly annoying theme song "In the Tiki, Tiki, Tiki, Tiki, Tiki Room" is preserved for the ages.

But the story line is a bit more interesting, made all the better because of a greatly improved audio system. Now you can hear all of the corny jokes, including Iago's taunting insult to the Polynesian gods. They warn: "When you mess with Polynesia, the Tiki gods will squeeze 'ya."

Among the musical highlights is a rendition of "In the Still of the Night," when all of the Tiki icons around the room come to life, complete with a disco mirror ball. There's even a Tiki rap.

The Tiki birds were among Disney's first attempts at Audio-Animatronics, representing the state of the art as it existed around 1963 when a very similar show was introduced at Disneyland.

We know some young children who have been absolutely enchanted by the birds; the very young and the very cynical may want to pass. In any case, the show is blissfully short, and it's nice and cool inside on a hot Florida day.

Shrunken Ned's Junior Jungle Boats. A set of coin-operated remote-control boats near the Jungle Cruise. If you say the name quickly, you'll get the minor joke.

Frontierland

Almost anything goes in this wild western corner of the Magic Kingdom, home of Davy Crockett, Tom Sawyer, a bunch of vacationing bears, a runaway mining train, and the park's newest, wettest, and wildest big splash.

WOW Big Thunder Mountain Railroad. One of the best rides at the park, it is at the same time much more than and much less than it appears.

Big Thunder is a Disneyfied roller coaster, one of only three "thrill" rides in the Magic Kingdom (along with Space Mountain and Splash Mountain). As roller coasters go, it is fairly tame, with about a half mile of track and a three-and-one-half-minute ride with a few short drops and some interesting twists and turns. But in the Disney tradition, it is the setting and the attention to detail that make this one of the most popular places to be.

You will ride in a runaway mining train up through a quaking tunnel, across a flooding village, and back down around and through a 197-foot-high artificial mountain, bedecked with real mining antiques from former mines out West. As you enter the waiting line, you'll see part of a "stamping mill" made by the Joshua Hendy Works in San Francisco, possibly made for one of the mines of the Comstock in Nevada. Stamping mills were used to crush large pieces of rock into smaller pieces to allow the removal of ore.

Look, too, at the Audio-Animatronic animals, birds, and an old coot of a miner in a bathtub as you zoom by. The telegraph office lists the manager's name as Morris Code; get it?

Construction of the ride, completed in 1981, cost $17 million, which equals the entire price tag for Disneyland when it opened in 1955.

Picking the right time to visit the railroad can make a real difference at this very popular attraction; waits of more than an hour are common at midday in peak season. The shortest lines are early in the day or just before dinnertime. Coaster fans say the best ride (meaning the wildest) can be had with a seat in the last row of seats; we also like the very front of any coaster ride because it gives you a view of the perils ahead, over the top of the engine in front.

The line outside, near the rafts to Tom Sawyer Island, is only a small portion of the waiting area. There is a large upper corral and a winding path down through the mining station to the railroad. The ride takes on a very different feeling at night, and true fans should experience it then as well as during the day.

One-upsmanship. Big Thunder Mountain Railroad at Disneyland Paris has a much sharper drop than its older American cousin.

Children younger than seven must be accompanied by an adult; no one under 42 inches is allowed to ride. Warn young children about the loud noises they will hear as their railway car is pulled up the first lift on the ride.

Big Thunder Mountain Railroad at night is like another ride altogether. Like Space Mountain, the fun is increased because the darkness hides the track ahead of you.

WOW Splash Mountain. Disney's "highest, scariest, wildest, and wettest" attraction is a wild ride to contemplate; you may have a long time to contemplate it as you wait your turn on a busy day.

Splash Mountain includes three lifts and four drops, with the biggest plunging about 50 feet at a 45-degree angle and a top speed of about 40 miles per hour—Disney claims it's the steepest flume ride in the world. The big drop, visible to the crowds along the Rivers of America in Frontierland, will make it appear as if the log car has fallen into a pond.

Some of the best special effects take place within the mountain, with a story based on Disney's classic *Song of the South* cartoon, made in 1946. The ride follows Brer Rabbit as he tries to outwit Brer Fox and Brer Bear on a wild journey to the Laughin' Place.

The entrance to Splash Mountain is beneath the reconstructed Frontierland railroad station. (As you approach on the train, you will be able to see a small portion of Splash Mountain—it's the *Zip-a-dee Lady* paddlewheeler that is at the end of the ride, *after* the big drop.)

Be aware that Disney has hidden the waiting lines within an open inner courtyard not visible from the entrance, and then a long and winding queue within the building itself; be sure to ask the cast member at the measuring pole (44 inches for youngsters) about the length of the line. We'd suggest you come back another time—very early or late—if the line is unreasonably long. As usual at many of the attractions, you often will save a few minutes by picking the left-side line over the right. The capacity for the ride is about 2,400 passengers per hour, with 50 log boats in use at a time.

Once you enter the Splash Mountain building itself, there are a few interesting exhibits including a series of Brer Fox story needlepoints ("Some critters ain't never gonna learn" and "You can't run away from trouble. Ain't no place that far" among them). Check out the animated shadows on the wall in some of the dark areas.

How wet do you like it? Splash Mountain is a watery place, and the log cars make a huge wave as they land at the bottom of the big drop, but the fact is that you won't get very wet on the ride. The two wettest places seem to be the very first row of seats and the last—the wave flies over the car. The front row has the best view of the drop; the last row has the most suspense.

No charge. Splash Mountain, because it is one of the high places in the park and because of the watery path, is occasionally forced to close when a lightning storm is in the area. **Extra charge.** When you get off Splash Mountain, you'll be greeted by a wall of video monitors that have color pictures of each log car as it goes down the big drop. You can buy a large print (it includes everyone in your car, strangers and all).

Inside Splash Mountain. Disney engineers carefully control the amount of water in the flumes. Too much water will cause too much turbulence and splashing; too little can cause a loaded boat to bottom out. On the big drop, about one-quarter of the water is diverted around the boat to control the speed of the drop.

In any case, there's an emergency braking system at the bottom of the big drop; the brake is turned on if an infrared beam determines that two boats are too close together for safety. Pressurized air inflates a set of air bags that lift the underside of the moving boat and push it against rubber strips in a safety channel on the side of the boat, bringing it to a halt.

By the way, the big splash at the bottom of the drop is not caused by the boat—it's an artificial splash produced by water cannons.

Department of Redundancy Department. There is a fire sprinkler system in the ceiling of the water tunnels within Splash Mountain.

The interior waiting line for Splash Mountain is not the place for claustrophobics. It is dark in places and tight—closer than the waiting queue for Pirates of the Caribbean. Actually, once the Splash Mountain ride is underway, you'll probably think of Pirates of the Caribbean with a bit of It's a Small World mixed in.

You'll start by loading into your "log"; you may find the seats slightly wet. The logs will climb up into the mountain—you'll see the bottom of the big drop, and first-time riders will certainly be expecting a sudden sharp drop over the precipice they've seen from the ground. And, just to build up the tension, there are a few small teasing drops.

But instead of the great fall, your log will move gently through a beautiful, tuneful, and peaceful water world filled with some 68 Animatronic characters and lots of delightful details. At the end of the first room there's a drop—but again it's not the big one.

Midway through the ride you'll pass through an opening to the outside and you'll be treated to one of the better views of the park—Thunder Mountain to your left, Cinderella Castle straight ahead, and Space Mountain and the distant Contemporary Resort behind it. (This peek is reminiscent of another Disney classic—the Matterhorn at Disneyland in California.) You'll also likely see a crowd of people staring up at you from below—actually, they're looking beyond you to the big drop over your shoulder.

All of a sudden you're back in the mountain and it's dark. Is this the big drop? Actually, no; you enter into another large room, this time illuminated with black light. Check out the bees circling around the bee hive. There's lots of water now, with splashing fountains and little squirts of water overhead. And there are now some signs of warning: "Enter at your own risk," "Danger," "Go Back, Beware, Watch Out."

But instead of going down, you'll go up one more sharp climb. Why do you suppose there are a pair of vultures hanging over the top of the hill? Listen to what they say: "Everybody's got a laughing place, maybe this is yours."

This is it, folks. The big one, the spectacular waterfall you've seen from the walkway below. You're over . . . and down in about four seconds.

There is one final surprise at the very end, yet another pretty inside room with a "Welcome Home Brer Rabbit" party.

Splash Mountain is actually one of the longer rides at the Magic Kingdom at nearly 11 minutes, and despite the brevity of the final drop it does give you a lot more for your waiting time than Thunder Mountain or Space Mountain. If you can convince the kids (or the adults) to look past the short drop, they are sure to love the rest of the ride which is pure Disney. And try the ride in the day and the night; the view of the park from near the top is worth the wait.

There are Splash Mountains at Disneyland and at Tokyo Disneyland; in California, guests sit one behind another while the Japanese and Florida versions load side-by-side.

WOW! **Tom Sawyer Island.** Another essential, at least for the youngsters, is the raft ride over to this little island in the middle of the Rivers of America. Based vaguely upon Mark Twain's classic book, you'll find dark caves, waterwheels, a barrel bridge, and a rope bridge to bounce on; at the far end of the island is a little bridge to Fort Sam Clemens, where kids can scramble around the parapets and fire air guns at passing sidewheelers.

The little snack bar at the fort sells, along with beverages, a most unusual fast food: whole sour pickles. There's also an interesting little gazebo out on the water known as Aunt Polly's Landing, selling picnic basket fare: things such as peanut butter and jelly sandwiches, cold fried chicken and apple pie. Nearby is a half-whitewashed fence with notable graffiti, including a declaration that Tom♥Becky.

Parents will appreciate the space to let their children burn off a bit of energy after standing in lines all day; be advised, though, that it is fairly easy to misplace a youngster in one of the simulated caves or on a trail. Discuss with your children a meeting place in case you become separated.

Lines for the raft rarely require more than 10 minutes waiting. The island closes at dusk.

Country Bear Jamboree. A doggedly cute show starring some 20 robotic bears of various sizes, shapes, and personalities, full of corny jokes and strained puns. Where else but at a Disney park could you possibly expect to see a trio of bears named Bubbles, Bunny, and Beulah singing a bowdlerized Beach Boys hit, "Wish They All Could Be California Bears"? (The soundtrack is changed annually for a Christmas Hoedown.)

For our money, we find this 15-minute attraction just barely (sorry) easier to take than the Enchanted Tiki Birds; youngsters and fans of Disney Audio-Animatronics will probably want to argue strongly in its favor. And the Hoedown is a very popular show, despite our opinion. The best time to visit is early, late, or during one of the parades. The best seats are at the very front or back of the hall.

Frontierland Shootin' Arcade. A durn-fancy shooting gallery, sort of a live video game and not like any other shooting gallery you have seen at a county fair. Players aim huge buffalo rifles at a Disney replica of an 1850s frontier town. The rifles fire infrared beams at targets on tombstones, clouds, banks, jails, and other objects; direct hits make the targets spin, explode, or otherwise surprise. Some of the signs on the objects tell a story: "Old Tom Hubbard died with a frown, but a grave can't keep a good man down." If you hit the skeleton of a steer, his horns will spin around.

To use the rifles you must pay an additional charge for a specific number of "bullets."

Diamond Horseshoe Saloon Revue and Medicine Show. Disney's squeaky-clean version of a Western dance hall revue is a lot of fun for young and old. Expect some funny crude humor, mostly made at the expense of the visitors. This is a good place to take a break for lunch; come early or late to avoid crowds.

Check the daily schedule for the shows, which last about 30 minutes, and show up about half an hour early to grab one of the limited seats. You can order sandwiches priced at about $6, salads from $4 to $6, and ice cream at the bar.

Eating Your Way Through the Magic Kingdom

There are three types of restaurants at the Magic Kingdom: overpriced and bad, overpriced and barely acceptable, and overpriced and almost good. Well, OK, there are a few meals that are overpriced and good.

In any case, we'd recommend that you not consider meals to be an important part of your experience at the Magic Kingdom; save your time and money for one of the somewhat better Epcot Center or Disney-MGM Studios restaurants or for an evening outside of the Disney borders.

You do, though, have to eat. Disney has a rule against bringing your own sandwiches or other food into the park. In dozens of visits to Walt Disney World, though, we have never seen an attendant search a backpack or shoulder bag for tuna fish on rye, and you certainly can pack a baby's formula and a few candy bars for the kids.

If you don't pack your own, it is possible to pick and choose among the offerings at the park. Disney does offer a few nonstandard and more healthful offerings, like pasta salads, turkey hamburgers, and smoked turkey legs at some of its stands. Nevertheless, each year guests at Walt Disney World eat more than 7 million hamburgers, 5 million hot dogs, 5 million pounds of french fries, 265,000 pounds of popcorn, and 46 million Cokes.

KEY:

🍽️ = Fast food

🍺 = Pub

🏠 = Full-service restaurant

We include general price ranges in our listings and mention specific prices for some items. Pricing on food and menus is subject to change. All food establishments within Disney World offer soft drinks at prices of almost $3. (Did I hear someone say, "Why, I'll just throw a few cans of soda in a backpack."? Thought so.)

Main Street, U.S.A.

[icon] **Main Street Wagons.** Located throughout the Main Street area. Espresso, cappuccino, soft drinks. Hot dogs and baked goods. Fresh fruit and vegetables and fruit drinks priced from about $1 to $3. A few umbrella-shaded tables are available on East Center Street beside the Main Street Market house.

[icon] **Main Street Bake Shop.** On Main Street near the Plaza Ice Cream Parlor. Unusual baked goods and beverages, $2 to $4. Cookies about $1. Watch cookies being made from scratch through the large window fronting on Main Street. There is a small seating area inside the pleasant, floral decorated shop, but most customers take their goodies to go, either to sit at one of the nearby umbrella tables or to carry with them as they move deeper into the park.

Very crowded at opening time, this shop is popular for breakfast sweets and coffee. Check out the oversized iced and glazed donuts and sweet rolls. A separate cookies and pastries line is available to the right of the entrance if that is all you want.

[icon] **Plaza Ice Cream Parlor.** Near Main Street Bake Shop, across from Refreshment Corner. Lines can be long in this pleasant, old-fashioned ice cream shop, but they move rather quickly. About $2 to $3 for most items.

[icon] **Casey's Corner.** At the top end of Main Street. Hot dogs, soda, soft drinks, and coffee. Serving staff in vintage baseball outfits offer hot dogs ($2.50 and $3.95) with a toppings bar, plus other snacks.

[icon] **The Crystal Palace.** At the top of Main Street, toward Adventureland. Breakfast, lunch, and dinner buffets. Breakfast $13.95 for adults and $7.95 for children ages 3–11. Lunch for $14.95 (adults) and $7.95 (children). Dinner $19.95 (adults) and $9.95 (children). Breakfast offerings include scrambled eggs and omelettes, French toast, and breakfast lasagna. At lunch, there is an assortment of salads, soup, pastas, and deli sandwiches. For dinner, you can choose from carved meats, pastas, and chicken, beef, and fish dishes. A children's buffet of chicken tenders, pizza, and macaroni and cheese is also offered.

The building is a replica of the Crystal Palace, built for the first International Exhibition in New York in 1851. The atmosphere is bright and airy with floral designs in a Victorian gazebo setting and a Dixieland jazz group often entertains diners.

[icon] **Tony's Town Square Restaurant.** Just inside the entrance gate to the right. Italian food, steaks, seafood, hamburgers, and salads, $15 to $21; appetizers, $3 to $8. Breakfast, lunch, and dinner from 8:30 A.M.; closing time depends on park hours. Reservations recommended; check in at the restaurant lobby.

The restaurant is modeled after the cafe in Disney's classic *Lady and the Tramp* movie. Seating for about 200. Entrees, priced from about $15 to $25, include Steak Fiorentino, a T-bone steak rubbed with garlic and peppercorns; chicken Florentine, grilled breast served with spinach cream sauce and polenta; and Veal Marsala with wild mushrooms and marsala wine. Breakfast specialties include Italian frittatas, Lady and the Tramp waffles, and traditional favorites.

[icon] **The Plaza Restaurant.** At the top of Main Street toward Tomorrow-

land. Gourmet hamburgers, soups, sandwiches, and salads. Lunch and dinner. Open from 11 A.M. Entrees, $7 to $9.

This pleasant 19th-century-style dining room offers table service inside and bright yellow and white umbrella tables outside. Specialties include Reubens and other sandwiches, basic burgers and grilled mushroom-and-onion burgers with provolone cheese, and supercalifragilisticexpialidocious sundaes.

Adventureland

🍴 **Sunshine Tree Terrace.** At the north end of Adventureland, behind the Enchanted Tiki Birds' Tropical Serenade, this is worth a quick stop for a drink or light snack. Offerings include citrus drinks, frozen yogurt, shakes, and desserts, $2 to $3. A few umbrella tables give you a place to rest while you snack.

🍴 **Aloha Isle.** Pineapple and fruit drinks, about $2. Try fresh pineapple spears for about $1 or raspberry/vanilla swirl.

🍴 **El Pirata y el Perico.** Mexican fast food for lunch and dinner. Specialties include tacos and nachos.

Frontierland

🍴 **Pecos Bill Café.** Just past the Country Bear Vacation Hoedown. Burgers, chicken barbecue, salads, and hot dogs, $5 to $7. Western saloon atmosphere in the side-by-side restaurants that share a common menu. Look carefully at the animals mounted on the wall; they're talking and singing robots.

The chicken and bean salad or a barbecue chicken sandwich is a good burger alternative, but if hamburger fits your fancy, try the Pecos Bill Trail Bacon Cheeseburger Basket. A large fixings bar offers a range of toppings that include pickles, relishes, tomatoes, and more.

🍴 **Turkey Leg Wagon.** One of the strangest sights you are likely to see in Frontierland are visitors walking along the pathway absently chewing on what looks like the leg of a large dog. Actually, they're smoked turkey legs available from a stand directly across from the Country Bear Vacation Hoedown for about $4. Just follow the smell to the end of the line. As you carry along one of these interesting treats, watch out for seagulls; they'll sometimes fly right at the turkey leg trying to take a bite out of it!

🍴 **Diamond Horseshoe Saloon Revue.** Sandwiches, ice cream, and snacks with a free Old West vaudeville show. Check daily schedule.

Liberty Square

🍴 **Columbia Harbour House.** On Liberty Square across from Ichabod's Landing. Battered shrimp and chicken, cold sandwiches, pasta salads, salads. Lunch and dinner, $3 to $7. Children's menu includes a chicken sandwich or hot dog for about $4.

Seafood dining in seafaring atmosphere. Multiple small rooms break up the dining area. The dark, cool decor provides a comfortable respite from the sun. Larger tables seat six to eight. A few, small, semi-private dining rooms accommodate groups.

For an unusual appetizer or full meal, try the clam chowder served inside a large, round loaf of dark bread. When the chowder is gone, you can eat the bowl. A fruit plate is about $5.25. Sandwiches include smoked ham and cheese, tuna salad, and smoked turkey. Apple cobbler or chocolate and banana cream pies for dessert are about $3. A children's menu named the "Little Mariner's Meal" includes an entree, cookies, and a child's beverage for $2.49.

🍴 **Liberty Square Wagon.** On the walkway between Columbia Harbour House and the Hall of Presidents. Baked potatoes with toppings and beverages, $2 to $3. There's also a fresh fruit and pickle stand nearby.

In an area where sandwiches and other fast foods average about $5, the potato wagon is a popular alternative for a filling, low-cost lunch or snack. Fresh-baked white and sweet potatoes with a variety of toppings, about $2.50.

🍴 **Fruit and Vegetable Wagon.** Usually on the square behind the Columbia Harbour House and the Liberty Square Wagon. Various fruits and vegetables from a "farmer's market" wagon.

Attractively presented fruits and vegetables for alternative snacks and additions to meals. The selection includes apples, peaches, grapes, star fruit, and even pickles, squash, and potatoes.

🔺 **Liberty Tree Tavern.** Next to Diamond Horseshoe Revue and open for lunch (11:30 A.M. to 4 P.M.) and dinner (from 4:30 P.M.). Sandwiches, beef, chicken, seafood, salads, $7 to $16. Reservations recommended; request a seating time at the door.

Sit-down dining in a colonial atmosphere with a lot of interesting details, including maple bench seats, fireplaces, and simulated peg flooring. A variety of sandwiches is available from $7 to $10. Seafood and other entrees from about $9.50 to $13.50. Luncheon specialties include New England Pot Roast, Pilgrim's Feast turkey dinner, and Cape Cod pasta with shrimp and vegetables.

At dinner time, the Liberty Tree features a Disney characters family-style dinner for about $20 for adults and about $10 for children age 9 and younger. The meal includes salad, roast turkey, glazed ham, and marinated flank steak.

Fantasyland

🍴 **Pinocchio Village Haus.** Next to It's a Small World under the Skyway. Turkey hamburgers, turkey hot dogs, chicken, salads, pasta. Lunch and dinner.

A large dining hall in a Disneyfied Tudor style. Several small rooms, including a favored location overlooking the It's a Small World ride. Meals from about $5 to $6 with french fries or grapes and a regular beverage include choice of cheeseburgers (beef or turkey), a quarter pound turkey hot dog, or a grilled bratwurst. The eatery now includes a relish bar with pickles, tomatoes, onions, mushrooms, sauerkraut, barbecue sauce, cheese sauce, and more. The entrees are available a la carte, too.

Also available is a smoked turkey sub with provolone cheese, lettuce, and tomatoes for about $4.50.

As at many Disney fast food restaurants, the service lines move slowly at peak time. Come early or late to avoid wasting time.

🍴 **Mrs. Potts' Cupboard.** Ice cream and soft drinks from about $2 to $3.

🏰 **Cinderella's Royal Table.** (Formerly King Stefan's Banquet Hall.) Upstairs in Cinderella Castle. Character breakfasts, lunches, and dinners.

If you enter the castle from the Fantasyland side, the restaurant is on the outside left. Lines for lunch begin early because seating is limited. Among the more expensive restaurants in the Magic Kingdom, Cinderella's Royal Table has a special draw for some children, especially little girls who dream of meeting Cinderella herself. Reservations are accepted at the door on the day you wish to dine; guests at Disney hotels can make telephone reservations up to two days ahead of time.

You enter the restaurant through a "great hall" entrance on the ground floor. This interesting room is complete with torch lanterns and swords on the wall. The slate floor and high, exposed-beam ceiling enhance the "castle" feeling of the restaurant. You'll move upstairs via an interesting, winding stairway or in an elevator.

Tomorrowland

🍴 **Cosmic Ray's Starlight Café.** Cosmic Ray's (get it?) is the largest fast food eatery in the Magic Kingdom, the former Tomorrowland Terrace. Decorated in brushed aluminum, purples, and blacks, there's a little stage at the back of the room for presentations. Food includes burgers, cheeseburgers, vegetarian burgers, chicken, soups, salads, and other offerings at several food court–like stands within. Specialties include the Chick Encounter family meal for three to four, featuring a whole rotisserie chicken, and the Coop Canaveral chicken drummettes.

🍴 **Plaza Pavilion.** In the walkway between Main Street and Tomorrowland. Pizza, sandwiches, salads, $3 to $5. Covered outdoor dining in a pleasant setting for about 650 people. There are three dining areas, one overlooking a portion of the central lagoon and offering an excellent view of Cinderella Castle. The area offers cool shade and ample seating away from the main service area and transient crowds.

Try the Italian hoagie at about $4.25 or the chicken Parmesan sandwich for a dollar more. Deep dish pizza is available by the slice for about $3.25 to $4.75. Fix up your ice cream with the brownie sundae ($2.75) or an ice cream float for about $2.30.

🍴 **Auntie Gravity's Galactic Goodies.** Across the broad plaza from Space Mountain at the base of the Astro Orbiter tower. Juice, snacks, frozen yogurt, $2 to $3.

MAGIC KINGDOM

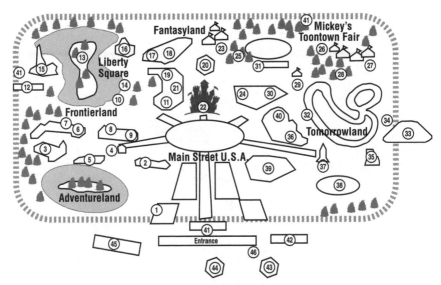

1. City Hall
2. First Aid
3. Pirates of the Caribbean
4. Swiss Family Treehouse
5. Jungle Cruise
6. Enchanted Tiki Room
7. Country Bear Jamboree
8. Jungle Cruise
9. Diamond Horseshoe Saloon Revue and Medicine Show
10. *Liberty Belle* Riverboat
11. The Hall of Presidents
12. Splash Mountain
13. Tom Sawyer Island
14. Mike Fink Keelboats
15. Big Thunder Mountain Railroad
16. The Haunted Mansion
17. Skyway to Tomorrowland
18. It's a Small World
19. Peter Pan's Flight
20. Cinderella's Golden Carrousel
21. The Legend of the Lion King
22. Cinderella Castle
23. Dumbo The Flying Elephant

24. Snow White's Scary Adventures
25. Ariel's Grotto
26. Toontown Hall of Fame
27. Mickey's and Minnie's Country Houses
28. The Barnstormer at Goofy's Wiseacre Farm
29. Mad Tea Party
30. The Many Adventures of Winnie the Pooh
31. Fantasyland Character Festival
32. Tomorrowland Speedway
33. Space Mountain
34. Tomorrowland Transit Authority
35. Skyway to Fantasyland
36. Alien Encounter: The ExtraTERRORestrial
37. Astro Orbiter
38. Carousel of Progress
39. *The Timekeeper*
40. Buzz Lightyear's Space Ranger Spin
41. Walt Disney World Railroad Station
42. Magic Kingdom Bus Transportation
43. Ferry Boat to Parking
44. Boats to Discovery Island and Fort Wilderness
45. Monorail Station
46. Stroller rental

Chapter 8
Epcot Center

Epcot Center will be the centerpiece of Disney's 15-month-long millennium party, "Celebrate the Future Hand in Hand," which will run from Oct. 1, 1999 through Jan. 1, 2001.

Spaceship Earth will be the focal point of the front of the park, redecorated with the help of Mickey's hand, sprinkling pixie dust. Also at the front of the park, near the entry, guests will be invited to "Leave a Legacy" at a set of crystalline monuments. There you can have a digital image of your face etched onto a tile and installed as a remembrance of a visit in the millennium year.

All of the exhibits at both Innoventions halls were due to be changed for the celebration year as well.

At Millennium Village, a new pavillion constructed in World Showcase between the United Kingdom and Canada exhibits, countries from around the world will have special demonstrations of their cultures and products.

And then there is the daily moving party, performed once or twice a day in World Showcase.

Lead by the "Sage of Time," a convoy of some 120 huge figures, controlled from 20 feet below by puppeteers who look like marionettes to the figures, will appear from hiding places around the lake. The puppets and costumes were created by the costume designer of the Broadway production of the Lion King. To the accompaniment of music, the puppets will join 16 percussion units, designed to resemble colossal timepieces. Visitors will be encouraged to participate in the party that will circle the lake.

The evening performance of the show will segue into a new IllumiNations 2000 celebration on the lake. The excitement will begin with the lighting of 19 large torches. A large globe, circled by video screens, will move about the lake, which will be filled with fire. And then with the grand finale the globe will open like the petals of a flower to reveal the 20th torch, in a salute to the end of the 20th century.

Facts and figures.
Epcot, at 260 acres, is more than twice the size of the Magic Kingdom. The World Showcase Lagoon is about 40 acres in size; the promenade that circles it and leads to the national showcases is 1.2 miles in length. Initial construction costs were about $1.3 billion in 1982; at the time, one of the largest private construction jobs ever completed.

The Epcot Story

Walt Disney's original concept called for construction of a modern city from scratch: homes, offices, farms, and factories. It was intended as a showcase for new ideas and technologies from American industry and educational institutions.

Disney called his dream the Experimental Prototype Community of Tomorrow, which is the almost-forgotten name behind the Epcot acronym.

Disney lived long enough to set the broad outlines for Epcot, but the park as built was quite different from the prototype community he first planned. Instead, the second theme park at Walt Disney World is like a permanent World's Fair.

Roughly half the park is given over to imaginative pavilions that explore the frontiers of science: communication, energy, human life, transportation, technology, creativity, agriculture, and the seas. And then spread around the World Showcase Lagoon are exhibits, films, and a handful of rides that share some of the cultures of the globe: from Canada, the United Kingdom, France, Morocco, Japan, America, Italy, Germany, China, Norway, and Mexico.

Although it is most likely the lure of Mickey and Minnie's Magic Kingdom that brings most visitors to Walt Disney World, many adults and quite a few children will tell you that the memory they bring home from Florida comes from Epcot: the wild ride at GM Test Track, the dinosaurs at the Universe of Energy, Alec Tronics at Innoventions, the troll at Norway, or the film view of the Great Wall at China.

The biggest draw at Epcot in coming years is sure to be the wild GM Test Track.

Spend the time at Epcot and talk about the things you learn there; that may be the greatest legacy of Disney.

Epcot includes an interesting range of special events. In recent years these events have included Holidays Around the World at Christmastime, featuring a candlelight processional, the Christmas Story presented at the America Gardens Stage with 400 voices and a 50-piece orchestra, and a "living" Christmas tree. The events were free to all ticketholders, but Epcot also made available a specially priced ticket that offered entrance to the park, reserved seating at the processional, free preferred parking, and special discounts on Epcot merchandise.

Disney's **Candlelight Processional**, a retelling of the Christmas story at America Gardens Theatre in World Showcase, is presented at least twice nightly from just after Thanksgiving through December 30.

Each program features a guest celebrity narrating the traditional story of Christmas, interwoven with music of the season by 450 choral voices, a 50-piece orchestra, and a handbell choir. A limited number of seats are available to guests at Epcot, with lines forming several hours before show time. Disney also sells Candlelight Processional packages that include dining at select Epcot restaurants and preferred seating at one of the shows. In recent years, the packages began at about $40 for adults, not including admission to the park; a special package with an after-4 P.M. admission to Epcot sold for about $60.

Also at Epcot, the Lights of Winter—a sparkling canopy of 30,000 synchronized lights above the bridge from Future World to World Showcase, plus nightly tree-lighting ceremonies with carolers, fanfare trumpeters, and holiday storytellers. And in recent non-Millennium years there has also been **Holiday IllumiNations**, a seasonal version of the nightly laser, light, and fireworks show. The score includes "Greensleeves," "Nutcracker Suite," and a Hanukkah medley.

And gardeners and nature lovers can soak up the grandeur of the gardens, topiaries, and flowers from late April through the end of May at the Epcot International Flower & Garden Festival. For information about this and other festivals at Epcot, call (407) 824-4321.

Many of the international pavilions have special celebrations on their national holidays. Chinese New Year is celebrated in February at China; Moroccan Throne Day is observed on March 3, and Italy holds a Carnivale Celebration at the opening of Lent.

Epcot operates on a split schedule, with Future World open for much of the season from 9 A.M. to 9 P.M., and the World Showcase at the back of the park open from 11 A.M. to 9 P.M. One more thing: on most days the gates actually open at 8:30 A.M., with Spaceship Earth and some of the restaurants ready for early arrivals; when the park starts to get very busy with the opening of the GM Test Track, I'd recommend an early spot in line. And remember that operating hours are subject to change; call the park or check at the front desk of one of the hotels within the park for current information.

MUST-SEES

Millennium Celebration
(Until January 2001)

GM Test Track

Spaceship Earth

Universe of Energy

Body Wars
(Wonders of Life)

Cranium Command
(Wonders of Life)

Journey Into Imagination
(New show opens in late 1999)

Honey, I Shrunk the Audience
(Journey Into Imagination)

Living with the Land
(The Land)

Circle of Life
(The Land)

Innoventions

El Rio del Tiempo
(Mexico)

Maelstrom
(Norway)

Wonders of China
(China)

The American Adventure
(United States)

Springtime treat. If you arrive at Epcot in March, April, or May, pay attention to the trees just at the base of the golf ball. The striking ornamental trees with blue trumpet-shaped flowers are jacaranda, native to northwestern Argentina.

Epcot is unique among the three parks at Walt Disney World in that it has two entrances—the main door, which leads directly to the Spaceship Earth, and a second, less-used International Gateway at the World Showcase, between the pavilions of the United Kingdom and France. Trams or little ferry boats run between the International Gateway and the BoardWalk, Swan, Dolphin, Beach Club, and Yacht Club resorts.

Here's an insider tip for a classy way to spend the day at Epcot: take the launch from World Gateway to the BoardWalk Resort for lunch or dinner to escape the madding crowds.

Power Trip

This plan is based on the split schedule that opens Future World two hours before the World Showcase.

The key to getting the most out of a visit to Epcot, as with every other attraction, is once again to adopt a Contrarian View of the park. Most visitors saunter into the park in mid-morning and join the crowds at the pavilions of Future World before beginning a slow—and crowded—circle of the World Showcase section in a clockwise direction. Another important bit of information is the fact that **Spaceship Earth** and the surrounding Innoventions usually open a bit before the rest of Epcot.

Get there early. If you're up for a thrill ride, this is the time to make tracks to the **GM Test Track.** Bear to the left from the entrance and follow the signs. You may be able to go for a second ride in the early morning; it will probably be late in the day before lines drop back down to reasonable lengths.

While you're in the neighborhood, backtrack a bit to the **Universe of Energy** pavilion and see the show there. If you're determined to see all the big draws before the lines build up, sprint across Future World to the Imagination pavilion and visit the "Honey, I Shrunk the Audience" show.

By this time, it should be near 11 A.M. and time to jump out ahead of the crowds. Move into the **World Showcase.**

The biggest crowds at the World Showcase can usually be found at the Norway, Mexico, and American pavilions, although the new **Millennium** pavilion between the United Kingdom and Canada will likely be a major draw. If you are at the head of the throng, go immediately to **Mexico** and then next door to **Norway** and then continue in a clockwise circle around the lagoon. If you find yourself behind the madding crowd, you might want to travel in the opposite direction, going counterclockwise and starting at **Canada.**

After you come out of the World Showcase, tour the remaining pavilions of **Future World,** this time moving in a clockwise direction—starting at the new **Imagination** pavilion when it reopens sometime in 2000, and heading toward the front of the park and Spaceship Earth. Double back at the golf ball and visit **Innoventions** and **Wonders of Life** to complete your tour.

With luck, you will complete the tour of Epcot at nightfall and can enjoy a leisurely dinner before coming out to the lagoon for a view of the spectacular **IllumiNations** show.

Here's a by-the-numbers Power Trip, pavilion-by-pavilion. 1: **GM Test Track**; 2: **Universe of Energy**; 3: **Honey, I Shrunk the Audience**; 4: **Mexico**; 5: **Norway**; 6: **China**; 7: **Germany**; 8: **Italy**; 9: **The American Adventure**; 10: **Japan**; 11: **Morocco**; 12: **France**; 13: **United Kingdom**; 14: **Millennium**; 15: **Canada**; 16: **Imagination** (when it reopens); 17: **The Land**; 18: **The Living Seas**; 19: **Spaceship Earth**; 20: **Innoventions**, and 21: **Wonders of Life**.

Attractions at Future World

Spaceship Earth

WOW Spaceship Earth. The huge geodesic sphere that is the symbol of Epcot—referred to by most visitors as the "golf ball"—is 180 feet (18 stories) high and 165 feet in diameter with 2.2 million cubic feet of space within. It weighs almost 16 million pounds, including 1,750 tons of steel. Actually, the building is not a dome; it is a sphere.

As impressive as the shell is, the real excitement of Spaceship Earth can be found on the ride within, which is sponsored by communications giant AT&T. (Each of the major exhibits at Epcot's Future World is sponsored by a major American corporation, but the commercialism is relatively low-key.)

The original exhibit was designed by an interesting collaboration that included science fiction author Ray Bradbury, the Smithsonian Institution, and newsman Walter Cronkite. The ride was updated in 1995 with some new areas, a new narration by actor Jeremy Irons, and a new musical score. (The cloying "Tomorrow's Child" song is gone.) There's nothing here that will set your heart to pounding, but the lighting, video, and computer special effects are among the best at Walt Disney World.

Tubular, dude. The Spaceship Earth sphere is built from four structural parts. The outer shell is strictly for decorative purposes and is connected to an inner waterproof sphere by hundreds of small support columns. A column that runs up the center of the ball supports the internal ride, which circles around the column like a spiral staircase. And finally, a platform at the bottom of the sphere supports the inner structure and the ride itself.

Who's counting? The outside of the sphere is made up of some 11,000 triangular tiles, made of a composite of ethylene plastic bonded between two aluminum panels.

Hard ride. As befits the unusual building, the time machines in this ride take an unusual route. You'll slowly spiral up, up, and up around the sides of the ball until you reach the starfield at top; then your chair will turn around for a steep, backward descent to the base. Some riders might find the trip down a bit uncomfortable.

You'll board "time machine" chairs for a trip through the sphere that will take you back through history from the age of the Cro-Magnon man some 30,000 years ago to the present, along the way passing through the great ancient civilizations of Egypt, Phoenicia, and Rome. The narration may be a bit beyond the comprehension of young children, but they'll still enjoy and learn from the sights.

You'll note some of the truly important developments of our time, including the development of an alphabet and written language, the first books, the development of the printing press, and on to modern communications. You'll also see great cultural figures from Michelangelo (the painter, not the Ninja Turtle) at work in the Sistine Chapel to Howdy Doody and Ed Sullivan. At the very top of the ball is the most spectacular sight of all, a huge sky of stars and planets. Not all of the special effects of this ride are visual ones; Disney engineers created smell cannons that fill the air with odors, including those of burning Rome.

The page from the Bible that Johannes Gutenberg is examining is an exact replica of a page from one of his early Bibles. In the Egyptian scene, the hieroglyphics on the wall are reproductions of actual graphics; the words being dictated by the Pharaoh were taken from an actual letter sent by a pharaoh to one of his agents.

And then we move into the near future, where we see a young boy communicating in his room over the information superhighway. At the very top of the golf ball we move into a startlingly beautiful planetarium-like dome with Spaceship Earth and the stars all around it. Our chairs move into a view of a futuristic classroom embarking on a virtual field trip.

The dazzling finale puts the audience in the heart of interactive global networks that tie all the peoples of the earth together. Fantastic special effects, animated sets, and laser beams that surround and encase the visitors will finish off the experience with a simulated trip into a microchip.

From there, it is on to the **Global Neighborhood** for hands-on demonstrations of new technologies in voice recognition, video telephony, and the information superhighway.

Because of its position at the front of the park, lines for this ride are usually longest at the start of the day, although early arrivals can still expect to be able to walk right on. If the line builds up, though, we'd suggest coming back in the afternoon or on your way out of the park at the end of the day.

Early Value Meals. Epcot sometimes offers discount early bird meals at many of its restaurants for diners who arrive between 4:30 and 6 P.M. Check at Earth Station when you arrive at Epcot to see if this unadvertised special deal is in effect when you visit.

🎡 Innoventions

Innoventions is a highly commercial version of a World's Fair or a major trade show like the Consumer Electronics Show. Although products will not be sold in exhibit areas, representatives will be on hand to explain and demonstrate. Guests may use interactive computer terminals to receive information by mail.

Disney planned an unprecedented changeover of every exhibit in the two Innovention halls to coincide with the opening of the Millennium year celebration.

What Disney has done is truly an amazing thing: they have found a way to charge visitors more than $40 each to enter a somewhat ordinary convention hall–like building and look at exhibits of commercial products. Even more amazing is the fact that Disney is able to charge major corporations millions of dollars for the right to build their own exhibits.

"Epcot visitors may never go to Mars," said Michael Eisner, chairman and CEO of The Walt Disney Company, "but they will use the machines, computer games, toys, phones, musical instruments, televisions, stoves, refrigerators, vacuum cleaners, and toilets which they will see, probably for the first time, in Innoventions."

Youngsters and fans of electronic gadgets will likely want to bear to the right of Spaceship Earth to **Innoventions West**, home of exhibits by companies that include AT&T, IBM, and Sega of America. On the left side of Spaceship Earth in **Innoventions East** are exhibits aimed mostly at adults, including displays from Apple, General Electric, Hammacher Schlemmer, Honeywell, General Motors, and others.

Eating establishments included within the Innoventions area are the **Electric Umbrella Restaurant**, **Pasta Piazza Ristorante**, and **Fountain View Espresso & Bakery**.

Parental Guidance: Innoventions is a tremendous lure for the video kid generation. I don't know about you, but I'm not very happy about the thought of spending thousands of dollars and traveling thousands of miles to Orlando to see my children head off to play video games for hours at a time. Other parents might be willing to trust their kids to stay in one place for a few hours while they head off to a leisurely dinner. In either case, be sure to have a plan of action with your children in the sprawling Innoventions building.

Epcot ecology. As a planned community, Epcot includes many interesting experiments in ecology.

The huge Disney development uses a tremendous amount of water, which is a particular problem in the wet Florida environment. Some of the effluent of the wastewater treatment plant is sprayed on the 145-acre Walt Disney World Tree Farm to make use of nutrients in the water. Another project involves the growth of water hyacinths in a pond fed by the wastewater plant; the plants help purify the water by absorbing nutrients and filtering solids through their roots. Grown plants are harvested and composted for use as fertilizer.

The light fantastic. Disney designers snuck a little extra bit of magic into the construction of the Innoventions building. Fiber optics embedded in the tiles of the walkways outside are computer controlled to dance along with the nightly IllumiNations show on the lagoon.

Innoventions West

One of the stars of Innoventions West is Bill Nye the Science Guy, host of a television show of the same name (not coincidentally produced by Disney's television division). He appears in a videotaped multimedia show explaining the basic principles of science that underlie many of the products on display at Innoventions.

In recent years, exhibitors at Innoventions West have included:

AT&T. Voice and data-transfer technologies that include a wrist telephone, recognition devices, video computer phones, on-line computer libraries, and a variety of new computer games.

***Discover* Magazine Awards for Technological Innovation.** A display of the current year's winning inventors and their inventions.

IBM Corporation. The Thinkplace presents the latest advances in information technologies, from electronic field trips to videoconferencing to thrilling special effects.

Lego Dacta. Hands-on models of equipment, buildings, and molecular structures that demonstrate principles of physics, engineering, architecture, biology, and other areas of science. That's right: Lego, as in Lego blocks.

Sega of America. Sonic the Hedgehog, almost as famous as Mickey Mouse, is the host to a demonstration area of more than 100 new video games.

There may be a potential problem with the video games on busy days, by the way. I saw several instances where a youngster was parked in front of a game with no intentions of moving until the lights were turned out. According to Disney staffers, there is no rule that requires players to give up the controls after a particular time. In the case of my own son, I had to lean over a teenager and ask him repeatedly to step aside after half an hour with a single game. He finally left, muttering some distinctly un-Disney-like language.

Innoventions East

In recent years, exhibitors at Innovations East have included:

General Electric. The wide-ranging operations of GE were represented here, from the National Broadcasting Company to jet engines to home appliances.

General Motors. The display features the Impact prototype electric car. (Does anyone else out there think that "Impact" is a less than reassuring name for an automobile?)

Hammacher Schlemmer. A display from the pages of the catalog of this specialist in unusual gadgets and devices, including a body-activated video control, a digital player piano, and an aroma steam personal sauna.

Honeywell. At Comfortville, see new for the home, including temperature control, security, and energy-saving systems; electric windows; and the latest communications and entertainment products.

Universe of Energy

WOW **Universe of Energy.** Forward to the past, and back to the future: one of the favorite pavilions at Epcot has been given a new jolt of . . . energy.

The pavilion is based around an entertaining film known as *Ellen's Energy Crisis,* starring comedian Ellen DeGeneres and featuring some exciting special effects. In the movie, Ellen dreams she is a contestant on the *Jeopardy* television game show. She's up against the reigning champion Dr. Judy Peterson, played by Jamie Lee Curtis. The third contestant: Albert Einstein. And the categories?

Relativity. All of Disneyland in California could fit within the lagoon at Epcot Center, or within the boundaries of the parking lot at the Magic Kingdom.

They're all about energy, a subject that is clearly not Ellen's specialty.

Ellen has a secret weapon, though: her neighbor Bill Nye the Science Guy. She summons him for some hints, and he responds by taking Ellen—and all of the guests seated in the pavilion's famous moving grandstands—on a tour that travels back in time to the birth of the planet, and then on to a world tour of today's energy need and research.

The show begins with a standing-room-only preshow where we are introduced to Ellen, her cats, her neighbor Bill, and her nemesis, the brainy Dr. Peterson—Ellen insists her nickname was "Stupid Judy." Also making cameo appearances are game-show host Alec Trebek, Willard Scott with the 1 million B.C. weather, and Len Berman with the back, back, back sports report.

From the preshow, guests move into the old moving theater cars for an expedition 220 million years back to the Big Bang and from there to the dawn of the dinosaurs, with Ellen wisecracking all the way along.

(There are six sections of seating; the seats all the way forward to the left lead the parade, while the back right section moves out last. We prefer to be in front.)

The show is a major draw at Epcot and contributes to a lopsided draw to the west side of the park along with the new GM Test Track. Head there early, or come back late in the day to avoid lines that may stretch for eons.

Wonders of Life

A world of its own. Under one geodesic domed roof you will find two of Epcot's best attractions, plus a healthful Fitness Fairground for children of all ages and a set of entertaining and informative films and presentations on subjects from exercise to reproduction.

You could easily spend a few hours here; it's an especially good place to escape bad weather.

WOW **Body Wars.** Strap on your seat belts and prepare for blast-off on a journey to inner space. Body Wars is a fantastic simulator ride that takes you on a repair expedition inside a human body—a training mission to remove a splinter from *within.* (Check out the pilot's cockpit for the Body Wars vehicle; we like the pink baby shoes hanging over the windshield.)

As usual in a sci-fi story like this, something goes wrong within the body and the medical craft begins to lose all power from its fuel cell. So, our pilot decides he must go to the brain and cross the blood-brain barrier and park next to a synapse in hopes that it will fire and recharge the cell.

Secret Mickey. There is a hidden image of Mickey Mouse in the mural above the waiting area for Body Wars.

How'd they do that? The geodesic dome for the Wonders of Life pavilion is 250 feet in diameter and 60 feet tall at the center; to construct it, engineers built a temporary tower crane in the center. Rings of triangles were then hoisted by cables attached to the tower and anchored to columns around the circumference. When the dome was up, the crane was dismantled and removed.

Super helix. The huge sculpture at the entrance to the Wonders of Life pavilion is a 75-foot-tall representation of a DNA molecule, the basic building block of life. A human built to the same scale would be several million miles tall.

The simulation cabin bounces and twists through the veins and arteries of the human body, ending up with an electrical bang.

Amazingly, for a vehicle that doesn't really go anywhere, this ride carries as many health warnings as a roller coaster. No pregnant women or persons with back or heart ailments are allowed aboard, and children under seven must be accompanied by an adult. Those less than three years of age cannot ride. If you're the type who gets queasy on an elevator—and you know who you are—you might want to pass this one by.

By the way, any serious sci-fi fan will recognize the Body Wars story as a spin-off of the classic science fiction movie, *Fantastic Voyage,* which featured Raquel Welch in a body suit.

WOW Cranium Command. One of the wildest and most offbeat shows anywhere in Walt Disney World, this is a combination Audio-Animatronics and film journey into one of the most unstable places on earth. Your screaming leader, General Knowledge, will inform you that you have been assigned to pilot the most erratic craft in the fleet—the mind of a 12-year-old boy.

This is a presentation that has something for everyone, from corny jokes and a food fight for the kids to smart one-liners and comic performances from well-known comedians, that include George Wendt (Norm from *Cheers*) as superintendent of the stomach, Bobcat Goldthwait as a hysterical adrenaline gland, and Charles Grodin as the smug, all-knowing Right Brain. All this to teach about the benefits of stress management!

It's a very clever show and rarely more than a 15- to 30-minute wait; don't miss it.

Fitness Fairgrounds. The various exhibits in the center of the dome can occupy visitors for hours and are a great place to get out of the sun or rain. Our only warning about this place is that it is quite easy to misplace young children in the busy aisles.

- **Goofy About Health.** You wouldn't ordinarily include our old friend Goofy on a list of contenders for the Olympic team, but this very entertaining film presentation teaches about the value of exercise and health habits as it entertains.
- **AnaComical Players.** A lively and pun-filled tour of the human body,

presented by a clever improvisational theater group. Are you really ready for "Flossed in Space"?

- **The Making of Me.** OK, parents: here's an opportunity to teach your children some of the facts of life in an entertaining 14-minute film starring comedian Martin Short. He begins with a visit to the birth of his mom and dad and follows them right through his own conception (lovemaking is described as a private moment between lovers, with just enough detail to guarantee your kids will come up with their own questions). There is spectacular footage of the beginnings of life and childbirth. Lines for this show—presented in a tiny theater—can begin to stretch to as much as an hour at the most crowded parts of the day; go early or late. Highly recommended.
- **Coach's Corner.** Step up to the batting tee, the tennis net, or the fairway for a quick sports lesson. Your swing will be videotaped and you'll receive a quick taped comment from one of sport's greatest players. It's all in good fun, although some adults seem to take their moment of stardom *very* seriously.
- **Wondercycles.** A very high-tech set of exercise bicycles that present videodisc images keyed to your pedaling speed. You can "visit" Disneyland, scoot in and among the floats in the Rose Bowl Parade in California, or enjoy a hilarious low-level pedal through Big Town, U.S.A., in which your cycle passes humans, dogs, cars, and furniture at rug rat level.
- **Sensory Funhouse.** A set of interesting demonstrations of human senses, including sight, sound, and touch. It includes some unusual demonstrations including an area where you stick your hands through a black curtain so you can't see what you are touching; like the old story of the blind men and the elephant, it's amusing to hear the descriptions visitors make of items that include a pair of ski goggles, a chess piece, a gyroscope, a toy train, and a toy dinosaur.
- **Met Lifestyle Revue.** A computer will ask you all sorts of personal questions and then offer a personalized set of lifestyle suggestions.

The best way to tour Wonders of Life is to keep an eye on the waiting lines for Body Wars and Cranium Command and dive in when they seem reasonable. There is plenty to occupy visitors between trips to those attractions.

Horizons: The Sun Has Set

Horizons. One of the sentimental favorites of Epcot, the Horizons pavilion may ride off into the sunset; the switch was turned off and the doors locked in early 1999 when the much-delayed GM Test Track finally opened next door. Horizons was an extension of the Magic Kingdom's Carousel of Progress theme, presenting a vision of the future that includes the **Omega Centauri** space colony, the **Sea Castle** underwater city, and the robotic farm station **Mesa**

Verde. The rumor mill says the next tenant of the building will be a pavilion that celebrates space exploration, perhaps a moving theater/coaster ride.

GM Test Track

WOW GM Test Track. Fasten your seat belts for the longest, fastest, and most technologically complex ride at Walt Disney World, a wild salute to GM's proving grounds for automobiles. You'll climb hills, experience hairpin turns, jounce down bumpy roadways, zip along straightaways, and enter into a 50-degree banked turn at 65 mph, zooming across the front of the pavilion. Trust me, it feels like twice that speed.

The Test Track climbs, spirals, and snakes through the 150,000-square-foot pavilion; the former home of the World of Motion was completely gutted and rebuilt for this new attraction at Epcot. About half of the 5,246-foot-long track loops outside the pavilion where maximum speeds are obtained; a full ride takes about 5-and-a-half minutes. (Space Mountain lasts about three minutes, reaching a top speed of just 32 mph, half that of the test vehicles.)

This is sure to be the number one draw at Epcot for some time to come; if you have any doubt, consider the fact that the ride is set up with the largest waiting area in Walt Disney World. If the outside queue is filled, the last person in line can expect as much as a 90-minute wait. Once you set foot inside the building, the wait should be about 45 minutes.

On the plus side, the inside queue is actually one of the more interesting places I know of to stand around and wait. You'll pass through a simulation of a GM test facility with all sorts of torture devices for vehicles—from door slammers and seat belt twisters to crash test dummies in all sorts of extreme distress. The much-abused star here is Chester, who allows himself to be repeatedly thumped in the chest by a swinging weight. By the way, real crash test dummies cost as much as $100,000 each, wired with as many as 120 data channels for instruments.

You'll also learn about emissions, braking, and safety engineering at GM.

At the end of the waiting area, the line is split into groups of 24 and ushered into small theaters for a briefing by the test track coordinator. You'll learn about acceleration, braking, and rollover tests . . . oops, no rollovers today. Note the pictures on the walls of actual GM test tracks around the world.

Your guide will select a menu of tests for you and your vehicle:

Hill Climb Test. An accelerating climb up a three-story, 18-degree hill, demonstrating testing of generation of heat and stress on engine and transmission.

Road-Surface Test. Your vehicle will clamber across stretches of rough German and Belgian blocks in a trial for the suspension system.

Brake Test. The car will make a high-speed run at a set of traffic cones, with and without computer-controlled ABS braking. Without ABS, of course, the cones become orange road kill. A set of monitors give you an instant replay of both sequences.

Environmental Chamber. The vehicles move into a 120-degree heat lamp oven and then an indoor 20-degree arctic in a test of the effects of temperature and corrosion on the body and system; from there the car (and passengers) endure a corrosive mist sprayed by industrial robots.

Ride and Handling Test. A pass through a hairpin and loops set the stage for high-speed trials to come.

Barrier Test. Off to the left side of the car you can watch another test vehicle—with test dummies instead of vacationers—crash into a barrier. And then your vehicle will accelerate rapidly and slam at full speed into a solid wall. NOT! But it will come very, very close.

High-Speed Test. On the other side of the wall is the outdoor high-speed test track, a wild ride into the backyard of the pavilion and then a great swoop around the front on a 50-degree bank where the vehicle reaches its top speed of just under 65 mph.

GM and Disney chose to limit the top speed of the vehicles to a street-legal 65 mph, actually just a hair under the limit at 64.8. Passengers will experience about two Gs of force on the banked turns, at an angle of up to 50 degrees.

Heading back inside, each vehicle is examined by a thermal imager, a device that displays the areas of heat generated on the vehicle—and its passengers—during testing.

The ride draws its inspiration from GM's famed Milford proving ground northwest of Detroit; the facility dates back to 1924 and includes 132 miles of test roads of nearly every construction. The vehicles are not derived from an actual GM car but instead are adaptations of a HYGE sled. HYGE, which stands for hydraulic-controlled gas-energized, is a test sled that allows engineers to simplify and standardize the proving grounds process.

Guests enter into a six-passenger Test Track vehicle; vehicles pull up four at a time. When they leave, cars are spaced about 10.5 seconds apart; the ride should be able to accommodate about 1,800 persons per hour.

There are three seats in front and three in back, and each passenger has a shoulder harness and seat belt. (There is no steering wheel, accelerator, or brake pedal—the vehicle is entirely under the control of the computer.) A video screen in front of each row of seats helps explain the testing process.

Passengers will feel the wind; I'd recommend angling for a front seat—there's a bit more protection from the wind and the view of the track is clearer. The ride will likely continue to operate in light rain but shut down in heavier conditions. Trust me, you wouldn't enjoy the ride in a Florida thunderboomer.

The ride is fun anytime of the day, but I particularly recommend the experience by night when darkness accentuates the outdoor experience.

The gas caps on the body of the car are strictly for show. The vehicles use electric motors in the rear that draw 480 volts of power through a slot in the bottom of the track, like a super-sized slot car racer. The motors generate about 250 horsepower and can accelerate from 0 to 65 mph in about 8.8 seconds; the electric motors are also part of the braking system.

A pair of accumulator tanks in the rear compartment of the car controls air pressure for the pneumatic system that keeps the car adhered to the track and is used in the braking system as well.

A trio of onboard computers manages acceleration, deceleration, and braking; together the computers perform more calculations per second than the brains of the Space Shuttle. A central computer in the ride's control room manages distance between the cars on the track.

The vehicles are constructed entirely out of composite material, with no steel between the front and rear wheels. Cars run about 145 miles per day on a "Tailhook" track surface, based on the coating material used on aircraft carriers. The abuse is tough on the tires, which must be replaced several times a year. During the course of a year, each vehicle will travel the equivalent of 21 roundtrips from Orlando to Detroit.

A two-year delay in opening the ride was directly related to the complexity of the technology, a Disney spokesman acknowledged. It is by far the most intricate ride at Epcot and anywhere else at Walt Disney World.

At Test Track, Disney had to invent everything, he said; there were no off-the-shelf mechanisms to be customized. (By comparison, the Rock 'n Roller Coaster at Disney-MGM Studios uses a track and car system already proven at other parks, albeit within a building fitted out with Disney theming.)

The show is not over when you exit your vehicle; you'll walk into an impressive simulation of a robotic assembly line with a stamping mill shaking the floor, and parts of vehicles moving by overhead.

In the Driving Technologies Lab you'll have a chance to sit at one of 10 high-tech driving simulators to test out new automotive technologies, including night vision. Your chair will rumble and bounce in sequence with your driving, and you'll feel the thud of any collisions. (Two of the ten stations are set up with hand controls for drivers who have disabilities.)

Finally, there is a display of some of the latest real cars from General Motors, backed by a flashy set of video walls. Here's where the ride turns from thrills to marketing, although for many visitors there's a lot to be said for a car showroom without a car dealer in sight.

Journey Into Imagination (Reopening in late 1999)

WOW Journey Into Imagination. We're waiting with our imaginations in full gear for the new version of this much-loved attraction.

In its previous incarnation, the attraction included some of the most unusual special effects at Epcot and was a clear favorite among youngsters. The ride introduced us to Dreamfinder and his pet purple dragon Figment (as in "of imagination") on an expedition to collect colors, sounds, shapes, and stories with which to create new ideas.

The new show is based on the Imagination Institute that is featured in the fun-filled Honey, I Shrunk the Audience show.

Imagination will reopen about October 1, with a new show offering a behind-the-scenes at the Imagination Institute.

By the way, Figment wants his fans to know that he will be back in a new role at the show.

WOW Honey, I Shrunk the Audience. A spectacular 3-D thriller that takes off where the two shape-altering Disney films (*Honey, I Shrunk the Kids* and *Honey, I Blew Up the Baby*) left off. In this case, it's the audience that shrinks instead of the kids. This is a theatrical performance that is simply not to be missed.

It begins outside the theater with a preshow sponsored by Kodak and based on their "true colors" advertising theme, an attractive and somewhat inspiring collection of photographs on the general idea of imagination and an extension of the imagination exhibit upstairs.

Then we find ourselves as honored guests at the presentation of the "Inventor of the Year" award to Wayne Szalinski, played by actor Rick Moranis. Other members of the film cast also appear in the feature, and are joined by funnyman Eric Idle of Monty Python's Flying Circus.

And finally we are invited within to see a demonstration of some of Wayne's greatest new inventions, including the Dimensional Duplicator and the No Mess Holographic Pet System. You'll go through the doors on the left side of the preshow auditorium into the theater. You'll be asked to move all the way across a row to fill up all the seats; if you want to try to grab one of the best seats hold back a bit until about 25 people have entered a row and then enter.

As far as what happens next, we don't want to spoil the fun or play a cat-and-mouse game with you; oops, disregard that last hint.

The wild conclusion of the show comes when one of the machines goes berserk and ends up shrinking the entire audience down to toy size. "Stay in your seats and we will blow you up as soon as possible," says Wayne.

The auditorium conspires with the 3-D images to complete the illusion with moving seats, spectacular lighting, special film effects, and unusual effects that will tickle your fancy and sprinkle you with laughter.

The large theater seats 575 guests and will eat up a full waiting line inside the building; if the line stretches out onto the plaza you can expect at least a 45-minute wait.

Lines will ebb and flow at the theater, reached from an entrance inside the doors of the Journey Into Imagination to the left of the loading area for the theme ride. Go early or late to avoid lengthy waits.

The Land

Everyone has to eat, and The Land is a tasty collection of informative exhibits about food and our environment. The building, in part a gigantic greenhouse, also includes a popular food court restaurant. The sprawling pavilion is as large as all of Tomorrowland in the Magic Kingdom.

WOW **Living with the Land.** A boat ride through the past and future of agriculture. Disney Imagineers created a storm scene as an introduction to a tour that passes through a rain forest, desert, and plain—traditional sources of food—and then into some amazing experiments with hydroponic farms, cultivated seafood farms of shrimp and fish, and a desert made to bloom with crops through high-tech irrigation.

The opening storm scene now includes some very nice special effects with lightning and a rain forest, and a cast of Audio-Animatronic creatures. Another significant change is that the opening segment of the ride is introduced by a

Wide world. The Land is one of the largest attractions at Walt Disney World. It covers some six acres and is as big as the entire Tomorrowland area in the Magic Kingdom. Stop and take a look at the huge mosaic at the entrance: some 3,000 square feet in size, it is made of 150,000 separate pieces of marble, granite, slate, smalto (colored glass or enamel), Venetian glass, mirror, ceramic, pebbles, and gold in 131 colors.

woman, one of the few female voices in the park; once the boats enter into the farming areas the guide at the front of your boat will take over.

Among the advanced techniques you will see are "intercropping" of different plants to make the best use of soil and nutrients (coconut, cacao, and sweet potatoes in one example); growing plants vertically in hydroponic (soilless) containers, which makes them easier to feed and inspect for pests; and an experiment in growing plants in simulated lunar soil, based on analysis of the real thing brought back from the moon by American astronauts.

Plants you will see inside include bananas, papayas, ferns, rice, peanuts, pak choi, sugarcane, casaba, sweet potatoes, and some incredible varieties of squash. The simulated tropical and desert farms of The Land create vegetables for some of the restaurants in the pavilion.

One section of the farm includes a computer-controlled watering system that delivers individual amounts of moisture to plants as needed.

A fish farming "aquacell" grows crops of fish selected for their ability to thrive in a crowded environment. Fish under development on various trips have included sunshine bass, tilapia, catfish, pacu, sturgeon, and the strange-looking paddlefish, which is cultivated for its caviar. Some fish and vegetables you see here are served at some of the restaurants.

Among the most educational of all the exhibits at Epcot, Living with the Land is also a good place for a quick break. Preschoolers may be bored, but anyone else is sure to find something to learn. Lines build by midday to as much as an hour in length; come early or late.

On the walls by the waiting line are thoughts about nature from thinkers great and small. They include poet William Wordsworth's "Nature never did betray the heart that loved her" and "Take care of the Earth if you care for yourself," by the Kids for Saving the Earth Club in Valley, Washington. And there is 10-year-old Jessica Lee of Hong Kong: "The Earth is like my mother. You get punished if you make a mess. Why do you think this planet is called Mother Earth?"

The Land Backstage Tour. Serious gardeners and eaters will want to sign up to take this one-hour walking tour of The Land's greenhouses and labs, concentrating on soil-free gardening, fish farming, plant biotechnology, and pest management. Sign up for the tour at the desk near the Green Thumb Emporium on the lower level. There are only a limited number of places on the tours, which are offered from 10 A.M. to 4:30 P.M. Tickets are $6 for adults and $4 for children ages 3 to 9.

Food Rocks. This revue gives new meaning to the term "vegetable." Only Disney would dare give us edible versions of our favorite rock 'n' roll stars. The Peach Boys (Beach Boys) sing about "good, good, good, good nutrition," Pita Gabriel (Peter Gabriel) wants to be your High Fiber, Chubby Cheddar (Chubby Checker) tells you "Come on baby, let's exercise," Neil Moussaka (Neil Sedaka) sings "Don't take my squash away from me; don't you leave me without broccoli. Eat your spinach. Yes, it's true, cause vegetables are good for you."

Cher-acudda (Cher) begs you to "Just keep him lean," and The Wrapper (Tone Lōc) discusses nutrient information labels. But wait, there's also Refrigerator Police (Sting) watching every little knish you eat, and The Get-the-Point Sisters (The Pointer Sisters).

At the end of the show, all of the stars come back and harmonize on the stage in the ultimate rock concert.

The Food Rocks Theater has a capacity of 250 for the 13-minute show and there should rarely be more than a 15-minute wait. This exhibit replaced the overly cute Kitchen Kabaret show.

Before you enter the theater, by the way, take a moment to read some of the interesting food facts in the waiting area. There I learned why cashews are never sold in the shell: they are related to poison ivy and their shells contain an irritating oil. I also found out that many famous French sauces, including Mornay and Hollandaise, were not named for the chefs that created them but instead for the nobleman who featured them at his table.

Real or artificial? Neil Sedaka, Cher, Little Richard, and Chubby Checker actually performed their own songs for the "Food Rocks" show. The other stars had singing stand-ins.

WOW **Circle of Life.** The animated stars of *The Lion King* reappear as the "actors" in an environmental spectacular.

Simba the lion, Timon the meerkat, and Pumbaa the warthog appear in 70-mm glory, along with actors in a fable that begins when King Simba finds that Timon and Pumbaa are planning a new subdivision in the jungle, the "Hakuna Matata Lakeside Village."

Simba warns his friends about the mistakes made by a creature who has from time to time forgotten how everything is connected in The Circle of Life. Those creatures, of course, are humans.

You'll learn about some of modern science's efforts to deal with thoughtful use of land in urban and rural settings around the world. The film includes scenes of polluted wildlife and an oil spill, an ironic antidote to the Exxon Pavilion across the way. There is some very spectacular photography that builds off *The Lion King* film. For example, the famous thundering herds of animals of the cartoon move into a film of the real thing.

The auditorium for the Circle of Life is a bit strange for Disney World; once you leave the waiting area, you'll go down a series of narrow stairways into the seating area. It may be a difficult climb for some. Those who climb all the way down will have to put up with a sometimes overly loud soundtrack.

The Living Seas

An ambitious but ultimately unsatisfying bust. There are a few interesting exhibits here, but if you or your children are truly interested in learning about the watery two-thirds of our planet, you would be much better off visiting SeaWorld or a big-city aquarium.

But, as long as you are in here, check out the exhibits and interactive areas, including some of the antique diving equipment in the entrance and waiting area. When you enter the auditorium for a short film, lag back a bit and get a seat along the left side so that you will be first in line to enter the "hydrolators." The film—a superb explanation of the birth of the oceans and the origin of life from within them—is about 12 minutes. The ride that follows is about three minutes; allow a total of 30 to 45 minutes for the exhibit.

The movie does make one interesting point: humans have spent less time at the deepest points in the ocean than on the surface of the moon.

Caribbean Coral Reef Ride. The idea was great—take visitors on a tour within a huge saltwater aquarium filled with strange and wonderful marine life that include sharks, stingrays, parrot fish, and more. But the trip takes just three minutes and the setup to the ride—the trip deep down below the sea in elevator-like "hydrolators"—is hokey and there's no chance to stop and study. Check out the "Dept. of Pelagic Safety" certificate in the hydrolator.

Don't read this. We don't want to spoil the illusion here. So, if you don't want to know an inside tip about the hydrolators, stop reading this sidebar right here. OK? You've been warned. The hydrolators don't really dive down beneath the sea; the floor moves a few inches to simulate movement and bubbles move up the sides of elevator. Then you walk out the door on the other side of the wall. It's the same principle used in the Haunted Mansion and in more dramatic fashion in other simulator rides.

Sea Base Alpha. A series of sometimes interesting exhibits about underwater technologies and sea life. Spend a few moments studying the wave tank to understand the physics of breakers at the beach. Youngsters will enjoy climbing into the diving suits, and adults can grab a good picture when they poke their heads into the breathing bubbles.

Dolphins at the exhibit are participants in a project that uses a large keyboard to communicate with humans; scientists believe the dolphins are responding to instructions given them by humans, and are able to communicate with their handlers using the same device.

Certified Open Water SCUBA divers can go for a 30-minute swim with guaranteed calm seas, no current, clear water, and more than 65 species of marine life that includes sharks, turtles, eagle rays, and much more. The Epcot DiveQuest is offered twice daily at 4:30 and 5:30 P.M. The $140 fee includes all gear, the dive, a training session, and a T-shirt. For information, call (407) 939-8687.

Eating Your Way Through Epcot's Future World
Innoventions

Electric Umbrella. A large fast-food eatery inside Innoventions East, offering burgers, chicken, and salads. An outdoor terrace is a good bet in temperate weather. The restaurant features an unusual electronic scoreboard for menus (easy to adjust offerings and prices). Items include a chicken sandwich with fajita seasoning for $6.59, hot dogs for $4.34, cheeseburgers for $4.34, and a meatless burger with fries for $5.24.

Fountain View Espresso & Bakery. Baked goods. Espresso, cappuccino, latté, cafe mocha, and other hot drinks ranging from about $1.50 to $2.50. Also available are coffees with Amaretto, Bailey's Irish Cream, Frangelico, or Sambucca for about $4.29, plus beer and wine. This is a good place—if you can get one of the relatively few seats—to sit and watch the fountain show.

KEY:

= Fast food

= Pub

= Full-service restaurant

Ice Station Cool. An unusual bit of marketing, this little igloo celebrates a bit of the Coca Cola culture. More interesting is a section of free soda fountains dispensing soft drinks from around the world. On one of my visits samples included Smart Watermelon from China, Kinley Lemon from Israel, Lilt Pineapple from the United Kingdom, Vegitabeta from Japan, and Krest Ginger Ale from Mozambique. You can also purchase Coke T-shirts in languages that include Japanese, Arabic, Russian, and Korean.

Pasta Piazza Ristorante. Pizza, pasta, and more.

Wonders of Life

Pure & Simple. Within Wonders of Life, across from the AnaComical Players' stage. Waffles and fruit, salads, sandwiches, frozen yogurt, and sundaes. "Guilt-free goodies," $1.50 to $5.

Well named for its small offerings of frozen yogurt, shakes, muffins, and other healthful fare, presented in an attractive cafe-like setting. Seating is at colorful blue metal tables and chairs, like something out of the Jetsons.

Special offerings priced from about $3 to $5 include a beta carotene salad (assorted veggies with a cantaloupe–balsamic vinaigrette dressing), venison chili soup, Oriental chicken salad, and a submarine with turkey pastrami, turkey ham, turkey breast, turkey salami, low-fat mozzarella, lettuce, and tomato with tomato-basil vinaigrette served on a multigrain roll. Sweets include nonfat yogurt sundaes, fruit cups, and frozen fruit juice "smoothies."

The Land

Sunshine Season Food Fair. An attractive food court downstairs in The Land pavilion. Items range from about $1.25 to $7 for breakfast, lunch, or dinner.

Stands include the **Barbecue Store,** offering beef and chicken sandwiches ($4.50 to $5) or chicken and ribs ($6 to $7); the **Picnic Fare** with cheeses, sausages, and fruit; the **Bakery,** a fine place for bagels, rolls, muffins, luncheon breads, cakes, and cookies; the **Cheese Shoppe,** offering quiche, pasta, vegetable lasagna, and . . . cheese, and the **Potato Store,** selling baked potatoes with stuffing that includes cheese, bacon, and beef ($2 to $3.25). Dessert counters include the **Beverage House** ($1.25 to $2.50) and the **Ice Cream Stand** ($1.50 to $2.75). Also, select a double chocolate brownie, giant cookie, or apple pie. There is also a selection of regional beers. The Beverage House has added alcoholic drinks to its offerings, including beer, wine, piña coladas, and margaritas.

> **Hold the grease.** One of the best things about eating at The Sunshine Season Food Fair in The Land is that everyone in your party can eat something different, shopping at the various stands and meeting at a table in the court. Just don't promise your kids a hot dog, a greasy burger, or fries when you arrive to eat; you'll have to get those elsewhere.

Note that all of the stands share the same kitchen and there is some duplication; the same excellent brownie, for example, is available at several counters.

The Garden Grill. Upstairs in The Land pavilion. One of the most attractive and interesting full-service restaurants in the Future World section of Epcot, the entire room revolves around a portion of the "Listen to the Land" boat tour down below. It is now given over to character dining "experiences" for breakfast, lunch, and dinner starring Mickey, Minnie, and Chip 'n' Dale. Breakfast includes scrambled eggs, grilled smokehouse ham steak, grits, and biscuits. Lunch and dinner specialties include rotisserie chicken, hickory-smoked steak, and a variety of fresh vegetables, including some from the gardens on site. Breakfast costs $14.95 for adults and $8.25 for children ages 3 to 11; lunch is priced at $16.95 for adults and $9.95 for children ages 3 to 11, and dinner is priced at $17.50 for adults and $9.95 for children.

> **Fast food?** The speed of rotation of the Garden Grill is adjusted to about one revolution per meal. The lunchtime speed is slightly quicker (about 448 feet per hour); dinnertime slows the turntable down to about 422 feet per hour. Either way, you're not likely to suffer from jet lag.

Parties holding confirmed reservations are permitted to bypass any lines and enter directly into The Land pavilion within 15 minutes of their reservation time.

Outside the entrance is a display of some of the fresh herbs and vegetables grown in the pavilion's greenhouses and served in the restaurant. You will see basil, chives, rosemary, parsley, thyme, and some beautiful cucumbers, peppers, beans, squashes, and eggplants.

The Living Seas

Coral Reef Restaurant. In the lower level of The Living Seas exhibit, to the right of the main entrance. Fish, shellfish, beef, chicken, and salads. Lunch,

$6 to $15; dinner, $19 and up. Children's lunch and dinner menu. Beer, mixed drinks, and a full wine list. Reservations are suggested; make them at the Earth Station on the day you wish to dine. Open for lunch from 11:30 A.M. to 2:45 P.M., and for dinner from 4:30 P.M. to the closing hour for the park.

This place gives a new meaning to the idea of a seafood restaurant; the restaurant was given a full renovation in late 1998. You see food, the food sees you. We kept seeing diners nervously eyeing the passing sharks in the coral reef behind the huge windows alongside the tables; we suspect they worried *they* were going to be the seafood.

Glassy-eyed. The best seats in the tank, er . . . restaurant known as the Coral Reef are eight tables along the glass wall. Other tables are as much as 20 feet from the fish. However, the restaurant is arranged in three terraces that give all guests a relatively good view of the aquarium wall.

Anyhow, there is a fine selection of fish and shellfish; there are also some beef and chicken selections. Specialties include grilled filet of tuna wrapped in plantains, the Coral Reef Clambake with half a lobster and shrimp, maple-glazed salmon, and steak and chicken offerings.

Attractions at World Showcase

The rest of the World's Fair at Epcot is the World Showcase, a group of enter-tainment-education-tourism-trade exhibits from an unusual mix of countries. With the possible exception of the United Nations, nowhere else will you find Germany between Italy and China, or Mexico beside Norway.

And though other parts of the vast Disney empire may be individually more impressive, there are few vistas more spectacular than the viewing area at the six o'clock position on World Showcase Lagoon. Displayed in a circle before you are the pavilions of the select nations of the world; all around is lush vegetation (sometimes adapted to the vagaries of Central Florida weather) including tens of thousands of rose bushes and trees, Callery pears, Washingtonia fan palms, and camphor trees.

Most of the young staffers come from the country of the pavilion they work at, participating in the World Showcase Fellowship Program. During a one-year stay, the young people take part in a work-study curriculum.

Now, as at any World's Fair, it is important to draw an important distinction here: going to the Mexico pavilion is not the same as experiencing the ancient reality of Mexico. Seeing the spectacular movie at the Chinese exhibit does not mean you have been to Mongolia or Beijing. And taking the water ride at Norway does not qualify you to say that you have explored the Norwegian fjords.

Instead, the pavilions—some better than others—do an excellent job of whetting the appetite for travel and educating us all on how different and alike we all are. If you can get your kids excited about a visit to England or Canada or Italy, then a trip to Orlando may pay dividends all around; or, maybe it's your kids that have always wanted to go to Japan and they needed to convince you.

One welcome addition in the World Showcase is the Kids Zones outside most of the pavilions where young visitors can engage in arts and crafts and educational activities related to each international destination; check the schedule when you arrive.

Mexico

The pavilion is set within a striking pre-Colombian-style pyramid, festooned with giant serpent heads and sculptures of Toltec warriors and patterned after the Aztec Temple of Quetzalcoatl at Teotihuacán. Quetzalcoatl, the god of life, is represented by large serpent heads that can be seen along the entranceway.

The arid desert regions of Mexico are portrayed with the landscaping around the Cantina de San Angel; the moist tropics of the Yucatan jungle are echoed with the lush greenery around the Mayan temple.

Inside is a magical wonderland of a happy Mexican village. You'll enter into the colorful **Plaza de Los Amigos,** filled with carts selling handcrafted sombreros of varying sizes, toys, sandals, and other objects—sold at prices that are relative bargains within Walt Disney World. On a terrace near the "river," a mariachi band lets loose with its almost impossibly happy sound.

And down by the water, there's a charming Mexican cantina. The food is good, not great, but in our opinion the **San Angel Inn and Restaurant** is one of the most spectacular settings for dinner within the park, a magical indoor setting.

Take a few moments on your way into or out of the pavilion to look at the small but spectacular collection of ancient Mexican art.

WOW **El Rio del Tiempo.** A charming, happy journey to Mexico—sort of a south-of-the-border version of the Magic Kingdom's It's a Small World. This six-minute boat ride, though, is sure to appeal to children of all ages. There's a touch of Mexico's majestic past as a regional power, a greeting from a Mayan high priest, a humorous acknowledgment of the country's present day as a tourist mecca (enjoy the salespeople who scuttle from screen to screen to try to sell their wares), and a dazzling indoor fireworks salute as dozens of animated dolls dance around you. The indoor fireworks of El Rio del Tiempo (The River of Time) are produced with cool fiber optics.

The Mexican pavilion can become quite crowded at midday; we suggest a visit before 11 A.M. or after dinner.

Norway

The Land of the Midnight Sun has constructed one of the more interesting exhibits at Epcot. You'll enter on cobblestone streets of a simulated ancient village; take special note of the wood-stave church modeled after one built in 1250 A.D. There's also an interesting—and very expensive—set of stores offering clothing, crafts, and toys. Children will love the Legos table in the gift shop; Legos are made by a company in neighboring Denmark.

The wooden building outside the main pavilion is a "stavkirke" or Stave Church, styled after the Gol Church of Hallingdal, which dates to about 1250; within is a display of Norse artifacts.

There are four distinct Norwegian architectural styles displayed in the pavilion. The Puffin's Roost and Kringla Bakeri are built in Setesdal style with grass roofs and thick log walls. The Fjoring shop uses the gables of Bergen style. The castle represents the Oslo-style 14th-century Akershus, which still stands guard in the harbor of Oslo. And the stucco and stone Informasjon building is built in Alesund style.

WOW Maelstrom. A dramatic and entertaining look at Norway from Viking times through modern days on a storm-tossed oil platform in the North Sea. You'll board Viking longboats like those used by Erik the Red 1,000 years ago and set sail into a world of fjords, forests, and the occasional troll. Some very young visitors may be momentarily scared by the "monsters"; all riders are likely to be thrilled by the indoor lightning storm in the North Sea.

You'll know you are in trouble near the end of the short four-minute ride when one of the trolls will get angry: "I cast a spell: back, back, over the falls." Sure enough, your boat will appear to travel over a cliff to land in the World Showcase Lagoon of Epcot, before reversing direction for a gentle plunge down a waterfall.

The Maelstrom ride can become quite crowded at midday; visit early or late.

Shops feature trolls, beautiful (but pricey) knit sweaters from Scandinavia, trolls, leather items, trolls, candy, and trolls.

China

One of the most successful of all of the Epcot pavilions at transporting the visitor to a foreign land. The building is a small-scale but beautifully replicated version of Beijing's Temple of Heaven. On busy days, look for dragon dancers and acrobats performing outside near the replica of the Zhao Yang Men (Gate of the Golden Sun).

WOW *Wonders of China: Land of Beauty, Land of Time.* Simply breathtaking and not to be missed. A Circle-Vision 360 tour of China guaranteed to open your eyes to the beauty and vastness of this still scarcely known nation. We've all seen pictures of the Great Wall, although never so spectacularly as presented here. And recently, we've been granted views of the fabulous Forbidden City of Beijing. But consider the thrill of being able to look back over your shoulder at the gate through which you came. But then, there is more: the incredible Shilin Stone Forest, the Gobi Desert, the Grand Canal, tropical palms, and snow-capped mountains.

In making the film, a Disney film crew had to carry the 600-pound camera up the 4,500 steps of the steep slopes of Huangshan Mountain in Annui Province for what ended up as just a few seconds on the screen.

By the way, if you are thrilled by the images

How high's the water? You probably didn't even notice it was there as you crossed it, but there is a small drawbridge between the Chinese pavilion and the Village Traders shop. Each day at about 5 P.M. the bridge lifts and some of the floating props for the IllumiNations parade are taken through onto the lake for the nightly show.

Twelve by twelve. The Hall of Prayer for Good Harvests is a half-scale reproduction of the actual hall within the Temple of Heaven near Beijing. There are 12 outer columns supporting the roof, representing both the months of the year and the 12-year cycle of the Chinese calendar. Near the center of the room are four columns representing the four seasons; the columns support a square beam, which stands for the Earth, and the assemblage is topped off by a round beam, representing heaven.

of China presented in the film, you may want to make a visit to the Splendid China theme park in Kissimmee; read about it later in this book.

Lines for the 19-minute film build during the day, but rarely add up to more than about half an hour; come early or late to avoid them altogether. The only drawback to this presentation is the fact that the theater has no seats. There are rows of rails to lean upon—sitting on the rails is frowned upon—and small children and short adults may have a hard time seeing the screen without a lift. To make things worse, no strollers are allowed.

Land of Many Faces. An impressive exhibit introducing some of China's many ethnic minorities.

Yong Feng Shangdian Department Store. An indoor shopping mall of Chinese merchandise, including silk clothing, embroidered items, and crafts. A huge collection, it includes some of the more interesting foreign items at Epcot, including silk robes, wooden toys, jewelry, and prints. You can also have your name written in Chinese characters on a scroll, T-shirt, or sweatshirt at a booth outside.

Germany

Wunderbar! A visit to a make-believe German village complete with a beer garden, teddy bear toy shop, wine cellar, and a pastry shop of your dreams. The high wall at the back of the showcase is based on the Eltz Castle on the Mosel River, and Stahleck Castle on the Rhine.

Biergarten. Almost as loud and fun as a hall at the Oktoberfest in Munich—especially as the night goes on. The lively restaurant offers an all-you-can-eat banquet-style dinner that includes rotisserie chicken, sausages, sauerbraten, smoked pork loin, red cabbage, and salad. Desserts include apple strudel and Black Forest cake. Next door is the **Weinkeller,** which stocks several hundred varieties of German wines, as well as a selection of beer mugs, wine glasses, and other drinking items.

Big thirst. Germans are serious about their beer; if you have any doubts, check out the mugs for sale at the **Weinkeller.** One of them is big enough to hold a couple of gallons of brew.

Der Bücherwurm. A bookworm's delight, filled with books from and about Germany. The facade of the building is modeled after the Kaufhaus, a 16th-century merchants' hall in the Black Forest town of Freiburg.

Der Teddybär. You've been warned: this is a

children-parent-grandparent trap full of fabulous toys, dolls, and various stuffed animals.

Die Weihnachts Ecke. It's Christmas every day in this shop full of ornaments, decorations, and gifts.

Glas und Porzellan. An outlet of Goebel, a large glass and porcelain maker best known as the maker of Hummel figurines.

Süssigkeiten. We're uncertain whether to recommend you visit this shop on an empty or a full stomach. Let's put it this way: a full stomach will save you a lot of money. The cookies, candies, and pretzels are unlike anything you will find this side of Germany, and are worth a trip from anywhere.

Dragonslayer. The statue in the center of the square is of St. George and the dragon he slayed on a pilgrimage to the Middle East. St. George is the patron saint of soldiers, and statues in his honor are common in Bavaria.

Volkskunst. A wondrous crafts mart of carved dolls, cuckoo clocks, clothing, and more.

Italy

Like China, the Italian pavilion is one of the more successful efforts in terms of giving the visitor a feeling of walking the streets of a foreign land. Take the time to study the various architectural styles. Out front is a 105-foot-tall campanile, or bell tower, a version of one of the landmarks of St. Mark's Square in Venice, and the replica of the square itself is beautifully constructed; all that is missing are the pigeons, which explains why this version of St. Mark's is so Disney-clean.

The detailed replica of the angel on top of the campanile in the re-created Venice is covered with real gold leaf. The marble stones for the buildings, though, have no marble in them: they are actually fiberglass that has been painted and treated.

At the top of one of the columns at the entrance to St. Mark's Square is a likeness of St. Theodore, an important military leader in early Venetian history. Topping the other column is the winged Lion of St. Mark's, the mythical guardian of the city of Venice. The stairway and portico alongside the Doge's Palace are drawn from Berona, while the town hall is reminiscent of the style of northern Italy.

Landscaping around the garden area includes bougainvillea, citrus plants including orange and lemon trees, and colorful blue, white, and pink hanging baskets. Down at the edge of the World Showcase Lagoon is a gondola mooring. And around the square is a collection of delicious and attractive stores. Outside the square, look for the lively and irreverent performances of Il Commedia di Bologna.

Delizie Italiane. An open-air market with sweet delicacies of all description.

La Cucina Italiana. Gourmet foods and wines, and cooking accessories.

Il Bel Cristallo. Fine crystalware, including Venetian glass and porcelain figurines.

United States

WOW The American Adventure. In our early visits to Epcot, the United States pavilion was one we passed by as the day got long. It's located at the very "back" of the park, and besides, we're Americans, so why should we be interested in something known as "The American Adventure"?

Boy, were we ever wrong! The exhibit here is the ultimate in Disney Audio-Animatronics, a rip-roaring, flag-waving show on a larger scale than almost anything else at Walt Disney World or anywhere else. The unlikely co-stars of the production are author Mark Twain and statesman and inventor Ben Franklin. Never mind that Twain wasn't born until 45 years after Franklin died; such things don't matter when figures from history are brought back as robots.

No mistake. The clock on the facade of the building uses a IIII instead of IV for the four o'clock hour; this is an accurate reproduction of Georgian architecture of the time.

The walls of the main hall are adorned with an interesting group of quotes from an unusual collection of Americans, including:

Wendell Willkie. "Our way of living together in America is a strong but delicate fabric. It is made up of many threads. It has been woven over many centuries by the patience and sacrifice of countless liberty-loving men and women."

Walt Disney. "Our greatest natural resource is the minds of our children."

Charles Lindbergh. "I don't believe in taking foolish chances, but nothing can be accomplished without taking any chance at all."

Ayn Rand. "Throughout the centuries there were men who took first steps down new roads armed with nothing but their own vision."

Herman Melville. "Our blood is as the flood of the Amazon, made up of a thousand noble currents all pouring into one . . . we are not a nation so much as a world."

Grumpy and Dopey were absent that day. In the auditorium of The American Adventure, the 12 statues flanking the stage are said to represent the "Spirits of America." On the right, from the back of the hall to the front, are Adventure, Self-Reliance, Knowledge, Pioneering, Heritage, and Freedom. On the left, from back to front, are Discovery, Compassion, Independence, Tomorrow, Innovation, and Individualism. The 44 flags in the Hall of Flags represent the banners that have flown over the colonial, revolutionary, and independent United States.

The 29-minute show starts with the Pilgrims landing at Plymouth Rock, moves on to scenes including the Boston Tea Party and General George Washington's winter at Valley Forge. There's an eclectic collection of well-known and lesser-known figures of American history and culture, including—to Disney's credit—women, Native Americans, and African-Americans. The audience will meet characters such as Teddy Roosevelt, Alexander Graham Bell, Susan B. Anthony, Charles Lindbergh, Frederick Douglass, Chief Joseph, and Martin Luther King, Jr. On the cultural side are representations of Lucille Ball, Muhammad Ali, Marilyn Monroe, John Wayne, and even Walt Disney himself. And don't overlook the imposing Georgian building itself and the various paintings and statues in the hallways.

Among the special effects employed in The American Adventure is multiplane cinematography, first developed by Disney technicians to add the illusion of depth to animated films, including *Snow White and the Seven Dwarfs* and *Pinocchio.*

The buildings at the pavilion echo American architecture from the late 1790s through 1830, including English Georgian, developed during the reign of King George III. Other examples are

Good luck charm. The red Gate of Honor (Torii) at the entrance to the Japanese pavilion is a sign of good luck. The gates were originally intended as perches for roosters to welcome the daily arrival of the sun goddess. The one at the pavilion is modeled after one in Hiroshima Bay.

drawn from Williamsburg, Independence Hall, the Old State House in Boston, and Thomas Jefferson's Monticello home.

By the way, the 110,000 "bricks" on the exterior of the main building are made from fiberglass formed and colored to appear the correct age. The landscaping evokes a formal Philadelphia garden.

Lines at The American Adventure can build at midday but, except on the busiest days, are rarely larger than the seats in the large auditorium. The best seats are in the first few rows nearest the stage.

Japan

A typically understated but elegant Japanese setting, featuring a reproduction of an eighth-century pagoda from the Horyuji Temple, the oldest completely preserved temple complex in Japan. Each of the five levels of the Goju-no-to (five-story pagoda) symbolize one of the five basic elements: earth, water, fire, wind, and sky. Amateur gardeners will marvel at the detail in the rock gardens and ponds. Fish fanciers should check out the koi in the ponds. Rocks symbolize the long life of the earth; the water symbolizes the sea, a source of life.

Most of the plants and trees of the Japanese garden are native to the Southern U.S. but were selected because they were similar in appearance to those in Japan.

Bijutsu-Kan Gallery. A small museum of Japanese arts, culture, and craft. The exhibition is changed from time to time, making it worth a repeat peek if you've seen it before.

Mitsukoshi Department Store. The farthest west branch of a large Japanese department store, offering a selection of clothing, dolls, toys, and trinkets. The food section includes some unusual items such as fried sweet potatoes, shrimp flavored chips, and tomato crackers. Gardeners may want to bring home a grow-it-yourself bonsai kit.

Morocco

Step through the Bab Boujoulad gate to a beautifully detailed replica of the Koutoubia Minaret in Marrakesh and a world of fezzes, saris, and belly dancers. Bab Boujoulad is the main gate to the ancient city of Fez, known as the Med-

Festival Marrakesh. The folklore, dances, and music of Morocco presented in the square outside the pavilion. Belly dancing and music and dance from the regions of Tangiers, Fez, Casablanca, the Andaluz, and Marrakesh are presented within the Restaurant Marrakesh.

ina. It was founded in the year 786 by the Idrissids. In the Medina section of the pavilion is a reproduction of the Chella Minaret in the capital city of Rabat. There is also a reproduction of the Nejjarine Fountain in Fez.

Check out the very full Senegal date palm to the right of the pavilion. The intricate tilework of the Morocco pavilion is among the most authentic recreations of a foreign nation at Epcot; note that none of the tiles are perfect, because Muslims believe that only Allah is without flaw.

Gallery of Arts and History. A museum of arts, crafts, and culture, with a changing display. Nearby is a branch of the **Moroccan National Tourist Office** with information for visitors who would like to make a journey to the real thing.

Within the courtyard is a collection of fascinating shops, including **Casablanca Carpets** for handmade Berber and Rabat rugs; **Tangier Traders** for leather goods, woven belts, and fezzes; **Medina Arts** for crafts; and **Jewels of the Sahara**, selling silver, gold, beads, and precious and semiprecious jewel items. There's a sign at the shops inviting shoppers to "make an offer" for items they want to purchase; we'd suggest you start with a large discount from the list price and be happy with a small break.

France

Vive la France! France lives in a small-scale reproduction of a section of the streets of Paris, complete with an elegant theater, shops, and a bakery and sweet shop of your dreams. There's even a one-tenth scale Eiffel Tower atop the pavilion. It's for appearance only, though—there is no top-level observation tower as there is in the real thing.

Take a few moments to look at the architectural styles, which include mansard roofs and ironwork harking from France's Belle Epoque (Beautiful Age) in the late 19th century. The park on the right side of the pavilion is stocked with Lombardy poplars, looking somewhat like the famous setting of Seurat's painting, *Sunday Afternoon on the Island of La Grande Jatte.*

Eiffel Tiny. The one-tenth-scale replica of the Eiffel Tower was constructed using Gustave Eiffel's original blueprints.

Impressions de France. Enter into the Palais du Cinéma for a lovely 18-minute film that hits all of the highlights of France—from Paris to Versailles to Mont St. Michel to Cannes, and lots of lesser-known but equally beautiful settings, accompanied by lovely and familiar music, including "Gaité Parisienne" by Jacques Offenbach, "Trois Gymnopédies" by Eric Satie, "Carnival of the Animals" by Camille Saint-Saëns, "Claire de Lune" by Claude Debussy, "Daphnis et Chloé" by Maurice Ravel, and other familiar French compositions. The large screens extend 200 degrees around the theater, which has the added advantage of seats for all viewers. Lines build at midday; visit early or late on crowded days. Stop and take a look at the postshow area, which is modeled after Les Halles, the former commercial marketplace of Paris.

Plume et Palette. One of the most high-tone of all shops in Epcot, with its entranceway modeled after one of the more famous decorative entranceways to the Paris Metro subway. The interior of the store and the showcases compete with the lovely gifts and artworks for sale here.

Ooh, la la. The costumes of the pretty jeune filles at France's pavilion are modeled after dresses worn in Edouard Manet's famous nightclub painting, Le Bar aux Folies-Bergère.

La Signature. Get a whiff of the perfumes and a peek at the clothing.

For the gourmand, there is **La Maison du Vin**, which, as its name suggests, is a Gallic House of Wines. And send your sweet tooth to **Galerie des Halles**, a bakery and candy store in a building that is modeled after the famous Les Halles market of Paris.

United Kingdom

Merry Olde England (and the rest of the United Kingdom) is represented at Epcot by a selection of attractive shops and a first-class pub that sports a nice selection of British beers; it may be one of the few places in Florida where you can get a decent kidney pie.

The streetscape includes a thatched-roof cottage from the 1500s, a formal square with a Hyde Park–like bandstand, a London city square, and an exterior facade of the style of Hampton Court.

If you fancy you have a Green Thumb, or wish you did, be sure to check out the perfectly tended little English garden next to the Magic of Wales shop. The gardens include all sorts of roses from many parts of the former British Empire. By the way, the secret garden also is an excellent place to watch the IllumiNations show on the lagoon.

The Toy Soldier. Playthings for men and boys, women and girls of all ages. The shop's exterior is modeled after an ancient Scottish manor.

Lords and Ladies. More toys, of a slightly nobler fashion: chess sets, dart boards, beer mugs, stamps, coins, and more, inside a hall where the Knights of the Round Table would have felt at home.

Pringle of Scotland. Lay down your chips for beautiful knit sweaters and other articles of clothing.

The Queen's Table. Her highness may be the

Disney reality. Look for typical attention to detail in the construction of the buildings in the interesting streets of the United Kingdom. Never mind that the thatched roofs are made from plastic fibers (for fire protection) or the smoke stains applied by artists with paint brushes; you probably didn't notice that until I pointed it out.

School ties. The crests for four of the realm's most famous schools (Oxford, Cambridge, Eton, and Edinburgh) are displayed in the upstairs windows of The Queen's Table.

only one among us with the available cash to do some serious shopping here, but it's fun to poke (carefully) among the fabulous Royal Doulton china, figurines, and Toby mugs.

The Magic of Wales. A gift shop of small items and souvenirs from Wales; prices are the most reasonable among U.K. emporia.

The Tea Caddy. Here you'll find considerably more kinds of leaves in bags and cans than you're likely to find at the corner grocery.

Canada

The vast range of experiences of Canada is reflected in the landmarks of the pavilion. At front is a native totem pole; out back is a scaled-down Canadian Rocky Mountain; and between is a scaled-down reproduction of the stone Château Laurier in Ottawa. The gardens of the Canada pavilion are based on the famed Butchart Gardens of Victoria, British Columbia, in western Canada.

O Canada! Another breathtaking Circle-Vision 360 movie that brings you up close and personal to bobcats, wolves, bears, and other creatures of the wild, to human glories such as the Cathédral de Notre Dame, to the ski slopes of the Rockies, and onto the ice of a hockey game in a scene so real you'll wish you had a goalie's mask on. Did we mention getting caught in the middle of the rodeo ring in the Calgary Stampede or the breathtaking camera ride down the toboggan slide at Quebec City?

The waiting area for the film is a cave-like mountain lodge from the Canadian Rockies. Be advised that you'll have to stand to watch this extraordinary 18-minute movie.

Northwest Mercantile. A modern-day version of a frontier trading post. You'll trade dollars (credit cards accepted, too) for sheepskins, lumberjack shirts, maple syrup, and Indian artifacts and crafts.

La Boutique des Provinces. Canadian products from its French regions.

Eating Your Way Through Epcot's World Showcase
Mexico

🍴 **Cantina de San Angel.** Tacos, salads, and burritos, $3.50 to $6. This outdoor cantina is located opposite the Aztec pyramid, beside the lagoon. Get a quick Mexican fix at this attractive outdoor cafe: tortillas, tostadas, and sweet churros (fried dough dipped in powdered sugar and cinnamon).

Night light. The outdoor Cantina de San Angel, outside of the Mexico pavilion along the lagoon, is an interesting place to view the nightly IllumiNations show over a cold beer or soft drink. Tables will fill up early.

Small, round, wooden tables seat four under colorful umbrellas during the day and under high, soft-light lanterns at night. Your meal is accompanied by Mexican music in a setting that includes native flowers on a tiled patio inside a stucco wall. The platos Mexicanos include corn or flour tortillas filled with chicken or beef, priced from about $4 to $6. Side dishes include refried beans or chips and salsa. Desserts, priced from about $2 to $3, include flan or churros. Drinks include frozen margaritas and Mexican beer.

San Angel Inn. Traditional Mexican dining. Lunch from $5 to $15. Dinner from $15. Children's menu. Reservations are suggested and necessary in busy season.

This restaurant is inside a simulated Aztec pyramid in the center of the Mexican exhibit, probably our favorite location for a restaurant at Epcot. Diners sit on a terrace overlooking the passing boats on the River of Time (El Rio del Tiempo), under a make-believe starlit sky. It feels about as real as any place north of Mexico City; in fact, the eatery is run by the same company that operates the well-known restaurant of the same name in Mexico City.

Live percussion music and a mariachi band add to the atmosphere and the enjoyment. Look beyond the River of Time to view pyramids, a volcano, and a campfire.

The food is above-average Mexican fare. Specialties include *carne asada Tampiquena, huachinango a la Veracruzana,* tacos, burritos, enchiladas, and much more.

On visits we have made, lunchtime offerings have included the interesting and traditional *mole poblano* (chicken and spices with a chocolate-based sauce) and a combination platter (beef taco, enchilada, quesadilla, and avocado dip). At dinner, we have been offered baked California lobster ($26) and *camarones enchiladas* (shrimp sautéed with pepper).

Lunch or dinner children's offerings include soft tortilla with chicken or beef, fried chicken, or grilled beef taco. Traditional Mexican desserts include flan or *capirotada* (bread pudding). Alone or with dessert, try Mexican coffee with Kahlua, tequila, and cream.

Dos Equis and Tecate beers, margaritas, and a full wine list also are available.

Norway

Kringla Bakeri og Kafé. Open-faced sandwiches, pastries, cakes, $3 to $4.

This interesting kafé is located on the left side of the Norwegian exhibit, behind the replica of the church.

What else would you expect from a Kringla Bakeri than fresh kringles? All right: a kringle is a candied pretzel. Also available are *vaflers*, which are waffles covered with powdered sugar and jam and other interesting sweets. Sample the wonderfully white rice cream pudding or chocolate ball, like a three-inch truffle.

Open-faced sandwiches ($3 to $5) are very well presented for a medium-to-small serving. Offerings include tongue, beef, smoked salmon, mackerel, and ham. And yes, there's a herring platter.

Chairs and tables are available outside, between Norway's Ancient Church and the shops at the pavilion.

Early bird meals. Oslo, the capital and major port of Norway, lies at the head of the Oslo Fjord. The earliest settlement was on the Akershus Peninsula, where a royal fortress was built about 1300. The building still stands, used for state banquets.

🏛 **Restaurant Akershus.** Buffet with hot and cold meat, cheese, pasta, and dessert. Lunch, $11.25 for adults and $4.25 for children; dinner $17.25 for adults and $7.50 for children. Reservations are available and necessary on busy days. Open from 11:30 A.M. to 3:30 P.M. for lunch, and 4:30 to 8:30 P.M. for dinner.

This restaurant is located inside a replica of the famous castle of Akershus in the Oslo harbor on the right side of the Epcot Norway exhibit.

Visitors are offered a version of a Royal Norwegian Buffet *koldbord,* or "cold table," with more than 40 items. You'll find more types of herring than you ever imagined possible, along with hot and cold smoked salmon, turkey, or mackerel. You can also find meatballs, scrambled eggs, lamb with cabbage, mashed rutabaga, hot smoked pork with honey mustard sauce, and more. Be sure to take advantage of the offer by the waiters and waitresses for guided tours of the *koldbord.* Desserts, wine, beer, and soft drinks are a la carte; free refills are offered on soft drinks.

Akershus is an interesting excursion for the adventurous, although most children we know will find the offerings a bit strange and unappealing. Even some adults will consider the buffet to be an unending selection of appetizers without the main course. In recent years, the offerings have been broadened to include more pedestrian fare: peel-and-eat shrimp, meatballs with gravy, and macaroni and cheese.

The white stone walls and tile floors offer a pleasant, cool atmosphere for lunch or dinner. The rustic elegance of high ceilings and exposed wooden beams are enhanced by the appetizing odor of cabbage and vinegar.

China

🍴 **Lotus Blossom Café.** Stir-fry, eggrolls, sweet-and-sour chicken, soup, and more, $2 to $6. Lunch, dinner.

This is a quality fast-food restaurant located near the entrance to the China exhibit beside the Nine Dragons Restaurant. It offers covered outdoor dining in a cafe or patio setting. The dining area is tastefully decorated; the food is better than most fast-food operations.

For the most variety for your money, try one of the combination platters. For a lighter meal, sample a bowl of soup for under $2. Chinese beer, tea, and soft drinks are available.

🏛 **Nine Dragons Restaurant.** Varied traditional Chinese cuisine in Mandarin, Cantonese, Kiangche, and Szechuan styles, plus appetizers. Lunch entrees range from $5 to $15; dinner entrees start at $15. Reservations required at busy times. Open from 11 A.M. through the closing time for the park.

This is a palace-like, Oriental setting located near the entrance of the China exhibit, on the left side as you enter. Look up as you walk into the waiting area to see an interesting golden dragon hanging from the ceiling. An ancient robe hangs on the back wall of the waiting area.

As fancy as it is, the selection of food is no better than many average Chinese restaurants, and not as impressive as gourmet Asian eateries. Spe-

Goes great with chili dogs. For an unusual treat, try the red bean ice cream offered as a dessert at the Nine Dragons restaurant in China.

cialties include *kang bo* chicken and red bean ice cream. Chinese beer as well as specialty drinks and Chinese cordials also are available.

Outpost

🍴 **Village Traders.** Located in a dead area (space for a new pavilion?) between Germany and China. A group of huts there offers vegetarian delights, including a "vegetable box" for $1.40 (you might call it a salad); the box with dips costs $2. A selection of fresh fruit is also available.

Germany

🏔 **Biergarten.** Traditional German fare including potatoes, pork, and bratwurst, served for lunch and dinner in all-you-can-eat banquet-style dining. The luncheon buffet, offered from 11:30 A.M. to 3 P.M. was priced at about $9.95 for adults, and $4.75 for children 11 and younger; offerings include sausages, rotisserie chicken, salads, red cabbage, and potatoes. At dinner, the menu expands to include sauerbraten and smoked pork; prices increase to $15.75 for adults and $6.99 for children 11 and younger.

Located at the rear of the German exhibit off the Sommerfest courtyard, the Biergarten offers a loud and raucous atmosphere that gets louder as the evening wears on.

Once inside you'll feel like you are in a German beer hall at night. You'll dine at long tables, served by waiters and waitresses in alpine dress. The setting also includes simulated small-town shops and a stage for the nightly music performances.

Wash it all down with a huge 33-ounce stein of beer (up to $7.50) or German wine and sit back and enjoy the floor show of oompah music and other lively tunes. All in all, a lot of fun.

🏔 **Sommerfest.** Bratwurst und strudel und Black Forest cake und beer for about $2 to $4. Lunch, dinner, snacks.

Sommerfest offers German fast-food treats served at an attractive outdoor cafe located at the right rear of the German exhibit outside the Biergarten. You won't have any trouble finding this interesting and different establishment; follow the sharp odor of wurst and sauerkraut.

Select a German beer to accompany one of

One million bottles of beer on the wall. . . . The famous Oktoberfest is celebrated in Munich, Germany, every October. Germany has the highest per capita beer consumption in the world, about 40 gallons per person per year.

the sandwich offerings. Ask for sauerkraut and all the fixings with your bratwurst sandwich.

Italy

▲ **L'Originale Alfredo di Roma Ristorante.** Veal, chicken, pasta, and seafood entrees plus appetizers and dessert in an Italian atmosphere; there are strolling musicians at dinner. Lunch entrees range from about $5 to $20; dinner entrees start at $15. Children's lunch and dinner entrees. Reservations are required; stop by the Earth Station on the day you wish to dine.

Enter by crossing the stone-paved square, beside the huge Neptune fountain and walled patio. The pink stucco exterior, complete with columns, stone benches, and lanterns, provides an appropriate atmosphere.

A semiformal decor with interesting wallpaper and upholstered seating welcomes you to the cool interior and pleasantly lively atmosphere. Check out the numerous photographs on the wall of the waiting area; you'll see many familiar personalities being served pasta.

Originally elsewhere. L'Originale Alfredo di Roma Ristorante is not the original Alfredo's; the real thing is in Rome and is credited with the creation of the creamy pasta fettuccine Alfredo.

The menu features a wide selection of freshly made pasta (including spaghetti, rigatoni, ziti, lasagna, and more) with various delectable sauces. Recent specialties have included Cornish chicken legs in focaccia bread and oregano crust, Ossobuco di Vitello, and grilled salmon with Italian ratatouille in basil sauce. House wines available by the glass or by the liter.

United States

🍴 **Liberty Inn.** Burgers, sandwiches, chili, and salads, $2 to $6. Lunch and dinner. Child's menu, $3.50 to $4. Indoor and outdoor seating with traditional stateside fare. There's nothing here to startle a youngster or, for that matter, to educate the palate of an adult, but the food is acceptable and typical of what many American families eat most of the time.

The outdoor patio is a very pleasant, tree-shaded affair that includes umbrella tables and colorful landscaping. The inside dining room is very spacious and has large window walls to maintain a bright, light atmosphere, even late in the day.

Lunch and dinner offerings are essentially the same, with a few more options for dinner. For example, you can select a chicken breast sandwich served with french fries or fresh fruit for about $5 for lunch or dinner. At dinner, you can also choose a roasted half chicken with french fries and cole slaw for about $6. The evening offerings also include jambalaya, a southern stew that includes pork, shrimp, crawfish, chicken, sausage, vegetables, and rice. For the children there is fried chicken and hot dogs.

Japan

🍴 **Yakitori House.** Japanese fast food including beef, chicken, seafood, and salads, for about $3 to $8. Lunch, dinner, snacks.

Yakitori is located in the rear left portion of the Japanese exhibit, behind the fountain, within the Japanese gardens in a replica of a teahouse in the 500-year-old Katsura Imperial Summer Palace in Kyoto. Dine indoors or outside; the rock-walled patio with fragrant landscaping is a pleasant getaway for lunch or dinner. Imitation paper lanterns give the evening meal a pleasant glow.

The restaurant offers Japanese fast food, serving yakitori (skewered chicken basted with soy sauce and sesame), teriyaki chicken and beef, and guydon (a beef stew served over rice).

The Shogun Combo offers a good selection, including beef teriyaki, seafood salad, and soups.

[🍴] **Japanese Shaved Ice.** In hot weather, the snack bar on World Showcase Lagoon just to the left of the Japanese pavilion sells *kaki-jori*, which is your basic snow cone done Japanese style with tasty fruit syrups. Flavors include cherry, strawberry, honeydew melon, tangerine, or mixed for $1.50.

[🍸] **Matsu No Ma Lounge.** Exotic drinks, sushi, and more, ranging from about $2 to $8. The lounge is located upstairs at the right side of the pavilion.

Here you can sample sake (warm rice wine), Japanese beer, or exotic mixed drinks. Nonalcoholic drinks include *Ichigo* (strawberries, pineapple juice, lemon), and *Mikan* (Mandarin orange and pineapple juice with lemon).

Appetizers include tempura, Kabuki beef or chicken, sashimi, and assorted Nigiri sushi.

[🏔] **Teppanyaki Dining Room.** Table-prepared Japanese entrees of beef, chicken, and seafood. Lunch entrees from about $10 to $20; dinner entrees from about $15 to $30. Children's menu available. Reservations are usually necessary; make them at the Earth Station on the day you want to eat.

Find this interesting restaurant on the second floor of the building on the right of the Japanese exhibit, above the Mitsukoshi Department Store.

An entertaining and tasty break from the hubbub of Epcot. Groups of diners are assembled around a hot table, facing a chef equipped with a set of sharp knives; he carries salt and pepper shakers in holsters. Depending on the luck of the draw, your chef may be a multilingual comic, playing games with the chicken, shrimp, and beef as he slices and stir-fries the food. Teppanyaki fare is fresh and simple, featuring vegetables and meat over rice.

Not invented here. What could be more American than burgers, hot dogs, and chili? Well, actually, there are some doubts as to the lineage of hamburgers (as in Hamburg, Germany), hot dogs (a sausage, such as those made in Frankfurt, Germany, but placed on a roll), and chili (influenced by Mexico well before Texas was a state).

Minimalist meals. The Japanese style of raw or lightly cooked foods in small, elegantly prepared portions is said to be derived from that nation's historical situation of being overpopulated and short of both food and fuel.

Sipping rice. Sake, pronounced sah'-key, is a colorless, sweet alcohol, sometimes called rice wine. It is made from rice fermented with yeast. It is traditionally served warm.

The dining experience is definitely not for someone who wants a quiet, leisurely, and private time. But children—and adults who enjoy a floor show with their meal—are certain to have fun.

Dinner entrees are the same as for lunch, but the prices are higher and the portions slightly larger.

Before and during your meal, sample exotic alcoholic and nonalcoholic drinks. For example, the Sakura includes light rum, white curaçao, strawberries, and lemon juice.

Note that there are several teppanyaki-style Japanese restaurants just outside Epcot, generally offering better prices and smaller crowds.

Tempura Kiku. Batter-fried meat and vegetables, sushi, sashimi, shrimp, scallops, lobster, and fried beef and chicken strips. Lunch entrees from about $10 to $12; dinner entrees from about $15 to $23. Open from 11 A.M. to 3 P.M. for lunch, and from 5 P.M. to park closing for dinner.

Tempura Kiku is located upstairs at the right side of the Japanese pavilion, next to the Matsu No Ma Lounge. Exotic drinks from the lounge are available at the restaurant. Reservations are not accepted; waits are rarely long. There are only 25 seats, though.

Morocco

Restaurant Marrakesh. Traditional Moroccan food. Lunch entrees range from about $10 to $15. Dinner entrees range from about $17 to $20. Children's lunch and dinner selections. Reservations necessary in busy season; stop by the Earth Station or sign in at the podium at the front of the Morocco exhibit. Best deal: lower-priced lunches.

One of our favorite spots at Epcot, this place does a good job of making you feel as if you have traveled to an exotic place. When you arrive, wind your way through the Fez gate to the back of the Medina to find the Marrakesh amid the narrow streets and quaint shops.

Waiters in ankle-length *djellaba* robes, strolling musicians, and belly dancers provide an interesting and entertaining backdrop for a delightful meal. Even if you have to wait in the lobby briefly for your table, you'll be entertained by the music, native costumes, and decor.

Veiled threat. Belly dancing first came to America in 1893 at the Chicago World's Fair when a Syrian dancer who called herself Little Egypt scandalized viewers with what later came to be named the "hootchy-kootchy." Belly dancing is believed to have originated in Persia (now Iran) and is still popular throughout the Middle East.

The dining area, with its raised, segmented dining rooms that overlook a central entertainment area, adds interest to your meal.

Among the traditional delicacies you may be able to sample for lunch are *meshoui* (lamb roast in natural juices with rice, almonds, raisins, and saffron) and *couscous* (rolled semolina) steamed with garden vegetables, chicken, or lamb. You might also consider ordering one of the sampler plates that have small portions of various offerings for yourself or to share with someone.

The dinner menu is similar, but with more variety and larger portions. Try the Tangier sampler for a selection of items, including specialties marinated in spices such as ginger, cumin, paprika, garlic with olives, and pickled lemon. It's all topped off with some delicious honey-sweetened pastries or crepes.

[🍴] **Moorish Café and Pastry Shop.** Baklava and other delectables for about $1.50 each. Moroccan Flag Beer for about $3.

France

[🍴] **Boulangerie Pâtisserie.** French pastries and fresh croissants, priced from about $2 to $4. Breakfast, snacks.

This quaint bakery shop is across the narrow French street from the Bistro de Paris. It's a wonderful place to grab breakfast or a sweet snack any time of the day. The bakery is managed by the Chefs de France, which is as tasty a recommendation as can be found at Epcot.

Any of the tarts, apple turnovers, quiche Lorraine, and chocolate treats are good. Dark, flavorful coffee makes a good accompaniment for the sweet treats.

[Y] **Bistro de Paris.** Traditional French cuisine in a light, quiet setting. Dinner and lunch (in peak season only). Dinner entrees start at about $15 and rise from there. Children's menu.

A window seat upstairs at the Bistro may be the best place in the park to view the nightly Illuminations show.

Reservations are available and necessary on busy days.

Upstairs over the Chefs de France, this bistro is entered through a rear door at the back of the building. A bistro is an intimate little cafe or pub, and that's what the designers of the Bistro de Paris had in mind in this lighter and (usually) quieter version of Chefs de France. The same master chefs designed the menu, which includes a variety of appetizers, soups, entrees, and desserts.

Specialties include grilled beef tenderloin with mushrooms, glazed onions, and green peppercorn sauce; grilled swordfish with a tomato-béarnaise sauce; and sautéed veal tenderloin with apple and Calvados sauce.

Appetizers and entrees vary by season and are occasionally changed. In recent years, offerings have included appetizers such as salad of duck liver pâté at $14, *gratin d'escargots de Bourgogne* (casserole of snails in herbal butter) at $7.50, cream of lobster soup ($4.50), or a mixed green salad with true Roquefort dressing and walnuts at $7.50.

Entrees have included a sautéed breast of duck with cherries and red wine sauce for $20, and a rack of lamb with vegetables for two is $48.

At least 10 dessert items are available and have included fruit and sherbet with raspberry sauce, and vanilla creme in a puff pastry shell topped with caramel sauce.

[Y] **Au Petit Café.** French cafe fare from soup to quiche, $4 to $14.50. Children's offerings, about $4. Lunch, dinner, snacks.

This is a Parisian-style sidewalk cafe located to the left of Chefs de France. You'll find it through the smell of fresh flowers coming from the many hanging baskets that adorn the posts that support the awning over the patio.

The World Showcase is not quite the Champs-Elysées, but the little sidewalk cafe here with its formal black-jacketed waiters gives a nice taste of the time-honored people-watching stations on the streets of Paris.

The menu includes traditional onion soup with cheese, *coq au vin,* and sautéed strip steak with Bordelaise sauce. Moderately priced offerings include such familiar items as quiche Lorraine and salads. Luncheon entrees range from $5 to $15; dinner plates begin at $15.

Fruit sorbets, ice cream, pastry shells filled with light cream and chocolate sauce, and ice cream soufflé with Grand Marnier sauce round out the menu.

No reservations are accepted, and the waiting lines can become quite long on busy days.

Chefs de France. Traditional French cuisine. Lunch, $8 to $15. Dinner from $15. Children's lunch and dinner menu. Reservations are suggested.

Chefs de France is located on the ground floor of the large building at the left of the entrance to the France exhibit, to the right of the Au Petit Cafe outdoor dining area.

C'est merveilleux! Right here in Epcot, just across the way from umpteen hot dog and pizza stands, is a restaurant nearly as fine as any in France.

Enter this intriguing restaurant under the red awning off the stone-paved street of the France exhibit. The building is of classic French architecture with stone walls and a metal roof. Inside is an elegant French dining room complete with fresh tablecloths, paintings, and chandeliers; table service in elegant continental style with a bustling, active atmosphere. Pleasant and helpful personnel speak French (English, if you insist) and are ready and willing to help you make selections.

To the right of the main dining room is a pleasant, glassed sunroom that provides bright, sunny dining in a dark green and wood tone motif.

Lunch and dinner meals include 10 or more salads and appetizers and about as many entrees. All of this comes at only a slightly high premium, compared to other Epcot table-service restaurants.

Menu items change from season to season. On recent visits we have seen fresh filet of snapper and spinach baked in puff pastry, sautéed scallops and crab dumplings with lobster cream sauce, and sautéed tenderloin of beef with raisins and brandy sauce.

As you might expect, desserts are worth drooling over, with plenty more than a dozen selections. We have dreamed about Crème Caramel (baked French custard with caramel sauce).

Beer and wine by the glass or carafe also are made available.

Recipe for success. The chefs of France who are behind the restaurant of the same name are Paul Bocuse and Roger Vergé, operators of two of the country's finest restaurants, and Gaston LeNôtre, considered a national treasure for his pastries and desserts.

United Kingdom

Rose & Crown Pub and Dining Room. English pub fare in a pleasant atmosphere. Lunch entrees from $5 to $15, and dinner from

$15. Children's menu. Lunch, dinner, snacks. Traditional afternoon tea at 4 P.M. Reservations for the dining room are recommended and necessary on busy days; no reservations are accepted for the pub.

Located across the street from the main portion of the United Kingdom exhibit, the Rose & Crown is an interesting British dining experience. Very ordinary pub food in England seems very exotic in Orlando. On previous visits, we have been offered steak-and-kidney pie, lamb and barley soup, chicken and leeks, and fish and chips. The dinner menu expanded to include Cornish game hen, herb-roasted lamb, and Argyle prime rib with Yorkshire pudding. A selection of sweets, such as traditional sherry trifle, was also available.

Warm comfort. Tea dates back several thousand years to ancient China and Tibet. It was introduced into England in the 1600s and soon thereafter into the American colonies by British merchants in the East India Company. The classic English breakfast tea is a Chinese black tea called Keemun. The popular Earl Grey tea is a black tea flavored with bergamot or lavender oil.

There is a decent selection of beers, stouts and ales, including Bass from England, Tennent's from Scotland, and Guinness Stout and Harp ale from Ireland. They're sold by the pint and "yard" for those with powerful thirsts.

The decor is appropriately rough and dark, with elements of both city and country drinking establishments in the United Kingdom. Frosted and etched glass adds an elegant interest to this beautiful setting.

The pub, which can become quite crowded, offers appetizer-sized portions of the dinner menu along with beers and mixed drinks.

Canada

Le Cellier Steakhouse. Steaks, pasta, and seafood in a quiet corner of the park. Lunch, served from noon to 4 P.M., has entrees priced from about $8 to $10; dinner is served from 4 to 9 P.M. with entrees from about $10 to $15.

EPCOT CENTER

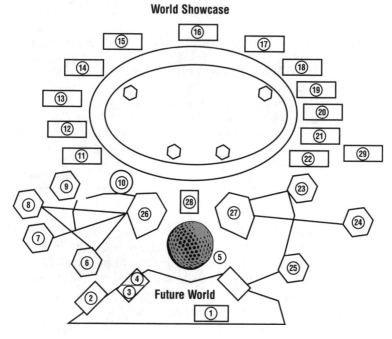

World Showcase

Future World

Epcot Center

1. Monorail Station
2. Pet Care Kennel
3. Banking
4. Strollers
5. Spaceship Earth
6. Universe of Energy
7. Wonders of Life
8. Horizons (closed)
9. GM Test Track
10. Odyssey Center (closed)
11. Mexico
12. Norway
13. China
14. Germany
15. Italy

16. United States
17. Japan
18. Morocco
19. France
20. International Gateway
    Ferry Terminal to Epcot Resorts
21. United Kingdom
22. Canada
23. Journey Into Imagination
24. The Land
25. The Living Seas
26. Innoventions East
27. Innoventions West
28. Fountain of Nations
29. Millennium Village

Chapter 9
Disney's Animal Kingdom

Disney's Animal Kingdom is a logical progression. After all, the entire Disney empire began with a mouse.

Now there is a cast of more than a thousand real animals at work at a wondrous new kingdom that celebrates the creatures real, extinct, and imaginary with rides and attractions, shows, dramatic landscapes, and close encounters with exotic creatures.

Mickey is still around, too.

From the moment you enter the park through a lush oasis, you are immersed in a meticulously re-created world: Africa and Asia brought to the swamps and meadows of Florida. More than 4 million trees, plants, shrubs, ground covers, vines, epiphytes, and grasses from every continent except Antarctica were planted.

The employees of the park include more than 1,000 birds and mammals, plus iguanas, chameleons, and other reptiles. On the human side, Disney recruiters traveled to Uganda, Zimbabwe, Ghana, Botswana, Cameroon and South Africa to hire nearly 100 college students, many seeking careers in the hospitality industry. You'll find Africans working at many of the gift shops and attractions in the park.

Disney's Animal Kingdom is 500 acres of sweeping vistas, including the wide-open plains of Africa populated by great herds of animals. By comparison, the Magic Kingdom is just 107 acres and Epcot just 260 acres.

The park is located in the southwest corner of Walt Disney World at the end of the Osceola County Parkway near All-Star Resorts. Although you wouldn't know it from the outside, it lies just north of U.S. 192.

Among the highlights:

- A safari across Africa, bringing us up close to real lions, elephants, and herds of zebras, giraffes, and dozens of other familiar and rare animals. There's a touch of an environmental message too, with a harrowing chase after a group of elephant poachers.
- A stroll through Asia, where tigers rule the ruins of a Maharajah's palace.

MUST-SEES

Kilimanjaro Safaris
(Africa)

Pangani Forest Exploration Trail
(Africa)

Kali River Rapids
(Asia)

Maharajah Jungle Trek
(Asia)

Countdown to Extinction
(DinoLand U.S.A.)

It's Tough to Be a Bug!
(Safari Village)

The Tree of Life
(Safari Village)

Conservation Station
(Conservation Station)

Festival of the Lion King
(Camp Minnie-Mickey)

Tarzan Rocks
(DinoLand U.S.A.)

- A voyage millions of years back in time to rescue a dinosaur moments before a fiery meteor slams into the earth, dooming the entire species.
- A 3-D glimpse of the world from a bug's-eye view.
- A striking sculpture known as the Tree of Life, which sets the theme for the park with images of animals large and small.
- A lively stage show that combines a bit of Broadway, a circus big top, and a Disney parade.
- And, of course, Mickey Mouse, Minnie Mouse, and other favorite Disney characters are in the park to greet visitors, including regular appearances in a beautiful garden setting.

The Park Is Born

Disney's Animal Kingdom opened on Earth Day, April 22, 1998.

"Just as this theme park has its roots in our films, it also represents a major departure," said Roy W. Disney, Walt's nephew and vice chairman of the company. "Once a movie is completed, it's done forever. On the other hand, Disney's Animal Kingdom—like the animal world itself—will evolve and grow. It's truly a living thing."

Speaking at the dedication of Conservation Station in the park, Disney lauded a group of "eco-heroes," including gorilla researcher Dr. Jane Goodall.

"Walt Disney advocated 'stealth education,'" he continued. "Remember the song: 'A Spoonful of Sugar Helps the Medicine Go Down.'"

And in a gesture reminiscent of the one 43 years before when Walt Disney read from the plaque dedicating Disneyland in Anaheim, Walt Disney Company chairman Michael Eisner read from the dedication plaque for Disney's Animal Kingdom at the formal grand opening of the park:

"Welcome to a kingdom of animals . . . real, ancient, and imagined: a kingdom ruled by lions, dinosaurs, and dragons; a kingdom of balance, harmony, and survival; a kingdom we enter to share in the wonder, gaze at the beauty, thrill at the drama . . . and learn."

A new section of the park, Asia, opened in March of 1999, adding a thrilling trek through habitats of extraordinary animals, including tigers, tapirs, and komodo dragons, and a wet river rafting adventure that has an ecological message.

About the Park

Disney's Animal Kingdom is a more leisurely experience than the Magic Kingdom, Epcot, or Disney-MGM Studios. The beauty is in the details, and you'll miss a lot if you rush from attraction to attraction.

There are seven main areas, each at the end of a spoke radiating out from the Tree of Life at the center of the park:

The Oasis. The entrance plaza leads into this very green and lush tropical garden. Most visitors will zoom right through; make a point to explore the Oasis later in the day or on your way out.

Safari Village. The island at the center of the park is home to the Tree of Life and "It's Tough to be a Bug!"

Africa. You'll enter through the East African port of Harambe to some of the most spectacular parts of the park: the Kilimanjaro Safari, the Pangani Forest Exploration Trail, and the Wildlife Express train to Conservation Station.

Conservation Station. An inside peek at the care and preservation of wildlife, and some hands-on participation at the Affection Section.

Asia. One of the most beautifully realized areas of the park, home to the very wet Kali River Rapids and the Maharajah Jungle Trek, a stroll through the jungles of Asia.

DinoLand U.S.A. About as close as you could hope to get to the world of the dinosaurs. Explore the Cretaceous Trail and the Boneyard, then load onto a Time Rover for a trip back in time to days when the dinosaur was king.

Camp Minnie-Mickey. An old-fashioned summer camp populated by Mickey and his pals, the Lion King and his troupe, and some fascinating smaller (and real) animals.

The layout of the park is somewhat confusing because you cannot see landmarks; the Tree of Life is only visible when you are in the center of the park and cannot be seen from outlying lands. Study the map and pay attention to the signs.

There's no Main Street or obvious gathering place, although the thriving port city of Harambe is likely to be a favored hangout for many visitors. Be sure to bring a hat and suntan lotion; parts of the park are about as hot and exposed as, let's say, Africa.

The park was open from 7 A.M. to 8 P.M. most days in its first year; Disney has installed lighting on the savanna and may operate the park into the night on some of the busiest days of the year.

There remains some additional space for expansion at the new park, including further sections near Asia. Disneyphiles note that the early renderings for the park included an area named Beastly Kingdom, the home of mythical creatures such as unicorns and dragons. And they point to the logo for Animal Kingdom, which includes a winged dragon in the middle of a march of real creatures. We can hope.

Wall Street analysts predict attendance will be similar to that of Epcot, which holds second place at Walt Disney World behind the Magic Kingdom. They estimate an average of about 20,000 visitors per day in the low season and 40,000 per day in peak periods, for an annual attendance of about 11 million.

Power Trip #1

Breakfast with the Animals

There are two good reasons to get to the park early and head for **Harambe**: First of all, the Kilimanjaro Safari is one of the biggest draws of the park and lines build by mid-morning. Secondly, many of the animals on the African savanna are morning creatures. (Lions, for example, sleep as much as 18 hours a day and are particularly fond of siestas in the heat of the afternoon.)

Dedicated animal lovers and photographers will want to arrive at the park as early as possible—it opens at 7 A.M.—and head for Harambe. If you're lucky, you may be able to make two safari trips before most visitors park their cars.

If it's a warm morning, head for Asia and the **Kali River Rapids** for a wet tour through a tropical rainforest; if there's a chill in the air, you might want to wait for later in the day, although lines will build in the afternoon. Walk through the thrilling **Maharajah Jungle Trek** while you're there. Move on to **DinoLand U.S.A.** for Countdown to Extinction and **Camp Minnie-Mickey** for the Lion King show. Leave the Tree of Life and the front of the park for last.

Power Trip #2

A Contrarian's Tour

OK, so we know that most visitors are likely to head first for the **Kilimanjaro Safari**, but you have other goals in mind. Take advantage of the major flow to the left side of the park in the morning by going the other direction instead.

Head first for DinoLand U.S.A. for **Countdown to Extinction** and then Camp Minnie-Mickey for the **Lion King show**.

Then move counterclockwise against the flow toward Africa and the safari. Catch an early lunch and then head out into the savanna during the noontime lull. If you bring your kids, see if they can wake up a few snoozing cats. The wet **Kali River Rapids** are definitely worth a visit; lines will build on warm afternoons.

The Oasis

You'll enter the park though the cool green of this lush garden. Colorful and unusual animals inhabit a miniature landscape of streams, grottoes, waterfalls, and glades. It's a place of cool mists, fragrant flowers, and the sights and sounds of playful animals.

Most visitors are going to sprint through the Oasis to get into the park itself . . . and that's not a bad idea on a busy day. But do take the time to revisit the area, or at least make a more leisurely stroll when you leave at the end of the day. This is Disney's horticultural and animal imagineering at its best, a lovingly created small world after all.

There are lovely and exotic plantings at almost every turn, and caves, waterfalls, and grottoes that offer welcome respite from the Florida sun.

And tucked away are hidden animal delights, including tropical birds and small animals such as anteaters, tufted deer, muntjac, two-toed sloths, otters, macaws, and scarlet ibis. My favorites include the tree kangaroos.

Disney's plant kingdom. The plant collection at Disney's Animal Kingdom includes 600 species of trees, 350 species of grasses, and 1,800 species of shrubs, vines, ferns, mosses, epiphytes, and perennials. All told, more than 100,000 trees and more than 4 million individual grasses and shrubs were planted or grown from seed.

At the far end of the Oasis, a stone bridge crosses the Discovery River to deposit you at Safari Village.

Hundreds of flowering trees from nearly every tropical and subtropical region on earth color the gardens. They include jacarandas, tabebuias, cassias, michellias, bauhinias, calliandras, and tipuana. Disney landscapers promise there will be plants and trees in bloom no matter what time of year you tour the park.

The Animal Kingdom's plant inventory is at least five times as large as the lush world of Epcot, and larger than all three other Florida Disney parks combined.

On the African savanna the challenge includes keeping the huge area looking like a piece of Africa while dealing with the fact that many of the animals will insist on eating the landscaping. Elephants, for example, can completely devour large stands of favorite grass. Handlers place pre-cut leafy branches and 1,300 pounds of fresh grasses in various spots each day to attempt to lure some of the larger eaters away from the live vegetation.

Absolutely no insecticides or other chemicals that might endanger the animals are used in the park, according to Disney.

The occasional freeze in Florida is another challenge, but lessons learned in the other Walt Disney World parks have been applied. Water sprays can help prevent frost, and heaters are used in some areas such as The Oasis where the plants are lush and tropical.

Safari Village

The crossroads of adventure at Disney's Animal Kingdom, this island of tropical greenery and equatorial architecture is the hub through which you'll pass to reach other lands. Safari Village is circled by Discovery River, where guests can board launches to journey past the forbidding Dragon Rocks, braving steaming geysers and mythical monsters on their way upriver.

There are some 1,500 hand-painted wooden folk art carvings scattered about, a fusion of pre-Columbian, Peruvian, African, and Polynesian forms. They were crafted on the island of Bali by native craft workers.

The Tree of Life

Towering 145 feet above Safari Village is the Tree of Life, 170 feet wide at its base and surrounded by shimmering pools and meadows filled with birds and small mammals noted for their playful behavior. The trunk of the tree is carved as an intricate swirling pattern of animal forms that symbolize the richness and diversity of animal life on earth.

> **Secrets of the kingdom.** Architectural scale is suppressed to allow trees to overshadow buildings; overall building height is limited to 30 feet, while the major trees of the park were at or above 40 feet at opening.

More than a dozen artists and Imagineers worked full-time for 17 months to create the 325 animal carvings from majestic lions to playful dolphins, from humble armadillos to camels, baboons, and elephants; they had between six and ten hours to finish each sculpture before the plaster hardened.

Hungarian sculptor Zsolt Hormay assembled a team of artists from around the world. Native Americans carved the bear, bald eagle, bobcat, and mountain lion. Hormay himself sculpted the baboon, koala, and scorpion.

The images were carved in a thin layer of cement attached to steel rods bent into the rough forms of the animals; some of the animals highest up in the tree are made of foam to reduce weight.

The tree itself has some 8,000 branches adorned with more than 103,000 artificial leaves that blow in the wind; the entire structure—built upon a framework designed with the assistance of an oil rig builder—sways a bit in the wind.

At its base are small pools and meadows that are home to animals that include otters, flamingos, capybaras, ducks, storks, cranes, cockatoos, lemurs, tamarins, tortoises, and red kangaroos.

Tree of Life Theater: *It's Tough to Be a Bug!*

Like Spaceship Earth at Epcot, the central symbol of Disney's Animal Kingdom also houses an exciting attraction. Guests step inside the Tree of Life to experience a 3-D adventure about creatures of a much smaller scale than most of the others in the park: insects.

Based on *A Bug's Life*, the animated film from Disney and Pixar (creator of *Toy Story*), the humorous film and special-effects theater provide a bug's-eye view of the world.

The queue for the 430-seat theater wends its way around the base of the Tree of Life before eventually ducking into a cool, dark room; listen carefully for the rustle, buzzes, and chirps of the stars of the show. While waiting, read some of the amusing movie posters promoting the greatest hits of insect cinema, titles include: *Web Side Story, Beauty and the Bee, My Fair Lady Bug, Antie, A Cockroach Line,* and my favorite, *Little House of Hoppers*.

When the doors open, pick out a place to sit on a log and admire the tangled-root and vine architecture all around. The orchestra of creatures tunes up below while a buzzing can be heard from the wasp nest projection booth.

Try to sit in the middle of the theater—midway in from both sides and halfway back from the screen—for the best 3-D effects.

The show is ready to begin. The announcer has a request: Please refrain from buzzing, chirping, stinging . . . or pollinating.

With a pair of 3-D "bug glasses" in place, you're right in the midst of things as Flick, the ant master of ceremonies, welcomes visitors as honorary bugs and introduces us to some of the cast of millions.

"Take it from an ant. It's tough to be a bug," says the MC. "That's why we've developed some amazing survival techniques."

Assisted by a pair of acorn weevils with a sling shot, Chili the Tarantula demonstrates his ability to throw poison quills. Yes, they're zooming out toward the audience.

Next, an acid-spraying soldier termite, "the Termite-ator,"—defends his mound by spraying intruders—that's us—in the seats below. The stinkbug soloist, Claire DeRoom, astonishes us with a malodorous performance.

But the big artillery arrives with a villainous grasshopper, a bug on a mission to wipe out the audience of intruders. "You guys only see us as monsters!" he says. "Maybe it's time you 'honorary bugs' got a taste of your own medicine!" Suddenly we're under assault by a giant flyswatter, a blinding fog of "Bug Doom" spray, and a nasty hornet squadron.

I won't spoil the ending, but it does have a certain biting edge.

The butterfly curtain closes, and the announcer reminds the audience to remain seated while all the lice, bedbugs, maggots, and cockroaches exit first.

Discovery River Boats

This leisurely river passage proceeds clockwise around the Discovery River to Asia's Upcountry Landing just east of Harambe. The free-floating canopied boats seat about 80 persons.

According to Disney, the boats were originally intended merely as an alternate form of transportation around the park, but visitors expected some entertainment along the way. When the park first opened, a Disney animal expert accompanied each boat with a few examples of smaller creatures from the park. In mid-1999, the boats were given a bit of a theme, however incongruous, with an audio presentation highlighting Radio Disney, a programming channel for youngsters. A search was on for a more permanent (and engaging) theme for the river ride.

The trip offers a great view of the base of the Tree of Life from the river. The boat passes riverfront beaches adorned with sailing dhows and fish nets at Harambe, and then alongside the temple-strewn coast of Asia. There's also a regularly scheduled close encounter with "Dragon Rocks," where legend says giant fire-breathing reptiles await unwary river pilots; you can see the singed armor of unlucky knights near the mouth of the dragon's lair.

Near DinoLand U.S.A., there's a dinosaur marsh where a 30-foot iguanadon feeds on marsh grasses just below the Countdown to Extinction ride. You don't suppose the iguanadon has escaped from Dr. Seeker's misguided adventures at the Dino Institute, do you?

Africa

The adventure across the wilds of Africa begins in Harambe, a well-aged, modern-day town on the edge of a wildlife reserve. Harambe (pronounced Ha-rahm-bay) is based on the Arab-influenced Swahili culture and architecture of coastal Kenya, with white coral walls, thatched roofs, and a *hakuna matata* attitude toward life.

Disney Imagineers lavished a tremendous amount of detail on Harambe; be sure to read some of the signs and notes on the wall. The hand-plastered walls often expose their coral rock substructures. I was at first surprised to find that Disney had allowed the place to look so dusty on Grand Opening Day until I realized that the piles of wind-blown dirt inside the hallways of some of the buildings were actually created by designers and cemented into place.

At the end of Harambe's main street an ancient gnarled baobab tree, a symbol of the African savanna, beckons visitors toward the Kilimanjaro Safari.

Check out the Ziwani Traders shop at Mombasa Marketplace; the store offers an interesting selection of hand-carved masks, sculptures, and other items from Kenya and other African nations. The decorative gourds on display are used by Masai tribes to hold milk until it is sour enough to meet their taste preferences.

⭐ Kilimanjaro Safaris

The adventure begins in Harambe beneath a 40-foot-tall baobab tree, where the queue winds its way through a warehouse stocked with safari gear. The waiting area is huge . . . and well-hidden from view; be sure to check the posted wait time at the outside of the safari shed before staking your claim in line.

Disney has added a few touches that make the wait a bit less painful. Near the start of the covered portion of the line you'll circle around the base of *Mzee Mbuyu baobab* (Swahili for "Old Man Baobab"), one of the signature trees of the Harambe reserve. A bit later on, the queue passes through a few live animal habitats, including that of a group of crowned cranes.

Have thatch, will travel. Disney designers went back to Africa to obtain tribal craftsmen and traditional thatching grass to create the pole-supported thatched roofs of Harambe and the research outposts along Pangani Forest Exploration Trail.

During construction, Disney imported 13 Zulu craftsmen from Kwazulu-Natal in South Africa and 15 trailer loads of thatch.

Trading their tribal garb for American blue jeans—and putting hard hats over familiar straw caps and bandannas—the builders did object to air conditioning in their hotel rooms. They were eventually moved to houses where they could open the windows and let in the mid-summer warmth of Florida.

The roofs were constructed with wild Berg thatch, which resists insects and decay and provides excellent insulation and waterproofing. The battens, which secure the thatch to hardwood rafters, are made of eucalyptus pods stripped bare, coated with mud, and kiln-dried to produce a mottled dark brown finish.

The roofs are expected to withstand the weathering of Florida's sun and rain for up to 60 years.

Environmental messages play from video monitors overhead. The safari will help you learn about the importance of protecting animal life; the game warden quotes a Swahili saying: "What you see with your eyes you value with your heart."

A woman's place. African lions live in large prides of one or two males with females and cubs. Female lions do the hunting, but males eat first.

Eventually you will be bouncing across the rugged terrain in an open-sided, 32-passenger motor lorry; you can call it a safari truck. In the driver's seat is an experienced guide who will help identify the animals and keep in radio contact with a bush pilot flying ahead in a spotter plane.

The trucks follow a twisting trail through a lush green forest, across small river crossings, and into the Serengeti grasslands rich with antelope, giraffes, zebras, baboons, rhinos, elephants, crocodiles, lions, hippos, and many more animals.

Crossing the Bongo Pool, where many animals come to drink, be on the lookout for black rhinos, among the most fascinating animals in Africa. They may be along the shores, wallowing in the water, or lurking just below its surface. If you're lucky you may spot a glimpse of a rare okapi, a large mammal related to the giraffe but lacking the long neck.

Rounding the bend, you'll come to a woodland of date and fan palms, the home of a colony of shiny black and white colobus monkeys.

A set of cascading waterfalls forms a pool that is home to African crocodiles, which can grow to as much as 20 feet in length, much larger than American alligators. A very rickety bridge crosses directly over their heads; do you think it's strong enough to support the weight of your safari lorry?

Safely across, the safari emerges from heavy vegetation for a spectacular view of the vast savanna, where you'll see spotted giraffes, black and white striped zebras, sable antelope, Thomson's gazelles, and speedy ostriches that are capable of outrunning the truck.

The landscape of the savanna includes strange vegetation such as maringa trees—known as sausage trees—with foot-long seed pods used by natives to make a lemonade-like drink. Termite mounds stand up to 20 feet tall.

Out on the grasslands, baboon families sightsee from rocks and trees as the trucks pass by. Around another bend, a herd of elephants moves among the trees. The truck fords a small stream and moves into elephant company.

If you're lucky, you may catch a glimpse of one or more lions; they are hard to spot, especially in midday when they're likely to be snoozing.

The driver communicates with the spotter plane in search of "Big Red" and her elephant newborn "Little Red," a favorite pair of pachyderms who got their name because they seem to enjoy rolling in the rust-red dust.

Keep your eyes open (and cameras ready) for a glimpse of white rhinos in nearby pools; you may spot kudu, scimitar-horned oryx, Zimbabwean Klipspringer, long-horned eland, and cheetahs out in the grasslands.

The beauty of the scene is soon disturbed by a radio message from a game warden: ivory poachers have wounded Big Red, and Little Red is missing. The

A home for the animals. Most of the animals in Africa spend their days working the crowds on the Kilimanjaro Safaris and from along the Pangani Forest Exploration Trail, and then retire for the night to their hotel suites.

Most of the animals at the park were born in captivity at zoos and other preserves. Among the tasks undertaken by Disney animal managers was to give them more room to roam than most have ever known, while conditioning them to come to shelters each night for their own security and for daily care.

Each area has its own sound signal used to summon animals to their "backstage" homes. The Thomson's gazelles have learned to come back to their shelter each night when they hear a "goose call." Giraffes respond to a coach's whistle, and zebras listen for a cowbell.

When the animals were first introduced to the African savanna and forest there were temporary fences erected to help them learn where they were expected to roam. Subtle barriers including water, gratings, and hidden wires help reinforce the training.

bush pilot asks us to help out by forcing the poachers east along the gorge toward the waiting wardens. We hear the sound of the poachers' jeep ahead of us and even the sound of bullets; off to our left we pass their hurriedly abandoned camp, fires still smoldering.

And then comes the good news from the spotter plane: the poachers have been caught. As we come around a rocky bend, we find a ranger training his rifle on a pair of poachers inside their crashed vehicle. Beside it in the back of a small flat-bed truck is a baby elephant still covered with rust-red dust; Little Red is safe and will be returned to his mother.

Detouring around several waterfalls and across a 100-foot pool, we rejoin the main road and enter the lushest vegetation in all of the safari, a place of giant bamboo, palm, and other big-leaf trees; we are near the heart of gorilla country and the start of the Pangani Forest Exploration Trail.

About the Safari

The trucks sit very high off the road and give good views; dedicated photographers will want to try to get one of the outside seats. No guarantee, but I found more action on the driver's side of the vehicle. There is a canvas awning overhead that provides some shade from the sun, but in heavy rain you can expect to get wet.

The safaris run all day until dusk, and you are likely to see different animals each time you travel. Be aware that most of the creatures are more active in the morning, often seeking cool shade for long siestas in the heat of the afternoon.

The Kilimanjaro Safaris are sure to be one of the major draws of Disney's Animal Kingdom, and they're likely to have long lines at certain times of the day. In the early days of operation of the new park, lines were as long as two hours at midmorning, but dropped to a reasonable 15 minutes at lunch time. My suggestion is to arrive early and ride the safari before the crowds form and while the animals are most active, and then come back again in mid-afternoon for a second pass.

The animals all perform their roles well, but for many visitors the unsung stars include Disney's landscaping crew. The trick was to find a way to simulate the wilds of Africa in an environment that includes moving safari trucks and free-ranging animals. Disney's planners laid out the plant bed lines using spray paint from a motorcycle moving at the same speed as the trucks because guests would experience the landscape at that speed.

The park's chief landscape designer took some horticultural tips from a wise old elephant while he was scouting Africa for savanna landscape materials; the animal grabbed some favorite snacking grass with its trunk and passed it over to the designer. The seeds from that eualopsis grass were eventually planted at Animal Kingdom.

The rutted safari road is also part of the landscape design. The Imagineering team matched concrete with the surrounding soil, then rolled tires through it and tossed stones, dirt, and twigs into it to create a bumpy, remote African road in the wilds of Walt Disney World.

This is central Florida, of course, and not central Africa and so some creative compromises were necessary. The seven distinctive baobab trees were re-created in concrete, and the towering acacias are actually 30-foot-tall southern live oaks given a carefully maintained crew cut.

🔳 Pangani Forest Exploration Trail

The end of the safari ride is also the beginning of the Pangani Forest Exploration Trail, where you can take a walk through the domain of two troops of lowland gorillas, observe hippos from an underwater viewing area, and get close to exotic birds in an aviary.

Highlights include close-up views of African mammals such as hippos (with an over- and underwater viewport); you'll also be able to see families of lowland gorillas through viewing windows in the gorilla observatory and from a swaying rope bridge that crosses lengthwise through a small valley. And you can spy herds of antelope from a thatch-roof observation station.

Many of the animals are too small or too shy to be seen from passing safari trucks and are instead presented up close along the trail. One

Snorkel-derms. Unless you've been to the continent of Africa, you might not know that elephants can swim. Most animal parks don't have pools big enough or deep enough. In Disney's African savanna, though, there are three pools 12 feet deep and 60 feet long where elephants can swim and even "snorkel," breathing from underwater through their trunks.

Tree farm. A Brazilian flowering tree named Markhamia normally grows as straight as a telephone pole in the rainforest. Grown from seed at the Animal Kingdom, the tree started out in a straight line until it reached a shade canopy above. Then it "turned on its blinker and made a sharp left-hand turn," said Paul Comstock, the park's chief landscape designer. The plant grew toward the light, then made another sharp turn toward the sky, ultimately resembling a giant stairstep.

Another of the trees in the "valley" of Pangani Forest is one with an exceptionally long Latin name: *Schizolobium parahybum excelsum*, better known as the flowering Bacurubu tree from Panama.

display shows cutaways into the burrows of naked mole rats—some of the most unusual creatures in the park. The creatures are actually not rats at all, but rather relatives of the common mole, with a unique organization similar to bees or ants with a queen who is the center of society.

Giant African bullfrogs hop around a lily-pad pool outside a wildlife research center that has interactive displays and maps. The various research areas include telescopes, video displays, and animal and bird spotting guides.

At the exit from the research office, you'll enter into a canopy of trees filled with 30 to 35 species of exotic tropical birds nesting among the palms and bushes. In pools below are many rare fish, including the colorful cichlid that is found only in Lake Tanganyika.

Moving across the aviary, you'll find another open air shelter that has a dam on the far wall with a large panel of inch-thick glass holding back the mill pond. The water is home to a trio of giant hippopotamuses and a pair of coal-black African cormorants; and the glass offers an unusual above- and under-water view.

Further along is a savanna overlook with a view of giraffes, tiny dik-diks, and other rare members of the antelope family grazing in knee-high grass.

Eventually the trail leads through a leafy canyon to the gorilla research camp. Here you will find research materials, displays, and experts who can answer questions. Just outside a large plate glass window a family of gorillas—two females and a silverback adult male—make their home. Disney hopes for the patter of little gorilla feet in the years to come.

Beyond the research camp, the path crosses a small canyon over a swaying suspension bridge to present another view of the gorilla family. On the other side of the bridge is another group of young male gorillas, part of a study of bachelor groups within the Gorilla SSP (Species Survival Plan), a program of the American Zoo and Aquarium Association.

The end of the trail leads to the Harambe station of the Wildlife Express train to Conservation Station.

Conservation Station

Wildlife Express to Conservation Station

The Wildlife Express departs from the East African Depot near Harambe. The colonial-style, narrow-gauge steam trains of the Eastern Star Railway offer a glimpse backstage at some of the nighttime homes for the animals and other veterinary facilities.

"Karibuni Harambe!" announces the conductor. "Welcome to Harambe." There's to be no drinking, no smoking, and "absolutely no cooking on board."

And while we're on the short trip, *"Kuwa macho wajangili!"* ("Keep a look-out for poachers!")

The puffing steam engines and open-air carriages hark back to old British railroads in the mountains and jungles of far-off colonies. For nearly 100 years, engines like these were shipped to South Africa, Rhodesia, and India to carry

European explorers and the native populations to mines, agricultural areas, and animal lands.

The passenger carriages are partially enclosed by waist-high, wood-louvered shutters; with carpetbags, boxes, crates, and wicker luggage are stacked high on the roof. The classic depot is patterned after the stucco structures with open air waiting areas built by the British in East Africa during the early 1900s.

The narrow-gauge (3.3-foot rail width) track was used in many areas where that design was easier to build along canyon walls and around horseshoe bends.

Three engines and two sets of cars were built in 1997 by the model-railroad firm of Severn Lamb in Alchester, England, a few miles from William Shakespeare's cottage in Stratford-upon-Avon. The company makes trains for parks located around the world, including one in use at Disneyland Paris.

Each five-car train seats 250 passengers on side-facing benches for the 1.2-mile circle tour that runs down a shallow valley between Africa and Asia. The tour offers a behind-the-scenes look at the modern animal care facilities, including nighttime shelters for lions, elephants, warthogs, and antelope herds.

On the return from Conservation Station, the train also offers some peeks into the Asia area of Animal Kingdom.

Train buff alert. The model for the engines at Disney's Animal Kingdom was discovered in the archives of the Indian Peninsula Railroad; they feature an unusual Aspinwall side-tank 2-4-2 design first built in 1898 at Horwich Locomotive Works in England. The stubby locomotives combine engines and tender in one car. Unlike the American-style engines at the Magic Kingdom with their bells and low-moaning whistles, the Wildlife Express' whistles sound like the scream of a wounded piccolo.

Although a handful of the 19th-century trains may still be operating in some isolated corners of the world, the Wildlife Express is believed to be the only train of its type now carrying passengers.

WOW Conservation Station

Conservation Station offers a backstage look at the veterinary headquarters and center for conservation programs at Disney's Animal Kingdom.

Located in the north side of the park near the edge of Africa, Conservation Station is reached by a short journey aboard the Wildlife Express train. From the depot it's a short walk through a jungle to a building dominated by a giant montage of animal faces, including those of the gorilla, elephant, lion, panda, wolf, turtle, baboon, and others. Just inside the building, in the Hall of Animals, another mural presents hundreds of other animals looking directly at human visitors. "The animals are looking *at* you and *to* you—the human species," says Dr. Jackie Ogden, curator. "Man represents both the greatest danger to the animals and their environment and the greatest hope."

Here guests can meet animal experts and learn about the behind-the-scenes operations of the park and how they can help the animals they have met.

Around the room are high-tech interactive computer displays and video observatories with a view into the park's veterinary operating room. Veterinarians may describe surgeries or procedures as they perform them; an attendant can relay questions and answers. The operating room includes blood analyzers, anaesthetic equipment, and EKG machines; it even has a laparoscope connected to an overhead television monitor so guests can see into the bodies of patients in certain surgeries.

Animal care experts are on hand to explain goings-on and to answer questions about many of the creatures. There are also regularly scheduled presentations allowing you to get up close and personal to live animals, including aardvarks, chinchillas, a miniature donkey, a golden eagle, goats, guinea pigs, rock hyrax, a great horned owl, porcupines, and rabbits.

To the right is Rafiki's Planet Watch, a giant screen that projects a world map spotlighting 11 areas of the world where animals are most threatened by destruction of habitats and the encroachment of human civilization.

Chow time. Food service for the 1,000 animal employees of Disney's Animal Kingdom is one of the more complex and demanding assignments in the park. Do *you* want to tell a 425-pound gorilla or a three-ton rhino that supper is late?

A full-grown elephant chomps down something like 125 pounds of hay and pelleted chow each day. Anteaters don't eat just ants—they prefer a mix of ants and grubs.

Giraffes have their own smorgasbord hidden high up in the re-created baobab trees: hidden 16-foot-wide turntables deliver a mix of bamboo, willow, and acacia shoots throughout the day.

The park includes an 8-acre "browse farm" to feed the animals with a stand of acacia, hibiscus, mulberries, and shrubs to replace natural forage for giraffes, gorillas, baboons, elephants, and antelope.

Nearby is Animal Cam, four sets of computer touch-screens that allow visitors to control cameras trained on some of the animal habitats. A video and computer system allows visitors to hear messages from well-known wildlife conservationists and to find out about ecological programs in their own backyards.

Research activities directed from the facilities include high-tech radio transmitters that allow scientists to track the movement of herds, and endocrine studies that let scientists check on the health of animals without disturbing them.

Next comes a series of rooms with large picture windows that allow visitors to peek in on baby mammal nurseries, brooder rooms for birds, reptiles, and amphibians, and veterinary laboratories and operating rooms.

Near the center of Conservation Station is the EcoWeb computer, where guests can learn about conservation efforts in their hometowns and around the world.

I don't usually make recommendations about visiting bathrooms, but you might want to take a side trip into the public facilities at Conservation Station; while you are attending to your business you can learn things such as the fact that an elephant pees as much as 20 gallons per day.

Affection Station

This is your basic petting zoo, done very nicely

in Disney style. Here you'll find such creatures as Nigerian dwarf goats, pygmy goats, rabbits, a miniature donkey, guinea pigs, Tunis sheep, plus live demonstrations featuring unusual and exotic animals such as llamas, porcupines, aardvarks, and lesser anteaters.

The animals have hideaways where they can escape over-handling from visitors.

There's a fanciful hand washer and dryer built into the snout of an elephant sculpture at the entrance.

Asia

As you cross the Asia Bridge, you enter the mythical Kingdom of Anandapur (place of delight), filled with the crumbling ruins of an ancient village, its temples, and even a maharajah's palace.

In many small ways, Anandapur is the most realistic and engaging area of the Animal Kingdom. We enter into a collage of Asian themes, including Nepalese, Indian, Thai, and Indonesian architecture, ruins, and animal carvings. A stand of trees grows from the ruins of a tiger shrine, and two massive monument towers—one Thai and one Nepalese—provide an idyllic setting for two rival families of gibbons who create a hooting racket all day.

The pathway from Harambe to Asia offers one of the best views of the Tree of Life.

Overall, this is a place to go slow and enjoy the scenery and the animals and the sense of place. Asia opened in the spring of 1999, almost a year after the rest of the park; plans call for continued expansion over the years, along the shores of Discovery River.

Humankind and animals have lived in relative harmony for centuries here in the rainforest. But today the lush Asian lands are in danger: fires are burning, trees are falling, and animals are losing their habitat. An environmental message about logging and development underlies much of this area.

〔WOW〕 Kali River Rapids

Aboard 12-passenger rubber rafts, adventurers zoom down the raging whitewater Chakranadi River through rapids and waterfalls and through dense jungles and into a modern-day parable about the effects of thoughtless development. Chakranadi is a Thai word meaning "river that runs in a circle."

Traveling into a huge bamboo tunnel, rafters are surrounded by a jasmine-tinged mist as they are lifted 40 feet to the river's headwaters.

The tour begins with a close-call with a geyser from the river bottom; if you're lucky you'll watch the people sitting opposite you take a surprise shower.

At the top of a climb, a giant carved tiger face peers from behind a waterfall. Gliding on through a rainforest and temple ruins, the raft emerges from a thicket of bamboo, and the smell of jasmine is lost to the acrid smell of smoke from burning trees. The raft twists and spins through the river, swollen by uncontrolled runoff from rain, the unpleasant result of environmentally careless logging.

Disaster narrowly avoided, more thrills await on a white-knuckle race through turbulent waters, some of the more energetic I've seen on a river raft ride. The large rafts move comfortably; take advantage of the dry storage section in the center of the boat for backpacks.

Depending on luck (and how heavily weighted down your raft is) you will end up somewhere between damp and drenched.

The setup to the ride has some lovely attention to details. The queue winds its way through a wooden temple; beyond the rails you can spot stone gods in the jungle. The counter at the entrance to the rapids holds a sign saying the owner is away, "gone to temple." The shelves are stocked with native guidebooks, and Kodak film in Indian-language packaging.

Speaking of queues: You can expect the water ride to be very popular on hot summer afternoons. I'd suggest heading there early or late on crowded days.

WOW Maharajah Jungle Trek

At the end of the river ride lies a trail through an Asian wonderworld, through temple ruins partially reclaimed by the jungle.

Komodo monitor dragons, which grow up to 12 feet long, perch on rocks near a stream bed. Across a wooden foot bridge are Malayan tapirs, families of bats, rare Asian birds, and other exotic creatures.

Tapirs are a strange black creature that look like a long-nosed pig wearing a gray Cardigan sweater. Related to the horse and rhinoceros, they are the most active in the early morning and late afternoon.

The ruins of a maharajah's palace are the home for a group of Bengal tigers. Beyond them lie a herd of blackbuck antelope and Elds Deer. The animals are visible from the top of a parapet, through a stand of bamboo, and from a bridge that stands amid the ruins near an old herb garden. On one of my visits, one of the tigers spent the morning swimming back and forth in a moat.

Gibbons let loose with hoots as they swing from a monument tower from Nepal to a Thai temple.

Near the end of the trek is a spectacular walk-through aviary, home to many species of ground-, mud-, and tree-dwelling birds. There's also a Bat-room, with visitors standing on the free side of an open wood grate with slats too wide for the creatures to pass through. (There's also a go-round for those too squeamish to face the bats up close and personal.)

Flights of Wonder at Caravan Stage

Birds swoop low over the audience gathered at Caravan Stage, a 1,250-seat amphitheater overlooking the Discovery River just across the bridge to Asia, on the outskirts of the expansion area.

Flights of Wonder demonstrates the skills of some of the world's most interesting birds, including falcons, macaws, vultures, hawks, and owls in a 25-minute show that is presented several times daily.

Here you'll meet Luke, the youngster whose discovery of a treasure map takes him back to the land of his ancestors, an Anandapur village in southern Asia. There's a cast of dozens of rare birds from at least 20 species.

And then there is the phoenix, the wise old bird of mythology who emerges from an explosion of fire and smoke to befriend Luke and, with the assistance of several trainers, reveals the wonders of birds.

The show is set in a crumbling fortified town in Asia, a centuries-old waystation on the fringe of the desert. The buildings are pockmarked to provide homes for some of the avian actors as they wait for their cues to perform. Others even fly from the top branches of the 145-foot-tall Tree of Life just on the other side of the Discovery River.

A Harris hawk or a Barbary falcon swoops down and swipes Luke's hat. Toco toucans catch grapes at 10 paces. A black-legged seriema, a large crane-like bird, body-slams a real-looking serpent. Tumbler pigeons do mid-air backward somersaults.

Other stars include a green-winged macaw, king vulture, Eurasia eagle owl, and moulacan cockatoo. At some shows, an augur buzzard flies out and lends a hand by scratching the head of the phoenix.

Although the presentation is carefully rehearsed, the birds are taught to show off their natural talent rather than perform tricks. Trainers demonstrate how birds respond to special audio or visual clues.

Casting will vary from show to show. At one performance, a troop of Indian runner ducks will dash across the stage on cue; another time the role might be taken by Abyssinian ground hornbills in flight.

Discovery River Boats

You can embark on a trip on the Discovery River from the Upcountry Landing just east of Harambe on the coast of Africa.

DinoLand U.S.A.

A celebration of America's fascination with all things dinosaur, this section of the Animal Kingdom looks like a quirky roadside attraction of the 1950s, complete with an old Airstream trailer, a Quonset hut, pink (plastic) flamingos, and other bits of dino-Americana.

It features the Boneyard playground, a rambling open-air dig site filled with fossils; kids can slide, bounce, and slither through the bones of Tyrannosaurus rex, triceratops, and other long-gone giants.

You will enter into the area beneath the skeleton of a 50-foot-tall brachiosaurus.

WOW Countdown to Extinction

Countdown to Extinction is housed within the "once-secret research project of the Dino Institute, built as a discovery center and ongoing research lab dedicated to uncovering the mysteries of the past." (Does this sound like Jurassic Park? More than a little, actually.)

Enter into the institute's rotunda, filled with murals, dioramas, and fossils telling the scientific theory of how the dinosaurs became extinct. A video starring Disney's in-house techno-geek Bill Nye explains that scientists now believe that an asteroid—six miles across and traveling 60,000 miles per hour—

Countdown to Extinction's cast of characters. Here is the dinosaur crew, in their order of appearance: Styracosaurus, Alioramus, Parasaurolophus, Raptor, Carnotaurus, Saltasaurus, Cearadactylus, Compsognather, and Iguanadon.

According to Disney Imagineers, the show was cast as if it were a movie, with a hero and a villain. The hero is the iguanadon, a plant-eating dinosaur large enough to make an impression anywhere he goes, but gentle-looking with a wise, beaked face.

Planners wanted to surprise visitors with a villain few had ever encountered in films, museums, or books: the carnotaurus. The name means "meat bull" and the creature matches its fearsome name with the blunt face of a bulldog, a gaping mouthful of savage teeth, and two huge horns. The creature in the show was based on a nearly complete skeleton of a carnotaurus that was uncovered recently in Argentina. The audio-animatronic version, though, is larger and even more fearsome than the real thing—that's show biz.

slammed into the earth in a fiery crash 65 million years ago at the end of the Cretaceous era. The resulting "nuclear winter" blocked the sun and dropped temperatures for several years, devastating plant life. Much of the planet's animal life, deprived of food, followed into extinction.

Guests are ushered into the briefing room (capacity 80 visitors) for a video conference with the institute's director, Dr. Helen Marsh. "I hope you enjoyed the quaint exhibits in the old wing," she says. "Today, that bare bones approach is history. The Dino institute has created the Time Rover—an amazing vehicle that can literally transport you to the age of the dinosaurs."

The idea is to transport guests back to the beginning of the Cretaceous era for a thrilling, but safe, excursion in Time Rovers for a romp amongst the dinosaurs. And, we'll all be whisked back to the present day well before that famous asteroid crashes into the planet. As Dr. Marsh promises, "The future is truly in the past."

Of course, nothing could possibly go wrong, right? Well, wait until you meet paleontologist Grant Seeker (nudge, nudge: Get the egghead joke?).

It seems that Seeker has a plan of his own: he wants to use the Time Rover—and us guests—to retrieve a living, breathing iguanadon. And to do so, he needs to send us very close to the end of the Cretaceous period. You know, when the asteroid is due.

Dr. Marsh is in charge, of course, and Seeker promises her the Time Rovers are properly programmed. But why is he winking at you?

Finally, we descend into the loading area for the 12-passenger Time Rovers, three rows of four seats. Buckle yourself into a seat and put your cameras and personal belongings into the pocket in front of you; you're going to need your hands to hold on tight.

And then we're off, into a cloud of fog and a blizzard of flashing lights . . . we're going back, back, back in time.

And suddenly we emerge into a sunless prehistoric forest, a place of strange insects and birds, and the honking and shrieking of giant beasts. As our Time

Rover climbs a small hill, the headlights reveal a styracosaurus. Nearby, an alioramus dines on a giant lizard.

As we move through the fantastic landscape, we can hear the voice of Grant Seeker as he helps us search for the iguanadon of his dreams. He doesn't seem all that concerned about the sudden hail of meteorites that is falling from the sky, smashing into the vehicle and making it swerve off the road . . . and directly into the path of a fearsome carnotaurus.

But wait! The big meteor is on its way. Will Grant Seeker manage to pull you back 65 million years to the Dino Institute before it hits the earth, or before you become a dino dinner? Everyone is going to enjoy the show, although some riders may find that the loud jumble of noises and flashes make the story a bit difficult to follow; others may find the ride itself a bit jarring.

As you stumble out of the institute and back to the present day, be sure to check out the security camera images near the exit; is that an iguanadon wandering the halls?

The CTX Rovers are versions of the vehicles used at Disneyland's Indiana Jones Adventure, Temple of the Forbidden Eye ride. The Rovers use a Disney-developed technology known as Enhanced Motion Vehicle, which controls the movement of the transport forward and backward, up and down, and side to side, as well as the sounds and some of the special effects of the ride. Each vehicle can stop, back up, slow down, or go faster based on computer decisions.

Guests must be at least 46 inches tall to ride, and pregnant women and visitors who have medical conditions are advised against travel.

The Boneyard

Not since the days of the dinosaurs has there been a playground like this: bones, fossils, and reconstructed dinosaur skeletons are everywhere. Children of all ages can dig in the sand to uncover the pieces of the past (returning them for other explorers). There's also a set of walkways, rope bridges, and slides that lead in every which way.

Cretaceous Trail

A walk through the past, where guests can wander through a garden of cycads, palms, ferns, and other surprising survivors from the age of the dinosaur, including soft-shelled turtles and Chinese crocodiles.

The cycad collection of more than 3,000 of the ancient fern-like plants is the third-largest in North America. It includes direct descendants of four botanical epochs of plant evolution dating back hundreds of millions of years, such as ferns, mosses, conifers, broadleaf plants, and the first flowering plants.

DinoLand U.S.A. features 20 species of magnolia, a flowering plant that dates back to the Cretaceous period.

WOW Tarzan Rocks at Theater in the Wild

A high-energy stage and rock show, based on Disney's *Tarzan* film. The show debuted in mid-1999, marking the first major change among attractions at Disney's Animal Kingdom. Tarzan replaced Journey Into Jungle Book, a musical show based on Disney's classic animated film, which in turn was loosely based on Rudyard Kipling's writings.

The 1,500-seat covered outdoor amphitheater is a nicely shaded setting. There's a good view of the developing Asia section of the park from the walkway to the theater.

Fossil Preparation Lab

One of the real stars of DinoLand U.S.A. is a display of a portion of "Sue," the largest, most complete skeleton of a Tyrannosaurus rex ever found.

Visitors will be able to watch staffers from the Field Museum in Chicago conducting painstaking preparation of the fossil bones for future assembly at the museum. Once that is complete, a life-sized replica of the 50-foot-long dinosaur will be created and displayed at Disney's Animal Kingdom. Two other replicas will tour the country, beginning in the year 2000.

The work at the Animal Kingdom will concentrate on the back legs and tail. Air abrasion is used to remove layers of stone and sediments.

The T-rex, 85 percent complete and including 350 bones, was uncovered in South Dakota in 1990 by fossil hunter Susan Hendrickson; it's her name the dino bears. Only 22 other T-rex remains have ever been found.

The skeleton was purchased in 1997 at auction by the Field Museum with support from Walt Disney World and other companies.

Chester and Hester's Dinosaur Treasures

A re-creation of a quirky roadside stand of the (believe it or not) pre-Disney era in America.

Camp Minnie-Mickey

Since the Disney empire did start with a mouse (and then his girlfriend, and then various dogs, ducks, and other creatures), it was obvious from the start that some of the most famous animals of our time would have an area of their own. (And yes, Goofy is a dog.)

Just across the Discovery River southwest of Safari Village, Camp Minnie-Mickey is a child's paradise of woodland trails and "meet-and-greet" pavilions, set in a Northeastern forest of cedar and birch trees.

🏆 Festival of the Lion King

Here's Disney's stagecraft at its best, a combination of Broadway, an indoor Disney parade, and a circus. Oh yes, there are also stiltwalkers, fire twirlers, singers, dancers, acrobats, and floats.

The theater is a 1,000-seat hexagonal timber structure. Guests are assigned to one of four triangular rooting sections: elephant, giraffe, warthog, and lion.

Giant stages move in from four directions to bring us up close to Simba and other animal heroes of *The Lion King*, along with singers, dancers, and acrobatic performers costumed in African tribal garb or dressed to depict exotic

African animals. The show opens with a rousing rendition of "I Just Can't Wait to be King."

A 12-foot-tall figure of Simba rises from Pride Rock. To the left is Elephant Waterfall, where a playful pachyderm spouts water from his trunk. Across the way is a pair of swaying giraffe heads. And nearby is a jungle mesa topped by Pumba and Timon.

> **Chairmen and chairwomen.** Benches and other furniture in Camp Minnie-Mickey were handcrafted by artisans from the Adirondack Mountains of upstate New York.

The unbilled stars of the show, though, are a troupe of acrobats who perform a comic—but impressive—routine on a trampoline and trapeze at center stage. A pair of adagio dancers performs to "Can You Feel the Love Tonight?" and the girl returns later in a flying harness to soar above the crowd. Kids from the audience are brought forth for a production of "Wimboweh."

The 28-minute show is performed eight times daily. Lines can build at midday; one strategy to avoid crowds is to visit the show early, or aim for a show that takes place near starting time for one of the two daily March of the Animals parades.

Pocahontas and Her Forest Friends at Grandmother Willow's Grove

Pocahantas takes the stage to help uncover the secret to saving America's forests and the creatures that live there.

With the help of Grandmother Willow—a spirit in a tree trunk—as well as a live armadillo, red-tailed hawk, skunk, boa constrictor, and several rabbits, Pocahantas and the audience learn that only humans can save the animals and the forest from civilization.

The 12-minute show is presented 14 times daily in a 350-seat amphitheater. Trees offer shade to part of the seats.

Character Greeting Area

The short hiking trails in the Character Greeting Area lead to kid-sized thrills:
- Mickey Mouse waiting in a rustic outdoorsy setting to give autographs and pose for photographs;
- Minnie and Goofy at the end of a trail beneath an arbor of vines and flowers, and
- Winnie the Pooh and Tigger, camped out in a grove of maples and oaks.

March of the ARTimals

The animals march daily through the paths of the Animal Kingdom. Don't expect to see hippos, elephants, and giraffes on parade, though; these are very strange creatures, ones that exist in the minds of very creative artists.

Before the march—and throughout the day—be on the lookout for the strange parade of the stilt birds, a troop of actors atop unusual metal and reed contraptions that seem a mix of ostriches, dinosaurs, and lawnmowers.

Beginning in Safari Village (entering from a gate between Pizzafari and the Creature Comforts shop), the march heads in a clockwise direction along the edge of Africa and Asia, nearby DinoLand U.S.A., and back to its starting point. The parade makes no stops along the way.

The art pieces worn as costumes by 55 performers represent prancing, bouncing, stilt-walking, and marching birds and animals. Most of the animals have their own distinctive whistle sound; the elephants play small saxophones, a reprise of a famous scene in Disney's *Fantasia*. The elements of the march include:

Oh, What a Tangled Web. Basket-woven ants, termites, beetles, spiders, and cockroaches dancing along to percussive rhythms; yes, of course, one of the tunes is "La Cucaracha" (The Cockroach). The spiders stand 11 feet tall; a puppeteer clad in black and hidden in the front of the creature controls eight stilt legs, while a second puppeteer moves the spider along.

Hop Sing Rides Again. With bullfrog lead singer Hop Sing, plus a quartet of toad tumblers, and a quintet Bolivian frog orchestra, tunes include bayou favorites "Jamabalaya" and "Louise."

Full of Light Under the Sea. Giant fish, seahorses, and a turtle on a bicycle, set to Cajun rhythms.

Busy Bees. Papier-mâché and brilliant paper-art cutouts create a swarm of bees around a rolling beehive, attended by a squad of playful Royal Jelly Bee dancers, worker bees, and a queen bee in royal Thai costume. The music includes "The Flight of the Bumble Bee."

Music Soothes the Savage Beast. A marching band like no other, with elephants on tuba, sax, and trumpet, an ape on piccolo, and a tiger on clarinet. A lion works the drums, accompanied by a gazelle troupe, playing tunes including "Elephant Walk" and "Hold That Tiger."

Carnival of the Animals Finale. Featuring fanciful metal sculptures that serve as a traveling montage of African animals. Bells, chimes, and metallic sounds perform "Dance of the Hours" and the "Carnival of the Animals Promenade."

Note: the entire parade takes as long as 30 minutes to make a complete circuit; if crowds are large you may find more space in areas late on the route. And the narrow roads in the park are completely blocked by the march, making it difficult to move from place to place until the animals have gone by.

One more note, though: the march will draw crowds away from the major attractions. This is a good time to visit the jungle safari or one of the shows or rides in the park.

Animal Kingdom's Top Ten

They're all stars, but here are ten of the most unusual and interesting creatures in the park:

• **Gerenuk.** An antelope with a pencil-thin neck, oversized ears, and delicate features, it stands on its spindly hind legs to feed on vegetation. Look for these other-worldly creatures on the savanna from Kilimanjaro Safaris or from the savanna overlook at Pangani Forest Exploration Trail.

- **Naked Mole Rat.** A homely, cold-blooded creature from Kenya and Ethiopia that lives in an underground colony centered around a queen, the only female in the colony capable of reproduction. Pink and virtually hairless, these members of the mole family seem to "moonwalk" along tunnels. A glass wall exposes the colony along the Pangani Forest Exploration Trail.

- **Marabou Stork.** It's been called the "world's ugliest bird" and it's not hard to understand why: it sports a pick-ax bill, two unsightly pouches, and a naked cranium that has scab-like spots. Standing as much as five feet tall, they were slaughtered in large numbers at the turn of the century for hat-makers who sought the downy feathers under their tails. One of the largest groups in North America can be seen on the savanna.

- **Okapi.** One of the largest mammals discovered in the 20th century, found only in the Ituri Forest of the Republic of Congo. Resembling a cross between a giraffe and zebra, it is a shy, solitary, and short-necked member of the giraffe family. They can be seen near the start of the Kilimanjaro Safaris tour, and from the Pangani Forest pathway.

- **Sable Antelope.** Large and aggressive antelope from southern Africa with scimitar-shaped horns that allow them to stand up to large predators, including lions. When at rest, they lie in a circular star pattern with their heads facing out and their young in the middle to protect them from predators. A herd of sable can be seen from the Kilimanjaro Safari.

- **Carmine Bee-Eater.** One of the most beautiful African birds, slightly more than a foot long with an iridescent turquoise head and a flaming carmine red body. It performs amazing acrobatics in pursuit of bees, one of its favorite foods. One of the largest flocks in North America can be seen in the aviary on Pangani Forest Exploration Trail.

- **Red Kangaroo.** This marsupial's unusual reproductive system allows her to have one offspring at foot while another nurses and grows in her pouch and a third is in the embryonic stage; she can produce two kinds of milk at the same time for these different-aged joeys. Boomers (males) are reddish in color, while females are bluish gray. They can leap distances of up to 40 feet, reaching speeds of 30 mph. A group can be seen in the Tree of Life area.

- **Ring-Tailed Lemur.** About the size of a large house cat, gray with a long black-and-white striped tail, they spend their leisure time sunbathing. One of the few primates that gives birth to multiple young, its horrific screaming is mostly bluster. A colony can be seen in the Tree of Life area.

- **White Rhinoceros.** Not really white—you tell him—but actually brownish-gray, its name comes from a mistranslation of the Afrikaans word for "wide," which describes the animal's upper lip. This creature, as much as three tons in weight, has been poached for years for its horn, which is used for ceremonial dagger handles in northern Africa and in Chinese folk medicine. Though they don't swim, they take dips to cool off. They can be seen from the Kilimanjaro Safari.

- **Black Rhinoceros.** More rare than white rhinos, these animals from eastern and southern Africa are also more aggressive. They use their hooked lip to grab the shrubs they eat. Fewer that 5,000 are left in the wild; like the white rhino, they have been poached for their horns. They can be seen on the savanna from the Kilimanjaro Safari.

According to Disney, most of the animals on display were born in zoological parks; others were rescued from endangered habitats or are orphans that have been saved by wildlife officials.

Eating Your Way Through Disney's Animal Kingdom

There are several interesting fast-food restaurants in the park as well as one sit-down restaurant, the Rainforest Café, near the entrance. You'll also find snacks that include dinosaur legs (well, OK, they're large turkey legs) in DinoLand U.S.A., fresh-baked cookies in an Adirondack-style cabin at Camp Minnie-Mickie, and ice cream bars that have the imprint of Simba's paw from stands throughout the park.

The park can be quite hot in the Florida sunshine; be sure to drink lots of water to avoid dehydration. Bottled water is available from vendors and there are free fountains in many locations.

And, unlike the Magic Kingdom, Disney's Animal Kingdom fully embraces alcohol. You can purchase beer in many of the restaurants, and there's even a house brand of wine at a bar in Harambe.

Rainforest Café

Somewhat hidden behind a 65-foot waterfall to the left of the entrance is a branch of the quirky Rainforest Café chain, the second outlet at Walt Disney World (the other Rainforest is at Disney Village). There are entrances from inside and outside the park. (You'll need to have your hand stamped and hold on to your ticket to re-enter the park; visitors coming just for the restaurant will have to pay for parking in the Animal Kingdom lot.)

The Rainforest Café was the only full-service restaurant at the park when it opened, and its operators were expecting long waits for lunch and dinner in its 575-seat dining room—as long as several hours. Reservations are not accepted, but arriving guests will be given a "passport" with an expected departure time for a dining "safari." Not coincidentally, a large gift shop lies between the check-in desk and the dining room, and your presence—and money—will be welcomed there while you wait. If your safari time is several hours in the offing, you could go back into the park.

There are other sights while you wait, though, including real parrots on perches below giant toadstools, giant cylindrical aquariums, and a bubbling water wall at the base of the juice bar. And you've got to love the stools at the bar—I wonder where the front halves of those animals went?

Safari Village

Pizzafari. Open-hearth oven pizzas, offered with unusual toppings. One of the more Disneyesque places in the park, the inside of the restaurant is nevertheless worth a peek; the walls are covered with animal murals and the ceiling is lined with colorful animal figurines. Small pies sell for about $5 to $6. Also available is a mesquite-grilled chicken Caesar salad. Open for lunch and dinner.

Flame Tree Barbecue. Wood-roasted meats with a choice of tomato-based or mustard sauces. The restaurant offers indoor seating as well as an outdoor dining pavilion along the river for lunch and dinner. The menu includes smoked beef brisket, pork shoulder, and turkey for about $7, and barbecued rib platters for $8.50.

DinoLand U.S.A.

Restaurantosaurus. A fast-foodery with a somewhat altered McDonald's menu, minus the golden arches. You'll find Chicken McNuggets, Happy Meals, french fries, plus hot dogs, sandwiches, and salads. Complete meals are priced at about $6.

A daily character breakfast starring Mickey Mouse, Donald Duck, Goofy, and Pluto is also presented here.

Africa

Tusker House Restaurant. Chicken cooked on the rotisserie, roasted, grilled, or fried, plus prime rib, lasagna, and roasted vegetable sandwiches with tabbouleh. The restaurant sprawls out onto a weatherbeaten outdoor patio. Open for breakfast, lunch, and dinner. Prices range from about $7.25 to $9.

Kusafiri Coffee Shop and Bakery. An attractive eatery that features warm cinnamon rolls, coffee, espresso, cappuccino, and other delicacies. Kusafiri is designed like an east African bazaar, with Arabic archways and ceilings draped in exotic fabrics.

DISNEY'S ANIMAL KINGDOM

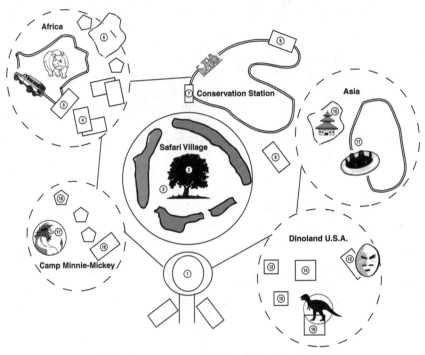

1. Oasis
2. The Tree of Life
3. *It's Tough to Be a Bug*
4. Harambe
5. Kilimanjaro Safaris
6. Pangani Forest Exploration Trail
7. Wildlife Express
8. Conservation Station
9. Flights of Wonder
10. Maharajah Jungle Trek
11. Kali River Rapids
12. Tarzan Rocks
13. The Boneyard
14. Fossil Preparation Lab
15. Cretaceous Trail
16. Pocahantas and Her Forest
17. Festival of the Lion King
18. Character Greeting Area
19. Countdown to Extinction

Chapter 10
Disney-MGM Studios

Let's go to the movies: The Disney-MGM Studios celebrates the magic of movies and television.

For several years, the park has been struggling to come out of the shadows of the splashier Magic Kingdom and Epcot. The first step was the installation of the **Twilight Zone Tower of Terror**, a spectacular journey into a story from the revered television show.

In 1999, the park came front and center with a whole raft of major new attractions: the **Fantasmic!** nighttime show, the **Rock 'n' Roller Coaster**, new shows including **Doug Live!** and **Sounds Dangerous**. And just to make things interesting, the Tower of Terror was reprogrammed to make it even more terrifying.

The idea behind Disney-MGM Studios is to allow guests to step into some of the greatest—or at least the most popular—movies and television hits of the 20th century. Not surprisingly, many of them are Disney hits, including *Beauty and the Beast, The Little Mermaid, Mulan, Toy Story, The Hunchback of Notre Dame,* and *Honey, I Shrunk the Kids.*

The overall theme of Disney-MGM Studios seems to be "Nothing is what it appears to be." This will be apparent from the moment you spot the park's distinctive Earffel Tower (a set of mouse ears atop a 130-foot-tall water tower) to when you first see the movie-realistic New York street scenes or see some of the inside magic of the studio production tours.

Also visible from the road is the Twilight Zone Tower of Terror, a creepy derelict hotel. It's fun to think of the Tower as a counterpoint to the squeaky-clean real hotels spread throughout Walt Disney World.

The Fantasmic! show is absolutely not to be missed. It is quite simply one of the best outdoor entertainments at any theme park anywhere.

The new **Rock 'n' Roller Coaster**, just off Sunset Boulevard, is Disney's first serious coaster in Florida.

Be sure to find time to stroll **Hollywood Boulevard** near the entrance-way—we suggest coming back to this area at midday when lines are longest at

MUST-SEES

Fantasmic!
(the best nighttime spectacular at Walt Disney World)

Rock 'n' Roller Coaster
(an outrageous coaster for thrill-seekers of all ages)

Twilight Zone Tower of Terror
(more white-knuckle drops than ever)

The Great Movie Ride

Star Tours

Sounds Dangerous
(eyes shut)

The Voyage of the Little Mermaid
(adults excused)

Doug Live!
(adults not wanted)

Honey, I Shrunk the Kids Movie Set Adventure
(adults won't fit)

Jim Henson's Muppet*Vision 3D 4D

Backstage Studio Tour

the attractions. The boulevard is a constant street theater. Pretty girls may be approached by "producers" handing out their business cards. Would-be actresses looking for work will give you the eye; vain stars will expect you to swoon at their feet. Actors perform skits and gags from old silent films. The street actors stay in character all of the time they are "on"; for fun, try asking one of them for directions, or some personal questions about their careers.

In recent years, Disney beefed up its shopping district on **Sunset Boulevard** to include a Planet Hollywood shop, joining the store already in place at the restaurant at Disney Village Marketplace.

The area now includes the four biggest draws at MGM: Fantasmic!, Rock 'n' Roller Coaster, Twilight Zone Tower of Terror, and the Beauty and the Beast show.

If you arrive late or are visiting on a crowded day, be sure to stop by the **Studios Tip Board** at the top end of Hollywood Boulevard. A chalkboard here will tell you how long the waits are for many of the attractions at the park; the hosts are kept up to date by walkie-talkie reports from head counters. You may need to alter your Power Trip based on unusual conditions.

One more note: the layout of the park seems to make it one of the hottest areas of Walt Disney World. Be sure to bring a hat and sunscreen lotion any time of the year.

How does Disney-MGM Studios compare to the other movie-themed park in town, Universal Studios Florida? In my opinion, the Disney operation—like everything within Walt Disney World—offers a more polished and better planned experience than almost anywhere else we know. Universal Studios is larger and has several rides and attractions that are unlike anything else at Walt Disney World, including the Twister, Terminator 2, Earthquake, and King Kong attractions. If you have the time, I suggest you visit both Disney-MGM and Universal; if you are on a very tight schedule and must choose between the two parks, I'd suggest Disney-MGM if you are with young children and Universal for older parties. Universal's new theme park, Islands of Adventure, has offerings for the very young, including Seuss Landing and Toon Lagoon, as well as some of the hairiest roller coasters for older kids of all ages.

Christmastime at MGM Studios

Speaking of wild fantasies, MGM is also home each Christmastime to the Spectacle of Lights show on its Residential Street and Washington Square backlot.

The display began as a private show that lit up the house of businessman Jennings Osborne; he—or at least his show—was eventually run out of Little Rock, Arkansas because of its electrical excess.

The street is open for strolling each evening from just after Thanksgiving through early January. The backlot tram tour ends early each day to allow pedestrians to walk around.

The rest of the park is hardly neglected. Live plantings of poinsettias line the paths, a giant set of mouse ears adorns the landmark "Earful Tower" near the road entrance to the park, and a spectacular Christmas tree occupies the plaza outside The Great Movie Ride.

Power Trip #1

For Adults and Adventurous Kids

Arrive early. This tour allows time for a quick fast-food lunch and a more leisurely dinner. Stop by the **Production Information Window** just inside the gates on the right side to see if there are any tickets for tapings of television shows.

Head up Hollywood Boulevard and turn right and head down Sunset Boulevard to the **Twilight Zone Tower of Terror**. If the lines are short and you are so inclined—if you can pardon that pun—check into the hotel again before the lines reach intolerable lengths later in the day.

Next stop for the brave is the **Rock 'n' Roller Coaster** in Studio 15 to the left of the Tower of Terror.

Once your stomach is back in its customary position, zoom out of Sunset Boulevard and back to Hollywood Boulevard; make a left at the first corner along Echo Lake. Note the Hollywood & Vine and '50s Prime Time Cafe as possible dinner stops; you may want to make a reservation as you go by.

The goal is **Star Tours**. (Pass by the Indiana Jones Epic Stunt Spectacular—it'll wait for later.)

After Star Tours, make a sharp left turn and head for **Jim Henson's Muppet*Vision 3D 4D**, a treat for all ages. While you're in the area, check out Mama Melrose's Ristorante Italiano, another interesting food stop, or the Sci-Fi Dine-In Theater Restaurant, a must-see eatery; make reservations early for these dining options.

The next stop is **The Great Movie Ride** at the top of Hollywood Boulevard. (Along the way, you have passed by Doug Live! and Sounds Dangerous.)

Continue moving in a counterclockwise direction through the archway to the studio section of the park.

It should be time for lunch now; the Soundstage Restaurant is in the studio area and is as good a fast-food stop as any other.

Go next to **The Magic of Disney Animation** tour; don't let youngsters talk you out of this visit—they'll enjoy the Peter Pan movie in the preshow and you'll want to see the artists at work.

At this point, you have visited all of the attractions that have the longest lines. Backtrack or continue in a counterclockwise direction to see shows such as the **Indiana Jones Epic Stunt Spectacular** (consult the daily schedule for show times), **Doug Live!** (for younger visitors) and the clever **Sounds Dangerous** for movie and Drew Carey fans.

Remember that crowds at many rides and restaurants will be shorter during the afternoon parade; check the schedule on the day you arrive.

And finally, you'll want to end your day at one of the nighttime showings of **Fantasmic!** On a busy day you may need to secure a seat as much as an hour before show time.

Power Trip #2

For Young Children and Adults Who Are with Them

This tour skips three rides that may be too wild for youngsters: Twilight Zone Tower of Terror, the Rock 'n' Roller Coaster, and Star Tours.

Arrive early. Make restaurant reservations for lunch or dinner. Then head up Hollywood Boulevard and go straight to **The Great Movie Ride.** When you're through, enter into the studio section of the park and join the line for the **Voyage of the Little Mermaid** stage show.

The next stop is the **Backstage Studio Tour.**

Now cross over the top of the park to visit the **Honey, I Shrunk the Kids Movie Set Adventure** and one of the outdoor stage shows such as the Hunchback of Notre Dame.

It's time to go inside for some inspired silliness at **Jim Henson's Muppet*Vision 3D 4D,** a treat for all ages.

Go next to **The Magic of Disney Animation** tour.

Depending on the ages of your children, you may want to visit the **Indiana Jones Epic Stunt Spectacular** (consult the daily schedule for show times, and be aware that there are some loud noises and flashes in the show), **Doug Live!,** and **Sounds Dangerous.**

And then end the night at **Fantasmic!,** a treat for all ages. Get there an hour early if the park is crowded.

Attractions at Disney-MGM Studios

 Fantasmic!

The fabulous Fantasmic! nighttime music, light, water, and animation show, which has been thrilling visitors to Disneyland in California for years, made its way east to the Disney-MGM Studio.

The show is presented twice nightly at a 6,500-seat amphitheater behind the Twilight Zone Tower of Terror off Sunset Boulevard. Half-circling a newly created 1.9-million gallon lagoon, the theater can accommodate another 3,000 standing guests, making it the largest amphitheater at Walt Disney World.

Fishy statue. Note the statue between the Studio Catering Co. and the Special Effects Tour. It's the actual mermaid fountain from the 1984 film *Splash.*

Under the baton of Mickey Mouse himself, the spectacular attraction features 50 performers and combines lasers, dazzling special effects, animation, and dancing waters synchronized to the melodies of beloved Disney classics. Three water mist screens are used to project Disney animation.

The 25-minute show takes guests inside the dreams of Mickey Mouse—into a world where his magic creates dancing waters, shooting comets, animated fountains, swirling stars, balls of fire, and other amazing wonders. When Disney villains intrude on Mickey's fantasy and turn his dreams into nightmares, he uses the power of good to triumph over the evildoers.

The show opens subtly, with a faint musical note in a darkened theater. As the music swells, a brilliant light bursts in the night sky, illuminating the entire island and casting a spotlight on Mickey Mouse. Mickey's imagination gives him the power make the waters dance as he conducts the musical score.

Next, an animated comet soars across the sky, sprinkling stars against a giant water-screen backdrop. Under Mickey's direction, the stars dance in unison to the "Sorceror's Apprentice"; as the stars burst forth in color, they transform into blooming floral images.

To the sounds of African drums and the chatter of wild animals, costumed animal characters emerge from behind the water screens to perform a version of "I Just Can't Wait to be King" from "The Lion King."

A cascade of bubbles fills the water screens for a medley of hits, including "Under the Sea." Old friend Jiminy Cricket rises up the screen, trapped within a bubble; Jiminy escapes only to find Monstro the whale in pursuit.

Love is in the air as we are visited by Pocahontas and John Smith, Cinderella and Prince Charming, Belle and beast, Aladdin and Jasmine, Ariel and Eric, and Snow White and her Prince.

The merriment fades rapidly with rumbling thunder and crashing waves. The Evil Queen from *Snow White* brews a magical spell amidst lightning, flares, and smoke effects. Her plan to defeat Mickey also involves classic Disney villains Ursula, Cruella, Scar, Jafar, Maleficent, Hades, and others to harness the positive energy of Mickey and turn it to evil. Mickey is terrified when Maleficent unexpectedly transforms into a 40-foot-tall dragon whose breath ignites the waterway into a sea of flames that overtakes the island.

But once again, it's Mickey to the rescue as the mouse rises high above the water, summoning forth a giant water curtain to surround the island.

The fountains begin to dance again, smothering the fierce flames while Mickey defeats the dragon. When MM triumphs, Tinkerbell heralds the arrival of the good guys, and the Steamboat Willie River Boat full of all-time favorites comes steaming around the bend.

Fantasmic! is sure to be a major draw at the theme park every night, which means two things: Get to the amphitheater early to claim a seat (the gates open 90 minutes before showtime), and if you're not going to the show, take advantage of the fact that thousands of people will be out of circulation and not on line at major attractions such as The Twilight Zone Tower of Terror.

There are no bad seats, although the best view is about 10 rows up from the water in the center of the amphitheater, roughly rows I through L. If it's a cool night and the wind is blowing from the stage, I'd recommend sitting a bit further back—the wind can carry some cold mist into the seats.

There's also no cover in the theater—the show will go on in light rain, but is likely to be canceled in heavier weather.

WOW Rock 'n' Roller Coaster. The Mouse meets hard-rockers Aerosmith for some bodacious partying at Walt Disney World's first serious roller coaster.

The coaster is hidden within a building styled to look like the other working soundstages at Disney-MGM Studios. Stage 15, we find, is the headquarters of G-Force Records. We enter beneath a 40-foot-long Fender guitar into the record company's lobby, beautifully decorated with details that include carved guitar-head columns.

Here's the buzz: the mega-rock group Aerosmith is in the house, recording a new song. Even better, this must be the VIP Tour, for we are ushered through the Artist's Entrance to the recording studio. Music blasts through the closed doors of Studios A and B, and then the door opens to Studio C. Alas, the recording session is over, but wait: there's the band listening to playback in the control room beyond. And they're happy to see us, too; what's a rock band without a following of frenetic fans?

But then a producer rushes in to tell the boys they're already late for a major concert across town. Time to go . . . but not without the fans. It's time to order up the largest, fastest limousine in town.

We step out of the studio and into a wonderfully seedy Hollywood alley, the back door to the Lock 'n Roll parking garage and the Down Under Club. The concert is about to begin and there is no time to waste; we're ushered into our stretch limo, a 24-passenger pink Caddy that shines with chrome. (There are six coaches, each with two rows of two seats.)

Before you've got the time to ask yourself, "How'd a nice person like me end up in a place like this?" your vehicle is launched into a traffic tunnel and the chase is on. And I do mean "launched." The coaster accelerates from 0 to 57 mph in 2.8 seconds. The takeoff is unusual because it is flat rather than up a hill; once the cars reach maximum speed they will climb up to the top of the building under their own momentum.

From there it's a wild trip through Beverly Hills, downtown Los Angeles, over the traffic jam intersection of I-10 and the 101, and through one of the "O"s of the HOLLYWOOD sign. The large signs and 30 sets are illuminated with black light.

All of this is accompanied, of course, by a rock 'n roll soundtrack performed by Aerosmith and blasted through 108 speakers in each train. (There are five different songs, so serious fans will have to ride at least that many times to hear all of the music.)

I visited the coaster during the final days of testing and was treated to an unusual view of the interior of the building with the lights on. The most amazing sight was the first climbing hill at the end of the launch tube—it heads almost straight up the rear wall; it's probably just as well that you won't have to see that stretch of track. At the top of the hill the coaster almost immediately goes into a double inversion. There's a third inversion a bit further along in the ride.

Disney is proud to point out that the coaster was not adapted to fit within an already-built structure. Instead, the tracks were designed and installed at the park and a building was put up around them. This is one reason, Imagineers say, the ride is as smooth as it is.

Disney planned to institute height minimums for riders of at least 48 inches, perhaps a few inches more. The coaster is located off Sunset Boulevard to the left of the Hollywood Tower of Terror.

WOW **Twilight Zone Tower of Terror.** Behold the mysterious Hollywood Tower Hotel, a relic of Tinseltown's golden age moved to Disney-MGM Studios, complete with a set of high-speed elevators guaranteed to fail on a regular basis.

The Tower of Terror was an instant hit when it opened several years ago; in the spring of 1999, Imagineers put into effect the third major reworking of the popular ride, ratcheting up the terror factor.

The ride begins with a launch skyward. There's a brief moment of panic when the cables of the elevator seem to snap in a shower of electrical sparks. The vehicle then plunges 13 stories, falling faster than the force of gravity. Then it lurches back upward, only to fall again and again.

I counted seven drops of varying lengths and intensity, including a final plunge that delivered a few moments of palpable weightlessness. I might have missed a few drops, too; it's not easy taking notes in a falling elevator.

Computer technology allowed ride engineers to make changes to the ride with adjustments to the software. According to Disney, engineers tested 33 versions to come up with the most exciting new variation. The amount of time in the elevator shaft is about the same as it was before the changes.

You'll approach the hotel across its beautifully landscaped grounds; if the waiting line extends outside the building, you are in for a lengthy wait.

Even before you enter the lobby of the abandoned hotel, there are signs of impending danger high on the side of the 199-foot-tall building: a sparking electrical sign hangs above a gaping hole in the tower walls. (The hotel is the tallest structure at Walt Disney World.)

Legend has it that an entire guest wing was once attached to that damaged wall. What happened to the wing? And more important, what happened to the people who were in the tower when it disappeared?

Well, you'll receive a not-too-subtle hint of what lies ahead as you see an out-of-control elevator cage plunge past you through exposed doorways high on the outer wall.

Once inside the hotel, you'll enter the lobby where you will see the concierge's table and the front desk. On the left side you'll see a dusty, interrupted mah-jongg game and a stack of newspapers from the 1930s. Many of the furnishings of the lobby came from old hotels in Hollywood and Los Angeles, including the famed Jonathan Club, an L.A. landmark built in the 1920s.

Eventually, you'll make it to the bellhop's podium where you will be assigned to one of the four libraries. (Warning: if you're prone to claustrophobia, you may feel uncomfortable in the library; then again, if the library scares you, then the elevator will definitely terrify you.)

The introduction begins in the darkened hotel library as a flash of lightning energizes a television in the corner. Our host, Rod Serling (long dead, but that doesn't matter in the Twilight Zone), tells the story of the dark and stormy night—Halloween of 1939, to be exact—when the guests disappeared from their elevator and stepped into a nightmare.

"This elevator travels directly to . . . The Twilight Zone."

When the lightning bolt struck, service in all the main elevators of the building were lost; only the creaky old service elevator still functions.

And then the library doors open to reveal the entrance to the hotel's basement, a creepy world of boilers, generators, and electrical boxes. It even smells like a basement.

There's another waiting line down in the basement; the line splits into left and right queues that head to one or the other of the two elevator shafts in the building. The rides are the same, although the shaft to the right offers a brief view of the park from the top, while the left shaft overlooks the Disney road system.

The cars seat 22 passengers with three rows. If you want to sit in the front row of the car, you'll need to camp out on one of the spaces marked 1 or 2 in front of the elevator; to snag the center seat on the top row—a seat with an unobstructed view and a seat belt instead of safety bar to hold you in place, you'll want to ask for seat four in Row 5. The elevator operator at the door may be able to help you with your choice.

The doors of the elevator will open on the first floor where you will see a happy family and bellhop suddenly struck by lightning; the view changes to a star field. Your car will move forward into the lights and the shaft.

When you arrive at the "fifth dimension" you will look out at what seems to be an elevator shaft. Wait a minute! Are you going up or sideways? And who are those people who seem to have hitched a ride in your elevator? They seem like ghostly doubles of you and those around you.

Finally, you are in the vertical elevator shaft in the most severely damaged part of the hotel; your cab rises up higher and higher. At each floor, you can catch glimpses of the happy theme park outside. At the very top, you will reach the damaged elevator motors; they are sparking and flashing ominously.

The door opens for a view of the park—guests down below will be able to see the elevator cab hanging in space for a few seconds.

The elevator cab is actually driven downward by high-power motors so that it travels faster than it would in free-fall. The rest of the way down, the cab travels in what the engineers call controlled deceleration. That means putting on the brakes. And, by the way, the drop is advertised as a 13-story drop but the top floor is the twelfth. Ah, but you got on the elevator in the basement.

How good is the ride? Well, it definitely is worth a **WOW** in this *Econoguide*. But it is a very short experience once you are in the elevator, about two minutes with just ten seconds or so of drop. Personally, I love the ride but I work real hard to avoid waiting in line for two hours for ten seconds of thrill.

On busy days, be sure to get to the park early and ride the Tower of Terror immediately, especially in the summer and in holiday periods. On one of my visits in March, the official opening hour for the Disney-MGM Studios was 9 A.M. but the gates opened at 8:30 A.M. and people poured into the park. We were on the ride by about 8:40, off by about 8:45, and back on ten minutes later. By 11 A.M., the wait was up to nearly an hour. But during the midday parade, the lines fell away and the wait was a reasonable 10 minutes.

WOW **The Great Movie Ride.** A celebration of some of the most famous movies of our time within a reproduction of the famous Mann's Chinese Theater in Hollywood.

The interior of the Chinese Theater is a bittersweet reminder of how full of marvel were the grand theaters of the early years of movies and how ordinary are our local quintupleplex mall theaters. In the lobby, you'll find what may be the world's most expensive slippers: Dorothy's ruby shoes from the 1939 MGM classic *The Wizard of Oz*. You'll also find a carrousel horse from the 1964 *Mary Poppins* movie, and a portion of the set from the 1979 *Alien* film.

Your first stop is a waiting area in a theater that is continuously showing original trailers from some of the most beloved movies of all time, including *Singin' in the Rain, Fantasia, Footlight Parade* with Jimmy Cagney, Joan Blondell, and Ruby Keeler, and a stark preview of *Alien*. You'll go within all of those movies and more in the ride to come.

Your moving auditorium will be presided over by a host or hostess who will narrate the tour. The excitement begins soon, when your leader will be hijacked by a 1920s gangster or a Wild West desperado (depending on which set of seats you are in). Don't worry, though: the good guys will prevail later on in the ride.

The heart of darkness. The spaceship that is invaded by a murderous alien—the most chilling scene of the Great Movie Ride—was named "Nostromo." That name comes from a 1904 book by the Polish/English novelist Joseph Conrad, who spent much of his early life as a seaman on a succession of freighters.

In addition to the West and old Chicago, you will visit a re-creation of the "By a Waterfall" scene (with more than 60 Audio-Animatronic dancers) from

Going my way?
The Great Movie Ride brings to Disney-MGM the same "moving theater" cars first introduced at the Energy pavilion at Epcot.

Fly it again, Sam.
According to the Hollywood myth-makers, the Lockheed Electra 12A on display in the *Casablanca* set was actually used in the real movie, a happy accident.

Busby Berkeley's *Footlight Parade*. You will also travel into and through the Nostromo spaceship, home of the Alien himself; an extended *Raiders of the Lost Ark* set, including wriggling robotic snakes; the jungle world of *Tarzan;* Mickey Mouse's *Fantasia;* and finally a drive down Oz's Yellow Brick Road.

The last stop on the ride is a high-tech theater that will surround you with the sound and images of a well-done short film with some of the best-known scenes of all time. See how many stars and films you can recognize as they fly by.

The lines for this attraction build at midday. If the lines extend outside of the building, we'd suggest you come back at another time; there is still a lengthy queue within the theater. The ride itself takes about 20 minutes once you're seated.

The ride is worth a visit, although it has remained essentially frozen in time since the Disney-MGM Studios park opened; it could use a freshening.

The sidewalk outside the ride includes hand- and footprints from all sorts of celebrities minor and major. Look carefully to find Pee-Wee Herman, dated 1984, before he became persona non grata at Disney. Leonard Nimoy's handprint gives the V-shaped Vulcan "Live long and prosper" salute.

WOW Doug Live! The Beets are coming to town, but Doug is worried that his beloved Patti may go to the concert with Roger. Will love conquer all? Will Quailman and Quaildog triumph over the evil Dr. Rubbersuit? Do you have any idea what I'm talking about here?

If you do, then you are either a preteen, or hang around one. This musical stage show, based on the ABC Television show "Doug," follows 12-year-old Doug Funnie, his dog Porkchop, best friend Skeeter, secret crush Patti, and class bully Roger through the ups and downs of preteen life.

It's a lively and fun show for kids, with a talented group of young singers and actors, along with an onstage rock group drafted from audience members. The characters move in and out of doors in the screen.

The message of the show: Be yourself. "That's a cool theme," says Doug. "Why do you think they call this a theme park?" answers Patti.

Outside the building, you'll find the **Academy of Television Arts and Sciences Hall of Fame Plaza** honoring television legends. The Academy was founded in 1946, the same year network television was born; the real Hall of Fame is located at the Academy's headquarters in Hollywood. Plaques in Orlando honor Red Skelton, Bill Cosby, Mary Tyler Moore, Sid Caesar, Rod Serling, James Garner, Andy Griffith, Milton Berle, Danny Thomas, Barbara Walters, Carol Burnett, and, of course, Walt Disney.

WOW ABC Sound Studio: Sounds Dangerous. How better to demonstrate the power of audio in storytelling than to take a whole audience of visitors and lock them up in the dark . . . with a high-tech stereo and 3-D sound system, that is.

That's the idea behind Sounds Dangerous, starring comedian Drew Carey as a bumbling police detective.

Everything starts out like your basic television sitcom, with Drew in search of a smuggling ring. He's equipped with a hidden video camera and he's in broadcast communication with headquarters. Ah, but something goes wrong and the video camera shuts off . . . and we're all left in the dark. Very dark, actually; there's barely a peep of light in the auditorium.

Ah, but we can still hear Drew in our headphones and we learn the entire story from his description and some truly amazing sound effects. Have you ever experienced a haircut and shave in the dark? There's a trip to the circus—watch out for those elephants. And then there is that jar full of killer bees; you don't suppose the glass will break, do you? Can you imagine the sound?

Justice triumphs, and the smuggling ring is unmasked. It's all a clever lesson in how important a role sound plays in movies and television.

Outside of the theater is an interactive playroom where you can experiment with some of the arts of movie sound, including a Foley stage for sound effects and computer stations where you can put your own voice or noises you select into a classic Disney cartoon.

> **Sounds like . . .** The Foley Stage is named after the acknowledged creator of the Hollywood sound-effects stage, Jack Foley. The same sort of devices were used in adding sounds to live radio dramas of the 1930s and 1940s.
>
> The work of the audio engineer is known as "sweetening" and includes the use of sound filters, the addition of echo, and the inclusion of sound effects.

Indiana Jones Epic Stunt Spectacular. A huge covered outdoor theater, but it still fills up within 10 or 15 minutes of afternoon showtimes, even earlier on busier days. It's a good place to park at the busiest, hottest times of the day. The best seats are in the center of the theater; they are filled first and it is from this section that the "casting director" usually selects a dozen or so "extras" to participate. All must be over the age of 18; there's a ringer among them—see if you can spot him or her. The extras don't have an awful lot to do.

The stunt show starts with a real bang as a double for Indiana Jones rocks and rolls across the huge stage; most of the later actions rely less on mechanisms and more on the skills of the stunt actors. It's a 30-minute world of Nazis, Arab swordsmen, fiery explosions, and bad jokes.

WOW Star Tours. "Whenever your plans call for intergalactic travel," say the travel posters, "please consider flying Star Tours to the vacation moon of Endor."

Disney builds the atmosphere and excitement beautifully from the moment you walk beneath the huge space machine outside; it continues as you walk through the indoor waiting area that simulates a gritty space garage. Our favorite flaky robots, R2D2 and C3PO, are the mechanics.

Most of the queue for Star Tours is inside the building; if visitors are lined up outside the building onto the plaza, you've got about a 45-minute wait; if the line extends outside and into the covered space "forest," you might want to plan your expedition to Endor for later in the day.

Another big adventure. The original voice of the robot pilot at Star Tours was none other than the exceedingly strange Paul Reubens, also known as Pee-Wee Herman. After Pee-Wee was, err, exposed as someone a bit out of the Disney mold, a new (less interesting) voice replaced his.

When your time comes, you will enter a 40-passenger simulator cabin and meet your pilot, Captain Rex. The doors will be closed and your seat belts tightly cinched before he informs you that this is his first trip. Too late—you're off. You'll make an uneasy takeoff and then blast (accidentally) into and through a frozen meteor, stumble into an active intergalactic battle zone, and finally make a wild landing at your goal, the vacation moon of Endor.

This is quite a wild ride, at about the same level of twisting, turning, and dipping as the Body Wars show at Wonders of Life in Epcot Center. It's a short ride, but a bit rough for the very young; pregnant women and those with health problems are advised to sit this one out.

After the ride, note the travel posters for other Star Tour destinations, including lovely Hoth and Tatoine.

Disney insiders say a new film is in the works for the attraction.

WOW Voyage of the Little Mermaid. This is presented throughout the day at a theater that includes all sorts of bits and pieces of Disney magic, including snippets from the movie, more than 100 puppets, lasers, holographic projections, live performers, and Audio-Animatronic robots. The 15-minute show can draw huge lines on a crowded afternoon; it is presented 22 times a day. If this film is a favorite of your youngsters, you would do best to head there early. Very young kids may become a bit startled by some of the special effects; prepare them ahead of time.

At the start of the show, the curtain becomes running water, and laser beams overhead create the effect of descending beneath the waves. Especially enchanting is the opening sequence of black-light puppetry.

Beauty and the Beast Live on Stage. Off-off-Broadway, this 20-minute live-action show at the outdoor Theater of the Stars showcases live performers in fanciful and spectacular sets, costumes, and special effects.

All of your kid's favorite characters—and your own—are there: Belle, Gaston, Lumière, and Mrs. Potts among them. Check the daily entertainment schedule for times.

Hunchback of Notre Dame. A 32-minute stage spectacular based on Disney's cartoon of the same name, presented at the Backlot Theater near the Muppet*Vision show.

WOW Honey, I Shrunk the Kids Movie Set Adventure. A most inventive playground based on the hit movie about a mad inventor whose shrinking ray accidentally reduces his children and a few friends. Play areas include giant cereal loops, ants, spiders, a huge roll of film, and a leaky garden hose. The ground is carpeted in a spongy rubber.

It's a great place for youngsters to burn off some energy; be advised, though, that it is quite easy to lose a child in the playground. The best strategy is to station an adult by the single exit from the playground, rather than chasing through the various adventures.

WOW Jim Henson's Muppet*Vision 3D 4D. We have to admit that we passed by this attraction the first few times we brought our kids to the studios—Bert and Ernie and Kermit the Frog seemed a bit too silly, even for an 8-year-old. Were we ever wrong!

The fun begins once you enter the theater, which is designed as Muppet World Headquarters. Pause just inside the entrance to read the office directory on the wall. Listings include the Institute of Heckling and Browbeating—Statler and Waldorf, Curmudgeons-in-Chief; the Sartorial Accumulation Division, run by Miss Piggy, of course; and the Academy of Amphibian Science, under the tutelage of Kermit the Frog. The security desk at the door advises that the guard will be back in five minutes, but the key is under the mat.

The preshow area for Muppet*Vision includes a wonderfully goofy collection of packing cases with equipment for the Muppet Labs (Tongue Inflators, Gorilla Detectors, and Anvil Repair Kits) and roadshow suitcases for the Muppet band, Dr. Teeth and the Electric Mayhem, including paisley bell bottoms, Nehru jackets, Beatles boots, and love beads. There's a big pink trunk that bears the label, "Miss Piggy Satin Evening Gowns"; below that is "More Satin Evening Gowns," and finally, "The Rest of the Satin Evening Gowns." Another favorite: a cargo net filled with orange and green cubes and labeled "A-Net-Full-Of-Jello" in a tribute to original Mouseketeer Annette Funicello.

But the real fun is within the beautiful 584-seat theater, which is decidedly more opulent than your neighborhood quintupleplex. There's a robotic all-penguin orchestra in the pit (they took the job just for the halibut) and a private box at the front for Waldorf and Statler. The film includes some marvelous 3-D special effects, as well as flashing lights, a bubblemaker, smell-o-vision, and a surprise from the skies, as well as a live actor and a cannon.

Don't pass this extraordinary multimedia show by. If you don't have a kid with you, you can pretend you're with the ones in front of you in line.

And when you leave, be sure to check out the statue outside: It's Miss Piggy as the Statue of Liberty.

WOW Backstage Studio Tour. Disney-MGM Studios is a working movie lot, and the backstage shuttle tour is a great way to see some of the real—and not-so-real elements of moviemaking. Films and TV shows under production vary, but have included in recent seasons *Star Search*, *Mickey Mouse Club*, professional wrestling shows, and bits and pieces of major films, including *Honey, I Blew Up the Baby* and the HBO Films series *From the Earth to the Moon*.

The tour now begins with a visit to the Water Effects Tank. This pool, home of the *Miss Fortune* tugboat and other miniature or partial boat sets, demonstrates how technicians use fans, explosions, and a 400-gallon splash tank to re-create a raging storm and a battle at sea. Two volunteers from the audience will get to play captains courageous.

From there it's onto a walk through a portion of the prop warehouse. Signs indicate some of the more recognizable objects; pay attention to the little tags on some of the items on the shelves for clues to the more obscure.

The large trams run continuously, and lines are generally short in the morning and late in the day. Remember this: the left side of the cars (the first person into each row) is the wet side, no matter what the guide says at first. (Not very wet, by the way—more of a splash than a soaking.)

As you pull out of the tram station, you will first pass by the **Car Pool,** which includes some of the vehicles used in your favorite movies. In recent years, the lot has included a futuristic vehicle from *Blade Runner* and an assortment of gangster cars from *The Untouchables* and *Dick Tracy.* The trams next pass through the **Costuming** shops.

Carpenters and designers at the **Scenic Shop** construct just about anything and everything for the movies; you'll also glimpse the huge stock of lighting fixtures for filmmaking. The interior of the 747 was used for scenes in *Passenger 57*; it is part of an actual plane retired from the Delta Airlines fleet.

The backlot of Disney-MGM Studios includes a **Residential Street** that has some familiar sights—you may recognize the homes from *Golden Girls, Empty Nest,* and other television and movie settings. These are empty shells, of course, and are used for exterior shots; interior filming is performed within soundstages in California or elsewhere.

At the end of the street, you'll make a right turn past the **Boneyard,** home of some of the larger props from former movie productions. Look for the trolley from Toontown in *Who Framed Roger Rabbit* and the UFO from *Flight of the Navigator,* among other props. A recent addition is a Gulfstream airplane owned by Walt Disney and used in 1964 during the scouting for land for Walt Disney World in Florida.

Two pants, one jacket. Tailors at the costume shop make as many as 12,000 costumes a year. Disney claims the world's largest working wardrobe, with more than 2.5 million items available. Among articles on display is a hot red dress from *Pretty Woman* and Michael Jackson's "Captain EO" suit.

And finally, it is on to a demonstration of large-scale special effects in the area known as **Catastrophe Canyon,** which simulates a working oil field in a narrow desert canyon. We won't spoil the fun except to point out that the "set" includes hydraulic shaker tables, a series of tanks storing 70,000 gallons of water, and flames, and explosions, and . . . .

The tour includes a stop at the AFI Showcase, honoring American film heritage. Presented by the American Film Institute, the Showcase includes rare movie artifacts and memorabilia, a video wall, and exhibits on the careers of AFI's 25 Life Achievement Award recipients.

Among the many pieces of movie history that have been exhibited are Rosebud, the sled from *Citizen Kane*; Humphrey Bogart's suit from *The Maltese Falcon*; the cheesy little miniature saucer used in the 1955 sci-fi classic *The Day the Earth Stood Still*; and sketches from *Toy Story.* The Showcase will also feature displays on film preservation and the many disciplines of filmmaking taught at the AFI Conservatory, including directing, producing, editing, cinematography, screenwriting, and production design.

Funds raised from sale of items at the Showcase will go to AFI's preservation efforts, such as the restoration and distribution of the newly discovered 1912 film *Richard III*, the oldest surviving American feature film, found in the basement of a Portland, Oregon, home where it had languished untouched for some 30 years.

Lines build by midday; come early or late in the day to avoid a long wait.

Sorcery in the Skies. With the debut of Fantasmic!, the popular laser and fireworks show, choreographed to classical and Disney music (which are not the same), was put on hold. Disney officials said it might be brought back as a special event or in peak season when the park is open late. The finale of the show included a gigantic inflatable Mickey dressed as the Sorcerer's Apprentice. The best view of the show was from near the Chinese Theater, but you could also see the fireworks and hear the music from the parking lot—a good place to beat a quick getaway with the kids.

Fill 'er up. The oil field at Catastrophe Canyon bears the markings of Mohave Oil, a fictitious company that is also represented at the old-timey Oscar's Super Service Station on Hollywood Boulevard.

Movie souvenirs. If you are a movie fan, Sid Cahuenga's One-of-a-Kind shop near the entrance gate at Crossroads of the World offers large color posters for many classic movies from Disney, MGM, and other studios (we found *Bambi*, *Sleeping Beauty*, and *Pinocchio* for about $15 each). Also available are small lobby cards for about $3 and even original press kits for major motion pictures.

Eating Your Way Through Disney-MGM Studios

Disney-MGM Studios includes some of the more interesting eateries at Walt Disney World. Be sure to check when you arrive for Early Value Meals offered at some of the restaurants, and for special meal deals for youngsters.

🍴 **ABC Commissary.** A large fast-food cafeteria offering basic fare that includes burgers, large hot dogs, chicken breast sandwiches, and stir-fry chicken, prices range from about $4 to $5. Children are offered hot dogs, chicken strips, and more for about $4.

🍴 **Starring Rolls Bakery.** A small bakery almost hidden along the right side of the Brown Derby. A good place to stop for a quick breakfast, or anytime during the day for dessert. Offerings include bagels, small loaves of bread, croissants, pastries, donuts, muffins, and cheesecake, prices range from about $2 to $4.

🍴 **Min and Bill's Dockside Diner.** On Echo Lake, near SuperStar Television. Belly up to the hatchway in the S.S. *Down the Hatch*, moored at a dock on the studio pond. Snack offerings include nachos with cheese, fruit cup, danish, soft yogurt, and ice cream sodas, prices range from about $2 to $3.

🍴 **Dinosaur Gertie's Ice Cream of Extinction.** Across from the Indiana Jones Epic Stunt Spectacular. Cold treats from within the belly of a dino,

KEY:

🍽 = Fast food

🍸 = Pub

🏛 = Full-service
      restaurant

or so it appears. Some of the same items can be purchased from wagons around the park. The eatery's name is a tribute to Gertie the Dinosaur, one of the first animated cartoon stars; Gertie was a big hit in 1914 in vaudeville shows.

🍽 **Backlot Express.** In the Studio Shops between Star Tours and the Indiana Jones Epic Stunt Spectacular. An interesting setting for a burger and hot dog fast foodery, set among the props of the Studio Shops. Offerings include charbroiled chicken with flour tortillas, burgers, hot dogs, chili, and chef's salad, prices range from $4 to $7. Make good use of the condiment bar, which includes about two dozen toppings.

🍽 **Studio Catering Co.** Off the streets of New York, next to the *Honey, I Shrunk the Kids* playground. It's an outdoor fast-food restaurant under a corrugated tin roof. Just outside is an ice cream and sundae bar.

🏛 **The Hollywood Brown Derby.** At the end of Hollywood Boulevard, near the entrance to the studios; this is one of the nicer restaurants within any of the Disney theme parks. The Brown Derby was the "in" restaurant and night spot of Hollywood in the 1930s. Owner Bob Cobb reportedly told his friends that food was all that mattered—in fact, he said, his menu would be so good that people would eat out of a hat. So he built his restaurant in the shape of a derby.

A replica of the Hollywood landmark, featuring an art deco interior and drawings of stars on the walls. Lunch includes the famous Cobb salad introduced at the original Brown Derby, as well as corned beef and cabbage, and pasta with seafood; prices range from about $9 to $18. Dinner entrees include peppercorn-crusted tuna with balsamic syrup, sautéed grouper, rack of lamb, and tomato-garlic penne, prices range from about $15 to $24.

🏛 **Hollywood & Vine Cafeteria of the Stars.** At Hollywood and Vine, on the main gate side of Echo Lake. An old-style cafeteria that offers a hot table and an art-deco interior. Offerings include Back Lot Ribs, Casting Call Catfish, and Cahuenga Chicken, for about $9 to $11.

🏛 **'50s Prime Time Café—Tune In Lounge.** Along Echo Lake, near the Indiana Jones Epic Stunt Spectacular. Step right into a kitchen of the 1950s; Mom will greet you at the door, and your waitress will stand by to make sure you clear your plate. Luncheon appetizer offerings include Mom's Chili over angel hair pasta for about $4, Dad's Bachelor Chili for about $2.50, and fried zucchini for about $3. Entrees include Magnificent Meatloaf, Chicken Pot Pie, Granny's Pot Roast, and the All-American Burger, for about $8 to $15.

Dinner offerings include Auntie's Roasted Lamb and a charbroiled T-bone steak, prices range from about $13 to $23. Book reservations early.

🏛 **Mama Melrose's Ristorante Italiano.** In the streets of New York near the Muppet*Vision theater and Star Tours attractions. A very attractive eatery, filled with the enticing smells from the wood-fired pizza oven.

"Tutta La Pasta Che Puoi Mangiare" (all the pasta you care to eat) costs about $10.50; grilled tenderloin of beef goes for about $14. Other offerings include fresh fish, vegetable lasagna, and chicken marsala. Your basic (small) pizza sells for about $9.50 and is available in basic, Italian combo, four-cheese, chicken, and pesto varieties, among others. There are also vegetarian, ham, Mexican, and other varieties. The child's menu includes spaghetti, pizza, hot dogs, and chicken strips, for about $4 to $6. There are 292 seats available, but things can become quite hectic between 1 and 3 P.M. Reservations are accepted.

Disney's Toy Story Pizza Planet Arcade. A pizza parlor with a collection of the latest in video games—or is it the other way around? Located near the entrance to Star Tours.

Sci-Fi Dine-In Theater Restaurant. Behind Monster Sound and across from Star Tours. Ya gotta see this place—it's a must-see eatery, among the most unusual settings of any restaurant anywhere. Each group of diners is shown to their table—inside a little convertible—by a parking attendant. Each four-seat car with a 1955 license plate faces a large drive-in movie screen showing coming attractions for weird and wonderful science fiction movies of the 1950s and 1960s. Reservations are essential.

On a recent visit, the films included *Cat Women of the Moon* starring Victor Jory, *Devil Girl from Mars* (a creature without mercy), *The Horror of Party Beach* (teenagers, beach, rock 'n' roll, bikers, and atomic monsters) and Peter Graves in *It*, and the original trailers for *Attack of the 50 Ft. Woman*. (The girl in one of the horror films says to the guy she is with, "I expected to be frightened on my wedding night, but not like this.")

The reel of trailers also includes a few newsreels; it runs about 45 minutes before repeating itself, which is enough time to order, eat, and leave.

All in all, the Sci-Fi Restaurant is a hoot. The food is appropriate for a drive-in theater—very ordinary, but that's not really the reason you came.

Luncheon offerings include Journey to the Center of the Pasta, Attack of the Killer Club Sandwich, Return of the Killer Club Sandwich, Revenge of the Killer Club Sandwich, and Beach Party Panic (filet of fish, of course), prices range from about $8 to $12. At dinner, look for some of the same dishes, plus Red Planet (linguine and tomato sauce) and Saucer Sightings (a rib-eye steak), priced from about $10 to $17.

Sunset Ranch Market. As you rush to or from the Twilight Zone Tower of Terror, don't overlook the attractive outdoor eatery on Sunset Boulevard. Included in this area is **Rosie's Red Hot Dogs**, **Catalina Eddie's** frozen yogurt stand, and **Echo Park** and **Anaheim Produce** fruit and vegetable stands. The market is a tribute to the famed Los Angeles Farmer's Market.

Another Magic Kingdom?

Magician David Copperfield, who has seemingly made the Statue of Liberty disappear, has seen his hopes to make a magical restaurant showplace appear near the Disney-MGM Studios fade because of financial difficulties. **Copperfield Magic Underground** was to be a $30 million marvel, with entrances from inside and outside the Disney-MGM Studios.

It remains to be seen whether the plans can be brought back from the dead.

DISNEY-MGM STUDIOS

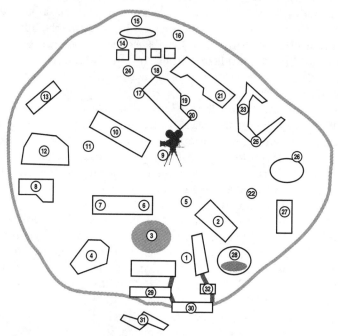

① Hollywood Boulevard
② Beauty and the Beast Live on Stage
③ Echo Lake
④ Indiana Jones Stunt Spectacular!
⑤ Plaza
⑥ Doug Live!
⑦ ABC Sound Studio: Sounds Dangerous
⑧ Star Tours
⑨ The Great Movie Ride
⑩ Honey, I Shrunk the Kids
   Movie Set Adventure
⑪ New York Street
⑫ Jim Henson's Muppet∗Vision 3-D-4-D
⑬ Hunchback of Notre Dame
⑭ The Backlot
⑮ Catastrophe Canyon
⑯ Residential Street

⑰ Inside the Magic
⑱ Soundstage I
⑲ Soundstage II
⑳ Soundstage III
㉑ Production Center
㉒ Sunset Boulevard
㉓ The Voyage of the Little Mermaid
㉔ Backstage Studio Tour
㉕ The Magic of Disney Animation
㉖ Rock 'n' Roller Coaster
㉗ Twilight Zone Tower of Terror
㉘ Fantasmic!
㉙ First Aid
㉚ Entrance Plaza
㉛ Guest Relations
㉜ Lockers/Strollers

Chapter 11
Disney Water Parks

On hot New York City summer days when I was a kid, we sometimes managed to unscrew the covers from fire hydrants and turned them on: instant water park!

Over the course of years, water parks have grown much more ambitious. All over America you'll find 100-foot towers of fiberglass and steel, lubricated with rushing water. Beneath them you will find swimming pools that have massive wave machines.

But once again, leave it to Disney to take what has become the ordinary water park and make it extraordinary. It's all in the setting.

Disney's watering holes Blizzard Beach, Typhoon Lagoon, and River Country, are state-of-the-watery-art. They are a great way to cool off and have a ton of fun on a hot summer or summer-like day—a season that in Florida can extend from March and sometimes February through December.

If you've got an all-parks admission ticket, it's not a bad idea to plan on splitting your day into thirds: start at one of the theme parks in the morning, break away to a water park in the heat and crowds of the afternoon, and then head back to a theme park in the evening for more rides and the nightly fireworks or parade.

The water parks have fast food eateries. You can also bring your own lunch in a cooler; no bottles or alcohol are allowed.

If you're on an a la carte plan, jump at the chance to unwind at a water park on the hottest day of your trip. And don't overlook Wet 'n Wild, an independent park near Universal Studios.

Blizzard Beach

You are, of course, perfectly willing to suspend disbelief—that's why you are at Walt Disney World in the first place. So you'll have no problem getting this concept: after a freak storm dumped a ton of snow on Orlando, Blizzard Beach was planned as Florida's first ski resort. Unfortunately, temperatures quickly returned to normal.

And so, what we've got here is a ski resort for swimmers. Blizzard Beach is

Electricity overhead.
Thunderstorms can
come up quickly and
powerfully in Florida,
especially in the late
afternoons of hot days.
Lifeguards will clear the
pools and slides of
Typhoon Lagoon or
Blizzard Beach if a storm
is near, and they may
even close the park if
necessary.

Whoa! It's you against
gravity as you plunge
down the flumes at River
Country, Typhoon
Lagoon, and Blizzard
Beach. You can
somewhat control your
speed, though, by the
way you lie down.
Fastest: Lie on your back
with your hands over
your head. Arch your
back so that only your
shoulders and heels
touch the track.
Fast: Lie on your back
with your hands crossed
on your chest and your
ankles crossed.
Slow: Sit up.
Slowest: Walk back
down the stairs.

built around 90-foot **Mt. Gushmore**, which is
served by a chairlift to the top of the ski jump.
This is no bunny hill; nearly all of the 17 slides
are a few notches above the level of Typhoon
Lagoon on the other side of Walt Disney World.
It also features the only chairlift I have ever seen
with a beach umbrella over the chairs.

The 42-acre park is located north of Disney's
All-Star Sports Resort, across World Drive from
Disney-MGM Studios.

Downhill Double Dipper. New in 1997, the
world's first side-by-side racing slide.

Summit Plummet. This is the big one, the ski
jump starting 120 feet up. (It actually begins from
a platform 30 feet above the top of Mt. Gushmore!) As far as we know, it is the highest free-
fall water slide in the world. Sliders may reach a
top speed of 55 mph down the 500-foot-slide at
an angle of 60 degrees; the slide passes through
a ski chalet on the way down. From below, it
looks as if skiers . . . err, sliders . . . are heading
off a ski jump at the top of the mountain. For
those in training for the water slide Olympics,
there's a timing clock at the bottom to report
your results.

If you make it to the top of Mt. Gushmore but
don't have the courage to take the plummet,
there's an easier slope to the bottom: **Slush
Gusher**, a double-humped slide about half the
length and speed but still a spectacular plunge.

Another way off the top is **Runoff Rapids**, an
inner tube ride that includes a dark section
within a pipe.

Snow Stormers is a twisting and turning inner tube slide that looks like a slalom ski course.
"Snowmaking" jets spray water over the course as
you bounce your way to the bottom.

Ski Patrol Training Center. Activities for the hotshots include the **T-bar**
at the **Ski Patrol Training Center**, where you can hang on to an overhead
trolley for a trip over—or into—a pool. You'll also find the **Thin Ice Training Course**, which presents a pathway across treacherous icebergs in the pool.
And the **Krinkle Tin Slide** is an enclosed water pipe that deposits sliders into
a deep pool.

Teamboat Springs. A record-setting five-person, 1,500-foot raft ride
through waterfalls.

Toboggan Racer. An eight-lane competitive waterslide; unlike the other slides, this one puts riders head-first on a mat. Nearby is another mat slide, **Snow Stormers**; this trio of flumes races down the mountain on a switchback course through slalom gates.

Melt Away Bay. A 1.2-acre wave pool at the base of Mt. Gushmore.

Cross Country Creek circles the park, pushing visitors on inner tubes on a half-mile circuit; the creek passes through an ice cave where the "icicles" melt onto the paddlers below.

For the youngest visitors, there's **Tike's Peak**, which has miniature versions of Mount Gushmore's slides and a snow castle fountain.

Blizzard Beach is a hot draw and may attract crowds beyond your tolerance during busy times of the year; a contrarian approach calls for taking advantage of Typhoon Lagoon instead. Disney planners will close admission to the park once the lot is full; only guests at Disney resorts arriving by bus will be admitted; come early during peak times. Note that during the off-season in the early months of the year, Blizzard Beach is closed on Sundays.

Typhoon Lagoon

According to Disney legend, this was once a beautiful tropical resort until a rogue typhoon roared through. What was left standing was knocked down by an earthquake. Oh, and then there was a volcanic eruption. (Sounds like a lovely place to vacation.) But the villagers refused to give up, and they rebuilt their paradise in and among the ruins.

The fabulous water slides are built into realistic miniature mountains; the huge wave pool has a sandy beach; and the river rafting ride passes through jungle canopies, a rain forest, and caves. There is hardly any sign of the artificial nature of the park—the water that cascades down the mountainside emerges from rivers and creeks without a pipe in sight.

Mount Mayday is one of the tallest peaks in Florida, even if it is a Disney-created simulation. It rises some 90 feet into the air and is topped by the wreckage of the shrimp boat, **Miss Tilly.** The smokestack on the boat erupts in a plume of water every once in a while, adding to the cascades all around.

The namesake central pool is **Typhoon Lagoon**, which is almost three acres in size. Every 90 seconds, you can catch some of the world's

Up before down. As enjoyable as Typhoon Lagoon is, be aware that there is quite a bit of climbing involved in using the slides. There is a bit less climbing if you use the ski lift at Blizzard Beach, but you can expect long lines at busy times there.

Slip, sliding away. According to local myth, more than a few women have lost their bikini tops on the old Kowabunga. Always trying to please, Disney has built a little viewing stand at the bottom. I spent part of an afternoon there—strictly for research purposes—but the only lost articles I observed were sunglasses.

By the way, I'd strongly recommend wearing an eyeglass strap or carrying your glasses in your folded hands when you ride one of the slides. You should also use plenty of sunscreen.

largest man-made waves, walls of water as high as six feet tall. You'll hear a thunder-like rumble as the wave is generated and a scream from the bathers as the water is released. Two sheltered pools, **Whitecap Cover** and **Blustery Bay**, serve the less adventurous, with shallows for young children.

Hang on to your bathing suit as you drop 51 feet at speeds of up to 30 mph, down the 214-foot-long **Humunga Kowabunga** water slide. Do we actually pay good money and wait in line for the privilege of falling this far, this fast? The moment of truth will come when you reach the top; try not to stop and consider the folly of it all. Just lie down on your back, cross your ankles, and fold your arms over your chest. Once you've survived, come back another time and try the slide with your eyes open.

And just to make things more interesting, Disney Imagineers added a third Kowabunga slide and enclosed all three in dark tunnels at the start of 1999.

Or, try the nearby **Storm Slides.** The trio of body slides, **Rudder Buster, Jib Jammer,** and **Stern Burner,** crash through waterfalls, caves, and geysers. Each of the slides is somewhat different—on a busy day you'll have to take the slide assigned to you by the lifeguard at the top of the stairs. Our favorite is the center slide, which passes through an unexpected dark tunnel midway down the hill. Top speed on the slides is about 20 mph.

Mayday Falls and **Keelhaul Falls** send you down a slide on a large inner tube on a tour through caves, waterfalls, and more. Mayday is the taller and longer ride, about 460 feet in length. Keelhaul is shorter, about 400 feet, but includes sharper twists and turns.

Entire families can go for a relatively tame white water adventure at **Gangplank Falls.** Your circular boat will work its way down the mountain in and among waterfalls and obstacles. Don't say the wrong thing to the person who loads your raft at the top of the slide—with the flick of a wrist, he or she can send your raft under the waterfall at the loading zone. The rafts can hold up to five or six persons, and you may end up with strangers if lines are long.

For the youngest swimmers, **Ketchakiddie Creek** features water slides, boats, squirting animals, and other toys for children only.

And finally, you can take a tour on the lazily flowing **Castaway Creek** that circles the park for almost half a mile; it takes about 30 minutes to circle completely around. If the traffic gets too thick or if the float is *too* lazy, you can get out and walk in the three-foot-deep creek or even leave and cross the park to your starting place.

Perhaps the most unusual attraction at the park is the **Shark Reef,** where guests get to strap on a snorkel (provided) and float through an artificial coral reef in and among small nurse and bonnethead sharks, and thousands of other colorful little fishies. We're assured that these are peaceful creatures. In fact, naturalists worry more about visitors damaging the fish with their suntan lotions and other pollutants; you'll be asked to take a shower first. It's an absolutely captivating experience and highly recommended; the shark pond was renovated at the start of 1999.

Lockers and sometimes-crowded changing rooms and showers are available along the right side of the lagoon as you face Mt. Mayday. You can also rent towels. During the summer, the park is open into the evening; in spring and fall, it often closes as early as 5 P.M. Typhoon Lagoon typically closes for maintenance in January or February.

We have found that dragging a towel and shirt around the park is more of a nuisance than it is worth—you can't bring the towel up the waiting line for slides, and the exits are usually not in the same place as the entrances. If it's warm enough to go swimming, you might want to do without a towel. Although you are allowed to wear water shoes and glasses, you should take care to hold on to both in the water and on slides.

Night slide. Consider ducking out of the Magic Kingdom or Epcot some hot summer afternoon for a cooling dip as the sun goes down. River Country is open until 8 P.M. during summertime, and ticket booths have in past years offered lower-cost tickets after 3 P.M.

Snack bars in the park include **Lowtide Lou's, Leaning Palms, Typhoon Tilly's,** and **Let's Go Slurpin'.** Items range in price from $3 to $5 for basic burger, chicken, and fried fish dishes; you can also get soft drinks, beer, and ice cream.

There's also a gift shop, **Singapore Sal's Saleable Salvage,** where you can buy bathing suits, T-shirts, and souvenirs. They also have suntan lotion; you can save a few dollars or more by shopping at a drug store outside the park.

Note that during the off-season in the early months of the year, Typhoon Lagoon is closed on Saturdays.

River Country

River Country is Disney's version of Huck Finn's swimmin' hole. Get there by driving to the Fort Wilderness parking lot and taking the Disney bus from there to the park. Or you can hop a short boat ride from the Magic Kingdom across Bay Lake.

The walk from the bus stop to River Country takes you past the small Fort Wilderness **Petting Zoo,** a pleasant shaded area that has goats, sheep, horses, and other animals. Admission to the zoo is free; there is a $2 charge for pony rides, with an adult leading the very docile pony around the track.

Bay Cove at the heart of River Country includes rope swings, a ship's boom, and other interesting ways to fly out over and into the water below. Bay Cove is actually a part of Bay Lake, which is itself connected to Seven Seas Lagoon at the Magic Kingdom. Across the cove from the beach are the **Whoop 'n Holler Hollow** corkscrew flume rides. Also emptying into the cove are the inner tube rafts coming down **White Water Rapids,** which despite its name is actually a rather slow, 330-foot-long meander.

Be aware there is a health warning about swimming in Bay Lake—and most every other pond or lake in the state of Florida. Swimmers are advised not to swim underwater near the bottom of the pond because of the presence of certain bacteria and algae that thrive in the warm waters.

The **Upstream Plunge Pool** is a large heated swimming pool that includes **Slippery Slide Falls,** a pair of water chutes that end about seven feet above the water; you're on your own for the rest of the way down.

River Country is a pleasant break from crowds at higher-energy water parks Typhoon Lagoon and Blizzard Beach; parents can watch children from the comfort of the sandy beach. From the beach, you can see across Bay Lake to the monorail, the ferryboats, and a distant peek at Space Mountain.

In the summer, though, the park can become quite crowded, and the gates are sometimes shut before noon; they'll reopen in late afternoon, and the park stays open late in season.

You don't need to pay a parking charge for River Country; head for the Magic Kingdom, and move all the way to the rightmost toll booth. Tell the attendant you are going to River Country and bear right after the toll plaza.

Discovery Island, RIP

Disney's 11-acre zoological park, stocked with a small but interesting collection of wild animals, closed in the spring of 1999, a victim of the success of Disney's Animal Kingdom. The island was reached by ferryboat from a dock near River Country, and joint tickets with the two smaller attractions were offered.

As we go to press, Disney is mum on plans for the small island, which lies in an attractive location. One rumored use is as a super-luxury honeymoon island.

TYPHOON LAGOON

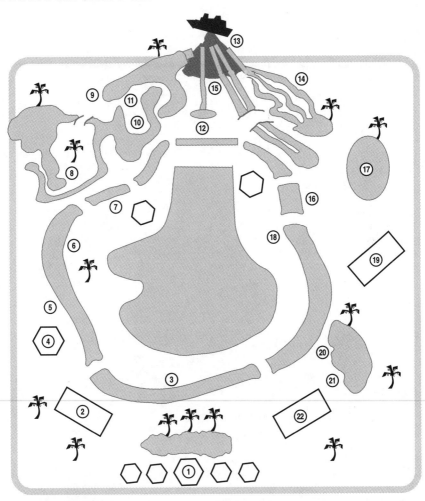

1. Entrance
2. Leaning Palms
3. Castaway Creek
4. Swiss Family Treehouse
5. Starfish entrance to creek
6. Rain Forest
7. Shell entrance to creek
8. Ketchakiddee Creek
9. Keelhaul Falls
10. Gangplank Falls
11. Mayday Falls

12. Forgotten Grotto
13. Mount Mayday
14. Storm Slides
15. Humunga Kowabunga
16. Shark entrance to creek
17. Shark Reef
18. Snail entrance to creek
19. Typhoon Tilly's
20. Sea Horse entrance to creek
21. High & Dry Towels
22. Singapore Sal's Souvenirs

Chapter 12

Downtown Disney: Disney West Side, Pleasure Island Marketplace, Cirque du Soleil

A city of entertainment the size of Walt Disney World deserves its own downtown, a place to unwind at the end of a long day of business, do some shopping, and catch a meal at a place that doesn't use paper napkins and plastic forks. Of course, the business of Walt Disney World is Disney entertainment, and so Disney has created its own very quirky metropolis of restaurants, nightclubs, shops, and theaters.

Set in a crescent curve along one shore of Buena Vista Lagoon, Downtown Disney is made up of:

- **Downtown Disney West Side.** The hottest area of downtown, home to a collection of "celebrity" restaurants, the indoor virtual theme park Disney Quest, and one of the world capitals of weird, Cirque du Soleil.
- **Downtown Disney Pleasure Island.** The original adult downtown district, it includes a collection of unusual clubs and restaurants.
- **Downtown Disney Marketplace.** Formerly known as Disney Village Marketplace, here you'll find all things Disney as well as a mega-LEGO store and an outpost of the Rainforest Café.

Parking is free at Downtown Disney, but sometimes you may feel as if you have parked in East Overshoe, Iowa; valet parking is available for $5 after 5:30 P.M. Disney added some 1,800 spaces in 1998, bringing the total to more than 7,000. If you are staying somewhere at Walt Disney World, consider using bus transportation from your hotel to Downtown Disney.

Downtown Disney West Side

DisneyQuest. Disney's most far-out park exists within the purple walls of DisneyQuest, a place that stands at the cutting edge of virtual entertainment.

How different is this theme-park-in-a-box? Check out its icon: "Hurricane Mickey," a swirling variation of Disney's classic mouse.

The 100,000-square-foot building is a five-story flagship for Disney's plans to build DisneyQuests in 20 to 30 major domestic and international locations; a center in Chicago is due to open in the summer of 1999.

When DisneyQuest first opened at Downtown Disney, it was on a pay-as-you-go basis using a magnetically encoded "stored value" card. That proved unpopular with visitors used to a one-price admission at the theme parks, and by early 1999, the ticket policy was revised.

Admission for adults is $25, and children (3-9) are charged $20. The ticket provides all-day use of the facility, including all the video games and pinball you can play. Everyone must have a ticket to enter, and guests 12 and under must be accompanied.

Disney estimates people will make visits of two to three hours. The attraction will have a capacity limit, and long lines can be expected from time to time—probably in the evenings and on rainy days. For more information and hours, call (407) 828-4600.

You enter DisneyQuest in a trip through the "Cybrolator," guided—not all that well—by Aladdin's madcap Genie of the Lamp. When the doors open, you find yourself standing at the Ventureport, a crossroads of adventure leading to four entertainment environments.

Though you're probably going to be anxious to begin your quest, do take a moment to soak in one of the most amazing interiors at Walt Disney World. The crossroads puts you in the middle of a gigantic armillary sphere, an ancient astronomical instrument that is composed of rings representing the positions of important circles of the celestial sphere.

• **Explore Zone.** The gateway is through the tiger's head from Aladdin's Cave of Wonders. The entrance is through a 150-foot-long slide that drops two stories (there are stairs, too, for those who prefer to stay on their own feet).

The Explore Zone is a place where the rules of time don't seem to apply.

You'll be able to navigate a primeval world in **Virtual Jungle Cruise**, where dangers include hungry dinosaurs and a cataclysmic comet. You'll strap your feet into toeholds on a real raft and paddle your way in a virtual reality re-creation of the wildest whitewater expedition ever.

You can drive a miniature camera-equipped, radio-controlled car on a hunt for the **Treasures of the Incas** beneath the glass floor at your feet.

You can fly through the streets of Agrabah on a hunt to release the Genie in **Aladdin's Magic Carpet Ride**, an entertainment that was previewed in a prototype version at Epcot several years ago. Sitting on motorcyle-like simulators and wearing virtual reality headgear, players become Abu the monkey on a tour on Aladdin's flying carpet in search of the Genie of the Lamp. Participants compete against the clock and each other.

And you'll be able to join Herc and his friends in a battle against Hades in **Hercules in the Underworld.**

• **Score Zone.** A dimensional rift slashed through a comic book grants passage to a "competition city."

Go sword-to-sword with supervillains as you fly through a 3-D comic book world in **Ride the Comix!** As many as six visitors at a time put on head-mounted virtual-reality helmets and brandish laser swords against Disney villains.

Rescue earth colonists under attack in **Invasion! An Alien Encounter** while piloting a planetary walker. This is an extension of the Alien Encounter attraction at the Magic Kingdom. You travel in X-S 5000 Rescue Units, developed to defend human colonists from a succession of nasties. Creatures include Alien Warbeasts and riders, slow but numerous Alien Grunts, and bloodthirsty Alien Heavy Weapons Commanders.

And you can become the joystick on a human-sized motion base—a Hover-Disc Motion Base—and hip-check your friends in **Mighty Ducks Pinball Slam**. A hydaulic system lifts the discs slightly off the floor, and players maneuver their ball on the screen by moving their bodies. It's fun to play and to watch.

• **Create Zone.** Enter through a digital artist's palette to an Imagineering studio.

Design the roller coaster of your dreams . . . and then buckle up and ride your creation on **CyberSpace Mountain**, a 360-degree pitch-and-roll simulator. You'll begin at a computer console where you can select ride elements—lifts, drops, rolls, loops, and just about any diabolical twist of fate you'd like to try with some 10,000 feet of virtual track to play with. Ride elements include figure-eights, spirals, barrel rolls, loops, banked s-curves, camelbacks, and straightaways. You can also choose a backdrop for your ride, including the Land of Lava, Ice Planet, and Astronomical Anomalies. And then you're off on a 90-second ride inside a simulator that can roll like a barrel, climb, and drop—in some ways it is more radical than the real thing.

Learn the secrets of Disney animation at the **Animation Academy**, an 18-seat video training classroom.

Create a toy from a menu of parts at **Sid's Create-a-Toy**, and then take home a copy.

Indulge in a virtual makeover at the **Magic Mirror**, and create a painting of color and movement at the **Living Easels**.

• **Replay Zone.** The doorway leads through a retro art collection from the moon-crazy '50s to three levels of classic rides and games with a futuristic twist. Climb into a bubble-top bumper car and shoot it out with oversized playground balls in **Buzz Lightyear's AstroBlaster**. There are two passengers in each car—one driver and one gunner. If you hit a target on another vehicle, they'll spin out.

And there's a section of carnival games with rewards, including **Dumbo's Water Race** and **Mickey's Lunar Rally**. There's even a **Game Graveyard** where the golden oldies of video gaming live on.

DisneyQuest includes a pair of unusual fast food eateries as well:

FoodQuest. Fresh salads, sandwiches, pizza, and fun food.

Wonderland Café. Indulgent desserts, including offerings from The Cheesecake Factory. While dining, guests can play Wonderland Web Adventures over the Internet.

Disney plans to change 20 percent to 30 percent of the attractions each year, keeping the place fresh for returning visitors.

WOW **Cirque du Soleil.** Wonderfully more weird than most anything else at Walt Disney World, Cirque du Soleil unveiled La Nouba in late 1998. A cast of 60 performers from around the world perform twice daily, five days a week, in a 70,000-square-foot, 1,671-seat theater that resembles a concrete circus tent complete with a 160-foot-tall mast.

The Montreal-based circus has no elephants and dancing tigers, and its aerialists and clowns march to a decidedly different beat from what you'll find under any other big top. Created in 1984 by one-time street performer and visionary, Guy Laliberté, Cirque du Soleil is a striking mix of the circus arts and street entertainment. The circus has permanent show facilities in Las Vegas at the Treasure Island and Bellagio casinos. Other shows tour in Europe, Asia, and North America.

The name of the show comes from an Algerian French phrase, "faire la Nouba," which means to party hearty.

The strangeness begins with a nightmare opening scene in a startling moment when a bicyclist pedals by upside-down suspended from a wire. And it goes on from there, including the introduction of a raft of creatures who rise up from beneath the floor.

There's a bit of a story involving a cleaning lady who seems to discover this strange world going on behind the scenes, and there's the wonderfully bizarre strong man who prances about making comically menacing poses.

Four tiny Chinese girls, ages 11 to 14, steal the middle of the show with a display of incredible acrobatics using the diabolo, a Chinese yoyo. The girls are under contract through the end of 1999, and a new troupe of youngsters now in training in Beijing will take over that segment of the show in 2000.

Another star turn is performed by Vasily Dementchoukov with his chair act, first introduced in Cirque du Soleil's Nouvelle Experience in 1992. Dementchoukov somehow defies the laws of physics and gravity while balancing precariously on a stack of eight chairs atop a table 25 feet in the air, all the while spinning a birthday cake lit with candles. You'll have to see it not to believe it.

A group of bicyclists in modern dress climb and descend stairs, performing some heart-stopping maneuvers at the edges of the stage and open pits. One of the bikers hops his bike over the body of a draftee from the audience.

But my favorite act came near the end when a whole troupe of acrobats perform on the power track and trampoline that rise from beneath the stage. They become human Spider-men, launching themselves and climbing the walls of a building that rises from the stage.

And then somewhere in the amorphous story, the cleaning lady kisses a frog and finds her prince.

All in all, this is a spectacular way to spend 90 minutes. In mid-1999, tickets for the La Nouba were priced at $56.50 plus tax, and $45.20 plus tax for children. Shows are presented at 5:30 and 8 P.M. daily from Wednesday to Saturday, and at 2:30 and 5:30 P.M. on Sunday. Sight lines in the U-shaped theater are very good; the best seats are in the center about midway up from the

Cirque du Soleil's La Nouba at Downtown Disney West Side

Photo courtesy of Cirque du Soleil

stage. Tickets in the 100 series are on the lower level and those in the 200 series are in the balcony.

No photography or videotaping of the show is permitted. The music and sound effects are rather loud, which may be a problem for some guests and children. La Nouba is under contract to Walt Disney World through the year 2010; the show may change slightly over that time as some of the acts rotate in and out.

AMC 24-Screen Theater. Already the most successful multiscreen theater complex in Florida when it had a mere 10 screens; its expansion to two dozen makes it the largest in the state. Sixteen of the theaters feature "stadium seating"—two with balconies and three-story-tall screens. Call (407) 827-1300 for show times.

Virgin Records Megastore. A state-of-the-art music, video, and book mecca; the circular, three-level store also features 300 CD listening stations and an elevated exterior stage for live performances.

Downtown Shops. Also on the West Side is a collection of eclectic shops, including:

- **Guitar Gallery.** Selling one-of-a-kind and celebrity model acoustic and electric guitars.

- **Magnetron Magnetz.** All things magnetic, and we're not just talking refrigerator magnets, although you can buy those, too. Every few minutes, the store's "magnetic generator" comes to life, energizing the whole place in wondrous ways.
- **Celebrity Eyeworks Studio.** Somewhere out there, someone is looking to buy a replica of eyewear worn by movie stars; this is the place.
- **Sosa Family Cigars.** Stogies from a renowned Cuban family in a store modeled after the living room of founding father Don Juan Sosa Acosta.
- **Hoypoloi.** An unusual gallery of art glass, ceramics, sculpture, and other decorative items.
- **Starabilia.** Nostalgic and collectible old stuff, run by the founder of a similar store at the Forum Shops at Caesars Palace in Las Vegas.
- **Copperfield Magic Underground—The Store.** Magic tricks and souvenirs, part of the David Copperfield empire.
- **Forty Thirst Street.** A high-tone coffee and juice bar with a computer-operated lighting system and fiber optic menus.

Disney West Side Restaurants

House of Blues. Out front of the huge 500-seat restaurant and 2,000-seat music hall, television production, and radio broadcasting facility hangs a sign: "In Blues We Trust."

The place is modeled after an old-time Mississippi jukejoint, with rusted metal and fall-down wood trim. It gets even funkier inside, with a collection of folk art paintings and sculptures.

Live blues, R&B, jazz, and country music are presented nightly, plus a rollicking Sunday Gospel Brunch. The restaurant features eclectic delta-inspired cuisine. Signature dishes, priced from about $9 to $22, include jambalaya, the Elwood (chicken breast Cajun style), the Jake Burger, and étoufée.

There is, of course, a gift shop that sells souvenirs and, more importantly, books about blues music and folk art and well-known and obscure blues recordings.

There's even a blues time for youngsters ages 4 to 15. Gumbo Yo Yo a live, interactive stage show, is presented Saturday mornings, focused on teaching the House of Blues mission of "Unity in Diversity" through comedy, music and storytelling.

Tickets are available at the door, or by calling (407) 934-2583; parents and children of other ages are free. A portion of the proceeds from ticket sales go to the International House of Blues Foundation to support various educational outreach programs.

KEY:

🍴 = Fast Food

🍸 = Pub

🏠 = Full-service restaurant

Wolfgang Puck's Café. The world-famous chef's first Florida restaurant features his innovative California cuisine in a casual setting adorned with colorful mosaic tiles. Specialties include wood-fired pizzas with toppings such as spicy chicken and smoked salmon.

There are 550 seats inside in three dining

rooms, plus a walk-up Wolfgang Puck Express restaurant outside. Inside is a sushi and raw bar, a casual dining restaurant downstairs with some seats allowing a view of the kitchen, and a more upscale, reservations-only restaurant upstairs with a view of Buena Vista Lagoon.

Wolfgang devotes his creative energies to the food, while his wife and partner Barbara Lazaroff designs the eating places—the bill was said to reach $8 million for interior decorating. Be sure to check out the bar counter, which includes a spread of $30,000 worth of semi-precious stones, and the tile work out front.

Bongos Cuban Café. A Cuban café/nightclub, created by Latin superstar Gloria Estefan and her husband, Emilio, brings the sizzle of Miami's South Beach to Disney.

A giant concrete pineapple outside and elaborate mosaic murals inside that speak of the hot, hot, hot heyday of Cuba in the 1940s and early 1950s; there's even a Ricky Riccardo look-alike as greeter.

The 471-seat restaurant includes a Cuban menu created by Quintin and Carmen Lario, founders with the Estefans of Larios on the Beach, a very popular eatery on Miami's South Beach.

The Cuban style of cooking, comidas criolla or Creole, combines tropical and European elements. Staples include white sweet potatoes, squash, corn, rice, beans, and simmered sauces known as soffritos.

Planet Hollywood. Planet Hollywood's three-story 400-seat restaurant, on its own plot of land between West Side and Pleasure Island, is one of the busiest eateries on the planet. The club, which has several major film stars among its owners, including Sylvester Stallone, Arnold Schwarzenegger, Bruce Willis, and Demi Moore, is a cinema equivalent to the Hard Rock Cafe chain. (Not at all coincidentally, there is a Hard Rock restaurant at Universal Studios Florida across town.)

The restaurant is decorated with movie and TV scripts, artifacts, and costumes and the sounds of music and film clips echo throughout. Surprisingly, the food is above average, including huge Caesar salads, Cajun chicken breast, hot wings, burgers, and pizza. Entrees start at about $10. Open daily from 11 A.M. to 2 A.M.

Pleasure Island

Merriweather Adam Pleasure, also known as MAD Pleasure or the Grand Funmeister, disappeared in 1941 on a circumnavigation expedition of the Antarctic. By 1955, his beloved home island was in disrepair; the coup de grace was administered by a rogue hurricane.

The six-acre island languished in ruins until it was rediscovered by Disney archaeologists, who painstakingly rebuilt the town.

If you believe that story, perhaps you'd like to join the Pleasure Island Historical Society, whose plaques dot the landmarks of Pleasure Island, which is located next to Disney Village. Even if you don't, a visit to Pleasure Island is a worthy nighttime entertainment.

It's New Year's Eve every night of the year at the nightly **New Year's Eve**

Half the pleasure. You can enter Pleasure Island during the day without buying a ticket; this will allow you to visit the shops and restaurants for free. Guests who are within the gates at 7 P.M. can stay at Pleasure Island and see all the outdoor shows without buying a ticket, although a Pleasure Island ticket is required to enter any of the clubs. The clubs generally open at 8 or 8:30 P.M.

Designated drinkers. Note that the drinking age in Florida is 21, and visitors to Pleasure Island who are not obviously over that age will be required to show proof of their birthdate; once "carded," you'll receive a wristband you can wear for the rest of the evening. There is, however, no requirement that you buy any drinks in any of the clubs—just say "no" and you'll be left alone to watch the shows.

Street Party. The celebration begins at 11:45 P.M. and includes music, dancers, confetti, and fireworks.

There's also a Mardi Gras celebration in late February, including a week's worth of partying, live music, and Cajun and Creole specialties. Twice nightly a Mardi Gras procession led by the Krewe of Caesar parades through Treasure Island. And then there's the Cinco de Mayo celebration of Mexico's Independence Day, held, naturally, on May 5 and featuring festive music, decorations, and authentic cuisine.

There is no cover charge or age restriction to visit Pleasure Island during the day, or at anytime to enter the restaurants. The shops open at 10 A.M. The ticket gates go up at 7 P.M., charging $18.95; after 7 P.M., visitors under the age of 18 must be accompanied by a parent.

Pleasure Island is included in park-hopper passes for Disney guests, and annual passes are available at roughly the price of three one-day admissions.

BET SoundStage Club. This upscale waterfront club features jazz, rhythm and blues, soul, and hip-hop in live performances, as well as programming from the BET SoundStage Network. (It replaced the Neon Armadillo Music Saloon.) BET operates Black Entertainment Television, a cable television programming service.

Mannequins Dance Palace. A contemporary club that has a rotating dance floor and a high-tech (recorded) sound, light, and dance show starring the Pleasure Island Explosion Dancers, presented several times each night. There are also a whole bunch of strange and wonderful mannequins scattered about, bubble machines, and more. You must be 21 to enter.

Pleasure Island Jazz Company. A new club celebrating America's native musical form with live performances in an old warehouse stacked with amusement park and carnival equipment.

Rock & Roll Beach Club. Live bands perform the classics of rock; a DJ spins stacks of vinyl—well, stacks of CDs anyway—during breaks. Be sure to check out the second floor where there is a selection of pool and air hockey tables and some video and pinball machines; check out the shark hanging from the ceiling with a bikini top in its teeth. Menu items include pizza by the slice.

8TRAX. If you can remember what an 8-track tape player was, you've got the basic concept of this celebration of the '70s (The Doors, Iron Butterfly, Janis Joplin, bell-bottoms, bean bag chairs, and lava lamps). It includes your basic disco mirror ball, fog machine, and a small dance floor.

The Adventurers Club. Kungaloosh! Welcome to the decidedly unusual private club of Mr. Pleasure and his friends. Don't worry, though, you'll be welcomed as a guest . . . and offered a free membership and a secret password. We're sworn to secrecy ourselves . . . but it begins with a K. Five strange rooms filled with strange actors and you, their guests. Stick around and see what happens.

> **We're impressed.** On one of our visits to Pleasure Island, a sign at the entrance to the parking lot read, "Impress your date. Use our Valet Parking services." Actually, though, you might consider it worth the fee to use the valet in bad weather because the outlying parking spaces can seem like they are in the next state.

The Adventurers Club is one of the most entertaining "performance spaces" you'll find at Walt Disney World. According to the cover story, this is the place where Mr. Pleasure stored all of the strange items he brought back from his journeys; it's enough fun just to cruise among them. You'll likely meet the curator, the maid, and other oddball friends of Pleasure who will share their stories, and you'll be invited to enter into the library for an oddball show, including the Balderdash Cup Competition, the Curator's New Discovery, the Second Annual Radiothon Talent Show, the Maid's Sing-a-long, and the Bon Voyage Party.

Get in early and grab a seat in the main parlor on the lower level. There's no pressure to buy drinks; you can just sit and watch the strange goings-on.

The Comedy Warehouse. This place is a hoot, presenting an evening of improvisational humor, with somewhere between a PG and R rating—by Disney standards it can get downright risqué. (I'll leave it to the comics to express themselves, but on one of my visits the skit—directed by instructions called out by the audience—progressed to a love scene on the beach in which Ariel the mermaid lost her strategically placed seashells and was revealed to be a man.) There were even a few gentle jibes at Disney, including a fake movie poster on the wall advertising a film dubbed as *Dumbo, First Blood.*

There are several shows each night; the club is small and seats are often filled well before showtime. If you want to sit through two sessions, you'll have to exit and get back in line for a later show. From time to time, television crews tape comedy specials here. When a "name" comedian is appearing there may be an extra charge for admission.

When you are offered a seat in the amphitheater-like club, think twice about whether you really want to sit by a telephone. You don't suppose it may ring during the show, do you?

As at all of the clubs in the park, you will be approached by a waiter or waitress but you do not have to purchase anything if you don't want to. Drink prices include small beers for about $3, up to a 60-ounce pitcher for $9. Special drinks include Laughter Punch, made with Midori, rum, and pineapple juice. Sodas, popcorn, pretzels, and banana splits are also available.

Pleasure Island Restaurants

The major restaurants on Pleasure Island are located outside the turnstiles between Pleasure Island and Disney Village and can be visited without purchasing a ticket.

▲ **Fulton's Crab House.** By the shores of Disney's inland sea is a seafood restaurant on a re-created paddlewheeler. Fulton's Crab House promises to change its menu daily to reflect the latest and greatest seafood available in season. (They'll even post the air freight bills on the wall!) Entrees, from about $15 to $35, include Nantucket Bay Scallops, Mustard Crusted Trout, and Fulton's Cioppino. Appetizers begin with a well-stocked oyster bar, and also include such delicacies as alderwood smoked salmon with potato crostini lemon chive cream. Open for character breakfast with seatings at 8 and 10 A.M., lunch from 11:30 A.M. to 4 P.M., and dinner from 5 P.M. to midnight. Dinner entrees about $20.

▲ **Portobello Yacht Club.** A first-class northern Italian eatery, with offerings ranging from thin-crust pizza cooked in a wood-fired oven ($7 to $8) to steak, chicken, and fish dishes. Lunch salads, priced from about $5 to $8 may include *insalata Caesar di pollo* (Caesar salad with chicken). A sample of entrees, priced from about $13 to $25, includes Spiedini di Gamberi, garlic shrimp charcoal-grilled on a rosemary skewer; center-cut pork chop with herb crust; veal rib eye breaded and sauteed with a balsamic vinaigrette topping; and Spaghettini all Portobello, a house specialty including Alaskan crab, scallops, clams, shrimp, and mussels with tomatoes, garlic, olive oil, wine, and herbs. A child's menu is also available. Open from 11:30 A.M. to midnight; call (407) 934-8888 for reservations.

The club is outside the gates of Pleasure Island and a ticket is not required to enter; Pleasure Island visitors can come and go if they hold on to their ticket for the evening.

▲ Ⓨ **Wildhorse Saloon.** Live country music, dance, and entertainment venue, plus American barbecue restaurant. This location is the first outpost of the world-famous Wildhorse Saloon in Nashville.

There is, of course, a gift shop, selling a mix of traditional and contemporary Western-inspired casual apparel for men, women, and children; plus jewelry, accessories, and souvenir merchandise.

Wildhorse is located in the former Fireworks Factory building.

Downtown Disney Marketplace

When the going gets tough, the tough go shopping, and the Marketplace is one of Disney's most interesting collections of shops, including a large Lego outlet and the mother of all Disney Stores. There's also another outlet of the unusual Rainforest Café chain.

You can drive to the Village and park in the huge parking lot (it adjoins and mixes with the spaces for Pleasure Island), or you can take a water taxi from the Port Orleans Resort, Dixie Landings Resort, or the Disney Vacation Club. The stores are open from 9:30 A.M. to 10 P.M.

During the holiday period, there's even ice skating on a 78-foot-diameter outdoor rink at Downtown Disney Marketplace, the only outdoor rink in Florida. Skate rentals are available.

Of course, there are lots of shops selling T-shirts, sweatshirts, and hats with pictures of Mickey or Minnie, but perhaps the single largest collection is at the warehouse-sized **World of Disney**, with 12 rooms of toys, clothing (including Disney lingerie!), and more.

Another favorite is the **Lego Imagination Center**, a one-of-a-kind retail shrine to the little plastic bricks. It features an outdoor play area and huge LEGO models, including a fire-breathing sea serpent rising out of Buena Vista Lagoon and a UFO model complete with an alien family. The store features every LEGO product available in the United States, including blocks, games, puzzles, bedsheets, and clothing.

It's Christmas all the time at **Disney's Days of Christmas**, where you can purchase American and European ornaments and Disney holiday merchandise. At **Toys Fantastic**, you'll find guess-what from guess-who, plus a selection of Barbie toys. **Eurospain** sells an interesting collection of hand-crafted Spanish crafts. **Harrington Bay Clothiers** and **Resortwear Unlimited** offer sportswear for men and women, respectively.

You'll be able to indulge that serious chocolate addiction with a visit to the **Ghirardelli's Ice Cream Soda Fountain and Chocolate Shop**. You'll find chocolate in all forms, as well as sundaes, shakes, malts, and more. The shop is designed like a turn-of-the-century San Francisco shop.

Downtown Disney Restaurants

Rainforest Café. Wild and wacky, with trees, birds, crocodiles, and rainfall . . . real and animatronic.

This is not your basic roadside café, unless your neighborhood eatery sports an animatronic gator at the door, an active (simulated) volcano, and a menu that emphasizes nonendangered fish, beef from countries that pledge not to deforest their lands for grazing, and some imaginative vegetarian offerings as well. Every once in a while the room lights dim and a (dry) thunderstorm breaks out inside the restaurant.

Be sure to check out the wishing pond to the right of the entrance. The spectacular parrots on perches are real; the huge alligator below is not.

Lines for the 550-seat restaurant, which cost $12 million to build, can become oppressive at prime lunch and dinner hours; your best bet is to come earlier or later than the crowds. Of course, you can also while away the time in the impressive gift shop.

Specialties include the Amazon Natural herbal burger constructed of nuts, grains, and beans; Rumble in the Jungle—roasted turkey tossed with Caesar salad and stuffed into a pita bread; Jamaica Me Crazy!—grilled pork chops dusted with Jamaican and Cajun seasonings; and Rasta Pasta with bow-tie pasta, grilled chicken, walnut pesto, broccoli, red peppers, spinach, and fresh herbs in a garlic cream sauce.

Open for lunch and dinner from 10:30 A.M. to 11 P.M. Another Rainforest Café is located at the entrance plaza to Disney's Animal Kingdom.

🔼 **Cap'n Jack's Oyster Bar.** Lunch, dinner. A little bit of Cape Cod in a pretty setting on a shack built into the village lake. Lobster tails, crab claws, clams, chowder, frozen margaritas. $5 to $15. Child's menu features pasta, $4. Open from 11:30 A.M. to 10 P.M.

🍴 **Wolfgang Puck Express.** Lunch and dinner service for California-style pizzas.

🍴 **Ronald's Fun House.** A one-of-a-kind outpost of the fast food chain featuring fanciful rooms and decor based on Ronald McDonald and his McDonaldland friends. Among the settings: Ronald's Dining Room, with a formal 20-foot serpentine dining area; Birdie's Music Room, featuring a giant french fry organ; and Grimace's Game Room, with video monitors. Oh, and they sell burgers and fries, too.

Chapter 13
Educational Opportunities at Walt Disney World

Feeling bad about taking your kids out of school for a vacation at Walt Disney World? How about giving them a little homework, Mickey-style?

Feeling too old to leave your job at the law firm to spend a week with Mickey and Minnie? How about coming to the Disney Institute to take a course on art or music? (While you're there, you can still sneak in a few circuits with Dumbo the Flying Elephant.)

Disney offers a range of educational seminars for youngsters and adults. You might want to discuss some of the options with your children's teachers.

Should You Take Your Kids Out of School?

In the best of all worlds, probably not. There are enough interruptions in the normal school year as it is. However, if work and school vacation times do not coincide, or if you are taking our advice seriously and trying to avoid crowds, there are ways to work with your schools.

We'd suggest you meet with your children's teachers to determine if there are particular times when an absence of a few days (wrapped around or including a weekend or minor holiday) will not make a big impact on school-work. Consult your school calendar in search of local holidays or "workshop" half-days.

See if you can coordinate special assignments for your children. If there is an upcoming unit on Mexico, for example, perhaps they could be assigned to produce a special report with research performed at Epcot Center's Mexican pavilion.

Disney Seminars and Camps

For information on any of the programs in this chapter, call (407) 939-8687.

Wonders of Walt Disney World

Here's a chance for kids from ages 11 to 15 to engage in a guided learning adventure; parents will receive a six-hour break for themselves, too. Programs cost $79; a theme park admission is not included or required for the programs.

Art Magic: Bringing Illusion to Life. An exploration of the Disney-MGM Studios for fans of animation, live theater, and theme parks. Young visitors learn about costuming and set making, and go backstage at Walt Disney Feature Animation. Offered Monday through Friday.

Passport: A Secret Mission to Other Lands. Go around the world at Epcot to solve a series of puzzles and games at selected pavilions. Offered Friday.

Show Biz Magic: The Walt Disney World of Entertainment. A backstage pass inside the Magic Kingdom, exploring the underground Utilidor system, parade and show setup areas, and more. Offered Monday through Thursday.

Wildlife Adventure: Exploring the Environment. Take a walk on the wild side in one of the few remaining cypress swamps in Florida, looking for alligators, egrets, turtles, and more. The tour finishes up at Disney's Discovery Island for a tour. Offered Tuesday and Thursday.

Camp Disney

Hands-on programs for 7- to 10-year-olds, within the theme parks and around the Walt Disney World resort. Morning sessions are from 8:30 A.M. to noon, and afternoon sessions run from 1:30 to 5 P.M. Two programs taken on the same day cost $89 per child and include lunch. One program costs about $59 per child, with lunch available for an extra charge. Advance reservations are recommended because of small class size. For information, call (407) 939-8687.

Broadway Bound. Behind the scenes at Disney shows. Tuesday mornings and Friday afternoons.

Face Magic! Special effects and illusions with makeup, at the Disney-MGM Studios. Wednesday afternoons and Friday mornings.

ArtSurround. Study the art of Epcot. Sunday, Tuesday, and Thursday afternoons.

Swamp Stomp. A nature safari through the cypress swamp. Monday and Tuesday mornings.

Discovery Island Kidventure. Wednesday and Saturday mornings.

Hands-On Programs for 11- to 15-Year-Olds

One six-hour adventure or two short programs taken on the same day cost about $89 per day, including lunch. One short program costs about $59, with lunch available for an extra charge. Because of small class size, reservations should be made well in advance. For information, call (407) 939-8687.

Art Magic. An inside view of how Disney Imagineers and designers create the magic of theme park attractions, and a hands-on demonstration of the animation process. Six hours. Monday, Tuesday, Thursday, and Friday.

Show Biz Magic. A backstage pass to Disney stage shows and a descent into the famed Magic Kingdom tunnel system to see the behind-the-scenes support areas. Six hours. Monday, Tuesday, and Thursday.

Rock Climbing for Youth. A seminar and supervised climb at the 26-foot-high Disney Institute rock wall. Two hours. Wednesday and Saturday mornings.

Discovery Island Explorers. Become a junior zookeeper with the Discovery Island zoological staff, caring for the animals and helping to set up one of the live animal shows. Three hours. Wednesday mornings.

The Funny Papers. Learn cartooning secrets, from pencil rough to final draft. Three hours. Sunday and Wednesday afternoons.

Disney Adult Discoveries

For the kid in all of us, from ages 16 and up, a chance to explore some of the hidden parts of Walt Disney World.

Keys to the Kingdom. Go beneath the streets of the Magic Kingdom to see the famous Utilidor underground tunnel system, and visit rehearsal and behind-the-scenes areas at some of the live shows of the park. $45 plus theme park admission. Call for schedule.

Backstage Magic. A seven-hour peek behind the curtain at Walt Disney World, including an exploration of the Utilidor system beneath the Magic Kingdom, backstage areas at all three parks, and special dining and entertainment. At the Disney-MGM Studios you'll have the chance to paint and keep a Mickey Mouse cel. Cost is $185 per person. Monday through Friday.

Epcot DiveQuest. A 30-minute dive adventure inside The Living Seas aquarium at Epcot for certified Open Water SCUBA divers. Offered daily. For information, call (407) 939-8687.

Hidden Treasures. A guided tour of Epcot World Showcase to learn about the art, culture, and history of the countries represented there.

Hidden Treasures East. A two-hour exploration of the Mexico, Norway, China, German, Italy, and American pavilions. $35 plus park admission. Offered Tuesday.

Hidden Treasures West. A two-hour tour of Canada, United Kingdom, France, Morocco, Japan, and American pavilions. $35 plus park admission. Offered Saturday.

Hidden Treasures. A five-hour journey to all 11 international pavilions, including lunch at Restaurant Marrakesh in Morocco. $75 including park admission. Offered Wednesday.

Gardens of the World. Explore the green side of the World Showcase in a three-hour walking tour led by a Disney horticultural expert. $35 plus park admission. Offered Tuesday and Thursday.

Inside Animation. An inside peek at Walt Disney Feature Animation including the chance to paint your own Disney animation cel. Two-and-a-half hours. Tuesday and Thursday. $45 per person.

Disney's Architecture. Learn how architects and Imagineers create the world of Disney. Three-and-a-half hours. Monday, Wednesday, and Friday. $45 per person.

The Disney Institute

One of Disney's principal goals in recent years has been to find ways to attract older visitors to Walt Disney World. Mickey and Minnie can only go so far once adults lose the excuse of bringing their children to the park.

Disney has had great success with its golf courses and other outdoor activities. Other expansions have seen such facilities as Sports Center Disney.

Now the attention has moved to the mind: In early 1996, the Disney Institute opened at an attractive new campus near the Disney Village Resort. The Institute began with an ambitious catalog of 80 courses with 27 studios, a broadcast-quality performance center, an outdoor amphitheater, cinema, teaching garden, and closed-circuit television and radio stations.

Courses at the Disney Institute in 1999 included: computer animation, clay animation, Disney architecture, topiary creations, television production, healthy cooking, portrait photography, outdoor photography, canoe adventure, golf, rock climbing, and much more.

Children ages 10-15 can enjoy most adult programs at the Disney Institute with their family. Camp Disney offers a variety of special programs and behind-the-scenes field trips just for kids ages 7–15.

Most students at the Disney Institute stay at the self-contained village; guests there are entitled to take two classes per day. Rates, including classes, range from about $275 to $340 per person per night for a three-night double occupancy stay in the Value Season from mid-July through early February. Peak Season rates in the spring and Christmas holiday period range from about $300 to $360 per person per night for three nights. Prices include accommodations, Disney Institute programs, baggage handling, daily use of the sports and fitness center, and scheduled evening entertainment. Package supplements including some meals are also available, as are packages including theme park admission.

You can also sign up for individual programs. In early 1999, rates were $69 for one program, and $99 for a Day Visitor pass, including a choice of two programs and access to the Sports and Fitness Center.

For information, call (800) 496-6337, and for reservations call (800) 282-9282. www.disneyinstitute.com

Chapter 14
Inside the World of Disney

Disney Cruise Line

Ahoy, Mickey! *The Disney Cruise Line* set sail in 1998, with the maiden voyage of the new *Disney Magic*. A second vessel, the *Disney Wonder*, began service in 1999.

Disney Magic and *Disney Wonder* are just like any other cruise . . . except for those six letters on the bow and all that they mean for guests.

A voyage on one of the ships is part of a seven-day vacation that includes three or four days at Walt Disney World plus a three- or four-day cruise to the Bahamas, featuring a visit to Nassau and Castaway Cay, Disney's private Bahamian island. The vessels depart from Port Canaveral on Florida's east coast, about an hour away from Orlando.

Disney has built its ships with adults as well as kids in mind. Youngsters have their own deck: Disney's Oceaneer Adventure is open late into the night. Features include Disney's Oceaneer Club, a play area for younger kids, and Disney's Oceaneer Lab that offers electronic games played on giant video walls and interactive computer activities. And teens have their own private hangout, Common Grounds.

Adults can join in the activities on the sports deck or catch the latest scores at the ESPN Skybox up top. They can dance the night away at Beat Street, an adult nightclub district with dance, jazz, and improv comedy clubs.

Guests rotate to one of three themed restaurants each evening. French contintental cuisine is offered at Lumières on the *Disney Magic* and Triton's on the *Disney Wonder*. The flavors and spirit of the Bahamas is featured at Parrot Cay. And then there is Animator's Palette, where the room magically transforms from a black-and-white artist's sketch to full color animation over the course of dinner. There's also Palo, an adults-only restaurant, and a kids-only pizza parlor.

After dinner, families can enjoy one of three Broadway-style shows at the

Walt Disney Theatre, or catch a movie at the Buena Vista Theatre. And there's Studio Sea, a nightclub for the entire family.

There's a day stop at Nassau and a visit to Castaway Cay, a 1,000-acre Bahamian island with miles of white sand beach. Activities include snorkeling, sailing, kayaking, paddle boats, and inflatables. The crew will offer an island barbecue.

The ships, built in Trieste, Italy, feature a "classic exterior design reminiscent of the majestic transatlantic ocean liners of the past." And they have in many ways delivered on the promise, with some of the most elegant shipboard spaces I have seen, and a vessel with stunning lines that will please even the most finicky cruise connoisseur. I don't recall the Queen Mary offering Disney character breakfasts and shows, though.

For full details on the Disney cruise line, you can consult one of the newest titles in the growing Econoguide series, *Econoguide: Cruises*.

Disneyland Paris

The French have an apt phrase: *Le plus ça change, le plus c'est la même chose.* It means: The more that changes, the more things are the same.

Disneyland Paris in Marne-la-Vallée near Paris is different from Walt Disney World in Florida and Disneyland in California, but it's the same thing.

After a few rocky years, Disneyland Paris has become France's leading tourist attraction, drawing more visitors than the Eiffel Tower and the Louvre.

When we visited Disneyland Paris we were able to convince our children to come to the United Kingdom and France with the promise of two days at Disneyland Paris as a reward for good behavior. As it turned out, the kids absolutely *loved* London with its museums and theaters, and were intrigued by incredible sights such as the Cathedral of Notre Dame in Paris, the palace of Versailles, and the ancient city of Provins, all within an hour of Marne-la-Vallée. Oh, and they liked Disneyland Paris real well, too.

The cost of the trip in off-season (similar to Walt Disney World, with lowest prices in winter and parts of the fall and spring) was just slightly more than a trip to Orlando.

Disneyland Paris is not a big draw for Americans, with only a few percent of visitors from this country. However, enough visitors from the United Kingdom and other non-French-speaking nations, plus the international allure of Disney makes it possible to get around the park without speaking French. The staff at the hotels within the park is multilingual, and guidebooks and signs are available in English.

If you do speak French, though, it's a bit of fun to see Disney Francified: the centerpiece of the park is *Le Château de la Belle au Bois Dormant* (Sleeping Beauty's Castle); favorite rides in Fantasyland include *Blanche-Neige et les Sept Nains* (Snow White and the Seven Dwarfs).

Beneath the castle is *La Tanière du Dragon* (The Dragon's Lair), with a rather scary, mechanical creature who comes to life every few minutes. *Indiana Jones et le Temple du Péril* in Adventureland is Disney's first real roller coaster, a wild ride through an archeological dig among the ancient ruins of the Lost City.

Phantom Manor in Frontierland is scarier than its cousins in Florida and California. And Big Thunder Mountain is faster and wilder, disappearing into a tunnel under the river at one point.

Space Mountain: De la Terre à la Lune is a spectacular version of Space Mountain. The ride extends the Jules Verne theme of a rocketship from the earth to the moon with a roller coaster that includes some upside-down spirals and twists and turns that was well beyond anything at an American Disney park before the raucous indoor Rock 'n' Roller Coaster opened in 1999 at Disney-MGM Studios.

> **Mouse mouths.** Walt Disney himself performed the voices of Mickey and Minnie in the earliest cartoons, including *Steamboat Willie,* which was the first Mickey Mouse cartoon with sound—but not the first movie starring the rascally rodent. That honor went to *Plane Crazy.* The current voice of the Mickster is Wayne Allwine.

Just outside the gates to the park is Disney Village, a cross between Pleasure Island at Walt Disney World, Church Street Station in Orlando, and CityWalk at Universal Studios in Hollywood. And absolutely not to be missed is Buffalo Bill's Wild West Show, one of the best dinner theaters I have seen. The show is loosely based on an actual touring company brought to France by Buffalo Bill.

We chose to make Disneyland Paris our base, venturing north to Paris and Versailles and southwest to Provins; you could also stay in Paris and commute down to the park quite easily.

Disneyland Paris is located about 20 miles east of Paris in Marne-la-Vallée. Direct shuttle bus service is available from Orly or Charles de Gaulle airports in Paris; or you can drive from Paris on the A4 motorway or take the new high-speed railway line that leads to a station directly at the gate to the park.

Disney has confirmed that it plans to eventually add at least one additional park at Disneyland Paris. Though the new park may end up with a movie theme, it apparently won't be called Disney-MGM Studios like the one in Florida. Disney has had an uneasy relationship with MGM in recent years.

Tokyo Disneyland

Hai, Mickey-san. If ever proof was required of the global impact of American popular culture, it came with the opening of Tokyo Disneyland in 1983. The park, six miles outside of Tokyo, is owned by a Japanese company under license to Disney. It includes familiar Disney attractions as well as new shows such as Pinocchio's Daring Journey, The Eternal Seas, and Meet the World.

Instead of Main Street, U.S.A., you'll find World Bazaar as the gateway to Adventureland, Fantasyland, Tomorrowland, and Westernland. Adventureland attractions include the Jungle Cruise, Enchanted Tiki Room, and Pirates of the Caribbean. In Westernland, you'll find the Mark Twain Riverboat, Tom Sawyer Island, The Golden Horseshoe Revue, and Country Bear Jamboree.

Fantasyland includes the Pinocchio ride, plus It's a Small World, Haunted Mansion, Snow White's Adventure, and the Mickey Mouse Revue. There are also venerable favorites Dumbo, the Flying Elephant, and Cinderella's Golden Carrousel.

Tomorrowland includes yet another Space Mountain, as well as Meet the World, an attraction based on Japanese history and the country's influence on the rest of the world.

A new park, Tokyo Disney Sea, is scheduled to open in late 2001 overlooking Tokyo Bay adjacent to Tokyo Disneyland Park. Surrounded by water (and aided by construction tricks that seem to extend the horizon of a small moat), the park will be centered around a globe-shaped fountain known as the AquaSphere, alive with the flow of water. Representing our Earth, the "water planet," the AquaSphere is intended to amaze viewers with dynamic cascades of water that flow down and around the globe, mysteriously clinging to its surface.

In a scheme that sounds somewhat like Universal's Islands of Adventure in Orlando, plans for the new Tokyo park call for seven distinct "ports of call."

Guests will experience the old world charm of the romantic southern European seaport of Mediterranean Harbor; discover portals to fantastic adventures deep within a smoldering volcano known as Mysterious Island; find the whimsical "under the sea" world of Ariel and all her friends from the classic Disney animated film "The Little Mermaid" in Mermaid Lagoon; encounter Aladdin and his playful Genie pal when they explore the exotic enchantment of "1001 Arabian Nights" along the shores of Arabian Coast; confront ancient perils and hidden mysteries in the jungles of Lost River Delta; travel across the horizons of time to Port Discovery, a futuristic marina that celebrates the thrills, adventure and excitement of new frontiers in the sea and sky; and take a step back in time to American Waterfront, which nostalgically showcases the harbors of New York and Cape Cod at the beginning of the 20th century.

In Mysterious Island, guests will venture to the ocean floor to explore the lost city of Atlantis in "20,000 Leagues Under the Sea," and take a thrilling journey far below an active volcano in "Journey to the Center of the Earth." In Arabian Coast, guests will board boats in "Sindbad's Seven Voyages " and set out with the famous sailor on a storybook journey through his treacherous travels. Boarding well-worn transports in the "Indiana Jones Adventure–Temple of the Crystal Skull," visitors to the jungles of Lost River Delta will join intrepid Indiana Jones on a perilous journey through the secret corridors of a foreboding Central American pyramid. Guests will also experience all the thrills of soaring high above the clouds and diving into the eye of a storm when they board "StormRider" in Port Discovery.

Located on the park's main waterfront in Mediterranean Harbor, the Tokyo DisneySea Hotel MiraCosta will offer breathtaking views of the park and Tokyo Bay. The MiraCosta will allow guests to stay overnight in the park.

The park will be connected to Tokyo Disneyland by monorail.

Suspended animation. A recurring rumor about dear old Walt Disney is that he chose to be cryogenically frozen when he died of lung cancer in 1966, in hopes of a defrost in another day and age. Actually, according to the company, he went to the other extreme and was cremated before burial at the famous Forest Lawn Memorial Park in California.

Part III
Universal Studios Escape

Chapter 15
A Burgeoning Universe

It's not a small world after all, anymore. In the summer of 1999, the kingdom of the mouse finally received some serious competition with the opening of a second Universal Studios theme park and a sprawling nighttime dining and entertainment complex.

It all comes together under the name Universal Studios Escape. Under that umbrella stands:

- Universal Studios Florida
- Universal Studios Islands of Adventure
- Universal Studios CityWalk
- The first of five large resort hotels. The elegant 750-room Portofino Bay Hotel opened in the fall of 1999, and the 650-room Hard Rock Hotel was due to open in 2000. Soon after then, work will be underway on the 1,000-room Royal Pacific Hotel. Two additional hotels planned for years to come will bring the total number of rooms on the park property to about 5,000.

And if that is not enough, Universal Studios also made a purchase of 2,000 more acres of land on the other side of I-4 that may one day hold a few more theme parks, another group of resort hotels, and other attractions.

On International Drive, Universal Studios also purchased Wet 'n Wild, a successful water park.

The bottom line at Universal: a doubling in size, and a claim on two or even three days of vacation time for Orlando visitors.

The Universal Story

It was almost 90 years ago that movie legend Carl Laemmle began to allow visitors—at 25 cents a head—to come to his studios to watch silent movies being made.

The tours at Universal Film Manufacturing Company in Hollywood were stopped when sound was added to film, but in 1964 the renamed Universal Studios reopened its doors to visitors.

Universal's Hollywood lot became the third most popular tourist attraction in the nation; visitors board trams that take them in and around the historic

Universal Studios Escape Tickets.
Prices were in effect for the summer of 1999 and are subject to change. One-day tickets are valid at either Universal Studios Florida or Universal Studios Islands of Adventure. Multi-day tickets allow moving back and forth between the parks on any day the tickets are in use. Add 6 percent tax to all prices

One-Day
Adult	$44.00
Child (3–9)	$35.00

Two-Day
Adult	$79.95
Child (3–9)	$64.95

Three-Day
Adult	$114.95
Child (3–9)	$94.95

Multi-day tickets never expire until used.

2-Park Annual Pass
Adult	$195.95
Child (3–9)	$154.95

2-Park Seasonal Annual Pass
Adult	$119.95
Child (3–9)	$109.95

Seasonal pass not valid in summer, Christmas, and Easter periods.

Universal Studios Florida Celebrity Annual Pass
Adult	$84.95
Child (3–9)	$69.95

Parking:	$6
Valet parking:	$12

For information, call (407) 363-8000, or consult www.uescape.com or www.universalstudios.com

backlot and soundstages of Universal City and along the way into some very special attractions based on some of the movie company's greatest hits.

In 1990, Universal moved east to Florida with the opening of its gigantic Orlando studios. Here are a few things to understand about Universal Studios Florida:

- It is a working studio, producing motion pictures, television shows, and commercials.

- Universal Studios Florida is more than 20 years newer than most of Walt Disney World, and Universal Studios Islands of Adventure is as state-of-the-art as theme parks come. Both parks include some of the most spectacular and state-of-the-art rides and attractions in the world, well beyond Pirates of the Caribbean.

- Universal Studios CityWalk offers some very sophisticated places to eat and to party, and best of all it sits at the entrance to both theme parks. You can break away from the rides for lunch or dinner, or end your day there. The somewhat equivalent Disney Downtown at Walt Disney World is a bus ride or automobile commute away from the parks or hotels.

The best times to come to Universal Studios Escape are the same as for other area attractions. Arrive between September and November, between Thanksgiving and Christmas, or in mid-January and you may be able to walk around like you own the place. Show up during Christmas break, Easter vacation, or mid-summer and you'll meet what seems like the entire population of Manhattan or Boston or Cleveland in front of you in line.

Universal Studios Escape is open 365 days a year. Hours of operation of the parks are adjusted based on projections for attendance and are subject to change. Check before you make plans for late evenings.

Also note that some of the shows are opened on a staggered basis. When

Universal Studios Islands of Adventure by night
© 1999 Universal Studios Escape

you first walk in the door at a quiet time of year, you may find that some of the shows don't offer performances before 11 A.M. or noon; head for the rides first.

Universal Studios sells VIP Tours for each of the parks through its guest relations desk. For about $110 each plus tax, a group of as many as 15 people will have their own guide for a four-hour half-day with the privilege of entering through "back doors" to most of the attractions at the park. For $1,500 plus tax, you can hire an "exclusive" tour with up to 15 people you choose. Neither tour includes lunch. As expensive as the tours are, they might begin to make sense if you are forced to visit the park on a day when all of the major rides have 90-minute waits. There are about a dozen tour guides available; Guest Services usually requires 48 hours notice before a tour. Reservations must

Orlando FlexTickets. Prices were in effect in the summer of 1999 and are subject to change. Add 6 percent tax to prices.

Visit any of the parks within the same day. Parking fee required only once each day at first park visited.

3-Park Orlando FlexTicket: $107.95 (ages 10 and above), $89.95 (ages 3 to 9). Unlimited admission to Universal Studios Florida, SeaWorld Orlando, Wet 'n Wild Orlando. Valid 7 consecutive days.

4-Park Orlando FlexTicket: $159.95, or $127.95 (ages 3 to 9) Unlimited admission to Universal Studios Florida, Universal Studios Islands of Adventure, SeaWorld Orlando, Wet 'n Wild. Valid 7 days.

5-Park Orlando FlexTicket: $196.95, or $157.95 (ages 3 to 9). Unlimited admission to Universal Studios Florida, Universal Studios Islands of Adventure, SeaWorld Orlando, Wet 'n Wild, Busch Gardens Tampa. Valid 10 consecutive days.

Universal Studios Islands of Adventure from above
© *1999 Universal Studios Escape*

be made at least 72 hours in advance and prepaid; call (407) 363-8295. One downside is that you'll miss some of the clever entertainments presented in the waiting lines; then again, you'll miss the waiting lines.

Upgrading your ticket. If you decide that you want to come back for a second day at Universal Studios, visit Guest Relations to upgrade your ticket to a two-day pass. You must do this on the day of purchase of the original ticket. During the off-season, Universal sometimes offers a "second day free" promotion. And if you are a regular visitor to Orlando, you might want to consider buying an annual pass, available for year-round or seasonal periods.

Travel to the park:

Universal Studios Escape is located near the intersection of Interstate 4 and the Florida Turnpike in Orlando. The main entrance is about one-half mile north of I-4 at exit 30B—Kirkman Road (Highway 435). Another entrance is located on Turkey Lake Road.

From Orlando International Airport: Take 528 West (the Bee-Line Expressway) toward Tampa and Walt Disney World. Watch for signs to Interstate 4 East (to Orlando); take the Universal Studios exit 30B.

From Walt Disney World: Take I-4 East (to Orlando) to the Universal Studios exit 30B.

Or, take Universal Boulevard (formerly Republic Drive) into the park.

Universal Studios Escape is jointly owned by MCA, Inc., and The Rank Organization. Rank's worldwide interests include the famous Pinewood Studios in England, one of the world's largest film libraries, video production, and film processing facilities and hotels, restaurants, and recreational services. Its brands include Hard Rock, Odeon, Butlin's, and Mecca. MCA in turn is a unit of the Seagram Company Ltd.

A Place to Spend the Night

Part of the master plan for Universal Studios Escape is to capture as many visitors as possible to spend their entire vacation time on Universal property.

The Portofino Bay Hotel at Universal Studios Escape is the first hotel on the theme park property. The beautifully detailed hotel is set alongside a lagoon, recreating a bit of the charm and romantic harbor setting of the Mediterranean seaside village of Portofino in Italy.

The Portofino Bay, managed by Loews, includes eight restaurants and lounges, two swimming pools, a pair of bocci ball courts, and a large convention and meeting space.

The Hard Rock Hotel, due to open in 2001, will showcase architectural styles of a California mission. Public areas will be decorated with pieces from Hard Rock's extensive collection of rock 'n roll memorabilia.

All of the hotels will be connected to each other and to Universal Studios, Universal Studios Islands of Adventure, and Universal Studios CityWalk by a chain of scenic waterways. Guests will be able to take water taxis ro various areas of the park.

Guests at hotels in the park will be allowed early admission to the theme parks, with VIP access to special attractions during the first hour the parks operate. Guests will also be offered priority reservations at restaurants in the hotels and the parks.

Portofino Bay Hotel at Universal Studios Escape
© *1999 Universal Studios Escape*

UNIVERSAL STUDIOS ESCAPE

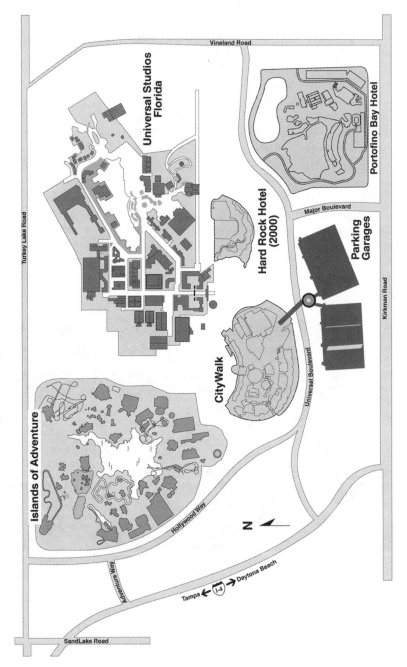

Chapter 16
Universal Studios Florida

Ride the movies, they promise. While you're at it, surf the TV shows, too. And immerse yourself in one of the most thematically consistent theme parks in the world.

Universal Studios Florida is a place where fans of Hollywood's greatest hits can extend the experience of the big screen into state-of-the-art rides and shows. This is the home of, among others, Jaws, King Kong, the Terminator, E.T., Hercules & Xena, and Beetlejuice. For kids of all ages, here you'll meet the universe of Hanna-Barbera, Woody Woodpecker, Barney, Feivel, and Curious George. Fans of the classics can pay tribute to Alfred Hitchcock, Lucille Ball, Hollywood makeup magicians, stunt men and women, and even animal star actors.

New in 1999 was an expansion of offerings to the youngest visitors, at the Woody Woodpecker Kidzone, which encompasses Animal Actors Stage, E.T. Adventure, A Day in the Park with Barney. Feivel's Playland, and the new attractions of Woody Woodpecker's Nuthouse Coaster and Curious George Goes to Town.

And sometime in the summer of 2000, look for the opening of Men in Black, the Ultimate Bug Hunt. A huge new building to house the techno-thriller was under construction between Back to the Future and the Wild, Wild, Wild West Stunt Show.

Power Trip #1

First Things First

Lines at some of the more popular attractions can build to as much as 90 minutes on busy days; the Power Trip puts you on a fast track for the major magnets in the morning, with a more leisurely pace for the rest of the day.

Once the new **Men in Black** ride opens sometime in the summer of 2000, it is sure to be the major attraction at the park; head there first or last to avoid the crowds.

Until then, the spectacular **Terminator 2 3-D** show, the **Twister** attraction, the **Jaws** ride, and the older but wilder **Back to the Future** simulator are the biggest draws at the park; therefore the smartest plan is to head for one of them as soon as you arrive at the park—and the earlier the better. Make your first right turn on Rodeo Drive and go directly to Terminator 2 3-D; if you're in the first crush of visitors you should be able to meet your robotic fate within half an hour. When the show lets out, continue up Hollywood Blvd. to Sunset Blvd. and head directly for Back to the Future. Lines should still be at manageable levels in the morning. When you're back to the present, continue around the lagoon to Jaws.

Warning: in our judgment, many young visitors and some older ones may find these rides to be too wild; if you're not up to the journey, go instead to the **E.T. Adventure** as your first stop.

When you are through with your early targets, you can check out the lines at the ride you missed, or make plans to come back late in the day.

Continue around the lagoon in a counterclockwise direction to **Earthquake— The Big One** and ride the subway to San Francisco. Exit that ride and continue to **Kongfrontation.**

Now, head to the front of the park and **The Funtastic World of Hanna-Barbera**, where you will probably find a growing line. It's worth the wait for youngsters; adults may choose to pass it by, especially if they've been to The Future already.

Youngsters will certainly want to visit **Nickelodeon Studios.** We also recommend to adults **Alfred Hitchcock: The Art of Making Movies.**

You have now seen the major attractions of the park. Check the daily schedule for show times and then make a second tour to visit **The Gory, Gruesome & Grotesque Horror Make-Up Show**, the **E.T. Adventure** if you missed it the first time around and if the lines are at a reasonable length, the **Animal Actors Stage**, the **Wild, Wild, Wild West Stunt Show**, **Ghostbusters**, and **Hercules and Xena: Wizards of the Screen.**

The **Dynamite Nights Stunt Spectacular** is worth a peek. At the same time, though, while it's on and drawing thousands to the sides of the lagoon, it's a pretty good time to duck into one of the major shows for a second ride or to catch one you've missed. Go back to Back to the Future or Jaws now.

Twister is a major draw; go there early or late to avoid being caught in a very slow-moving warm front.

Power Trip #2

Counter-Revolutionary

Here's an alternate plan for use on the very busiest days. It works especially well when you have a full day and the park is open late.

Start by going clockwise, against the crowds sprinting for Men in Black, Terminator 2 3-D, Jaws, or Back to the Future. Instead, your first stop should be one of the big draws near the entrance to the park. Try **Kongfrontation**, then **Earthquake** and then, depending on length of line, visit **Alfred Hitchcock**, and **The Funtastic World of Hanna-Barbera**. By this time, the park should be pretty crowded; have an early lunch. For the rest of the afternoon, visit the less-crowded shows including **Nickelodeon, Hercules and Xena: Wizards of the Screen,** the **Wild, Wild, Wild West Stunt Show, Animal Actors Stage,** and **The Gory, Gruesome & Grotesque Horror Make-Up Show.**

Have an early dinner. As the rest of the visitors collapse from waiting in lines all day, use the evening to see the biggest draws: **Terminator 2 3-D, Jaws, Back to the Future,** and **E.T. Adventure,** plus any other shows you missed in the morning.

Attractions at Universal Studios Florida

Expo Center

WOW! Back to the Future . . . The Ride. Dive into the world of the record-breaking movie trilogy, *Back to the Future* in Universal's incredible simulator adventure. This is about as wild a ride as anything you'll find in Florida, with the possible exception of the real Space Shuttle. There is absolutely nothing like it at Walt Disney World.

It seems that weird Doc Brown is back home conducting new time travel experiments. He has created his newest vehicle—an eight-passenger Time Vehicle that is faster and more energy efficient than anything before . . . or since. That's the good news. The bad news is that Biff Tannen has broken into the Institute of Future Technology and threatens to end the universe as we know it! It's up to you to jump into your own DeLorean and chase down Biff.

Surrounded by images and sound and buffeted by the realistic motion of your flight simulator, you will soar into Hill Valley in the year 2015, blast back to the Ice Age for a chilling high-speed encounter with canyons of sheer ice, explode into the Volcanic Era for a once-in-a-lifetime encounter with a Tyrannosaurus rex and then through a volcano and over the edge of a molten lava fall.

This is a state-of-the-art attraction that combines a spectacular 70-mm Omnimax film with simulator ride vehicles (bearing Florida license plates "OUTTATIME"). The 80-foot-diameter domelike screens of the Omnimax theaters occupy all of the viewer's peripheral vision, making the screen seem to vanish and take the viewer into the scene.

Production schedule. To find out what is "in production" at the studios, call the Guest Services office at (407) 354-6356.

Shopper's pass. Need to grab a quick souvenir on your way to the airport? You can purchase a Shopper's Pass at the Guest Services window; you'll put down a deposit equal to a full-price ticket, which will be refunded if you return to the window within an hour.

Universal on the Web. Visitors to the Internet's World Wide Web can check out the latest news from Orlando at www.usf.com

Triple A. Most of the gift shops and several of the sitdown restaurants within Universal Studios will give a 10 percent discount to AAA members; bring your card.

MUST-SEES

Men in Black
(Don't bug anyone until the summer of 2000)

Terminator 2 3-D

Back to the Future . . . The Ride

E.T. Adventure

Animal Actors Stage

Earthquake— The Big One

Jaws

Twister

Kongfrontation

Hitchcock's 3-D Theatre

The Funtastic World of Hanna-Barbera
(Children of all ages)

Nickelodeon Studios
(Kids and their escorts)

Woody Woodpecker's Nuthouse Coaster
(A little coaster for little coasters)

Curious George Goes to Town
(Don't get into trouble, kids)

The Institute of Future Technology in the waiting area features actual props from the *Back to the Future* movie series, including hoverboards (futuristic skateboards without wheels) and the all-important flux capacitors for time travel.

Check out the bulletin board in the waiting area where you will see the names of some of the visiting scientists who have offices in the building. They include guys named Thomas Edison, Albert Einstein, and Francis Bacon.

There are actually two identical rides in the building, each with its own set of 12 eight-seater DeLoreans and movie dome. Each area has cars on three levels with three cars at the top, five in the middle, and four at the bottom.

Universal insiders say that the very best experience can be had by sitting in the front row of the center car on the second tier; dispatchers call it Car 6. This particular vehicle is in the absolute center of the movie dome and you cannot easily see any surrounding cars that might distract from the illusion.

At about the midway point of the waiting line visitors will be divided among three ramps, one to each level. If you can at all arrange to go through portal number two to the middle level, you have a one-in-five chance of ending up in magic Car 6.

If you are concerned about getting motion sickness, you may want to try to get onto the lower level of the ride. (I prefer a Dramamine in the morning and Car 6.)

When you enter the holding room for the simulator, try to maneuver next to the door to get a seat in the front of the car. (Some visitors find the small waiting room a bit confining; you can ask the attendant to leave the door open if you feel it necessary. Trust us: a much more intense experience is coming.)

As you wait to board your simulator, pay attention to the little movie about time travel safety; we enjoyed watching crash dummies "Fender" and "Bender" at work. When you feel a rumble beneath your feet, you'll know the car is returning to its base.

The preshow film and the movie shown in the ride itself were made specially for the simulator. Doc Brown (Christopher Lloyd) and Biff Tannen (Thomas Wilson) took part in the movie, but Marty McFly (Michael J. Fox) is nowhere to be seen. According to rumors, Fox asked for too much money.

The glass case in the preflight waiting room includes some juicy little details for fans of the film. In the famous Car 6, you'll find a notepad discussing the results of various flights in which Doc Brown reports he discussed the theory of electricity with Benjamin Franklin and philosophy with Mark Twain. On one of the flights, Brown reports he attended a presidential inauguration, noting that "she is quite a woman."

The DeLoreans themselves rise about eight feet out of their garages at the start of the movie. Once in the air, four actuators drive the car—three for vertical movement and one for fore-and-aft movement. Although it may feel as if your car is soaring and dropping hundreds of feet, the entire range of movement for the vehicle is about two feet.

To give the feeling of traveling through space, the cars are surrounded with a fog made from liquid nitrogen.

On a busy day, lines easily reach to 90 minutes or more. Remember that the crowd you see out on the plaza is only about half the backup—there are internal walkways and hallways as well. Each ride takes about 4½ minutes, with about 96 persons entering each of the two simulator theaters at a time. By the end of the day on a quiet day, there may be no line at all. But it still takes 15 minutes or so to walk into the gate, up the stairs, into a waiting room for one of the simulators, and into your seat.

How long can the lines get at Back to the Future? Well, let's just say that this is the first waiting line I have ever seen with a beer vendor halfway to the entrance.

Coming attraction. If you have really sharp eyes and a good sense of balance, keep an eye out during your wild Back to the Future ride for the movie poster on the wall in Hill Valley; it advertises *Jaws 19.*

You're being watched. I took a backstage tour of Back to the Future, visiting the computer rooms and the security "tower" where operators monitor all 12 cars in each theater using see-in-the-dark video cameras. They are able to turn off individual cars if anything goes wrong or a rider becomes ill or faints.

From 2001 to the Future. The director of the Back to the Future ride-film was renowned movie special effects designer Douglas Trumbull, who created special effects for hits including *2001: A Space Odyssey,* and *Close Encounters of the Third Kind.* The 4-minute 70-mm movie portion of the ride took two years to make and cost as much as a feature film. Elaborate hand-painted miniatures were created for the filming.

Don't say you weren't warned. Back to the Future is described as a "dynamically aggressive ride." Visitors suffering from maladies including dizziness, seizures, back or neck problems, claustrophobia, motion sickness, and heart disorders, as well as pregnant women, are advised to sit this one out. The ride also won't work for persons of a certain size or shape who cannot fit into the seats and safety harness. We suspect you know who you are.

Meeting spot. If you're planning to do a baby swap, ask for advice from one of the attendants on the proper place to wait. And, if you need to meet someone after the ride, pick a specific spot such as the Jules Verne Train, because there are two exits from the building.

Before or after you join the line, check out the large prop to the left of the building. The Jules Verne Train was used in the closing scene of *Back to the Future III*, when Doc Brown returns from 1885 in this steam engine adapted to become a time machine.

Woody Woodpecker's Kidzone

WOW E.T. Adventure. One of the best-loved movies of all times is given life in this imaginative ride which begins where *E.T.* left off. You will share a bicycle with our favorite extraterrestrial in a voyage across the moon to save E.T.'s home, a planet dying for lack of his healing touch.

The huge miniature city beneath your bicycle includes 3,340 tiny buildings, 250 ultra-compact cars, and 1,000 street lights. The stars above include some 4,400 points of light. The music for the ride was written by Academy Award–winning composer John Williams, who was also responsible for the movie score.

As marvelous as the ride itself is, don't overlook the incredible fantasy world of the waiting area. It will start when you register at the door and are cast as an actor in the coming adventure; be sure to hold on to the special card you are given until it is collected as you climb onto your bicycle.

The entrance line wends its way through a mysterious redwood forest populated with all sorts of human and otherworldly creatures. All around you, government agents search for E.T.

Finally, you are at your bicycle. As with most of the other rides at Universal, the E.T. ride has been subtly improved over the years. The beginning is now much scarier as your bicycle is pursued by police cars with searchlights. Nicer effects include a gorgeous star field using fiber optics; throughout the rest of the ride the colors have been brightened. New fog and smoke effects were also added. It's the same wonderful ride it used to be, only better.

Higher and higher you climb, until the city looks like a toy beneath you. Director Steven Spielberg created a phantasmagorical cast of new characters for the adventure, including Botanicus, Tickli Moot Moot, Orbidon, Magdol, Horn-Flowers, Tympani Tremblies, Water Imps, Big Zoms, Gurgles, Squirtals, and Churtles. Will you arrive home at the Green Planet in time?

Well, yes: and the celebration begins as E.T.'s friend the Tickli Moot Moot laughs again, Orbidon sparkles, and Magdol sings. Baby E.T.s will dance and play all around you, and E.T. will thank you . . . personally.

WOW Animal Actors Stage. And you think you've a right to be proud when Bowser rolls over the third time you ask? Wait until you see the professionals at work—they've pawed and clawed their way to the top of animal show business.

I was especially impressed with the cat who opens the show. Yes, that's right: a trained domestic cat. He runs out onto the stage, gives the audience a glance, and then climbs up the wall, jumps into a basket, and sits there waiting for a dog to pull him up by rope. Then the cat runs across a catwalk and pushes down a sign that says "Welcome to the Animal Actors Stage." I don't know about yours, but our family cat Friskey would never stoop so low as to perform tricks for mere humans.

> **Mr. Ed, unmuzzled.** We hope we're not going to shatter any heartfelt illusions, but we trust you realize that Mr. Ed does not really talk. His trainers fill his mouth with peanut butter before he goes on stage, which makes him want to move his jaws any time his bit is loosened.

The cast of animals changes during the year. On one visit, the stars included Lassie (actually, one of many collies who have held that name over time), Benji, and even a horsing-around Mr. Ed.

Most of Universal Studios Florida's dogs and cats were rescued from the pound before they went on to stardom. Benji has appeared in four movies—three bearing his name, plus *Oh, Heavenly Dog!* with Chevy Chase. He has

Woody Woodpecker's Nuthouse Coaster
© 1999 Universal Studios Escape

twice been named the Animal Actor of the Year by the American Guild of Variety Artists. We've also seen stars of *Ace Ventura* and *The Flintstones*, and bit parts played by raccoons, skunks, and a sea lion.

The open-air stadium will accommodate 1,500 people for its 25-minute show; it is a good place to take an afternoon break when lines are longest at the most popular attractions and the sun is at its hottest.

WOW Woody Woodpecker's Nuthouse Coaster. Equal rights for kids: why should adults have all the thrills? In 1999, the Woodster arrived with his own kid-sized roller coaster, installing a brilliant red 800-foot-long track through a cartoon factory, and there's lots of small surprises for young riders. This ride is not The Hulk or Dueling Dragons–the monster rides next door at Universal Studios Islands of Adventure–but then kids aren't allowed on those coasters anyway. Think of Nuthouse Coaster as a thrill ride with training wheels.

The coaster's highest point reaches a top speed of 22 miles per hour, with a maximum height of 28 feet; the 16-car train takes 90 seconds from start to finish.

Riders must be at least three years old and able to sit up; kids under 48 inches must be accompanied by an adult.

WOW Curious George Goes to Town. Everyone's favorite mischievous monkey arrived at Universal Studios in the summer of 1999. (For the record, he pushed aside the creepy Psycho House movie false front that had stood on a hill nearby. We suppose that's a good thing.)

It seems that George has let loose a bit of havoc by freeing the animals from their cages, leaving them open for kids to climb through. Following George's footsteps into the town's plaza there's a dream of a playground, including a room with 12,500 foam balls to throw, shoot, and dump on each other. Outside, a pair of balconies face each other across the plaza with water cannons. Up above, two 500-gallon buckets fill up every few minutes and then dump their load on watchers below.

Fievel's Playland. Now here's *serious* entertainment for the very youngest visitors to Universal Studios, and a good place to burn off some energy.

The playground, based loosely on the *An American Tail* animated movies, is located between the E.T. Adventure and the Animal Actors Stage.

The playground is padded with a soft absorbent surface to protect kids who might fall. It includes a carnival-like air pillow for jumping, a 30-foot climbing net, and a kids-only water slide.

Actually, the sign at the water slide has a measuring post at about 40 inches that says: "If you ain't this tall, bring an adult." Another sign warns that the slide will give you wet breeches, and this is quite true. The slide itself, on a small raft, is short and not nearly as wild as bigger rides at water parks. The line for the slide can become quite long, and parents who do not accompany their kids will probably want to park themselves at the bottom of the slide to retrieve them.

It might be possible to let your kids run loose at the playground while an adult waits in line at E.T.; I'd suggest you keep them out of line for the water slide, though, since it would be impossible to retrieve them quickly if they were way up in the queue.

A Day in the Park with Barney. This interactive musical show and hands-on educational playground stars the ubiquitous purple dinosaur, his best friend Baby Bop, and her big brother BJ. The 350-seat theater-in-the-round teaches life lessons through song, dance, and play. Special effects take guests through the seasons of the year with wind, falling leaves, light rain, and even snow; clouds and stars appear magically on a 360-degree projection screen. Songs include some of Barney's favorites, such as "Mr. Knickerbocker," "If You're Happy and You Know It," and his chart-topping hit, "I Love You." Adults are excused unless accompanied by an insistent youngster.

Visitors enter the attraction through a landscaped park to a central court-yard where a statue of the dino-star is surrounded by playful streams of water. Gently winding paths meander through the park, inviting guests to try out the interactive Humming Stone, a kaleidoscope, or the sand sculpture wheel.

The centerpiece is the Barney Theater, of course. In the preshow area, visitors are met by a new character, Mr. Peekaboo, a bumbling but good-hearted fellow who introduces himself to the crowd with a lighthearted but forgetful song. When children remind him of whom they came to see, he urges them to use their imaginations . . . encouraged by a colorful waterfall wall that beckons them into the theater.

After the show, children of all ages are invited into Barney's backyard, which features interactive delights that include a water-harp that plays music as visitors run their fingers through its streams of water, and a woodpipe xylophone. Brightly colored rocks emit musical tones when stepped on, and rainbow lights sparkle everywhere.

San Francisco/Amity

WOW Earthquake—The Big One. Why in the world would any sane human being want to travel all the way to Orlando, fork over a not-small number of hard-earned bucks, and then wait in a long line for the privilege of walking right into a devastating earthquake?

Well, it has to be because this ride is devastating fun. This spectacular attraction is based on the motion picture *Earthquake,* which was the first movie in history to win an Academy Award for special effects.

Six visitors—usually three women, a man, and two kids—are picked as extras and "grips" for a demonstration of movie special effects. The kids

Out of business. On the streets of San Francisco, note the impressive facade of Ferries & Cliff, one of the biggest department stores in the city at the turn of the century. It collapsed in the great earthquake of 1906 and was never rebuilt, except at Universal Studios.

And then check out the photos along the walls of the preshow area. Universal researchers uncovered a treasure trove of photos from the family of a survivor of the 1906 San Francisco earthquake.

Heavy effects. The special effects of this ride are among the most spectacular ever created for an amusement park. To begin with, the rocking and rolling of the simulated earthquake would actually register a whopping 8.3 on the Richter scale. The mega-tremor releases 65,000 gallons of (recycled) water every six minutes. The falling roadway slab weighs 45,000 pounds.

Perhaps most interesting is the fact that the tracks themselves remain stable; all of the rocking and rolling takes place with lifters within the train itself.

Backstage at the earthquake. We took an exclusive tour into the control room and observed the computer controls for the sophisticated ride. You can see the room along the right side of the train in the catastrophe station; it's the operator who runs out with a megaphone at the end of each adventure.

get to fulfill a child's fantasy: dropping (foam) boulders on a bunch of adults; the male extra is in for a surprise dive.

Before the action, you'll see a short film about some of the special effects used in the film. Most interesting is probably the miniature city constructed for one of the most spectacular scenes in the movie. It took six months to build at a cost of about $2.5 million, and about six minutes to destroy; the actual sequence in the movie takes even less than that.

I'd suggest you move all the way across the rows in the demonstration area so you can move quickly to the train for your choice of seats. When the demonstration is over, you will enter into a realistic re-creation of a subway station in Oakland and board a train heading to Embarcadero Station in San Francisco.

The front of the 200-seat train is to your left; the best car for the ride is the second car from the front. The first row of each car has a somewhat blocked view; try to grab a seat in the middle. The right side of the train (the far side of the row as you get in) has the best view of the flood; the left side of the train (where the last person in the row gets on board) is closest to the explosions and the train crash.

The train pulls out of the station and under the bay to the Embarcadero station. Right away something goes very wrong. The train begins to shake violently, lights flicker, and the ceiling starts to collapse. The street above your head caves in, and a huge propane tanker truck crashes its way toward you. But that's only the beginning: another train bears down on you at high speed aiming for a head-on crash. Finally, a huge tidal wave races your way.

Cut!

Amity Games. Down by the waterfront, there's a movie set version of a boardwalk, complete with games of chance that include **Short Shot** basketball, **Milk Can Menagerie**, **Hoop Toss**, **Shark-Banger** (a version of the familiar whack-a-mole game), **Wave Roll**, **Goblet Lob**, **Quarter Pitch**, and **Dolphin Dash**.

WOW Jaws. Just when you thought it was safe to go back to Florida, Universal Studios went and opened **Jaws**, a spectacular new ride based on the movie classic that kept millions out of the ocean 20 years ago.

It's always the Fourth of July in the picturesque seaside resort of Amity. You can walk the boardwalk and try your hand at carnival games or stop for a seafood snack. And, of course, you are going to want to hop on board the Amity Harbor tour boat for a peaceful jaunt.

The five-minute cruise starts out innocently enough. The vicious little shark that had previously terrorized Amity hangs—dead—from a hook in the village. So what could possibly go wrong?

Well, OK, we imagine you have guessed what happens next. Your boat will motor gently around the corner, past a picturesque little lighthouse to find the wreckage of a tour boat just like the one you are in. A moment later, the harbor explodes with terror as a 32-foot, three-ton killer great white shark decides to invite you all to lunch. His lunch, that is.

It starts with a quick glimpse of a dorsal fin that zips past and then under your boat. Then he comes back!

Your boat captain will attempt to save the day, firing rifle grenades in a desperate attempt to stop the attacker. Somehow he will steer the boat into the safety of a deserted boathouse. Hah! Suddenly there's a loud crash on the side of the boathouse and the wall all but comes down with the force of Jaws breaking through.

Now it's a race for life as the boat is chased by the frenzied creature. This time the captain's shots hit a chemical tank along shore and the lagoon fills with burning fuel as he attempts to break for safety on a barge that carries the main power supply cable to Amity Island.

Once again the shark attacks, but this time he grabs hold of the main power cable: instant fish fry! At last, you're safe . . . right?

Some young visitors may find the explosions and the hot steam that envelops you at the end of the ride frightening; the fright level of the Jaws ride has ratcheted up a bit in recent years.

The left side of the boat is definitely the place to be for the more adventurous traveler; that's the side closest to the explosions, fire, Jaws, and . . . water. The fifth row of the boat lines up

Land line. How long is that line for Jaws? Here is a formula to estimate the wait: there are eight boats, each capable of holding 48 visitors, and the ride takes six minutes. Allowing two minutes to load and unload, that means each boat will carry about 336 passengers an hour. The eight boats, then, will move about 2,688 victims per hour across Amity Harbor.

By the way, the Jaws boat ride may be shut down if an electrical storm is in the area.

Vital stats. The Jaws ride employs space-age underwater technology never before used in an amusement attraction.

The 7-acre lagoon holds 5 million gallons of water and there are eight boats. Much of the New England memorabilia scattered about was found in Gloucester, Massachusetts, and surrounding fishing towns.

The 32-foot shark is made of steel and fiberglass, with a latex skin; its teeth are made of urethane. When it attacks, it moves through the water at realistic shark speeds of 20 feet per second, with thrusts equal to the power of a 727 jet engine.

Pool room. The lagoon at Universal Studios is actually a 15 million-gallon pool with a gunite bottom.

directly with the shark in some of the most spectacular scenes. By the way, when the ride first opened, Universal set decorators included a pair of mouse ears in the shark's mouth, but the top brass decided it was too scary for youngsters . . . and Disney.

Dynamite Nights Stunt Spectacular.
A wild demonstration of explosive movie stunts, performed on the lagoon. There's no waiting line for the show—just pull up a piece of the railing. In peak season the show is presented more than once each day; check the daily schedule for show times. There's a story line for those who care about such things: something about a high-energy shootout with desperate drug dealers.

Bottoms up. There is a block of seats at the Wild, Wild, etc. show that is marked "splash zone." Sit there if you are overdue for a shower. The water doesn't come from the "well" on the stage, though; that's a stunt pit, about six feet deep and padded on the bottom with a trampoline.

Wild, Wild, Wild West Stunt Show.
Guns blaze, cowboys brawl, and dynamite creates instant urban renewal in Universal's re-creation of a 19th-century western town. Hollywood stunt players demonstrate how they simulate the dangerous action.

The show, held in a 2,000-seat arena, is short, intense, and suitable for kids of all ages, although some of the explosions and gunfire are a bit loud. There's a little story about a rough and tough "Ma" and her gang of boys; the guys in the white hats win, but not before there's a terrific battle down in the corral, up on the roofs, and even out on the ropes that hold the sign ("Square Dance and Hanging, Saturday Night") across Main Street.

Watch out for the splash zone near the well at the left front of the stage.

New York

WOW Twister. Here's your chance to step into the room with a murderous tornado.

That's the storyline of the spectacular new attraction, based on the wildly successful movie of the same name and basically the same story.

Guests entering into the waiting line find themselves in an outdoor field littered with re-creations of some of the film's props and artifacts. The setting is Wakita, Oklahoma, population 585. You'll see old farm equipment, an Esmoo Dairy truck with its signature cow symbol, and a collection of storm-tracking vehicles. Monitors overhead show footage of actual tornadoes.

Eventually you'll make your way into the preshow area. There actor Bill Paxton deadpans his way through an introduction to the art and technique behind the film. The 300-mile-an-hour twister in the film, Paxton says, is classified as an "F5, a once-in-a-lifetime monster tornado." Some call a twister of that magnitude the "finger of God," he tells us.

Actress Helen Hunt livens up the place later with more details about filming in and around the real town of Wakita, in "tornado alley." Some of the scenes in the film, we learn, were enhanced with the winds produced by a commercial jet engine. The room is decorated with actual props from the film.

We enter into what is left of Aunt Meg's home, destroyed by a twister in the film, and from there into one last large area where we look out on the Galaxy Drive-In, a scene from the movie. The marquee at the theater promises "A Night of Horror."

Take a moment to drink in the details. You'll hear the sound of crickets. Look for the shadow of a worker inside Erik's Garage. If you watch very carefully, you'll see a snippet of the famous shower scene from *Psycho* on the screen.

But it's showers of another sort that grab our attention. Rain begins to pelt the drive-in; we're somewhat protected by the tin roof over the shelter where we stand.

The storm begins to intensify. A window in the projection booth shatters. A stormchaser truck, with the film's "Dorothy" experiment on its flatbed, blows in from the left and knocks over a fire hydrant.

A bolt of lightning splits a tree, and the wind and rain is suddenly very intense. The flimsy tin roof over our heads doesn't provide much shelter any more.

Finally, the event that has drawn us volunteers: a five-story tornado grows before our eyes. We feel the wind, see the finger of God, and hear its freight train rumble.

Was that an Esmoo cow flying over our heads?

And then a truck slides across the parking lot to strike the gas pumps outside of Erik's Garage. A line of flame moves toward the leaking gas.

Boom! And it's over . . . and we lucky survivors get to walk out into the giftshop, a place where you can buy souvenirs that declare to the world that you have been to a place where cows fly.

Twister replaced the *Ghostbusters* attraction that had a long run there; the building was almost completely rebuilt within its exterior shell. Twister was originally scheduled to open in early 1998 but was delayed out of respect for several Florida communities ravaged by real tornadoes in February of that year.

A trip through the Twister attraction will take about 20 minutes, plus the length of the waiting line. The tornado scene itself takes only about two-and-a-half minutes. If the outdoor queue is full when you arrive, you can expect about an hour's wait; if the line extends out the door and onto the street you'd probably be better off coming back later.

WOW **Kongfrontation.** It's the big banana himself, and you are a helpless captive in New York's Roosevelt Island tram. In fact, you're so close you can smell the bananas on his breath.

The 4½-minute adventure begins as you walk through a beautifully constructed replica of a Manhattan subway station, complete with advertising posters appropriately redecorated with graffiti. Up above are a series of television sets, and as you move through the building watch for news bulletins about the wild escapades of the famous ape.

Write if you get work.
When the park was first opened, Universal hired a graffiti artist from New York to decorate the walls of the tram waiting area. Since then, a lot more has been added by amateurs.

Kong's coat and other details. King Kong, the biggest computer-animated figure ever built, wears a 7,000-pound fur coat. Standing four stories tall and weighing six tons, he has an arm span of 54 feet. The rescue helicopters are molded from real National Guard OH6 choppers.

Expensive stains. The New York streets are made of concrete; a mold was applied to make the roads appear to be constructed of cobblestones. All of the cracks in the road, bubble gum on the sidewalks, and rust stains on the stone (styrofoam, actually) walls were applied by artists.

The Big Apple has been turned into a war zone, with wrecked cars, burst water mains, and massive fires. As your 60-seat tram makes a turn, you arrive at the Queensboro Bridge to find the big guy hanging from the supports. Uprooting telephone poles as if they were toothpicks, he reaches for your tram . . . until a helicopter makes a brave attempt to distract him.

Phew! You're safe. But are you, really?

The Kongfrontation set is based on Manhattan's lower west side in 1976, the setting for the remake of *King Kong,* starring Jessica Lange and Jeff Bridges. Pay attention to the little details along the way—peek into some of the windows of the tenements and see schoolkid drawings, posters, and boxes of food.

New Yorkers will note that the moviemaking magic ignores a few Big Apple facts. You enter into the ride through a replica of Penn Station which is on the west side of Manhattan; within, though, is the Roosevelt Island Tram, which is on the east side.

This is a must-see show, but be forewarned that lines can build by midday. Go early or late.

Beetlejuice's Graveyard Revue. This is the ultimate in graveyard rock, a tuneful singing and dancing show presented in a shaded outdoor amphitheater and starring everybody's favorite creep, Beetlejuice, and a monstrous cast of characters that includes Wolfman, Dracula, Frankenstein, the Phantom of the Opera, and the Bride of Frankenstein.

The background music is tape recorded, but the singing and dancing is live and very entertaining, although the very young and older adults may find it a bit loud. Pay attention to some of the inside jokes: Beetlejuice takes a gander at the creepy old horror set and comments, "Hey, it looks like Tim Burton's summer home." He introduces Frankenstein as "a man of many parts—all of them used." And the Bride: "this month's cover girl from *Popular Mechanics.*"

We especially enjoyed the stage performance of the "Banana Song" from the movie, as Beetlejuice dances with a pair of shrunken head dummies.

The Beetlejuice Revue is even better at night; the crowd is a little more rowdy and the lighting effects look especially impressive against the dark sky. Check the schedule for the hours of performance.

Beetlejuice is a character on loan from Warner Bros., while the rest of the awful actors are from Universal classics.

The Blues Brothers in Chicago Bound. They may be headed for the Windy City, but you'll find these two stand-ins for those strange rhythm and bluesmen performing on a stoop in New York's Delancey Street. Check the daily schedule for their next appearance.

Arcades. As if you needed any more excitement, there is a state-of-the-art video arcade in the New York section that offers a good selection of current games.

Production Central

Hercules and Xena: Wizards of the Screen. Hercules and Xena, among the top-rated syndicated action shows on American television, spring to life in an interactive live attraction based on *Hercules: The Legendary Journeys* and *Xena: Warrior Princess*. The show uses state-of-the-art digital and sound effects along with live-action stunt performers, allowing a few visiting "volunteers" to fight shoulder-to-shoulder with the superheros.

The presentation, which replaced the *Murder She Wrote* show, gives a behind-the-scenes look at how the shows are produced, and uses television wizardry to blend special effects with live action to move selected guests into an actual episode with stars Lucy Lawless and Kevin Sorbo.

Universal shot some footage for the show in New Zealand, reuniting Herc and Xena, who have gone off to their separate TV shows.

WOW Hitchcock's 3-D Theatre. At a theme park that celebrates the art of moviemaking, this show is the most serious exploration of the role of the director and a very entertaining stop.

Hitchcock, the king of cinema chills, made more than 50 motion pictures in his career, along the way creating some of the most famous scenes on film. From the dizzying heights of *Vertigo* to the terrifying shower scene of *Psycho* to the relentless aerial attack of *The Birds,* you will relive the terror—and learn the techniques behind

President Wasserman. The statue at 5th Avenue and Canal Street in the simulated streets of New York may appear to be Abraham Lincoln at first glance, but actually represents an insider moviemaking joke. The face on the statue is actually that of Lew Wasserman, the chairman of MCA, the parent company for Universal Studios; he is discreetly holding a pair of glasses behind his back, out of camera range.

Doubles. One of Hitchcock's signatures was that he always had a minor walk-on in his movies. In Anthony Perkins's film introduction to the *Psycho* set, pay attention when the technicians remove the set and lighting equipment; there is a Hitchcock look-alike walking off in the distance.

Rapid cutting. The shower scene in Alfred Hitchcock's *Psycho* is made up of 78 different shots, edited in rapid sequence to simulate the violence of the attack. However, the knife is never shown piercing the skin. Hitchcock shot the film in black and white to lessen the gore. The "blood" is actually chocolate syrup; stage blood photographs as grey in a black and white print.

Check it out. In the Bates Motel replica at the end of the tour, notice that the key to room #1 is missing. Even more interesting is what you'll uncover if you move the painting to the left of the check-in desk! The shop also offers some of the more unusual souvenirs of the park: Bates Motel towels and bathrobes.

Hidden behind an "employees only" door in the Bates Motel is a "Wall of Fame" with autographs of some of the celebrities who have toured the attraction. Signatures include those of Michael Jackson and Anita Baker.

Hitchcock's brilliance. Personal opinion here: the Hitchcock show, especially the assemblage of great clips shown in the theater, demonstrates moviemaking at its highest art form, while the *Murder, She Wrote* show across the way celebrates television at its most pedestrian.

Hitchcock made 10 movies with Universal, beginning in 1934 with *The Man Who Knew Too Much* and ending with *Family Plot* in 1976. Universal was also the company behind his television series.

The "filmstrip" that wends its way around the preshow area includes the names of all of Hitchcock's films. One volunteer will be chosen from the waiting line to participate in a re-creation of the shower scene. Sorry, girls, but the winner will almost always be a young man of average height, wearing tennis shoes. The reasons for the specifications will become apparent later.

Enter the 258-seat **Tribute Theater** for a giant screen film journey through many of Hitchcock's movie and television works, including a portion of the rarely seen 3-D version of *Dial M for Murder*. (The movie was filmed in 3-D, but while it was still in production the public fascination with 3-D seemed to have passed and the movie was released in a standard version.) You're also in for a surprise conclusion, courtesy of some of the flying fiends of *The Birds*.

Next, it's on to the **Psycho Sound Stage.** Anthony Perkins, who created the role of creepy motel owner Norman Bates, is your filmed host for a reenactment of one of the most terrifying scenes ever filmed. You'll see the scene as an unimaginative director might have shot it, and then learn how the master did it. The presentation includes actors (including a pretty model in a body stocking for the shower), our volunteer, reproductions of the *Psycho* house and the Bates Motel set, and clips from the movie.

Finally, you'll visit a fascinating interactive area where you can explore more of Hitchcock's technique. Actor James Stewart will be your guide in an exploration of the visual shocks of *Vertigo*. John Forsythe will assist you in the reenactment of the murder on a carrousel in *Strangers on a Train*. And Norman Lloyd, who played the villain in *Saboteur* and later produced Hitchcock's television shows, will lead you up the gigantic torch of the Statue of Liberty, the climactic scene in that film.

Be sure to climb the stairs for a fascinating simulation of the famous apartment building scene in *Rear Window*. You'll be able to peer through binoculars at a wall of windows, each showing a different scene—in one of them, a murder takes place.

Back downstairs, Shirley MacLaine narrates a presentation about Hitchcock's famous cameos—his brief appearances in each of his films. Note the lifesize mannequin of the director in the room; the master was only about 5'3" tall.

The first two acts, including the Psycho Sound Stage, may be too intense and frightening to youngsters. You might choose to go directly to the final, interactive area. You can also enter into the gift shop and the interactive area without waiting in line for the show itself.

WOW The Funtastic World of Hanna-Barbera. Yabba-dabba-doo. Children won't need to be persuaded, but adults: don't pass this one by. This show combines a wide-screen cartoon with state-of-the-art simulators—it's a wild ride for children of all ages. Think of it as a Junior Back to the Future.

Each group of eight seats in the 96-seat auditorium is actually a flight simulator without the cabin, offering an unusual glimpse at the technology—that is if you can take your eyes off the screen during the show. Remember the view when you ride the much wilder Back to the Future attraction, which uses similar technology.

The adventure begins with a three-minute preshow that introduces us to Bill Hanna and Joe Barbera, the rarely seen artists who launched some of our best-loved *non*-Disney characters, including Yogi Bear, the Flintstones, the Jetsons, Scooby Doo, and more. Their work has garnered eight Emmys and seven Oscars.

Hanna and Barbera will introduce us to the story of the adventure that lies ahead, if such things really matter. It seems that Bill and Joe have decided to make Elroy Jetson their star of the future. But along comes that diabolical dog Dastardly, who kidnaps Elroy. It's up to you, Yogi, and Boo Boo to rescue him.

While you are in the preshow area, if you listen carefully, you can hear from the other side of the door the screams of the people who are already riding. When it is your turn, the doors will open and you will be ushered into the auditorium full of simulator cars—it's an opportunity to see the motion of a simulator ride, because the mechanisms are usually hidden from view.

Yogi will lead the entire audience—seated in its simulators—to a giant spaceship for a blastoff into the stratosphere and then back down into

Medical news. If you are prone to dizziness or upset stomach on wild rides like Back to the Future or The Funtastic World of Hanna-Barbera, you might want to take one or two Dramamine motion sickness tablets at the start of the day (before you take any rides). They work like a charm. Check with your family doctor first if you are taking any other medications or if you have any allergies or unusual conditions. And be aware that the pills may make you a bit sleepy; you may want to assign a designated driver for the end of the day.

Back door. You don't have to wait in the sometimes-lengthy lines to the ride to get to the nifty play area of Funtastic Adventures. Enter through the Hanna-Barbera Store. This is a good place to let kids burn off some energy or get out the rain.

Studio lingo. As you walk through the back lot, try to spot the differences between three types of movie fake construction. A *facade* is a false front that has nothing behind it. A *shell* has a front, back, and side, but no useable interior space. A *practical set* is a shell that can be used for moviemaking or other purposes. For example, Louie's Italian Restaurant is within a practical set of a New York bank building.

Bedrock for a prehistoric tussle with Fred, Wilma, Barney, Pebbles, Bam-Bam, and the entire Flintstones family. From there it is on to Scooby Doo's weird world and eventually the fantastic future of the Jetsons.

The four-minute trip is every bit as silly as it sounds, but it's an exhilarating ride all the while. Lean back for the best ride. By the way, the auditorium includes a row of seats down front that don't move; the elderly, the very young, pregnant women, and those with back problems are advised to sit there. By the way, if you get queasy here, you will get sick at Back to the Future.

The fun and learning doesn't stop after Elroy is rescued, either. An interactive play area allows you to play with sound effects, color your own cartoon cel with an electronic paintbox and even see yourself as a cartoon character, shrunk in size to play in Pebbles' dollhouse.

The Boneyard. The storage place for some of the largest props from recent movies. In recent visits, we have seen the houseboat from *Cape Fear*, the Love Rock from *Problem Child 2*, and some of the topiary from *Edward Scissorhands*.

Films shot at the Orlando studios have included *Psycho IV: The Beginning;* Sylvester Stallone's *Oscar*, and *Problem Child 2*. Television projects include dozens of commercials and numerous Nickelodeon series.

WOW **Nickelodeon Studios.** If you have children, they'll already know the way to The Network for Kids once they spot the 17-foot-tall **Green Slime Geyser** out front; it's the planet's only known source of the stuff.

This is a real working television studio, producing nearly 300 episodes per year of Nickelodeon favorites.

Squarely aimed at an audience of children ages 2 to 15, the channel is on the air from 6 A.M. to 8 P.M. daily, reaching into more than 60 million homes. Nick at Nite fills the dark hours with reruns of classic situation comedies for children of all ages. Nickelodeon, which began in 1979, is owned by MTV Networks, which is itself owned by Viacom International.

Check out some of the funny signs overhead as you wait in line for a Nickelodeon tour or a television taping. One particularly interesting one offers translations of common proverbs from English to foreign tongues. For example, in English you might say, "Don't waste your breath"; in France you would say (in French), "Save your saliva." An American might observe that something is "nothing to lose sleep over"; in Hawaii you could say, "It's a heap of relish made of octopus liver." And finally, "All that glitters is not gold" is translated in Haiti as "not all hair is real."

Admission to the Nickelodeon studio tour is free to Universal Studios visitors. You'll be invited to tour the production facilities and the two large sound stages for the cable television network. From glassed-in catwalks above the stages, you can watch episodes as they are being rehearsed or taped as well as look in on control rooms, make-up rooms, and the "kitchen" where slime and gak are made.

At the end of each studio tour, kids and their families enter the **Game Lab**, where the youngsters can try out some of the stunts used on the shows; the kids, by the way, get the best seats while their parents are sent to the bleachers. And, of course, at least one kid will get slimed!

Inside slime. Try as we could, we were unable to obtain the secret recipe for Gak and Slime. We can tell you, though, that slime is the stuff that is poured over people while gak is dumped. And slime sorta tastes like applesauce while gak is a bit like butterscotch pudding gone wrong.

In addition to thousands of kids, movie director Steven Spielberg has also enjoyed a good sliming.

If you or your kids are hoping to be in the audience for the taping of one of the game shows, stop by early in the day and see if they are handing out tickets alongside the door to Stage 18. You can also call the Nickelodeon operator and ask to be connected to the "hotline" number to find out about tapings: (407) 363-8586. Most taping is done on weekdays. The odds are not great: there are only a few hundred seats for each taping and they are usually snapped up by the first few hundred youngsters through the gates.

Your child's chances of appearing as a contestant on a Nickelodeon show are pretty slim; most participants are drawn from the Orlando area because they must be available on short notice to meet the schedules of the producers.

Hollywood

WOW Terminator 2 3-D. He's back . . . and with a vengeance. Universal's newest major attraction is a tour-de-force of film and computer special effects that puts the audience in the middle of an epic battle between and among the fearsome "cinebotic" robots, live actors, and the reunited stars of *Terminator 2:* Arnold Schwarzenegger, Linda Hamilton, Robert Patrick, and Eddie Furlong, along with director James Cameron and special effects wizards from the series. In this newest "Terminator" adventure—which begins in the present day and jumps to the Los Angeles of 2029 covered in the film—Cyberdyne Systems, the dreaded creators of Skynet and its fearsome Terminator cyborgs, has moved its corporate headquarters to Universal Studios Florida's Hollywood Boulevard.

Guests will twist and turn in their seats as menacing Cyberdyne Systems "T-70" cinebotic warriors train their sights on random targets throughout the theater, firing across the theater. The audience will leap back in three-dimensional shock when the T-1000 Terminator "cop" from the *Terminator 2* movie morphs to life before their very eyes, then cheer with relief as Schwarzenegger's T-800 cyborg literally charges off the screen to save the day astride a 1,500-pound Harley Davidson "hog" that actually lands on the stage and then dives back into the screen and into the scene.

And we don't want to spoil the fun, but you'll want to hold on to your seats for the jaw-dropping finale. You'll understand what we mean when your feet are back on solid ground.

The show begins with a "super" entertaining preshow sales pitch by a Cyberdyne associate. "Imagine a world where butterflies run on batteries," Cyberdyne asks, expecting you to do so with happy anticipation, "where human error is a thing of the past. Our goal is complete control of global communication."

The associate unveils Skynet, a computer-controlled defense system, and then suddenly something goes wrong with the promotional video: it seems that hackers have broken into the system to warn us against Cyberdyne.

Terminator creator James Cameron, who directed this third installment of the saga, regards Terminator 2 3-D as a true sequel to his earlier blockbusters. "It's definitely the next film," he said. "The only difference is this film is only 12 minutes long and you can't see it in just any theater."

Because the audience is in the present day, the story uses T-70 cinebots, a design of robots not seen in the movies, which take place several decades in the future. The six T-70s each stand eight feet tall; they rise from their hiding places along the walls of the theater with the aid of a sophisticated hydraulic system.

This is the first time interlocking three-dimensional images are projected onto multiple screens, surrounding guests in 180 degrees of action. For its climactic third act, the film opens up from one 50-foot center screen to simultaneous projection on three screens, arranged at 60-degree angles for a sense of enveloping the audience. Spanning 165-feet, Terminator 2 3-D enjoys the distinction of being the world's largest 3-D installation and the first to use the triple screen setup and six 70-mm Iwerks projectors.

According to its producers, the 12-minute-long film is, frame for frame, the most expensive film every produced.

Live-action portions of the film took place in a two-week shoot at Kaiser Eagle Mountain, an abandoned steel mine in Desert Center, California, rebuilt in spectacular fashion to resemble Los Angeles after a nuclear war. More than 100 cars, trucks, and buses were hauled in from wrecking yards and strewn about the one-million-square-foot location set. The background consisted not of mockups but of actual buildings that were blown up during filming, lending a scale authenticity that surpassed many big-budget Hollywood action flicks.

Additional scenes were shot on a Los Angeles soundstage, where an elaborate 24-foot "miniature" of Skynet, the pyramid-shaped headquarters of Cyberdyne Systems, was constructed. Through the magic of cinema trickery it will appear to be 800 feet tall on screen.

The show has a seating capacity of 700, and can accommodate about 2,400 guests per hour. Much of the waiting area for the show is within the Cyberdyne building; if lines extend out onto the street you may want to come back later in the day. The best seats for the 3-D effects are from the middle to the back of the theater; the best seats to see the live action, including the arrival of the Harley on stage and the frozen breakup finale, is third or fourth row, center.

Lucy: A Tribute. On the left side of Rodeo Drive, keep your ears open for the world's largest indoor collection of Lucy screams. If you are a fan of Lucille Ball and everyone around her, you'll be enthralled at this collection of photos, scripts, and memorabilia and a continuous showing of episodes from her television show. Among my personal favorites is Lucy as part a barbershop quartet.

There is a diorama showing how the original television show was filmed in front of a live audience. The show was photographed (on 35-mm black-and-white film) on one large set; episodes were edited and combined for the final show.

We don't know very many other places in the world where you can see a collection of Desi Arnaz's conga drums or view some of the original scripts from *I Love Lucy.*

Lucy, I'm home! The original TV show was unusual in that the creators worked with three or four permanent sets that stood side-by-side in the studio, avoiding the flimsy looking sets typical of television shows at the time. The permanent setting also allowed for more advanced lighting, allowing cameras to move quickly from one area to another. All of the sets were painted in carefully chosen shades of gray to control the contrast of the finished black-and-white film.

There's also a *Lucy* trivia quiz, including questions like, "What was the biggest laugh in Lucy history?" Here's a hint: the answer involves Lucy, Ricky, a bunch of raw eggs, and a wild and romantic dance. You figure it out.

Desi Arnaz was born Desiderio Alberto Arnazey Acha III in Santiago, Cuba, in 1917. The son of a Cuban senator, he lived in great luxury until the Cuban Revolution of 1933 when the family left the country. Arnaz worked at various jobs, including cleaning bird cages for 25 cents.

Eventually, he got a job in a band and soon became one of the leading band leaders in New York. Signed to the lead in the New York musical *Too Many Girls,* he played a Latin football player. When he went to Hollywood to play his role in the movie version of the musical, he met the studio ingenue Lucille Ball, and in late 1940 they began a bicoastal marriage.

After World War II, looking for a way to work together in Los Angeles, Lucy and Desi hired the writers of Lucy's radio show *My Favorite Husband* and produced a pilot for *I Love Lucy.* Their new company, Desilu Productions, became the largest television and film production company in Hollywood. Arnaz died in 1986. Lucy passed on in 1989.

The Gory, Gruesome & Grotesque Horror Make-Up Show. It's nearly all in the name; they left out "gross."

Most everyone loves a good monster or horror movie. Here's your chance to learn some of the secrets behind the special effects. For example, where else would you find the recipe for gore: shrimp sauce, oatmeal, and red dye.

Among the devices demonstrated in the lively 25-minute show is the teleportation scene from *The Fly,* somewhat humorously reenacted on stage.

A film clip explains how Meryl Streep is turned around in her body in *Death Becomes Her*, a special effect that involved blue-screen technology. Streep was videotaped walking backward wearing a blue bag over her head, and then her face was electronically superimposed onto the bag for the effect.

One extra from the audience—usually a woman—gets her arm sliced open and suffers other simulated indignities. She is usually selected from one of the front rows.

Some children may find the GG&G show too gory, gruesome, and grotesque: parents be warned.

There are 355 seats in the theater, and visitors are often turned away at midday; go early or late on busy days.

AT&T at the Movies. An interactive electronic playground that may interest some visitors; it does have buttons for kids to push and, it is a good place to duck in out of the rain or the sun and enjoy a few Epcot-like science and computer games.

The **Movie Make-Up** screen is similar to an exhibit at the Imagination pavilion of Epcot; you pose yourself in front of a TV camera and then apply different ears or mustaches or beards or other facial adornments.

Nearby is what may be the world's largest working telephone, a booth where the entire family can enter to place a speakerphone call (on your dime, not theirs).

And there is the **Dawn of Sound** where you can listen to some of the most famous early sound clips of all time, including Al Jolson, news clips from Prohibition, the early talkies, and of all things, a bit of *Steamboat Willie*—the first Mickey Mouse cartoon with sound.

Special Events

Most any day in the summer and during holiday periods the rest of the year you can expect a high school or college marching band to high-step around the park at mid-morning. And Universal Studios also regularly throws itself a party for special events; call (407) 363-8000 for calendar updates.

New Year's Eve Celebration. A blazing fireworks show and other seasonal entertainment welcome the new year.

Spring Break and Daytona Speed Week. The park offers special discounts to college students during spring break.

Mardi Gras at Universal Studios Florida. Presented each year from mid-February through the end of March or early April, and featuring 15 or so full-sized floats direct from the streets of New Orleans, more than 200 costumed street performers, including stiltwalkers, fire-eaters, unicyclists, and 10 marching bands. In addition, more than 150 elaborately costumed characters—many of them guests selected from the audience will ride on the floats. The parade takes place nightly at closing time; admission is included in the day's ticket. In addition, major musical groups will perform on stage each Saturday during the Mardi Gras celebration, and the park's restaurants will add New Orleans favorites, including crawfish, jambalaya, and étouffée. You can also purchase a potent Hurricane, a rum-based drink concocted by Pat O'Brien's, a restaurant that now has its own location at Universal CityWalk. Here's an Insider's tip: a great place to watch the Mardi Gras parade is near the entrance to the Hercules and Xena show. The floats and bands actually pass by this spot twice.

Fourth of July. A special fireworks show, with music from E.T., Back to the Future, and other movie favorites.

Halloween Horror Nights. Hundreds of monsters, maniacs, and mutants crawl out from the back lot from mid-October through Halloween.

Eating Your Way Through Universal Studios

There are some interesting choices for food at Universal Studios, including a variety of foreign and ethnic foods.There are many more choices, too, with the opening of Universal CityWalk. You can leave Universal Studios Florida (get your hand stamped for re-entry) and go out to lunch or dinner at CityWalk, choosing from a nice variety of unusual to haute cuisine.

Near Nickelodeon Studios, there's a new exit from the park that leads to Hard Rock Café and NBA City, as well as offering a shortcut to Universal Studios Islands of Adventure.

The Front Lot

🍴 **The Fudge Shoppe.** Just like the sign says—no more, no less—The Fudge Shoppe is located beside the Studio Store across from the main Universal entrance. This is a good stop to get something special for the road or for a quick sweet treat on your way into the grounds.

🍴 **Beverly Hills Boulangerie.** Gourmet-style sandwiches and pastries.

At the corner of Plaza of the Stars and Rodeo Drive just inside the gate, the Boulangerie offers a selection of sandwiches, sweet treats, and drinks.

Sweets include cherry turnovers, cheese danishes, overstuffed muffins, macadamia chip cookies, flavored croissants, hazelnut eclairs, and slices of key lime pie, for about $2 to $3. There's also a huge chocolate chip cookie for $1.99.

Expo Center

🍴 **International Food Bazaar.** Gyros, brats, burgers, pizza, and more, $2 to $8. In the rear of Expo Center, next to the Back to the Future ride, this food court offers American, Chinese, German, Italian, and Greek fast food. The advantage of this eatery is evident to families: everyone in the party should be able to indulge their own tastes in one place.

Hollywood

🍴 **Mel's Drive-In.** Burgers, hot dogs, salads, chips, and drinks in a 1950s diner, modeled after the eatery from *American Graffiti*.

You can't miss Mel's. Just look for the garish pink and blue building with its large neon sign on the corner of 8th and Hollywood Boulevard. Unless you are a child of the '50s, you may not immediately appreciate the true beauty of the pink and white 1956 Ford Crown Victoria parked next to an absolutely cherry 1957 black Chevrolet out front.

Inside, a sock-hop theme prevails, with period music and booths that have individual juke box selectors. Check out the old 45-rpm records pasted to the wall and the pedal pushers worn by the attendants.

Notice I didn't say "waitresses." Forget the personal, at-table service you knew in the '50s, because you have to stand in line to retrieve your fast food here. You'll also have a lot of company in line at this popular place.

[🍴] **Café La Bamba.** This attractive eatery lost its Mexican flavor in favor of more ordinary fare such as barbecued baby back ribs, rotisserie chickens, and barbecued pork, for about $7 to $10.

The café is decorated within like an old villa, with fancy pillars and art; albeit with a cafeteria line within. During Universal's celebration of Mardi Gras, the restaurant takes on a New Orleans menu.

KEY:
[🍴] = Fast food
[Y] = Pub
[🏛] = Full-service restaurant

A bar near the entrance offers a variety of alcoholic and soft drinks.

[🍴] **Schwab's Pharmacy.** A classic old-time drugstore fountain just waiting to be discovered.

Hard to miss, on Hollywood Boulevard next to the Brown Derby Hat Shop. Look for the giant blue neon sign, and walk into the bright white drugstore fountain area.

This is a typical 1950s drugstore with a few booths and seating around a curved counter. Soda jerks in blue jeans, white shirts, and classic paper hats take your order and prepare the treats while you watch. The walls are decorated with vintage photos from the original Schwab's in Hollywood and some of its famous patrons.

If you remember the '50s with its custom, handmade ice-cream treats (or even if you don't), you'll have a hard time selecting from the familiar Schwab's offerings.

Main courses include hot dogs and turkey or chicken salad sandwiches for about $6 or $7. Ice cream cones and milkshakes sell for about $2.50 to$3.50.

Schwab's is also a good place to pick up an emergency supply of aspirin, Tylenol, Rolaids, or cough drops—some of which you may need after the treats you go through. They also sell Dramamine, useful to some for thrill ride relief.

San Francisco/Amity

[🍴] **Boardwalk Snacks.** Hot dogs, chips, fruit, and drinks. On hot days, this is the place to go for an emergency Slush Puppy.

For a quick, takeout snack or light meal on the go, stroll into the Boardwalk on the small wharf on Amity Avenue. The shop offers a nautical theme, with outdoor dining at picnic tables that offer a view of the lagoon.

Boardwalk fare includes hot dogs and chili dogs, and corn dogs for about $4 to $6; turkey drumsticks go for about $4.75. You can also buy cotton candy and frozen yogurt.

🍴 **Chez Alcatraz.** Quick seafood treats and drinks. Located over the water on the first wharf in San Francisco/Amity, this walk-up stand gives you a chance to sample shrimp cocktails, clam chowder, soft drinks, or beer and wine while you watch the activities in the lagoon.

An interesting crab salad "Conewich" gives you a one-handed shot at seafood salad on the go, or you can try a crab cocktail. Entrees range in price from about $3 to $6.

🍴 **Richters Burger Co.** Richter, as in Richter scale, and as in The Big One (a $6 burger with fries), The San Andreas (chicken breast on bun with fries), and The Trembler (a hot dog platter with fries). Entrees range from about $5 to $8. Located directly opposite the entrance to Earthquake, the tables in the back have a view of the lagoon.

🍴 **San Francisco Pastry Company.** San Francisco–style pastries and sweets, croissant sandwiches, plus espresso and cappuccino and the best selection of beers at any casual restaurant in the park.

At the front of Pier 27, on the Embarcadero across from Earthquake: The Big One. The European café design opens off of brick-paved streets, and the patio overlooks the lagoon.

🍴 **Midway Grill.** Carnival fare: grilled Italian sausage with peppers and onions for about $6, Philly cheese steak for about $6.50, plus hot dogs and chicken fingers.

🍴 **Pier 27.** Barbecue, hot dogs, clam chowder, beer, and chips.

You'd almost have to know this little eatery was here or find it by accident tucked into the back of Golden Gate Mercantile on Pier 27.

Draft ($2.50) and imported bottled beer ($3.50) complement the limited but rather nice selection of barbecue pork sandwiches ($3.75), clam chowder ($2), or hot dogs ($2.50).

🔺 **Lombard's Landing.** Steak, pasta, and seafood served in an elegant 1800s warehouse, this is, by most visitors' accounts, the most attractive restaurant in the park with a nice view of the lagoon. Lunch entrees range from about $8 to $15 for adults and $3.50 to $5 for children. Dinner entrees start at about $15 and reach to about $25 for adults and $5 to $8 for children.

Fish choices include swordfish, grouper, tuna, mahi mahi, salmon, and lobster, priced at market rates from about $15 to $25. You can begin your meal with New England Clam Chowder, or lobster bisque.Other entrees include Pan-seared bison ribeye for $24, and buffalo burgers for $10.

If you time your visit perfectly, you will have a front-row view of the stunt show in the lagoon; the best seats would be out on the balcony overlooking the water.

Located on the wharf next to the Pastry Company, Lombard's entrance is marked by a bright blue awning. Inside, the warehouse has been upgraded with jade green, simulated marble tables, fish fountains, and aquariums. Notice the exposed iron work and wooden beams with bright copper bases.

The large "port hole" aquarium in the center of the rear dining room is not to be missed. And while you select your food, you can read the newspaper reproduction of the story of the great San Francisco Earthquake of 1906.

Entrees for lunch include fish and chips, grilled chicken, crab cakes, New York strip steak, or chicken and chive fettuccine. The signature sandwiches include the Lomberger (a hamburger on a sourdough bun with swiss, cheddar, or boursin cheese), a fried grouper sandwich on sourdough with a dill *rémoulade* sauce, and a veggie burger on a seven-grain bun.

The catch of the day can be grilled, blackened, or sautéed; fish selections include swordfish, red snapper, tuna, salmon, and lobster.

Production Central

[icon] **Classic Monsters Café.** A gustatory celebration of Universal's greatest monster hits. You'll order your food from a cafeteria line and take it back to one of four monstrous dining areas stocked with artifacts and memorabilia from great movies: Egypt (including items from "The Mummy"), a Gothic haunted house ("Phantom of the Opera" and "Frankenstein"), outer-space (films including "This Island Earth", one of the worst sci fi movies ever made, so bad it's a classic), and a sea creature lair ("Creature from the Black Lagoon".)

Items on display include original scripts, props, posters, and costumes. The background music includes great hits from monster films and even some parodies such as "The Rocky Horror Picture Show." Video monitors show clips from Universal classics.

Appetizers include chef, Caesar, and chicken and shrimp Caesar salads priced from about $3 to $9. Pastas include four-cheese ravioli, penne pasta, linguine primavera, and wood-fired oven pizza from about $7.

The eatery replaced the Studio Stars Restaurant.

New York

[icon] **Louie's Italian Restaurant.** Italian antipasto, pizzas, salads, and more.

Located right on Universal's 5th Avenue at Canal Street, Louie's offers a wide selection of Italian specialties from antipasto to pizza, soups to salads, plus pasta and ices. You can also buy beer.

The dining area here is very large and open with studio-type lighting. The high ceiling and large front windows give an open, bright atmosphere. Two serving lanes offer the same fare on either side, but veteran Louie's visitors say the left side usually is shorter.

The portions are large and the food fresh. Pizza is available by the slice for about $3.50 or by the pie from about $16 to $18.

[icon] [icon] **Finnegan's Bar and Grill.** Traditional Irish fare, including stews and meat pies. About $10 to $15.

Finnegan's occupies a prominent position on 5th Avenue across the street from Kongfrontation. In movie-set style, the corner Regal Café is just another entrance to Finnegan's.

This is a typical New York City community bar, complete with brick-paved sidewalk and awning-covered entrance. The neon signs in the windows add to the festive saloon atmosphere. The pressed tin ceilings are high and accented with hanging lights and slow-moving fans.

Lighter items include a Blarney baguette filled with your choice of roast beef, corned beef, ham, or turkey with wedge fries for about $9, and a Shamrock steak sandwich, also for about $9. It's St. Patrick's Day every day here, including Irish Stew with lamb, potatoes, and fresh vegetable for $7.95. And there is London Times fish and chips (fish fillets in ale batter with fries and malt vinegar), served on the front page of the London Times for about $10.50. And, of course, there is corned beef and cabbage (about $11) every day.

Other offerings include Shepherd's Pie and bangers and mash (hot dogs and mashed potatos), each for about $10.

UNIVERSAL STUDIOS FLORIDA

N

① Production Center Information
② Nickelodeon Studios
③ Funtastic World of Hanna-Barbera
④ Hitchcock's 3-D Theatre
⑤ Hercules and Xena: Wizards of the Screen
⑥ The Boneyard
⑦ Production Studios
⑧ Twister
⑨ Men in Black *(coming in 2000)*
⑩ Kongfrontation
⑪ The Blues Brother in Chicago Bound
⑫ Beetlejuice's Graveyard Revue
⑬ Earthquake–The Big One
⑭ Jaws
⑮ Wild, Wild, Wild West Stunt Show
⑯ Back to the Future . . . The Ride
⑰ AT&T at the Movies
⑱ Animal Actors Stage
⑲ A Day in the Park with Barney
⑳ Fievel's Playland
㉑ E.T. Adventure
㉒ The Gory Gruesome & Grotesque Horror Makeup Show
㉓ Terminator 2 3-D
㉔ Lucy: A Tribute
㉕ Woody Woodpecker's Nuthouse Coaster
㉖ Curious George Goes to Town

Chapter 17
Universal Studios Islands of Adventure

Universal's Islands of Adventure is the most technologically advanced, wild and woolly theme park in Orlando. It's got something for everyone, with thrill rides, spectacular simulations, entertainment, worlds of wonder for children of all ages, and delights for the eye at most every turn.

And Islands of Adventure is also Florida's most beautiful theme park by night, a world of fire and water, fog and light.

On 110 acres, roughly the same size as Walt Disney World's Magic Kingdom, you'll find the world's first duel racing roller coasters; the first combined 3-D film, live action, and moving motion base simulator; and a high-speed coaster that has a zero-G heartline inversion.

The crown jewel of Islands of Adventure is the Amazing Adventures of Spider-Man, an attraction that is unlike anything else anywhere on the theme park planet; if comparisons must be drawn, think of Back to the Future and The Terminator 3-D . . . on wheels.

Then there are the awesome roller coasters. The glowing-green Incredible Hulk Coaster dominates the skyline as you drive by on I-4 and overhangs Marvel Super Hero Island to your left as you enter the park; a couple of times a minute the area rumbles with the launch of a train 150 feet up the takeoff tunnel and then echoes with the screams of the riders as they immediately enter into an inverted zero-G "heartline" roll. But not to be overlooked is the mind-boggling spaghetti bowl of red and blue tracks in the back right corner of the park; the two Dueling Dragons coasters run side-by-side, above, below, and straight at each other.

It does get hot in Florida, but you'll have plenty of opportunities to take a shower with your clothes on at entertaining water rides Dudley Do-Right's Ripsaw Falls, and Popeye & Bluto's Bilge-Rat Barges.

You can visit places heretofore only viewed in the mind's eye, at state-of-the-art simulations such as the Jurassic Park River Adventure, Triceratops Encounter, and Poseidon's Fury: Escape from the Lost City.

And then there is Seuss Landing, where the wonderfully weird world of Dr. Seuss comes to life for children of all ages.

At ceremonies at the opening of the park in May of 1999, Steven Spielberg, creative consultant to Universal Studios Escape, gave an interesting insight to the process that gave birth to Islands of Adventure: "Making a theme park is like making movies and plays, and then building an entire city to contain them."

A Tour of the Islands

The adventure begins at the Port of Entry and continues through five "islands" connected by walkways, bridges, and a water taxi. Clockwise from the Port of Entry, you'll find:

- Marvel Super Hero Island
- Toon Lagoon
- Jurassic Park
- The Lost Continent
- Seuss Landing

Power Trip

Everything Is New

Face it: this is going to be one bustling island for years to come. The biggest draws of the park are the major thrill rides, **The Amazing Adventures of Spider-Man, The Hulk,** and **Dueling Dragons.** On a Florida sizzler (which can happen almost any month of the year, but especially from May through September), **Jurassic Park River Adventures** and **Dudley Do-Right's Ripsaw Falls,** and **Popeye & Bluto's Bilge-Rat Barges** are likely to draw long, hot lines of guests in search of a cooling drench.

And if your heart is set on riding the simple but charming **Pteranadon Flyers,** don't wait too late in the day either.

Follow the basic Econoguide strategy: arrive early, head deep into the park to your number one goal, and try to stay one step ahead of the crowds who will likely work their way from front to back.

If you're heading to Jurassic Park or the Dueling Dragons, you might consider jumping on a water taxi at the landing where Port of Entry meets the lagoon; the shuttles run to a dock near the **Jurassic Park Discovery Center.** If there's a line for the boat, though, you'll probably do better by walking.

Remember that Jurassic Park, Dudley Do-Right, and Bilge-Rat Barges are not billed as water rides for nothing. (So, too for **One Fish, Two Fish, Red Fish, Blue Fish** for the kiddies.) Consider whether you want to start the day with a wet bottom, especially on a cool day.

Eat lunch and dinner early and head for major attractions while other park visitors wait in line for food.

Port of Entry

You'll present your passport (admission tickets, actually) at a dramatic plaza under the shadow of a towering lighthouse modeled after the famous Pharos light at ancient Alexandria.

Notable shops in the Port of Entry include Universal's Islands of Adventure Trading Company (the major souvenir shop of the park), Silk Road Clothiers (travel gear, leather bags, and jewelry), De Foto's Expedition Photography, Island Market and Export (gourmet foods from around the world), and Ocean Trader Market (carvings from Africa, mehndi skin colorings from India, and more exotica.)

Give yourself a few moments to stop and look at the attention to detail around you at eye level and up above. My favorite sign in the Port of Entry: "Sooths Sayed While You Wait."

At the end of the shopping district lies the entryway to the park itself, a pass through a set of gates held back by impressively large chains.

Island Skipper Tours. A fleet of three eccentric water taxis run from the Port of Entry across the Inland Sea to a dock at the Jurassic Park Discovery Center. It's a pleasant trip, only a bit faster than walking if your timing is right, but the taxis do offer some views of The Incredible Hulk Coaster and other sections of the park unavailable anywhere else.

Universal Studios Island of Adventure

Marvel Super Hero Island

Imagine: an entire island populated by super-heroes the likes of Spider-Man, The Hulk, and the Fantastic Four.

For most of us, this place is eerily familiar, a step into the fantasy comic book pages of yesterday and today. Just like in the cartoons, the storefronts are generic. You'll find a store named "Store", and arcade "Arcade" and a frozen ice stand advertised as "Frozen Ice."

You'll also find a trio of awesome thrill rides guaranteed to make you marvel.

WOW **The Amazing Adventures of Spider-Man.** You've got to see this, though you still won't believe it. Quite simply, this is the state-of-the-art in theme park rides, a 3-D video, virtual reality motion base simulator on wheels. There's nothing like it anywhere else in the universe.

There's an outdoor queue in the delivery docks of that well-known New York newspaper, the Daily Bugle, home of mild-mannered photographer Peter Parker. (Background information for the comically impaired: the bite of a radioactive spider changed shy high school student Peter Parker into a super-hero with the speed, agility, and strength of a spider-man. He earns his keep as a cameraman, acting as a one-man vigilante army whenever he can spare the time.)

Eventually, we make our way into the lobby of the Bugle. Spend some time to soak in the attention to detail in the waiting area. It begins with a collection of headlines of recent events you may have missed while you were away on vacation. For example, "Terror Coast to Coast: Magnetic Mutant Seizes Missile Base." There are also some Bugle editorials by the unknowing Spider-Man detractor J. Jonah Jameson, who asks: "Is Spider-Man Through?"

Past the hallway, we enter Peter Parker's office and darkroom. Look closely at the name on the door; it seems that the previous occupant of the small room was named "Broom Closet."

Signs on the wall give the Bugle's operating procedure: "Remember! First get the pictures. Then get the stories. And after that . . . safety first."

And next we enter the newsroom. Lights flash on old-style telephones, an incongruous mix with modern computer screens. Note the color scheme: most everything in the background is in pale green, like the muted backgrounds of a comic book. The foreground is decorated in bright posterish colors.

There is news in the air. Headlines on the computer monitors trumpet: "Emergency Declared! Statue of Liberty Stolen!" Who could possibly have done such a dastardly deed other than Doctor Octopus, Electro, Hydro-Man, Hobgoblin, and Scream, AKA The Sinister Syndicate?

Drafted as a civilian posse, we're given the chance to join with Spider-Man to retrieve the missing national treasure. Our vehicles are "Scoops," formally known as Surveillance Communications Patrols.

A funny cartoon describes the dos-and-don'ts about loading into the car. Watch carefully and see if you can spot the funny jab at the GM Test Track; it comes during the cartoon's recommendation that you be sure to use the Scoop's lap bars.

Each car holds a dozen volunteers in three rows of four. Two Scoops are loaded at the same time. The rows are numbered from the rear of each vehicle (and assigned a name for a section of the Daily Bugle's circulation area in New York City.) Row 1 is Queens, the back row of the second vehicle in line. Row 2, Bronx, is the middle row. Row 3, Brooklyn, is the front row. In the first vehicle in line, Row 4, Coney Island, is the back of the bus. Row 5, Staten Island, is in the middle. Row 6, Manhattan, is the front row.

All of the seats in the Scoop vehicle give a good view of the action, The front row offers the most dramatic views—without someone else's head between you and the action. But the middle and last rows offer the most motion.

And then we're off on a 20-block tour of New York City, a huge acre-and-a-half set where we are thrust into the middle of a battle between good and evil.

Seen through our 3-D glasses, Spider-Man greets us and then things go seriously wrong. Flaming pumpkins and spewing water pipes hurled by the forces of evil seem to fly toward riders and smash into our vehicle.

Short Story. Alas, the smallest visitors to Universal's Islands of Adventure will be unable to ride the fastest and wildest attractions. Don't fight the rules: they are there for the child's protection. Here are the minimum heights:

Pteranadon Flyers. 36 inches

The Amazing Adventures of Spider-Man. 40 inches

Jurassic Park River Adventure. 42 inches

Dudley Do-Right's Ripsaw Falls. 44 inches

Popeye & Bluto's Bilge-Rat Barges. 48 inches

Doctor Doom's Fearfall. 52 inches

Dueling Dragons, and The Incredible Hulk. 54 inches

Note that even if a child meets one of the lower height requirements, they must be accompanied by an adult on restricted rides if they are under 48 inches in height.

It all comes to a chilling conclusion when Doc Ock takes aim at us with his Doomsday Anti-Gravity Gun. One blast sends us 400 feet in the air and then into a 400-foot freefall. If you're wondering whether you should take out new flight insurance, remember that it's all simulated—a technology known as "sensory drop." That doen't mean it doesn't feel very real.

According to Universal Studios, the challenge in creating Spider-Man was to get guests directly involved in the action as they view 3-D films and move at high speed past props and special effects. The technology employs a "moving point of convergence" and uses 25 large-format movie projectors and dozens of smaller projectors.

I went for a behind-the-scenes peek at the control room for the high-tech ride. There I saw with my own eyes what my mind had refused to believe. The actual rise and fall of the vehicles—including the "400-foot drop" that is at the heart of the ride—is only about three or four feet.

Knowing the secret, I went back and rode the Scoop once more—and I still felt the bottom of my stomach rising to meet my throat as we "fell" 40 stories.

WOW Incredible Hulk Coaster. It seems that Dr. Bruce Banner is playing around with the rules of physics once again, conducting special gamma-ray accelerator tests.

We lucky visitors are offered the chance to become part of the experiment. How can we say no?

In a ride of about two minutes and 15 seconds, the 32 passengers, seated four-abreast, experience seven rollovers and plunge into a pair of deep subterranean tunnels.

Not that you're going to be able to read this book—or remember much of what I wrote here—while you're riding on The Hulk, here's a summary of your ride. Your trip begins when your car is catapulted in three seconds up a 150-foot launch tunnel with the same force as a U.S. Air Force F-16 fighter attack jet on takeoff. Exiting from the tube at 40 mph, there's an immediate twist onto your back in a weightless heartline roll more than 110 feet above the ground. The cars then dive at 60 mph in a steep plunge toward the water, and then straight back up 109 feet.

Still with me? OK, now we go into a sharp twist into an upside-down roll to the right, then a tight turn and upside-down roll to the left . . . followed by yet another plunge to the water. Back up we go, into a narrow oblong loop, upside down at the top, of course.

We complete the front side of the ride with a drop to—and below—the surface of the lagoon and beneath a bridge full of gawkers crossing from the Port of Entry to Marvel Super-Hero Island. Coming up from the tunnel, we make a slow, twisting climb to the left, which ends in a sideways loop. From there we're into an upside-down loop and into a semi-hidden area of the park behind the Hulk building.

Out back where there are few witnesses, we flip over and then plunge upside-down to earth and then immediately back up into another inverted loop and then another and then onto our sides in a small, tight loop upside-down at the top. If you have your eyes open, you may be able to see the end of the ride, but between here and there we've still got a few more high-G twists and turns to burn off our speed.

Whew! Now you can say that you've experienced The Incredible Hulk. Was it good for you, too?

The waiting queue for The Hulk begins outside and then wends its way into the Gamma Radiation Testing Zone, your basic sci-fi cartoon laboratory with flashing lights, green overhead pipes, and video monitors that tell the story of the experiment through the words of Dr. Bruce Banner.

(In case you're not a Marvel expert, scientist Bruce Banner's basic constitution was forever changed when he was caught in the rays of a gamma bomb explosion; he's a nice enough guy as long as you don't get him angry or agitated. When he does, he transforms into the rampaging Incredible Hulk, glowing a lovely shade of green.)

Just short of the loading area, the line splits. Keep to the left for a seat in the front car, or keep to the right for the faster-moving line for the rest of the train.

At night, the metal coaster track glows an eerie green, an especially dramatic sight for guests walking across the bridge to the island; the tracks loop over and then under the walkway.

WOW Doctor Doom's Fearfall. Looming above the island are a pair of 200-foot towers of steel. Victor Von Doom, absolute dictator of the otherwise insignificant nation of Latvaria has much bigger goals: total world domination. The creation is Dr. Doom's infernal device to drain fear from all visitors.

We enter through the portals of the Latvarian Embassy, guarded by a squad of Doctor Doom's army in their armored finery.

Dr. Doom's enemies, of course, are the Fantastic Four, although to tell you the truth these guys did absolutely nothing to prevent the bad doctor from sending me shooting up a tower into the sky.

We lucky visitors are strapped into four-passenger seats on the outside of the tower, feet dangling free below. With a sudden burst of energy, the seats zoom 150 feet up the tower; there's a brief pause of weightlessness at the top and then a powered descent back down the track to the bottom.

This ride gives many of us about as much of the feel of weightlessness as we're going to experience until we win a ride on the Space Shuttle. As we flew up the tower, the press credentials on a lanyard around my neck floated off and hung in space at the top. I had just enough time to reach out and grab it.

The chairs give you two or three bounces on the way down. And then when your feet and the rest of you are more or less back on terra firma, you'll exit the ride into a video arcade.

Toon Lagoon

A place where the funnies come to life, from the snow-capped peaks of Ripsaw Falls to Popeye's ship, the Olive to Wimpy's burger stand.

Comic Strip Lane salutes cartoon heroes old and new. In addition to Cathy and Shoe and the Marvel superheroes, you'll also find cutouts of classic toon characters such as Pogo, Snuffy Smith, Little Orphan Annie, Gasoline Alley, Beetle Bailey, Hagar the Horrible, Krazy Kat, Betty Boop, and Dennis the Menace.

Hanging from the storefronts and trees are cartoon blurbs. A few samples: "Don't have the mushroom pizza before you ride Ripsaw Falls." My favorite, hung outside of Blondie's: "I have a feeling people can read my thoughts."

Also outside of Blondie's is a fun photo opportunity. Pose a family member or friend pulling on Marmaduke's leash; turn your camera sideways and you can expect a picture right out of the comic books.

WOW Dudley Do-Right's Ripsaw Falls. Dudley Do-Right must save Nell from evil Snidely Whiplash in this wild flume ride. It's a familiar setting for Dudley, the dim-bulb Canadian Mountie who was part of the beloved Rocky and Bullwinkle Show.

It's our assignment to help Dudley on a wild and wet rescue attempt through a lagoon and log flume that ends with a drop through the roof of a ramshackle dynamite shack ("Danger Zone. Highly Kamboomable") and a dive 15 feet below the surface of the water.

You'll work your way up through queues that wind outside the building and then within. There is, of course, water, water, everywhere. The plunging logs splash onto the queue below, and water cannons fire spurts here and there.

When you finally enter the building, you'll learn the story of Ripsaw Falls, told with tongue decidedly planted in cheek. Movie posters advertise such slightly-skewed hits as "Saw Wars," "Paws," and "Three Men and a Grizzley."

You'll meet the Beaver and the Bear, performing a standup comedy routine (actually a hang-up comedy routine from their mounted position on the wall.) Listen carefully to the very bad jokes, including a few gentle jabs at the Mouse across town. I guess it is a small world after all.

My favorite sign at the loading platform: "Please remove hats and antlers."

There are three rows of seats in the log-like car. You can load as many as six per log if you're very friendly with another person in your party, one behind the other in the same seat.

The first lift takes you out on a floating pathway with a great view of Toon Lagoon and other parts of the Islands of Adventure. When we emerge from a mine section, we find our heroine Nell, fit to be tied.

Then Dudley loses his train of thought; we all regain it quickly when we seem to meet an oncoming locomotive. Get it?

After several false drops we come to the big one. In case you miss the point, a sign warns: "Scenic Overlook Ahead!"

The plunge down the falls is dramatic . . . and wet. The front row of the log gets soaked, the middle gets wet, and the third seat gets seriously damp. But a good time is had by all.

"And so," we are told, "our hero proves a Mountie always gets his man, but not always his girl."

Popeye & Bluto's Bilge-Rat Barges

❖WOW❖ Popeye & Bluto's Bilge-Rat Barges. The villainous Bluto is the proprietor of this establishment, and so you can count on things going awry.

Popeye tells us that "Bluto has taken me girlfrien' Olive down the White Waters of Sweet Haven. I need shipmates to join me rescue. Don't ferget to bring yer spinach."

You might want to bring a rain parka, too.

We start out on a path for Popeye's pleasant boat ride, but we come to a detour in the waiting line erected by Bluto. Suddenly, we are in the line for Bluto's boat, which seems like a much less friendly cruise line.

The long and complex queue eventually wends its way into Bluto's office. Among the awards and plaques for evil-doing is a framed greenback, labeled "First Dollar Stolen."

The 12-passenger circular rafts move along at a zippy 16 feet per second. There are lots of spins and tight turns, but only a short drop. That doesn't mean you won't get wet, though. If the splashes from the rapids and the unexpected geysers don't get you, one of the kids up on the deck of Me Ship, The Olive just may have you in the sights of his water cannon.

This is, after all, just another raft ride, not all that different from another Orlando attraction, Kali River Rapids at Disney's Animal Kingdom. Where the Bilge-Rat Barges shines, though, is in the theming. There are funny little surprises at every turn, including Bluto's Boatwash, and various other opportunities for some extra wet surprises.

You will get wet, especially in the seat of your pants. You're in most danger when your side of the raft is moving backwards into a wave. There is a covered storage area in the center of the raft, but you'd do better using a locker for valuables or leave them with someone on shore.

Me Ship the Olive. A fun spot for kids with some great slides and hidey-holes. There are also water squirters to aim at the Bilge Rat Barges passing by below. There are bells to ring and telescopes, and all sorts of toys.

Actually, this place is worth a visit by kids of all ages for the view of the lagoon and the rest of the park from the upper level.

Pandemonium Cartoon Circus. A 2,000-seat canopied theater for special events and a cartoon-based live stage show. Check schedules on the day of your visit.

Jurassic Park

The dinosaurs are back, and here's your chance to meet them face-to-face. The robotic creatures (you didn't really expect scaly flesh and blood, did you?) take over the Jurassic Park River Adventure. Elsewhere you will meet dinos up close and personal at Triceratops Encounter, check in on the DNA recombination process at the Jurassic Park Discovery Center, and hitch a ride on the back of a Pteranodon for a prehistoric bird's eye view of the park.

The entry to this part of Islands of Adventure wends its way through tropical jungle that is enclosed by electric fences and alarms. Beyond the mists of the ancient forests, you can hear distant roars. (Be sure to make a return visit to this area if you're in the park at night.)

WOW Jurassic Park River Adventure. Hop aboard a small boat for a pleas-ant little journey back in time, the ever-flowing river. We are, of course, in the ultimate theme park, the world of the dinosaur brought back to life by scientists who have extracted dino DNA from an ancient insect trapped in amber.

The boats carry 25 persons, in five rows of five seats, into a beautifully land-scaped, ferny recreation of earth as it existed millions of years ago.

"The river flows through a newborn world, where giants walked the earth," says our guide. "Welcome to . . . Jurassic Park."

First stop on our voyage is Ultrasaur Lagoon, home of a species of gentle veg-etarian giants who pose no threats to us. From there we float into Stegosaur Springs, where the natives seem just a bit more threatening, but we're harmless tourists, right?

And then there is Hadrosaur Cove, and here these guys are suddenly not very hospitable at all. In fact, one of them roars up out of the water so close to our boat that it diverts us into the wrong channel: we're pushed through the Juras-sic Park Animal Control Gate No. 13 into the Raptor Containment Area. And that's not good at all.

Alarms and flashing lights are everywhere. We see the destroyed remains of a crashed tour boat just like ours. (Shades of the crashed tour boat at Jaws in Universal Studios Florida.) Close by, a pair of small spitters fight over the rem-nants of a Jurassic Park uniform.

As we pass further along we come beneath a crane holding a large crate marked "Raptor Transport Unit." Something inside is moving around and making nasty noises. Will it drop on our heads?

And then we are into the warehouse building. We are pushed way back against our seats as the boat makes a very steep climb in near darkness. At the top, we seem to pause for just a moment . . . and then we plunge back to the surface of the lake, in an 84-foot plunge down one of the longest, fastest, and steepest water descents anywhere.

This is, of course, at heart a water ride and you will get wet—the first row gets soaked, with a bit less water as you move toward the back of the boat. You can use one of the lockers outside the waiting queue for valuables; when the park opened they were free for one hour, with a charge of $1 for each additional 30 minutes. (When the park is very busy, the waiting time may well extend more than an hour, putting you into the red.)

The long queue splits left and right to a pair of loading stations. As long as you've got to be waiting in line, you might as well learn something about the various species of dinosaurs in the park; there's an informative video on over-head screens.

By the way, gardeners will be thrilled by the plantings around the ride and along the river pathway.

The ride is a near-duplicate of the original ride at Universal Studios Hollywood.

Jurassic Park Discovery Center. An interactive educational experience where visitors can watch as a raptor is hatched from an egg, examine dinosaur skeletons, and learn how the biochemists of Jurassic Park brought these prehis-toric creatures back to life.

One of the stations demonstrates DNA sequencing in a process that is supposed to mix a bit of your personal characteristics with those of a compatible dinosaur. You begin by choosing between ancient creatures that were herbivores or carnivores, armored or camouflaged, large or small, and members of herding groups or solo folk. Then you lean into a "brain scanner" that takes a video image of your face, and give a simulated snippet of your DNA to a sampler that scans your hand.

The final step is an instruction to the computer to genetically recombine with your receptor dinosaur. The result: a new dinosaur with a bit of your face and personal characteristics. For some reason, the dino I created was not carrying a reporter's notebook.

At another station, a lab technician assists you in using a "pre-emergent nursery scanner" to examine the life growing within huge eggs. There's also a neutrino scanner that examines fossils in a wall of rock.

At Beasaurs, you can use a periscope-like device to get some idea of how the world looked through the eyes of a dinosaur—an unusual effect when you consider that for many of the beasts, their eyes were on opposite sides of their head.

The Discovery Center is an ambitious attempt at edutainment, but falls a bit flat; I expect Universal will step up the investment here in years to come.

WOW Pteranadon Flyers. Visitors can get a prehistoric bird's-eye view of the island, soaring in a chair beneath the ten-foot wings of one of these flying dinosaurs. This very simple ride is a charming diversion, and it immediately proved much too popular for its own good.

You'll clamber into your private seat on a two-seat metal bird, which climbs up a chain lift about 40 feet into the air and then descends under the quiet power of gravity along a winding track that circles above Camp Jurassic. The chairs move along at a brisk but unthreatening speed, swinging out from side to side a bit as they move around turns.

Some youngsters may be uncomfortable riding alone, but they must be willing and able to occupy their own seat. There is both a lap bar and a seat belt to hold riders in place, and there are no loops and dives on the track.

Universal planners thought of the ride as a diversion for the kids, and it surely is attractive to youngsters. But its simple charm and the view of the park it offers made it appealing to adults as well. The result: there can be lengthy lines for the very short ride. There are only three of the two-seater birds on the track at any one time. Lines can stretch to an hour or more, and, alas, the ride is way too short to justify that.

Insiders say park planners are considering ways to expand the ride and cut down on the lines. In the meantime, get there early or late in the day if you want to soar with the pteranodons.

Triceratops Encounter. A dino-petting zoo: for the first time ever, humans can pet a "living" dinosaur. At the feed and control stations, trainers teach guests about the biology of the 24-foot-long, 10-foot-tall Triceratops.

Here's your chance to get upclose and personal with a real, live triceratops. You'll meet Chris, making a visit to the veterinarian for a case of the sniffles.

Well, OK, she's not real, but she moves around, interacts with her concerned doc, and sniffles and sneezes. (You have been warned.)

Guests are escorted through in groups of about 30. The entire group will step onto a scale near the entrance for a group weigh-in. Our small contingent totaled about 6,315 pounds, or about the weight of a small triceratops we were told.

The walk-through to the encounter begins at the Jurassic Park Game Warden Station. There you'll be able to look at—and touch—all sorts of buttons and switches on the control system for the park. Yes, you really can play with the switch that turns on or off the electric fence systems and the surveillance cameras and all of the other safety systems that are there to protect us from the beasts outside the compound. I'm sorry to have to break this to you, though: the switches aren't really connected to anything. And, the dinosaurs aren't real. You knew that, right?

The next stop is a lab area (including lockers of Dilphosaurus Acid Protection Suits). You'll find huge bales of "Dino Chow" as well as samples of stomach contents and dino dung. And then we're in the examining room with Chris. Attendants there will check her temperature, listen to her vital signs, and collect a sinus sample and a urine sample, which is something you don't see every day. There are a few other bathroom jokes here, as well, which you can experience for yourself without my help here.

Chris, powered with high-tech hydraulics and robotics, moves and responds to trainers and visitors. And a lucky visitor will get to pet the gentle giant.

Camp Jurassic. A children's play area sitting in the shadow of Jurassic Park River Adventure, including a fantastic collection of climbing nets and slides. Some of the areas are nicely shaded.

The nets look a lot flimsier than they are. There are steel cables hidden within the webbing of many of the supports.

Best of all for parents: there is only one exit from Camp Jurassic, so you can let the kids run free and park yourself at the gate to catch them if they start to wander off toward the dinosaurs and other lures.

At the base of the climbing area is the Amber Mine itself, stocked with glowing gems (some including insects trapped in the amber, which according to the story of Jurassic Park, was the source of the dinosaur DNA for the resurrection of the beasts.)

Outside the mine be sure to step on the large dino footprints on the walkway. (If you don't step on them on purpose, you're almost certain to do so by accident.) Each print triggers a mighty or mini-roar from the maker of the mark, along with an accompanying rumble in the ground below your feet.

The Lost Continent

A crumbling statue of Poseidon, the Greek god of the sea, presides over a land long ago lost in the mists of time. Exotic traders peer from behind mountains of rich fabrics and precious metals, inviting guests to join them in the search for even greater treasures.

Dueling Dragons
© *1999 Universal Studios Escape*

WOW Dueling Dragons. A stroll through this forest can be a dangerous proposition," says the sorcerer Merlin. "Living within it are two fierce dragons. One breathes fire; the other breathes ice. In order to escape, you must prove your bravery by mounting the back of one of the creatures and riding it to freedom."

That's the good news; the bad news is that we're talking about a roller coaster here—one of the most terrifying yet conceived.

Dueling Dragons features two intertwined tracks that whiz guests over, under, and around each other through the trees of a medieval forest and out over Dragon Lake.

From the top of the 125-foot common lift, the Fire Dragon drops to the left and the Ice Dragon heads off to the right, with each track following its own layout. But they don't stay apart forever—three times the coasters zoom straight at each other, turning away or diving above or below each other at the last moment. At times, the two tracks and their passengers—their feet dangling below (or above) them, are separated by a mere 12 inches.

The seats in the dragons are four-abreast with eight rows, for a total of 32 volunteers; the cars are suspended from the overhead track except when they are upside down and the track is under your head. The tracks invert five times during the ride of about two minutes and 25 seconds. As each train is loaded, a computer calculates its weight and decides which of the two coasters should leave first and at what speed, so that the near-collisions will occur right on schedule.

And here's something you don't see in a press release every day: Universal says the queue for the Dueling Dragons, at 3,180 feet, is the longest and most elaborate waiting line in the world. Trust me, it just goes on and on and on.

The good news is that because there are two separate coasters, the line moves twice as fast, gobbling up about 3,264 riders per hour. The bad news is that nevertheless, this is one very long line; If you arrive at the coaster and find the line reaching to the outside of the queue, you're in for a wait that might reach two hours.

Just when you think you're heading for the loading station, the queue takes off in another direction into a whole new yard full of lines. Finally you enter into the building in a medieval churchlike setting, a place of shattered glass and crumbled stones that once was a castle so fair, where Merlin will tell you the story of the dueling dragons.

Slow down a bit to read the inscription in the open book in the next room, It's Merlin's entreaty to the gods to release us all from the thrall of the dragons. "Serpent of fire, obey my command. Abandon your hold upon this land." And, "Dragon ice, abominable scourge, from this blighted land diverge."

The next waiting area (yes, there's still more) is a creepy cavern, marked with the scrawls of ancient graffiti artists. "Don't be a bonehead," it says, just above a collection of skulls. And then there is "Enter in peace, exit in pieces."

And then finally, it is time to "Choose Thy Fate." The waiting line diverges into the final queues. Head left to Fire, right to Ice.

The two loading stations are next to each other. There is one final queue for those visitors who insist on sitting in the front of the car. The cars start off together, climbing the hill in tandem and taking off on their ride together.

The Fire track is a few seconds faster to the finish. Coaster experts say that the Ice side offers better twists and turns; sit toward the front for the best views of the next close encounter. Fire is a bit faster and wilder; ride at the back for the best whips.

Use the lockers outside of the queue to store your possessions. Trust me: anything that is not locked up will fall out.

WOW Poseidon's Fury: Escape from the Lost City. The "Keeper" seems to be extremely pleased with the unexpected arrival of guests to his cavern. After all, it's been hundreds—perhaps thousands—of years since his city disappeared into the sea.

This walk-through show puts visitors in the middle of a battle between the watery powers of Poseidon and the fiery authority of his archenemy Zeus.

You'll walk into the building through the moldy, crumbling ruins of an ancient city. Once you're inside, the hallway is very dark, damp, and cool, barely lit by flickering lamps. When your eyes finally adjust to the light, check out the interesting details on the walls and ceilings, including the shell sconces on the walls.

About 150 to 200 persons at a time are allowed into the first theater; you'll stand around the walls surrounding a circular platform in the center. A trap door drops from the ceiling, and we meet the "Keeper of Tales," who will be our guide. Call me Keeper, he says.

What we've got here, unsurprisingly, is a battle between the good and beneficent god Zeus and the evil Poseidon and his followers in the breakaway province of Atlantis. The battle went on for a thousand years or so, until Zeus triumphed and Atlantis and Poseidon were banished beneath the seas.

And so we move on to the next room, a creepy stone temple ruled by The Oracle, the Gatekeeper to Atlantis. But where has she gone? "Never trust a voice without a head," the Keeper advises. Ah, but there she is, speaking from a perch above a giant door; it is, we learn the portal to Atlantis.

The Oracle introduces us to some of a set of secret symbols we need to unlock the portal. And darned if the portal doesn't start moving around like a giant puzzle. It's like a giant bank vault door; when the pieces finally align, a vortex to Atlantis is revealed.

And as befits a visit beneath the sea, this is one wet and wild vortex. A huge tube of water flows up and around us as we move into the world of Atlantis. This is definitely a frizz-the-hair, fog the glasses kind of place, but you won't get wet.

And then we are welcomed to the spectacular Temple of Poseidon, with a view through windows into the undersea world. "It's beautiful," says the Keeper, "but I do not judge a shark by his smile."

Right he is, for soon thereafter Poseidon himself and his army of followers fill a dramatic water screen across the room. (The images are dramatic, an even better, indoor version of Disney's "Fantasmic" show across town.)

"Welcome to your new home," Poseidon tells us, but his welcome sounds like more of a threat. Who among us can stand up to a fearsome visage such as Poseidon? Not you or me, but what has come over old man Keeper? Suddenly, the Keeper reveals his true identity; let's just say we find out that he holds a much loftier position than a mere teller of tales.

The ensuing battle between the gods fills the room with fire and water and fog . . . and with victory, a sudden return to the other side of the vortex.

WOW The Eighth Voyage of Sindbad. Apparently, seven voyages were not enough for this great hero of the past, and so he sets out once again on a great search for riches.

Here's the story line in three sentences: "Sindbad: We're as rich as kings," says Kebab. "Yes, but only if we can make it back alive," replies Sindbad. And, look: "the princess is imprisoned in a circle of fire!"

So, you see, the goal is to escape the clutches of evil, with the riches . . . and the princess . . . intact.

Sindbad and his friend Kebab ("Shush, Kebab," says Sindbad at one point in the story) are entreated by the captive princess to snatch away the enchanted jewel, "The Sultan's Heart." But when they do so, the lovely princess transforms into the evil sorceress Miseria who proceeds to torment Sindbad, Kebab, and the real princess. ("That's so typical," says Kebab. "Give your girlfriend a big rock and she changes on you.")

The show involves some spectacular explosions, fireworks, and other pyrotechnics. And, there are also a few wet surprises. One splash zone is in the mid-section of the center of the theater near the mast; another is down low on the right side.

When Miseria and her henchmen battle against Sindbad and his buddy, you'll see just them throwing axes, hammers, knives . . . and a kitchen sink.

The finale features Miseria's flaming plunge from the upper level of the set into the pond below. (Watch carefully and you'll spot a stuntman in a flame-resistant suit substituting for Miseria at the last moment.)

There are 1,700 seats in the canopied theater, which should allow for enough space for last-minute arrivals except on the busiest of days.

While you're in the area, be sure to pause to contemplate the statue outside of the entrance to the theater. There's a hidden camera and speakers within, along with an array of water hoses. The controller talks with the guests . . . with his or her hands on the spray buttons. It's fun to watch or participate.

Mystics of the Seven Veils. One of the stranger offerings at a theme park, a team of rent-a-psychics operate under a tent near Sindbad's show. You can buy readers from five minutes to half an hour, for about $10 to $50. Or you can send the money to me and I'll send you the tea leaves from my last cup of Lipton's.

Seuss Landing

Ten whimsical acres where Dr. Seuss's famous characters come to life. This is the most fun part of the park, a draw for kids of all ages.

There's hardly a straight line to be found on the island, and Universal's horticulturists have even managed to find and grow some strangely misshapen trees to match the strange foliage of the books of Dr. Seuss. (Some of the palms were transplanted from southern Florida where they had been bent by the fury of Hurricane Andrew.)

Near the entrance to the land near the Port of Entry is a dedication to Theodore Geisel, better known under his pen name. "We dedicate this land to Dr. Seuss. May his genius forever be on the loose."

At the other end of the land, beneath an arch at the entrance to The Lost Continent is a Seussian quote: "Think left and think right. Think low and think high. Oh, the thinks you can think up, if only you try!"

WOW The Cat in the Hat. A ride through the pages of Dr. Seuss's best-known book, and one of the best "dark rides" anywhere. (This ride is the most Disney-like attraction at Universal's Islands of Adventure, the highest possible compliment for a ride aimed at youngsters.)

Up to 1,800 guests per hour travel on six-passenger couches through 18 scenes from the book, including a revolving, mind-bending, 24-foot tunnel. The couches twist and turn and spin on their bases.

The adventure features more than 30 robotic characters, including the Cat himself and the mischievous Thing 1 and Thing 2. Those Things tear the house apart in wonderful ways, then race to make everything right once mom comes back home.

"Should we tell her about it?" we're asked. "Well, what would you do if mother asked you?" We're not sure.

WOW Caro-Seuss-el. Claimed to be the most elaborate and interactive carousels ever built—who are we to argue with Dog-a-lopes and Cowfish?

Seven different Seuss characters, a total of 54 mounts, circle around; the creatures will respond to their riders in wonderfully weird ways.

Characters include Cowfish from McElligot's Pool; Elephant-birds from Horton Hatches the Egg; AquaMop Tops and Twin Camels from One Fish, Two Fish, Red Fish, Blue Fish; Dog-a-lopes and Mulligatawnies from If I Ran the Zoo, and Birthday Katroo from Happy Birthday to You.

〔WOW〕 One Fish, Two Fish, Red Fish, Blue Fish. Young visitors (and lucky adults in their company) steer one of 12 two-passenger Seussian fish up and down 15 feet in the air as they travel through water spouts and streams. Topping off the ride is an 18-foot-tall sculpture of the "Star Belly Fish" of the story.

You know which fish you are. If the song says that one fish should go down and red fish should head for the sky, pay attention unless you'd like a free bath from the water cannon on the next turn.

Sylvester McMonkey McBean and His Very Unusual Driving Machines (opening Summer of 2000). Based on the "Sneeches" tale that teaches children about discrimination, this indoor-outdoor elevated attraction is actually two rides in one.

Guests choose between the Star Belly side or the Plain Belly side, each offering a different ride experience on a track elevated 15 feet in the air. The 60 vehicles travel slowly on a track above Seuss Landing and through six show scenes, including the Circus McGurkus Café Stoo-pendous where the cars pass nearby a gigantic hanging mobile of Seuss characters.

Visitors will be able to honk their horns, control the speed of their vehicle, and gently bump into the cars ahead of them, setting off Seussian sound effects.

If I Ran the Zoo. An interactive playground that tells the story of Gerald McGrew and his quest to create a totally different zoo of strange and unusual animals. The three areas include Hedges, Water, and the New Zoo.

At McElligot's Pool, you can drop a coin in the creature's mouth if you'd like to see what happens. Let me give you a hint: the humor here is not dry. (By the way, Universal promises to give all of the coins to charity.)

Eating Your Way Through Universal's Islands of Adventure

Universal has done a good job of creating interesting food fare at Islands of Adventure, from green eggs and ham to Dagwood sandwiches, from burgers to exotic Asian noodle dishes. Fast-food meals will likely cost about $10 with a drink; the upscale Mythos and the quirky Confisco Grille offer restaurant service for about $12 to $20 for entrees alone.

Port of Entry

🏔 **Confisco Grille.** Run by a band of thieves (no, I wouldn't call Universal Studios such an unpleasant thing. These thieves are the wait staff within this unusual—and inventive—restaurant on the right side of the Port of Entry as you near the lagoon. The manager may warn you, though, that if you find something missing from your table to let him know; he'll see about getting it back for you.)

The slightly skewed lobby features some unusual mechanisms and stairways to nowhere. Inside, there's Kraft paper on the tabletops and the smell of a wood fire in the air.

Specialties, priced from about $10 to $20, include Thai chicken salad, a Portabella mushroom burger, Shrimp Alla Confisco, and a grilled sirloin steak. Side orders include Confisco fries for about $4, served in a cone with dipping sauces such as Buffalo-style (hot sauce and blue cheese) and Southern-style (peach chipotle barbecue sauce.)

[Y] **The Backwater Bar at Confisco's** includes an understated ad for Seagram's liquors on the exterior wall; Seagrams owns Universal Studios, which is partners with The Rank Organisation in Universal Studios Escape.

[🍴] **Croissant Moon Bakery.** A pleasant bakery with only a handful of inside tables. Specialties include soups and salads for about $3 each, and unusual sandwiches priced at about $7 include peppered roast beef and smoked Gouda cheese, and smoked turkey and brie. And then there is a sumptuous spread of cakes, cheesecakes, and cookies, priced about $2 to $3.

Marvel Super Hero Island

[🍴] **Café 4.** A salute to the Fantastic Four (scientist Reed Richards, his wife Sue, her kid brother John Storm, and Ben Grimm), to the left of the entrance to Spider-Man.

Offerings include pizza by the slice (about $3.50) or the pie (up to $17.45) with choices including cheese, pepperoni, and barbecued chicken with boursin cheese. Other choices, priced from about $5 to $8, include an Italian hoagie, sausage sub, minestrone soup, and Caesar salad.

[🍴] **Captain America Diner.** Good old American fare, including chicken sandwiches, burgers, and Freedom Fighter French Fries, with entrees from about $5 to $7.

Toon Lagoon

[🍴] **Blondie's: Home of the Dagwood.** We're talking real sandwiches here, huge stacks of stuff between slices of bread. Of course, the featured sandwich includes the Dagwood (ham, salami, turkey, bologna, Swiss and American cheeses). The Dagwood and other handfuls are priced at about $7. You'll also find vegetable soup and salads.

[🍴] **Comic Strip Café.** Just what you'd expect comic book heroes to order. You'll find counters serving fish and chips, Chinese, Mexican, and Pizza and pasta offerings.

[🍴] **Wimpy's.** You already know what kind of food this guy likes. Just head for the counter marked "bovine perfection." Wimpie promises, by the way, that he "personally supervises the culinary construction of each hamburger."

Alas, the burgers cost more than a nickel, and you'll have to pay for them today, or on Tuesday (if today is Tuesday). A basic burger with fries is about $5. If you insist, you can also order a chicken sandwich or chili dog for about $7. And attention Popeye, there's even a spinach salad for $3.

[🍴] **Cathy's Ice Cream.** The weight-conscious comic-strip heroine's favorite food is offered to all.

Jurassic Park

[🍴] **Thunder Falls Terrace.** A glass wall lets diners watch hapless guests plunge down the final drop at the Jurassic Park River Adventure.

The interior is Jurassic Park primitive, with huge wooden beams. It's an attractive setting with good food, albeit a bit on the pricey side for a cafeteria.

Some of the more unusual theme park offerings (Stegosaurus Starters, actually) include peel and eat shrimp for about $7, and roasted corn and conch chowder for $3. Entrees, priced from about $7 to $12, include rotisserie chicken salad, barbecued chicken wings, and chargrilled baby back ribs.

🍴 **Pizza Predattoria.** Small personal pies, including pepperoni and barbecued chicken with pineapple, are priced from about $6 to $7. Other entrees, priced similarly, include a meatball sandwich, and a Caesar salad in a pizza crust. There's also a combination platter of pizza, salad, and soda for about $9.95.

🍴 **The Burger Digs.** A basic fast food joint, offering burgers, cheeseburgers, and grilled chicken for about $6 to $9.

🍸 **The Watering Hole.** You've got to like a bar in Jurassic Park that advertises itself as the "home of the original lounge lizard."

The walk-up outdoor stand offers coffee and a full range of drinks, including rum runners, pina coladas, and margaritas, priced at about $3 plain, or $5 with a shot of alcohol. There's also a nice selection of imported and microbrews.

The Lost Continent

🏔 🍸 **Mythos Restaurant.** The showpiece of the Islands of Adventure, Mythos lies on the shore of the Inland Sea within a volcanic rock formation.

Stop and take a look at the intricate details on the Mythos building, with carvings and hidden figures, in some ways a rocky version of the striking Tree of Life at Disney's Animal Kingdom.

The interior is like a limestone cavern, with carvings in stone and jade.

A raw bar offers shellfish. Appetizers, priced from about $5 to $10, include tempura shrimp with wasabi and soy, grilled asparagus with citrus butter. Salads include poached artichoke.

Entrees from about $10 to $20 include linguini with Thai spices, including mint and cilantro, grilled yellowfin tuna Nicoise with kalamata vinaigrette, and grilled chicken sandwich with Vidalia onions, fontina cheese and green olive mayonnaise.

KEY:

🍴 = Fast food

🍸 = Pub

🏔 = Full-service restaurant

🍴 🍸 **Enchanted Oak Restaurant (and Alchemy Bar).** Designed to commemorate the oak tree trunk into which legend says Merlin was frozen by the Lady of the Lake. The eatery on The Lost Continent features oak-fired barbecue dishes and Dragon Scale Ale. The great sorcerer himself may make guest appearances if you're lucky.

Entrees from about $7 to $15 include chicken and ribs, barbecued spare ribs, and hickory smoked chicken.

Seuss Landing

🍴 **Green Eggs and Ham Café.** What else do you expect on the menu than this famed dish from Dr. Seuss? There's more, of course, but don't you want to try something green?

In case you were wondering, the eggs are colored with natural parsley puree. The outdoor counter with a set of umbrella-shaded tables offers entrees priced from about $5 to $6, including green eggs and hamwich, hamburgers, and cheese-burgers.

🍽 **Circus McGurkus Café Stoopendous.** A fun place for kids, with animated mobiles of Seuss circus creatures overhead. Also above is a section of track from Sylvester McMonkey McBean and His Very Unusual Driving Machines, and vehicles should pass through regularly. Private booths are named after Seuss characters, including "Rolf from the Ocean of Olf," and "The Drum-Tummied Snumm."

Entrées, priced from about $6 to $8, include a fried chicken platter with mashed potatoes, pepperoni pizza, lasagna with marinara sauce, spaghetti and meatballs, and cheese ravioli. There's also the old standby of alphabet soup for a relative bargain of about $3.

🍽 **Moose Juice Goose Juice.** A drink stand offering moose juice (also known as Turbo Tangerine) or goose juice (sour green apple.) Both are available fresh or frozen for $2 to $3. If you can't decide between them, order a mix of both.

A Musical Escape

Among the delights of the new park is a suite of original music composed and performed as a background theme. A different soundtrack is heard in each of the five islands, as well as in the Port of Entry.

Musicians from around the world came together in the resonant chambers of a de-sanctified monastery and professional studios in Seattle to make a recording that was one of the most ambitious musical events ever.

Four separate musical ensembles were created, including a gamelan orchestra from Java, a Celtic band, a Greco-Etruscan band, and a traditional Western symphony orchestra.

Port of Entry features music performed by a Javanese gamalan, a traditional orchestra, which traces its roots back to 230 A.D.; it consists mainly of percussive instruments, including gongs, drums, bells, and wooden-keyed xylophones, as well as violins, flutes, and zithers. Gamelan music, which features a pulsating, rhythmic beat, developed alongside the unique religious and secular dance and puppet plays of countries that include Bali and Java. The music changes as the visitor walks through an exotic bazaar, culminating in a grand, lush signature theme as guests pass under a grand arch and, like explorers discovering a new world, view the 100-acre vista of the Islands of Adventure for the first time.

A Celtic band recorded additional music for the Port of Entry and for The Lost Continent. The mournful sounds of Celtic music can be heard in Irish, Scottish, and Welsh music; the band includes some of the most ancient instruments in Western culture including the bagpipe, double oboe, flute, and harp. Also featured in the recording are a pennywhistle, a hand-held Celtic drum known as a *bohdran*, a concertina, and an Irish alto flute.

Also contributing to music for The Lost Continent was a Greco-Etruscan band, featuring instruments from the Middle East, India, and Greece. A variety of ancient instruments is employed, including a Greek lyre named a *kithara,* a wind instrument played with a double reed known as a *shawm,* a stringed instrument from Western Asia named a *cembalo* with strings struck by a pair of small hammers, an Indian stringed instrument named a *vina,* a sitar and its larger cousin the surbahar, a long-necked Indian lute known as a *tambura,* a pakawaj talking drum, and a bowed stringed instrument carved from a single block of wood called a *sarangi.*

At Seuss Landing, musicians were asked to bring the fantastic sounds of cartoons to life. The result was a score that involved some newly created but wacky instruments, including a harp that used rubber bands instead of strings. For Toon Lagoon, where two-dimensional cartoons populate the landscape, they worked with familiar meolodies such as "The Sailor's Hornpipe" (better known as Popeye's theme), and music from the beloved cartoons of Jay Ward, creator of Rocky and Bullwinkle.

For the more heroic, high-tech Marvel Super Hero Island, driving, rock-flavored music was composed. Each super hero has a unique theme that is heard at appropriate locales on the island.

John Wiliams's soaring orchestral themes from the blockbuster films *Jurassic Park* and *The Lost World* were performed in new arrangements as the soundtrack for the Jurassic Park island, where long-extinct dinosaurs come to life.

UNIVERSAL STUDIOS ISLANDS OF ADVENTURE

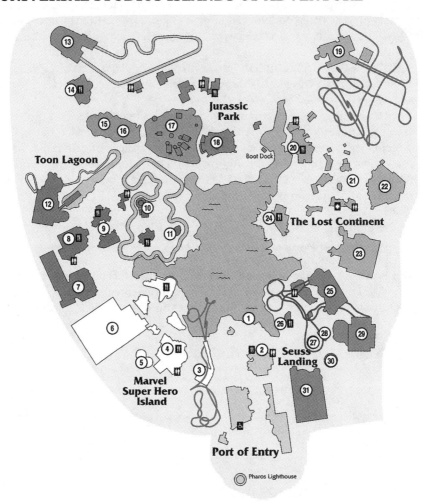

1. Island Skipper Tours
2. Confisco Grille
3. Incredible Hulk Coaster
4. Café 4
5. Doctor Doom's Fearfall
6. The Amazing Adventures of Spider-Man
7. Pandemonium Cartoon Circus
8. Comic Strip Café
9. Comic Strip Lane
10. Popeye & Bluto's Bilge-Rat Barges
11. Me Ship the Olive
12. Dudley Do-Right's Ripsaw Falls
13. Jurassic Park River Adventure
14. Thunder Falls Terrace
15. Camp Jurassic
16. Pteranadon Flyers
17. Triceratops Encounter
18. Jurassic Park Discovery Center
19. Dueling Dragons
20. Enchanted Oak Restaurant
    (and Alchemy Bar)
21. Sindbad's Village
22. The Eighth Voyage of Sindbad
23. Poseidon's Fury: Escape from the Lost City
24. Mythos Restaurant
25. Sylvester McMonkey McBean's
    and His Very Unusual Driving Machines
26. Green Eggs and Ham Café
27. Caro-Seuss-el
28. Moose Juice Goose Juice
29. Circus McGurkus Café Stoopendous
30. One Fish, Two Fish, Red Fish, Blue Fish
31. The Cat in the Hat

Chapter 18
Universal CityWalk Orlando

Even adults deserve a place all their own. (Kids can come along, too, most of the time.)

Universal CityWalk, a 30-acre day-and-night entertainment center, serves as the front door to Universal Studios Florida and Universal Studios Islands of Adventure. Visitors are deposited there when they exit one of the two gigantic parking garages.

The two-tiered promenade wraps around a four-acre lagoon.

Admission to CityWalk is free, and visitors can come and go between Universal Studios Florida and Universal's Islands of Adventure; your options for lunch or dinner are greatly improved by the addition. Some of the venues have a cover charge of about $3 to $5 in the evening when there is entertainment, and may have a higher entrance fee for some special events. A **Key to the Clubs** sold in 1999 for $18 including taxes, providing access to all venues of City-Walk on a single day. The Key does not include admission to special events that require tickets.

You will, though, have to park you car in Universal's lot and pay a $6 fee for the privilege; some restaurants and attractions at CityWalk have offered guests a credit for the expense.

On the moving sidewalk from the parking structure into Citywalk, to your right is the site of the Hard Rock Hotel, due to open in 2000. A bit further in the distance to your right is the elegant Portofino Hotel.

At the end of the walkway you will find yourself in Citywalk. Head right to Universal Studios Florida and left to Universal's Islands of Adventure.

The first CityWalk was opened at Universal Studios Hollywood, and was an immediate success. At Walt Disney World, Pleasure Island and Downtown Disney West Side were clearly influenced by CityWalk.

For many visitors, the best thing about CityWalk in Orlando is its proximity to the two theme parks at Universal Studios Escape. For the first time in Orlando, it is possible to exit a theme park and enter into a sophisticated dining and adult entertainment district for lunch or dinner and then return to the park.

A CityWalk Walkabout

Latin Quarter. Hot, hot, hot: a salsa beat and a delicious spread of hispanic food from 21 nations from Mexico to South America. Add in a dance floor and the infectious music, and you'll see why this place is one of the liveliest places in CityWalk. A dance troupe, including some outrageous costumes, performs salsa, merengue, tango, and other hot, hot, hot routines.

The extensive menu includes appetizers priced from about $5 to $8, including ceviche de corvina y camarones (Corvina fish and shrimp marinated in a spicy lemon and lime juice with jalapenos, tomato, and cilantro), nachos casi machos (plantain chip nachos with Monterrey jack cheese and jalapenos), and tamal en majo de maiz con mujo (cornmeal stuffed with seasoned pork wrapped in a corn husk and served on a black bean puree.)

Entrees, priced from about $14 to $20, include churrasco (grilled skirt steak with chimichurri sauce over garbanzo beans sauteed with ham and chorizo sausage), costillas de Cornero al morno (spiced rack of lamb), and atun a la cana de Azucar (sugar cane tuna loin on a bed of roasted garlic boniato).

Open from 11 A.M. to 1:30 A.M. for lunch and dinner. Cover charge $3.25 after 10 P.M.

Motown Café. The Motown Café is a temple to the icons of R&B and soul. The centerpiece is a revolving triple-threat statue of the Supremes in full spangle regalia. Around the room are other statues and pieces of memorabilia from other superstars such as the Temptations, the Four Tops, and the Jackson Five. There's also the Motown Moments, two house bands that perform hits by the Temptations and Supremes.

The menu features "slow cooked" homestyle Detroit dishes, including Smokey's Ribs and french-fried sweet potatoes. And there is, of course, a gift shop.

Open for dinner from 5 P.M. to midnight during the week, and until 2 A.M. on Friday and Saturday. Cover charge $3.25.

Bob Marley—A Tribute to Freedom. At Bob Marley's the room is hot, the music is hot, the dancing is hot, and some of the food is hot: the jerk chicken with black bean sauce will clear out your sinuses nicely.

The restaurant is a one-of-a-kind celebration of music and culture based around the music and philosophy of Jamaican reggae legend and cultural icon Bob Marley. The restaurant and club is patterned after Marley's actual home and garden in Kingston, Jamaica; in a touch of realism, it is not air conditioned. It includes an inner courtyard that is open to the sky and there's a stage for performances. The menu features light Jamaican fare, including meat patties, roti, Red Stripe beer, and grapefruit-flavored Ting soda.

Open for dinner weekdays from 5 P.M. to 1:30 A.M., and lunch and dinner on Saturdays and Sundays from 11 A.M. to 1:30 A.M. Cover charge $4.25 after 7 P.M.

Pat O'Brien's. A replica of the famous watering hole in New Orleans with a Main Bar and a Dueling Pianos bar next door. Famed for its old-world character and flaming fountain patio, Pat O'Brien's is also the birthplace of the world-famous Hurricane drink. The restaurant's wine collection features more than 4,000 bottles with many of them on display around the dining room; an extensive cigar humidor is located within the "chimney" of the eatery.

Founded in 1933 as Club Tipperary, one of the leading speakeasies of New Orleans, Pat O'Brien's moved to its current location in 1942. The CityWalk outpost is a close replica of the original, built of weathered red brick, wrought iron, and dark wood fixtures. Overhead in the entranceway are seven muskets representing the seven countries that once occupied New Orleans.

Pat O'Brien's does a great job of transporting Orlando to New Orleans. Upstairs over the open courtyard are a few handsome smaller rooms. Among them is the Briars Suite, named in honor of Napoleon Bonaparte's favorite retreat on the Isle of St. Helena. Napoleon came to visit and all but refused to leave.

I sampled a fiery Jambalaya, a lot different from the weak imitations you may find at your neighborhood diner.

Open for lunch and dinner from 11 A.M. to 1 A.M. Cover charge $3.25 to enter the Dueling Pianos bar, which is open from 6 P.M. to 2 A.M. and restricted to guests 21 and older.

The Groove. The Groove is a high-tech, high-end dance club, complete with all of the requisite toys: fog machines, strobes, spotlights, and video screens. Oh, and the music was so loud that I could barely take notes. I do remember, though, that the walls were decorated with all things dance, from funk to disco to Folies Bergere and even a bit of exotic dancing. One of the prized posters advertises an appearance by Josephine Baker at the Folies Bergere in Paris.

The Blue Room is like a set from the Jetsons, serving martini drinks such as the Hippie Chick and the Mood Ring. The Green Room is a spooky place lit by electric candles, featuring scotch and aperitifs such as Nectar of the Gods. The Red Room (reminiscent of an old old bordello, or so I am told), offers fruit drinks including the Scarlet Letter and the Red Velvet. The club includes live performances by Universal/MCA acts.

Open nightly from 9 P.M. to 2 A.M. Guests must be 21 or older to enter. Cover charge is $5.25.

Jimmy Buffett's Margaritaville Café. Perched like a parrot on the edge of the CityWalk lagoon, this quirky restaurant celebrates the island music and lifestyle of cult hero musician Buffett. There are, of course, margaritas on tap . . . in fact they may flow out of a bubbling volcano. The cafe is appropriately located overlooking the water near the bridge to Islands of Adventure.

Food is "high-end" bar food, including seafood, "cheeseburgers in paradise" and other fare related to Buffet's songs. The Volcano Bar erupts with margaritas, and there are also themed areas, including the Shark Bar, and the 12-Volt Bar. If you don't catch the references, just ask the nearest Parrothead: they'll likely sing you the appropriate line from the master.

Open for lunch and dinner from 11 A.M. to 2 A.M. Cover charge $3.25 after 10 P.M.

Emeril's Orlando. From the bayous of Louisiana, a sophisticated and "kicky" culinary adventure that features chef Emeril Lagasse's Creole-based cuisine. The focal point of the restaurant is a bustling open kitchen where diners can watch chefs prepare their meals. A squad of waiters descends on tables to deliver meals to every diner at the same moment—they call it "gang service."

Located in a separate building near the waterfront, this is a very upscale eatery—not a cheap date. A meal for two with wine can easily hit $200. And speaking of wine, the house collection is something like 12,000 bottles. Lagasse himself is expected to be at the restaurant about two weeks out of each month.

When the restaurant opened in Orlando, appetizers included Maine lobster cheesecake, Louisiana oyster stew, and lump crabmeat and fresh Florida hearts of palm strudel, priced from about $8 to $12. Entrees, priced from about $18 to $32, included Portobello mushroom confit, Andouille-crusted Texas redfish, grilled veal chop, and pan-seared filet of beef with parsley crust. Wood-fired pizzas included wild and exotic mushroom truffle pizza, sweet barbecue salmon pizza, and southwestern style seafood pizza with cilantro black bean sauce.

There's also a six-course "degustation" or sampler, served to the entire table.

Open for lunch from 11:30 A.M. to 2 P.M. and dinner daily from 5:30 P.M. to 10 P.M., and until 11 P.M. on Friday and Saturday.

CityJazz. CityJazz is very elegant, a wood-trimmed cathedral to jazz that is bestowed with impeccable acoustics. The Down Beat Jazz Hall of Fame honors the musicians hallowed in the pages of *Down Beat Magazine* since 1952. And the stars of today are featured at a live performance stage.

Nearby is an outdoor stage facing Central Plaza for small performances. A much larger stage offers seats facing the water; it is used for major concerts.

Open for downing from 8:30 P.M. to 1 A.M. The Down Beat Jazz Hall of Fame Museum is open from 3 to 6 P.M. Cover charge $5.25 after 8:30 P.M., with higher charges for special performances.

NASCAR Café. This is fast food of a different sort, with diners immersed within rows of gleaming Winston Cup Cars, a surround-sound video wall, electronic and multimedia games, and memorabilia and artifacts from the world of NASCAR racing. The atmosphere continues on to the menu and the pit-crew wait staff.

Car parts are everywhere, of course. An entire race car hangs over the bar on the ground floor, which is surprisingly close to the ground floor video arcade. The arcade features driving games, including a Virtual Reality Race Simulator, priced at $5 per ride.

The menu includes basic American food, some of the items named in honor of racing heroes. Offerings are priced from about $8 to $10 for burgers (including a Daytona chili burger and a vegetarian Gardenburger) and from about $11 to $20 for entrees such as the Bill France pork chop, the DW Dude Filet (Darrell Waltrip's steak of choice), the Crew Chief Roasted Chicken, and a Chicken Pastry Pot Pie.

Appetizers, priced from about $6, include Talladega Tenders, Winston Cup Wings, Supercharged Chili, and popcorn shrimp.

Open daily from 10 A.M. to 10 P.M. No cover charge.

Pastamoré. A lively outdoor street café, with a few indoor seats. Specialties include panini, a spiced and decorated bread, priced about $10. Offerings include panini al verdura with beefsteak tomatoes, grilled eggplant, fresh basil, olive oil and balsamic vinegar; panini capicola with Italian meats and

Fontina cheese; and panini di polle é pesto, with grilled marinated chicken, Fontina cheese, and pesto mayonnaise.

You'll also find antipasto and salad selections, along with a selection of Italian and domestic beers and wines. Desserts include gelato, ultra-rich Italian ice cream; flavors include cappucino, pistachio, spumoni, and chocolate with hazelnuts.

The café is open from 8 A.M. to midnight, and the small restaurant from 5 P.M. to midnight.

NBA City. A high-energy café, next door to the Hard Rock Café near the entrance to Universal Studios Islands of Adventure. This is the first in what is intended to be a new chain of theme restaurants, a partnership between the National Basketball Association and Hard Rock Café.

The restaurant includes the CityWalk Cage, a dining area featuring contemporary American cuisine and saluting the stars of the NBA and the WNBA, the NBA City Playground with games and attractions, and the NBA City Club where guests can watch live and classic games.

Open from 11 A.M. to 2 A.M. No cover charge.

Hard Rock Café Orlando. The world's largest Hard Rock Café includes a 650-seat restaurant. There is, of course, a gift shop. The spectacular eatery replaces the earlier version at Universal Studios Florida. (The old building near the Universal Studios Florida closed, but may be recast for another use.)

Hard Rock Café features classic American cuisine in a high-energy atmosphere, surrounded by rare and unique pieces of memorabilia from the past five decades of rock and roll. Signature dishes include Pig Sandwich, grilled fajitas, veggie burgers, and the Outrageous Hot Fudge Brownie.

Open from 11 A.M. to 2 A.M.

Hard Rock Live. The first live-concert venue in the chain is modestly fashioned after the Roman Forum in a modern "retro" style. Capable of seat-

Hard Rock Live at Universal CityWalk

ing as many as 2,500 people, Hard Rock Live hosts concerts by cutting-edge and rock-classic artists.

More than 140,000 square feet in size, complete with imposing columns, majestic archways, and a grand entrance, the hall includes the latest in sound and light technology. The arena includes opulent luxury boxes, as well as general seating.

The Hard Rock Live House Band, which includes members who have backed up some of rock's greatest names, performs from Monday through Thursday. Cover charge is $9.

Ticket prices for headliner acts vary by performer.

Universal Cineplex. A 20-screen, 5,200-seat Cineplex Odeon theater complex that employs state-of-the art projection and sound systems. The seating is laid out in a "stadium" design, assuring unobstructed views. One of the theaters, especially large and lavish, will be used for movie premieres.

CityWalk Shops

All Star Collectibles. Autographed, labeled, licensed, or otherwise touched by someone or something associated with just about every sport.

Captain Crackers. Your basic Florida T-shirt and nicknack shop, gone wild in a jungle theme.

Cigarz at CityWalk. Cigars, of course, and fine tobacco, as well as cordials, single malt Scotch, and coffees.

Dapy. Wind-up, flashing, beeping, and clicking toys and gifts. Dapy, which originated in Paris, is related to Spencer Gifts and Universal itself.

Elegant Illusions. Lower-priced, high-quality copies of expensive jewelry.

Endangered Species. A clothing and gift shop that has an environmentally aware message.

Fossil. An upscale version of the trendy watch, sunglass, and accessory marketplace.

Glow! An eclectic, electric, and glimmering collection of clothing, accessories, and gifts.

Quiet Flight. Beachwear and ware.

Silver. Retro jewelry in a re-creation of an old cruise ship.

Tabasco Country Store. Hot sauce, hot clothing, and hot toys.

The Universal Studios Store. Did you expect a Disney store?

Part IV
SeaWorld Orlando

Chapter 19
SeaWorld Orlando, Discovery Cove by SeaWorld

Four-fifths of the earth's surface is water, and almost five million Orlando visitors a year swim upstream to SeaWorld, the world's most popular marine life park.

Located 10 minutes south of downtown Orlando and 15 minutes from Orlando International Airport at the intersection of I-4 and the Beeline Expressway, SeaWorld is open every day from 9 A.M. to 7 P.M., with additional hours during the summer and holidays. Call (407) 351-4600 for more information or consult www.seaworld.com

SeaWorld has a decidedly different feel from Walt Disney World and many other attractions in Central Florida. Most of the scheduled events take place in outdoor theaters that seat 3,000 to 5,000 people. With rare exceptions, you don't wait in line here; you simply walk into the theater 15 or 20 minutes before the event and pick a seat. When the theater is full, you are told to return for another scheduled show.

The average attendance at the park is about 15,000 per day, with peak holiday levels in the summer of almost twice that level.

SeaWorld estimates it will require about eight hours to see the entire park. I recommend you see all of the shows first and then spend remaining time visiting areas that are not regulated by the clock. If you really want to see it all, plan on arriving at opening time (usually 9 A.M.) and staying through dusk.

Where possible arrive for any presentation at least 15 minutes ahead of the show time. This gives you the best chance at getting the seat you want and it lets you view the preshow activities offered at some of the theaters. Most shows are 20 to 25 minutes long. You can usually make the next show on your computer-suggested schedule, even if there are only 5 or 10 minutes between shows.

Although SeaWorld presentations tend to start on time, unless the theater is full, you can always slip in a couple of minutes late if you need to without disturbing the show.

Saturday and Sunday are usually the busiest days of the week at the park,

MUST-SEES

Kraken
(Spring of 2000, for fans of extreme coasters only)

Journey to Atlantis
(wet and slightly wild)

Shamu Adventure

Key West at SeaWorld

Wild Arctic

Shamu's Happy Harbor
(adults excused)

Manatees: The Last Generation?

The Intensity Games

Clyde and Seamore Take Pirate Island

Shamu: Close Up!

Terrors of the Deep

with Monday through Thursday the quietest. A big day's attendance would be about 15,000 visitors.

As you enter the park, stop to consider the introductory plaque near the entrance that quotes the African Environmentalist Baba Dioum: "For in the end, we will conserve only what we love, we will love only what we understand, and we will understand only what we are taught."

Power Trip

Begin your SeaWorld tour by stopping at the information counter to the left of the entrance gate. Ask for your own personalized park map and show schedule. This computer printout will guide you through an efficient schedule based on your time of arrival.

Notice that many of SeaWorld's shows and events occur only a few times each day. Decide which of these you definitely want to see (consult our must-see suggestions), then work the schedule.

We recommend that you see the scheduled shows in the order they occur from your arrival time; then spend the rest of your day viewing continuous-view exhibits. This may sound inefficient, but the SeaWorld property isn't all that large; you can crisscross a few times if you need to.

Here's one scenario: If you are ready, willing, and able, head directly for the new Kraken roller coaster, due to open in the spring of 2000; it is sure to be a major draw for years to come. You should also make a beeline to **Wild Arctic** in the morning to avoid lines. **Journey to Atlantis** is another top draw at the park in warm weather; if the morning is chilly, though, you might want to wait till late in the day before enjoying Atlantis's wet thrill. Next, move quickly to the **Manatees: The Last Generation?** exhibit area. From there it's an easy jog to the Dolphin Stadium in the northeast corner of the park for the **Key West at SeaWorld Show.** Depending on your time of arrival, you may have time to pass through the

Penguin Encounter after the Discovery show. Penguin Encounter is a continuous view show; after this brief look, you can come back if you want to.

After viewing the **Clyde and Seamore** show at the Sea Lion & Otter Stadium, pass by one of the lagoon-side restaurants for a sandwich on your way across the lagoon to the Bayside Ski Stadium for the Intensity Games stunt show. Don't worry if lunch takes a little longer than you'd like; simply sit dockside and you can see the start of the ski show from the back side of the lake.

After the water show, move into the Shamu Stadium (on the same side of the lagoon) for the **Shamu Adventure**. Before or after the show, depending on the timing, visit the **Shamu: Close Up!** research pool.

The afternoon may be the best time to visit Key West at SeaWorld. Then make your way back across the lagoon for **Terrors of the Deep**. Take time out for rest and snacks, walk through the Tropical Rain Forest (beside the dolphin pool), and end your day at the **Shamu Rocks America** finale at Shamu Stadium.

Attractions at SeaWorld

WOW Kraken (Spring of 2000). Rising up out of the sea, or at least up out of SeaWorld, is a new monster of a roller coaster, Kraken.

With the sudden explosion of roller coasters in Orlando, including the fabulous Dueling Dragons and the Hulk at Universal Studios Islands of Escape, and the raucous Rock 'n' Roller Coaster at Disney-MGM Studios, SeaWorld waited an extra season to come out with what it claims will be the highest, fastest, and longest coaster in town. It's due to open in the spring of 2000, alongside SeaWorld's Journey to Atlantis ride.

Kraken is a floorless and topless coaster. Before you get too excited, let me explain what that means; we're not talking about the dress code. The coaster seats are mounted on a pedestal a few feet above the wheels and track. There is no "car," no roof or sides, and riders' feet will dangle off the bottom of their chairs.

Think of being strapped into your favorite chair and taking off up a 149-foot-high hill and then careening off into space at speeds of up to 65 mph. Oh yes, and your chair will turn upside down seven times, with elements including a Cobra roll, a zero gravity roll, several vertical loops, and some flat spins. The first drop is an impressive 144 feet.

All this with a view of nothing but sky or ground.

A good portion of the 4,177-foot-long track runs over water. The track plunges below ground three times, including one trip into a tunnel in the lagoon. Riders will avoid the water, but onlookers will be rewarded with a major splash as the coaster goes by.

The lengthy ride will take about 3 minutes and 39 seconds. SeaWorld will operate three 32-passenger trains (eight cars of four passengers each), allowing about 1,500 passengers per hour to ride.

According to Greek and Norse myth, the Kraken was a massive underwater beast kept prisoner by Poseidon. At SeaWorld, the sea serpent has been set free

SeaWorld Tickets. Prices, which do not include 6 percent tax, were in effect mid-1999 and are subject to change. Note that SeaWorld regularly offers "second day free" promotions.

One-Day
Adult	$44.00
Child (3–9)	$35.00

Sky Tower
Per ride	$2.83

Guided Tours
Adult	$5.95
Child	$4.95

4-Park Orlando FlexTicket: $159.95, or $127.95 (ages 3 to 9) Unlimited admission to Universal Studios Florida, Universal Studios Islands of Adventure, SeaWorld Orlando, Wet 'n Wild. Valid 7 days.

5-Park Orlando FlexTicket: $196.95, or $157.95 (ages 3 to 9). Unlimited admission to Universal Studios Florida, Universal Studios Islands of Adventure, SeaWorld Orlando, Wet 'n Wild, Busch Gardens Tampa. Valid 10 days.

. . . and boy, is he ever angry. The waiting lines include displays of baby eels—Kraken's offspring, we are told.

The Swiss-designed ride is unique in Orlando, although it is similar to a ride named the Medusa at Six Flags Great Adventure in New Jersey.

WOW Journey to Atlantis. Part water ride, part roller coaster, totally wild: SeaWorld's first thrill ride—and by all descriptions a unique ride that has two of the steepest, wettest, fastest drops anywhere.

Journey to Atlantis plunges riders into the middle of a fierce battle between good and evil for the lost city of Atlantis.

According to historical lore, the city of Atlantis sank beneath the waves eons ago. Now it has risen again in the Greek fishing village of Thera. The Atlantis set spans an area larger than six football fields and towering taller than a 10-story building.

You'll enter into an eight-passenger fishing boat, two per row. The front and back seats may offer the best ride; you may get slightly less wet in the middle row.

The boats enter into an underwater setting with coral, an area filled with what SeaWorld calls "aqualusions." The attractive siren Allura, representing evil, and Hermes, as the force of good, play happily together for a few moments before the siren morphs into a wicked creature.

(Hermes, the golden seahorse that transforms into a glittering guide, may look like a horse but he is actually a fish. Hermes's live counterparts, yellow Indo-Pacific and lined Caribbean seahorses, reside in aquariums in the gift shop.)

Riders are pulled into Atlantis and the dark and mysterious depths of the siren's lair. (The piercing scream of the angry siren is actually made up of a combination of eight animal voices, including a lion, bear, and rattlesnake.)

Suddenly, the boats nose-dive 60 feet at a 60-degree angle, reaching a speed of 50 mph through a tidal wave of water. Just to add insult to injury, there is a bank of coin-operated water hoses at the bottom of the first 60-foot water drop.

You'll fall through a dark vortex with fog and light. A second drop of just nine feet may get you wetter than the big fall. Allura calls out: "Leaving so soon? I think not!" and then the fishing boats are drawn back up into the building, this time attached to the rails of a roller coaster. The coaster drop is also about 60 feet, with sharp S-curves and other elements . . . and there's one more splash at the base of the coaster's drop.

The last and most spectacular drop, unlike any other at a theme park, nose-dives at highway speeds down 60 feet into a series of careening, S-shaped curves until they finally emerge into the daylight.

The attraction adds some spectacular special "aqualusion" effects to give the illusion of a complete city beneath the water. Ancient statues come to life, transforming into rushing rivers of shimmering water. Entire sets appear and disappear, metamorphosing into Olympian vistas. The advanced technology includes hologram and LCD images. Nearly 24,000 fiber-optic lights illuminate the travels of Hermes, the attraction's hero who guides guests beyond the dark depths of the siren's dangers to safety. The ride is located at the back of the park between the Manatees display and Penguin Encounter; guests arriving at the park along International Drive can see the superstructure along the right side of the road.

The ride will likely be much more crowded on hot summer days, when the idea of a cool bath and high speed is relatively attractive. Avoid Atlantis or Wild Arctic just after one of the major shows lets out to avoid a mass arrival. Note there is a 42-inch height minimum for the ride.

The entire trip takes about 7-and-a-half minutes. You do not want to bring any cameras or other items not meant to get wet. There are unlocked storage cubbies for riders at the loading area; rental lockers with keys are also available before you get in line.

Be sure to check out the Jewels of the Sea Aquarium Gallery inside the gift shop at the base of the building that supports the ride; it includes eight aquariums, including an unusual glass tank set into the floor. Beneath your feet are stingrays and various fish; over your head are bonnethead sharks.

SeaWorld Florida/Busch Gardens Tampa Bay Value Ticket (One day at each park)	
Adult	$79.00
Child	$64.00
SeaWorld Annual Pass	
Adult	$75.00
Child	$65.00
Wild Card Pass (SeaWorld, Busch Gardens Tampa) Annual pass	
Adult	$119.95
Child	$104.95
Wild Card Plus 3-Park (SeaWorld, Busch Gardens Tampa, Adventure Island) Annual pass	
Adult	$149.95
Child	$139.95
Parking	$5

Open daily from 9 A.M. to 6 P.M., with extended hours in the summer and holiday periods. For general information, call (407) 351-3600. SeaWorld's Web site is at: www.seaworld.com

Realistic fantasy. The main building is modeled after a Greek palace, Knossos. Hieroglyphics on the walls of the attraction are duplicates of ones taken from murals and pictorial works in historical Etruscan books. In filming for the attraction, Santa Barbara, California, stood in for Greece.

WOW **Wild Arctic.** The Wild Arctic has arrived in balmy southern Florida, with the biggest new development in the history of any Anheuser-Busch Theme Park, a combination of a state-of-the-art simulator ride and an impressive re-creation of the wonders of the frozen north.

The adventure begins with a thrilling "flight" over the frozen north in the jet helicopter *White Thunder* to the remote Base Station Wild Arctic, surrounded by the beauty of the Arctic and kicking up snow at takeoff in a race to outrun an approaching storm.

As the chopper flies out of the hangar, the Arctic landscape unfolds. The journey is relaxing—at first—as the sweeping vista is filled with frozen mountains, glacier peaks, and clouds. The craft's diving and banking levels out over the sea, and passengers are treated to a spectacular view of narwhals, walruses, and other marine life.

Unsettled briefly by buffeting winds and blinding fog banks, the jet helicopter swoops toward the pack ice for a closer view of polar bears. The radio crackles a warning: the blizzard is bearing down.

Following the frigid Franklin Strait, the helicopter skims low over the Arctic sea. At Larsen Sound, a huge glacier fills the horizon. Gently touching down on the ancient frozen floe, visitors absorb the beauty . . . until a deep rumbling starts, and the copter starts to tumble into a deep crevasse. The copter smacks into the sea just as the rotors reach full thrust. The pilot makes a spectacular escape through the close walls of an ice cavern and eventually makes it to the base station.

There are three helicopter simulators in the Wild Arctic building, each seating 59 people. The attraction accommodates up to 1,800 guests per hour when all three simulators are in operation. Handicapped access is provided. High-definition video laser disk projectors provide the visual stimulation, backed up by 1,200-watt, six-channel laser-disc sound systems.

Each cabin moves six ways—yaw, pitch, roll, heave, surge, and sway. Sometimes the cabin moves as much as nine feet, and in some directions it moves at speeds up to 24 inches per second.

Stepping from the simulator, guests enter a chilly passageway into a frozen wonderland of **Base Station Wild Arctic** with ice walls, where they will encounter some of the real animals that live at the North Pole.

Forget you're in Florida and buy into the story: The base station was built by modern scientists around the decrepit hull of a 150-year-old British exploration ship frozen in the ice for all these years, a unique vantage point for viewing Arctic sea life, including polar bears, beluga whales, and walruses. The viewing position allows views of the animals above and below the water as they forage for food, dive, swim, and interact with Base Station workers.

High-tech equipment sits in and around the ship's remains, with measuring devices next to old anchors and video receivers perched on old shipping crates. The base station makes extensive use of computers and touch-screen monitors to allow guests to communicate with reports from field researchers, and guests can use computers to communicate with research base "scientists." You'll be able to gauge your own ability to hold your breath against polar bears

(2 minutes), beluga whales (20 minutes), walruses (25 minutes), and the local champion, harbor seals (27 minutes).

The Arctic is a mystery to most people, assumed to be a frozen desert. Instead, it is a vast, ever-changing ocean, teeming with life and closely linked to the rest of the planet.

Among the animal stars of Wild Arctic are Klondike and Snow, a pair of polar bears. Abandoned by their mother at birth, the bears were hand-raised by experts at the Denver Zoo. Weighing about 1.3 pounds at birth, by adulthood the male Kondike may weigh about 1,800 pounds and the female Snow about 900 pounds. Lack of space at the zoo demanded the bears be relocated, and in late 1995 the pair were brought to Orlando. They live in a special enclosure that includes a chilly pool stocked with fish (the cubs had never seen live food and had to learn how to fish for themselves). The bears' hunting instincts are further satisfied with morsels randomly hidden in nooks and crevices of the habitat.

Polar bears are among the most beautiful and dangerous of animals, and are found only in the Arctic. The animals are born white; coats turn yellow in the summer sun, and turn white again after a spring molt. The hair itself is hollow to trap warm air, oil coats their fur, and a thick layer of fat provides insulation from the cold. When awake, polar bears spend much of their time stalking or feeding on seals, walruses, and sometimes even beluga whales.

Beluga whales, sometimes known as "sea canaries," are born gray and turn white as they age, making a natural camouflage from predators as they move among the icebergs and ice floes. They weigh from 1,500 to 3,300 pounds and measure from 10 to 15 feet. Like other toothed whales, belugas "echolocate," sending out sonar-like sounds to find breathing holes in the ice and to locate prey such as squid, octopi, shrimp, and a variety of other bottom-dwelling fish.

Walruses have one pair of flippers in front and a second in back. A thick layer of fat, or blubber, helps regulate heat loss.

Children may explore polar bear dens (without the bears), or pop their heads through openings in a simulated ice floe, just as they saw the harbor seals doing before them.

The pool contains some 900,000 gallons of manufactured seawater, maintained at a cool 50 degrees in a two-story habitat that stands above and below the surface.

WOW **Key West at SeaWorld.** A showcases for the island beauty and funky tropical charm of the southernmost city in the United States, with a mix of New England and Bahamian architecture, framed by stands of palm trees, hibiscus, and bougainvillea. Visitors stroll along river rock and pathways and boardwalks; restaurants feature Caribbean cuisine. Street performers and vendors and perhaps a tightrope walker brighten the landscape.

The five-acre site is on the park's east side, alongside Manatees: The Last Generation. Naturalistic animal habitats allow up-close encounters and interaction with bottlenose dolphins, sleek stingrays, and one of the world's few saltwater-adapted reptiles, the sea turtle.

Life of a dolphin.
Bottlenose dolphins inhabit temperate and tropical waters throughout the world, and are the most common dolphin species along the United States, from Cape Cod to the Gulf of Mexico. They live in groups known as pods or herds, varying in size from 2 to 15 animals; the members of the pod rank themselves and establish dominance by smacking their tails against the water, butting heads, and other actions.

The largest section is **Dolphin Cove**, home to more than two dozen inquisitive bottlenose dolphins, the species most often seen in the coastal waters of the Gulf of Mexico and off Key West.

A wavemaker moves chilled seawater through the deep 600,000-gallon pool, creating tides that ebb and flow. There is also an area where guests can touch and feed the animals. And an underwater viewport allows glimpses of the dolphins below the surface.

At **Turtle Point**, visitors can come up close to threatened and endangered species of sea turtles, including the green, loggerhead, and hawksbill. The hunting of sea turtles was a major industry in Key West until federal laws protecting the animals were enacted in the 1970s.

Stingray Lagoon, a longtime favorite at Sea-World, was nearly doubled in size as part of the new area. The pool features a variety of graceful rays, including cownose, Southern, roughtailed, Atlantic and yellow stingrays, as well as guitar fish. Visitors are encouraged to touch and feed the 200 or so rays. These fascinating creatures swim close to the edge of the pool where you can easily rub their rubbery skin and feel their fins; their poison sacs have been removed, and these stingrays are used to humans. A new nursery cove will exhibit newborn rays.

In Key West, many rays are found in the shallow waters surrounding the island. These fish, relatives of the shark, often burrow into the sand at the water's edge.

Also part of the new area is **Sunset Square**, with streets of Key West–theme shops, restaurants, and entertainment.

Dolphin Cove, SeaWorld
© *SeaWorld of Florida 1995*

WOW Shamu's Happy Harbor. If you asked an active, adventurous kid to come up with the design for the ultimate outdoor playground, he or she might come up with something just like this. Shamu's Happy Harbor is, quite simply, one of the most spectacular playgrounds we have ever seen. In the learned opinions of the kids we asked, it stands head and shoulders over Fievel's Playground at Universal Studios; Honey, I Shrunk the Kids Movie Set Adventure at Disney-MGM Studios; and Tom Sawyer Island at the Magic Kingdom. We cannot imagine higher praise.

And higher is the word that comes to mind first. The central feature of the three-acre playground is a pair of gigantic nets that each extend about 40 feet in the air. The netting—actually double netting to prevent accidents—winds back and forth and makes turns like flights of stairs. Way up at the top is a tire swing, safely allowing youngsters to fly out as if into space.

The base of the net lets out into a long slide. Down below is **Pete's Water Maze**, a pirate ship with water cannon, a large sand play area, and other activities. On very hot days you might want to dress your children in bathing suits and let them cool off on the small wet slides there.

Parents can park at the bottom of the net and keep an eye on their kids as they climb; a snack bar serves the area. Most of the area is under a roof, blocking the sun and some rain.

If all of this is too rambunctious for your young ones, they can explore Boogie Bump Bay, a special area for small ones that includes bubble bikes, a mini-ball crawl, an air bounce, a fence maze, and many other activities appropriate to their size.

WOW Manatees: The Last Generation? SeaWorld is doing its part to answer the question it poses with a "no."

This is a fascinating 3½-acre attraction that winds through a river-like setting, filled with the gentle manatee giants, as well as turtles, fish (including tarpon, gar, and snook), and birds. A seamless, 126-foot-long acrylic panel permits underwater views. Nearby is a nursing pool built for manatee mothers and their babies.

The area includes the **Manatee Theater**, which presents a special film using Bi-Vision technology with stunning underwater footage to make it seem as if you are completely surrounded by manatees.

The manatee is an air-breathing marine mammal; when it submerges, special muscles pinch the nostrils tightly closed to keep the water out. If you look carefully, you will also see sparse hair on the manatee's skin. Manatee calves nurse from their mothers.

In the wild, an adult manatee dines exclusively on plants; a full-grown specimen may eat each day as much as 100 pounds of sea grass, water hyacinths, and other types of plants.

Hold the dressing, please. The favorite food for the manatees is romaine lettuce. The salad bill represents one of the bigger expenses of the park. If you're in the viewing area at one of several feeding times, watch as the manatees use their flippers almost as hands to grab the lettuce.

Close enough for us.
The fish that you see in the manatee ponds that look at first glance like an alligator are something known as alligator gar *(lepisosteus spatula).* From the side, they look ordinary but from the top and bottom they certainly could fool all but the bravest.

All of the manatees on display have been rescued from their only natural enemy—man. Most have been injured by boat propellers, fishing nets, or plastic items thrown in the water by boaters. Adults are released back into the wild once they are able to survive there. Orphans will probably spend the rest of their lives in the park.

Also on exhibit are some of the vehicles and equipment used by SeaWorld's Beached Animal Rescue Station. Since 1973, the park's marine animal experts have rescued more than 100 manatees found seriously injured, ill, or orphaned in the wild. The crews are also called upon to help at dolphin and pygmy sperm whale strandings.

One of the slogans in the manatee area is "Extinction is forever. Endangered means we still have time."

Pacific Point Preserve. This re-created coastal setting for California sea lions and harbor and fur seals is a great way to get up-close and personal with some of the most amusing aquatic creatures we know.

Able to swim at birth, a harbor seal pup stays close to its mother for short nursing periods. The female's fat-rich milk helps the pup to more than double its weight by the time it is four to eight weeks old. Then the pup is weaned, goes its own way, and fends for itself.

You'll be able to purchase a package of smelt to feed the seals. Washing stations are nearby to help remove the smell of smelt from your hands.

By the way, seals and sea lions are not morning creatures; they are most active in the midday sun.

Anheuser-Busch Hospitality Center. SeaWorld is owned by brewer Anheuser-Busch (which also owns Florida attractions Busch Gardens and Adventure Island), and the Hospitality House offers a bit of the corporate message along with free samples of the company's beers.

Clod reins. The driver of an eight-horse hitch pulling a beer wagon like the ones at SeaWorld must wrestle more than 40 pounds of reins to control the horses.

Set amid tropical lagoons and lush foliage, the center displays antique brewery equipment, including a turn-of-the-century Studebaker wagon used for hauling more than six tons of Budweiser beer behind a team of Clydesdale horses.

Adults can sample Anheuser-Busch products, including Budweiser and Michelob beers. A separate counter offers soft drinks and snacks at the going SeaWorld prices.

Bigfoot. Think your feet are tired at the end of the day? A Clydesdale horseshoe measures 20 inches end-to-end and weighs about five pounds.

An outside terrace offers a quiet, shady spot for sampling and resting and also provides a good view of the associated gardens and waterfalls, and the Clydesdale paddocks close by.

Ten or more of the giant Clydesdale work horses are on display at any given time, either in the outside paddock or in indoor stalls near the Hospitality Center. These huge horses, the symbol of Anheuser-Busch, are sometimes dressed in elaborate harnesses and hitched to their famous wagon to march in procession through the park.

Shows

Red, Bright, and Blue Spectacular. SeaWorld's spectacular nighttime show is one of the largest fireworks and laser shows in the country, with more than 2,000 explosions.

The show is presented in the lagoon with visitors in the Bayside Ski Stadium; the backdrop for projected images is a 60-foot screen of water.

Dolphin Stadium. As part of SeaWorld's Key West area, SeaWorld openedthe **Key West Dolphin Fest**. The show is presented in a stadium facing a large tank. You'll see dolphins swimming, flipping, and splashing in a variety of stunts with their trainers and with a young volunteer and his or her family from the audience.

On the trainer's command, the dolphins "dance" in time to the Key West–style music or stand up in the water to take a "bow" after they have done well. Among our favorite feats are Dolphin Powerboating, when two dolphins push a trainer around the tank by placing their noses on the bottom of his or her feet, and Dolphin "Roman Ride," when the trainer, riding with one foot on each dolphin, holds a loose harness around each animal and goes for a ride.

In addition to dolphins, this show features a pair of **pseudorca crassidens**, or false killer whales. Their beautiful, solid black color and smooth features make them unusual performers. These fast swimmers and fun performers are up to 25 feet long.

Perhaps the most spectacular trick in the show is the Bouncing Trainer, when a pseudorca surfaces with a trainer balanced on its nose, pushing him or her about 20 feet into the air.

Before and after the show you can walk up to the glass on the tank, nose to nose with the dolphins, but visitors are asked not to touch or slap the side.

The first four rows of the stadium, especially

Backstage at the ski show. After you've seen this show once, come back for the next showing, but view it from the gift shop in the middle of the walkway over the lagoon. Here you can see some of the backstage preparations for some of the special events.

Whale school. Many of the whale's actions are prompted by trainers' hand signals. For example, when the trainer holds up an open hand toward the audience, the whales face the audience and open their mouths. Also listen carefully for the faint sound of high-pitched training whistles during the show.

Sea food. Each dolphin eats about 20 pounds of fish a day, much of it as part of a performance reward during the show. Dolphin skin feels like a wet inner tube.

Rock fish. The show opening involves sea lions and an otter who appear to perform all by themselves. They're not that smart: trainers are hidden behind rocks high up on the set. Look carefully and you will be able to see fish for the animals fly out of the rocks to the animals.

toward the center of the arena, are the wet seats. The views from anywhere are good, but the best seats are mid-stadium within the first 10 rows.

Be aware that the stairs to the seats in the stadium are quite steep and might pose a difficulty for some people; the easiest seats are at the bottom, where you may get a bit wet, or at the top where you are the farthest away.

Dolphin Interactive Program. Here's a very special opportunity to swim with the bottle-nose dolphins. Guests meet early in the morning before the park opens for an educational session about dolphins and SeaWorld's training practices. Then they don wet suits, wade into the main pool at the Whale and Dolphin Stadium, and interact with the animals for about 20 minutes. Only about eight visitors, ages 13 and older, can take advantage of the program per day, at a charge of $148; each participant can bring along an observer with the purchase of a day ticket. For information, call the SeaWorld education department at (407) 363-2380.

WOW Clyde and Seamore Take Pirate Island. Some of the funniest bits at SeaWorld can be found here, at the 3,000-seat Sea Lion and Otter Stadium. It's a dramatic tale of treasure, treachery, and the quest for fish, beginning somewhere in the Caribbean as a pirate ship sails by an island inhabited by two marooned buccaneers. But when an otter purloins the treasure map and seeks the assistance of the stranded pirates, who will end up with the gold?

The humans in this show are more than mere characters: they are skilled animal handlers who are chosen for both their animal knowledge and their acting skill. The stars are the sea lions, a tiny otter, and the only trained walrus we've ever seen.

Depending on the time of day and season, much of the stadium may be facing the sun; come early to find a shaded area. The first four rows are marked as splash zones; we're talking about little spurts, nothing like the tsunamis at Shamu Stadium. Early arrivals also get to watch the talented mime make fun of late arrivals, one of the most popular minishows at SeaWorld.

Pelican Exhibit. On the left side of the walkway toward the Atlantis Stadium is a small spectacular collection of pelicans. Among the birds you will see there are American white pelicans, denizens of marshy lakes and the Pacific and Texas coasts; they winter chiefly in coastal lagoons from Florida and southern California south to Panama. Unlike Florida brown pelicans, white pelicans do not dive for their food. Instead they fish in groups, capturing their prey cooperatively by forming a crescent and beating their wings and driving the fish into shallow water where they use their large pouched bills to catch and then swallow their meal.

WOW The Intensity Games. The latest lagoon show includes SeaWorld's high-powered water stunt actors, wakeboarders, and skiers, mixing wild theatrical acts with gymnastics and athletic competition.

A 20-person team tests its mettle in contests that include speeding through a buoy course at 40 mph, an "air chair" competition, and freestyle wake-boarding. Barefoot skiers rip past the stands, and long-distance jumpers soar 120 feet in the air from a ramp in the water. The high-flying Ty Cobb Dare-devils perform incredible stunts and gymnastics on twin 40-foot tumble tracks.

Seats for the show are in the 3,800-seat Bayside Ski Stadium on SeaWorld's 17-acre lagoon.

WOW Shamu Adventure. A lone kayaker paddles into a fog-shrouded Alaskan bay. Through the magic of video, projected on the huge ShamuVision screen, animal expert Jack Hanna takes us to Alaska, Norway, and the Crozet Islands of the Antarctic.

An unusual feature of the show comes when a bald eagle in free flight soars from the rafters to pick up a lure on the water. (The eagle is actually an African Fisher Eagle, which looks like its American cousin but is not a protected, endangered species.)

The 5,200-seat Shamu Stadium, just down the hill from the Bayside Ski Stadium on the same side of the lagoon, was built around a 5 million-gallon saltwater pool that is home to the Shamu family of killer whales, including Baby Namu.

The stars of the show are the black-and-white members of the Shamu family. The youngest killer whale weighs in at a mere 1,000 pounds, while the largest weighs some five tons—10,000 pounds.

The majestic, mysterious killer whale mostly lives in a world unto itself, traveling in pods from frigid waters off the coast of Iceland to warmer climates near the tip of South Africa. On islands near Argentina, researchers have observed them hunting in packs, and have called them the "wolves of the sea."

But killer whales have also shown an unusual capacity for sharing special relationships with humans.

The best seat in the stadium—if you don't mind getting wet—is in the first six rows. Here you will be able to see under the water through the glass wall of the tank, as well as the show up above. If you prefer to stay dry, sit toward the front of the second bank of seats, in the middle of the stadium. You'll have a good view of the video screen and of the platform where the whales frequently beach themselves during the show.

Don't say we didn't warn you: The lower 15 rows are marked as the splash zone. That may at first seem like a bit of overkill—it does not seem possible that a whale can send water up that high over the glass. And in fact, for the first three-quarters of the show only those brave souls in the very closest seats are likely to be splashed by one of the animals as it passes by.

Whale wisdom. Whales are aquatic mammals and not fish, though they are good swimmers. Killer whales can remain submerged up to 12 minutes before surfacing for air. Newborn killer whales weigh about 300 pounds. Star of the show Shamu is 17 feet long and weighs about 5,000 pounds.

By the way, Shamu receives a physical examination once every two weeks, including a blood test and measurements.

But don't congratulate yourself too soon. The conclusion of the show is one wet finale. Wet as in water that washes over the top of the glass in a spectacular wave and soaks the people in those front 15 rows. Water. Wave. Soaks. 55-degree saltwater. Actually, it's two waves. Get the picture?

One problem with the stadium shows at SeaWorld is that when one of the presentations lets out, a large number of people are deposited onto walkways leading toward the restaurants. If you are planning to eat after a show, head directly to a restaurant or even consider sending someone ahead to place an order.

WOW Shamu: Close Up! SeaWorld's new 1.7-million gallon killer whale research facility allows visitors to get closer than ever to Shamu and his friends. It also allows scientists further opportunities to study the development of killer whales. The habitat is located alongside the Shamu stadium and includes shallows that will encourage the whales to engage in some of their favorite activities: back scratching and tummy rubbing. Special devices include a huge scale, capable of measuring weights up to 40,000 pounds in five-pound increments.

Nautilus Theatre. SeaWorld's 2,400-seat theater is used for special presentations. (The long-time favorite Big Splash Bash has been retired.) Check the schedule when you arrive at the park.

In 1999, the headliner show was Cirque de la Mer, which combines acrobatics, modern dance, music, and South American folklore, led by Peruvian comic Cesar Aedo. The unusual "circus" includes a music and dance salute to the traditional South American tale, The Flight of the Condor.

Special effects include aerial stunts, a dramatic water curtain, fog, lasers, and special lighting.

SeaWorld Theater: Pets on Stage. An all-star cast features pigs, cats, dogs, birds, the occasional rat, and a few not-so-well-trained humans.

One aspiring young actor or actress even gets into the act, co-starring with a sloppy-kissing Great Dane. Finally, guests receive training tips for their own pets.

And before you start making excuses for the limited repertoire of your own pets at home, consider that nearly all of the performers come from the local animal shelter.

The show is scheduled to run at least into the year 2000.

South Seas Revue. The Hawaiian Rhythms troupe performs songs and dances of the Polynesian isles on the beach at Atlantis Lagoon. Visitors sit on wooden benches over the sand, in front of a palm-shaded theater. Along with the music you will learn a little about Polynesian culture and the music of different locations.

If you're the uninhibited type, you can join hula dancers—male and female—on the stage for an impromptu hula lesson.

Continuous Viewing Exhibits

A number of SeaWorld exhibits are open all day without scheduled events. You can enter them for a quick walk-through or a leisurely study. The premier facilities of this type at SeaWorld include Key West at SeaWorld, Terrors of the Deep, Penguin Encounter, and Tropical Reef. You'll see a number of other interesting places as you walk through SeaWorld, including a tropical rain forest and Pacific Point Preserve.

WOW Terrors of the Deep. A unique collection of dangerous sea creatures. You will find yourself immersed in the secret hiding places of menacing eels, venomous fish, hungry barracuda, and . . . sharks. The creatures in this exhibit all can be potentially dangerous, it is true, but the message of this exhibit is clear: "Respect them, don't kill them." For example, sharks have a bad reputation for attacking humans, but there are few documented instances of wanton attack. As with most injurious encounters between humans and sea creatures, these attacks usually are the result of mistaken identity: the human was mistaken for food.

A short video at the start of this exhibit gives you some excellent background; don't rush through. The shark movie and aquarium portion of the show are timed to give you about 25 minutes to view the tunnel area and the other displays. If you rush through these sections you'll have to stand in line waiting your turn for the shark theater. The entire show takes about 40 minutes, including the film and the walk-through.

SeaWorld's education department occasionally schedules sleepovers within the tunnels for school groups.

The first aquarium in this exhibit focuses on eels—more than 500 of them in a 10-foot-deep tank full of artificial coral that looks like the real thing but is easier to maintain.

One of the really interesting facets of this exhibit is the acrylic tunnel at the bottom of the aquarium that allows you to walk through the tank to view the "terrors." Among the creatures you'll see are moray eels (some more than six feet long), spotted morays, and purple-mouthed eels.

Grouper, snapper, lookdowns, and jacks—predatory fish native to the same ecosystems inhabited by eels—also are housed there.

A high-tech system simulates the currents and wave action of the reef, and a single light source is placed to simulate the sun.

After the walk through the first tunnel, you next encounter venomous lion-

Shark tunnels. The clear viewing tunnels can support the weight of 372 elephants, which is more than strong enough to keep you and the 450 tons of water above you apart.

One of the scenes from the film *Jaws 3-D* was shot inside the shark tunnel.

Bad PR. Sharks have gotten a great deal of bad PR. Two times more people die of bee stings each year than succumb to shark attacks.

Last exit. If you are claustrophobic and choose to avoid the tunnel, simply exit to your left through the unmarked door beside the tunnel entrance. You can wait for the rest of your party at the end of the line.

Hungry sharks? Sharks eat only about once a week. Check with the park for the current feeding schedule; if you can make it, you will understand what the term *feeding frenzy* really means. This is not an experience for the squeamish.

fish and scorpionfish. The graceful lionfish will captivate you with their movement and the colors of the fins that hide their dangerous spines. The scorpionfish show their ability to camouflage themselves as they blend in with the sand and wait for an unsuspecting meal to swim overhead.

A separate tank showcases clown fishes, with beautiful but highly poisonous spines. Also on display are nasty surgeon fish. When agitated, they will sweep their tails and threaten antagonists with their spines; a swipe from one of the razor-sharp extensions can seriously slash another fish or injure a fisherman attempting to remove them from nets or hooks.

There's also a collection of barracuda, creatures that ordinarily feast on fish, squid, and shrimp, attacking with a single swift strike at speeds of as much as 28 miles per hour. Viewed from the side the barracuda is hard to miss, but from the front the slender fish is nearly invisible. Barracuda attacks on humans are rare and accidental. Murky water makes it hard to see and barracuda are apt to confuse shiny objects such as jewelry for fish; swimmers in tropical waters are advised not to be between the fish and the sunny surface of the water.

The final stop on the journey comes when you descend 15 feet below the surface to the territory of the shark through a six-inch-thick clear acrylic tube. You'll travel the 125-foot-long shark-filled habitat on a PeopleMover, as dozens of nurse, brown, bull, and sand tiger sharks swim overhead and in front. Among the shark skeletons on display is a set of jaw bones from a 16½-foot male great white caught in western Australia.

Penguin Encounter. The largest and most technically advanced exhibit of its kind, it is the home to hundreds of penguins (from the Antarctic) and alcids (from the Arctic). The science center goes beyond entertainment to educate guests about the need to protect and preserve polar life.

So realistic that it even snows inside, this exhibit moves you past living Arctic and Antarctic displays on a 120-foot PeopleMover. Tempered glass provides an unobstructed and unobtrusive view above and below the water of stately king penguins, gentle gentoos, and bounding rockhoppers.

At the alcid exhibit, you come face-to-face with more than 100 puffins, buffleheads, smews, and murres from the Arctic. While not related to penguins, they are considered their ecological counterparts.

SeaWorld animal experts match temperature and daylight as closely as possible to the animals' native territory so that their seasons change as they would if they were living in the wild.

Hot house. When it's snowing in the penguin exhibit, these fascinating animals are swimming in 55-degree water. That's cold to us, but compared to the 32-degree refrigerated air of their enclosure, it is relatively warm.

After the ride past the live exhibits, you enter a hall with many fascinating, lighted displays. Press on the kid-sized handprints within each display to hear a recorded message.

The largest penguins at SeaWorld of Florida are the king penguins from Antarctica; at SeaWorld California they have a colony of emperor penguins, which are the largest in the world.

And be sure to stop at the SeaWorld Learning Center just past the moving walkway. A globe depicts Antarctic explorers. You will see Scott's expedition of 1910 to 1913, and his somewhat friendly adversary Amundsen's from 1910 to 1912. Further back is Drake's route around South America from 1578 to 1579, and Cooke's expedition from 1712 to 1715, which was the first known circumnavigation of Antarctica—marked on the map as Terra Incognita.

> **Penguin and eggs.** If you see groups of penguins huddled along the back wall of the exhibit, chances are they are hatching eggs. SeaWorld has a very successful penguin breeding program.

Tropical Reef and Caribbean Tide Pool. More than 1,000 tropical fish live in the 160,000-gallon exhibit, the largest South Pacific coral reef display in the United States. The Caribbean Tide Pool gives you close-up views of tropical fish and invertebrates such as sea urchins, crabs, starfish, and anemones. Seventeen smaller aquariums contain exhibits that include sea horses, octopi, and clown fish.

Sky Tower. This 400-foot needle tower can be seen from miles around SeaWorld, marking the park location and helping you find your way in. Once inside the park, you can ride a sit-down, circular elevator to the top for a panoramic view of SeaWorld and much of Central Florida.

Admission to this ride is not included in the daily park pass. The elevator may not operate during heavy winds or other bad weather.

Take your SeaWorld map on this 5½-minute ride; it will help you orient yourself to the layout of the park as well as other attractions in the area such as Disney World, which you can see from your rotating, 400-foot perch.

Eating Your Way Through SeaWorld

In general, SeaWorld food offerings are a bit simpler than you will find at Epcot or Universal. Menus are more limited (fewer different offerings at each restaurant), but the food generally is of high quality, and the portions are large.

By the way, watch out for marauding seagulls too. They are quite capable of swooping down and grabbing some of your food if you are eating at one of the outdoor restaurants.

🍴 **Spinnaker's Cafe.** Hamburgers and sandwiches, $5 to $6. Interesting salads and desserts, $2. An outdoor café. The real forte at Spinnaker, however, are desserts. Select from Black Forest cake, key lime pie, cheesecake, strawberries and cream, and other delectables for about $2 each.

🍴 **Mama Stella's Italian Kitchen.** Near the Penguin area, this pleasant restaurant with indoor seating offers spaghetti for about $5 and pizza for about $4. You can also purchase a garden salad and garlic bread.

🍴 **Mango Joe's.** Chicken or beef fajitas, fried fish, and club sandwiches, priced from about $6 to $12. Children's meals include chicken or steak fingers served with french

KEY:

🍴 = Fast food

🍸 = Pub

🏠 = Full-service restaurant

french fries for about $4. The chicken fajitas at Mango Joe's are quite good. About those "fingers": they are grilled pieces of meat, not fried; we'd vote them among the best snacks at the park.

Bimini Bay Cafe. Seafood sandwiches ($7 to $8) and platters ($10 to $15). Entree salads and fruit, $6 to $8. For a different appetizer, try the Key West Conch chowder. Child's sandwich plate, $4. Domestic and imported beer about $3. The glass-enclosed dining room overlooks Atlantis Lagoon and offers a cool getaway for lunch; the tasteful decor has the feel of a hotel or resort restaurant rather than your typical theme park eatery.

Aloha! Polynesian Luau Dinner and Show. Polynesian luau and show, adults, $35.95; ages 8 to 12, $25.95; ages 3 to 7, $15.95. Seating begins at 6:35 P.M. and is limited. Reservations required. Call (800) 227-8048 or (407) 351-3600, or stop by the information desk to the left of the main SeaWorld entrance. The meal varies but usually consists of salads, seafood such as mahimahi with piña colada sauce, pork loin, sweet and sour chicken, rice, vegetables, and dessert. One cocktail or beer is included in the price of the meal.

Buccaneer's Smokehouse. Chicken and ribs. Entrees, $5 to $7. Hickory-smoked chicken or ribs, coleslaw, and roll. Picnic tables with umbrellas are available dockside overlooking the Atlantis Lagoon, with a backdoor view of the ski show from the lagoon-side seats.

Chicken 'n Biscuit. Fried or baked chicken, $4 to $6. Child's menu. Domestic beer, about $3.

Discovery Cove by SeaWorld

Theme parks are crowded, impersonal, harried, and expensive. Not so at Discovery Cove by SeaWorld, due to open in the summer of 2000 across the road from the existing SeaWorld Orlando.

Here you will be greeted by a concierge, escorted to your personal chaise in the shade of a thatched roof, make a reservation for dinner, and, most importantly, an appointment to swim with the dolphins, and get up close and personal with a pool full of bat rays, and 10,000 tropical fish.

At Discovery Cove, the experience will be uncrowded, personal, relaxing . . . and very expensive. Admission to the park will be limited to about 1,000 visitors per day by reservation, with an entrance fee of about $200 per person. The ticket includes lockers, snorkels, vests, towels, umbrellas, lounges, hammocks, and a restaurant meal.

The heart of the park is **Dolphin Lagoon**, home to about 30 of the marine mammals. Groups of three guests receive personal instruction from a trainer in shallow water and then enter the lagoon to swim and play with the dolphins. Each visitor will receive a special appointment for his or her time in the lagoon; children under the age of six are not permitted.

At **Coral Reef** swimmers and snorkelers can play hide-and-seek with rainbows of 10,000 tropical fish. Bright-colored angelfish and delicate butterfly fish compete for attention with silvery jacks, black-and-white spadefish, and more than 75 other species. Swimmers will also come within inches of barracuda and sharks—safely isolated from the pool behind clear panels in the water.

Discovery Cove by SeaWorld
© *SeaWorld of Florida 1999*

Ray Lagoon is a quiet protected area where guests can snorkel, wade, and play with hundreds of southern and cownose stingrays, gentle animals that can grow up to four feet in diameter.

Tropical River meanders its way throughout most of Discovery Cove, passing by beaches, walkways, and rocky lagoons. There is a dense tropical forest, an Amazon-like river, a tropical fishing village, and an underwater cave.

Swimmers passing under a waterfall along the Tropical River will find themselves inside an immense aviary, home to some 300 colorful birds from throughout the world. Many will be trained to eat from the hands of guests.

The aviary includes softbills such as thrushes and starlings, pink and white roseate spoonbills, multicolored Turacos, nectar-eating parrots known as *lorries,* and tawney frogmouths.

SeaWorld says its price is justified because of the high level of personal attention that guests will receive. Don't compare Discovery Cove to a major theme park, they say; think instead of a comparison between a small luxury cruise ship and a huge mega-liner. It is also worth pointing out that SeaWorld has operated a highly popular swim-with-the-dolphins program at SeaWorld Orlando for several years, priced at about $148 per person.

Visitors to SeaWorld Orlando may be able to grab a glimpse of Discovery Cove from the top of Shamu's Happy Harbor play area. For more information on the new park, you can consult a web page at www.DiscoveryCove.com

SEAWORLD

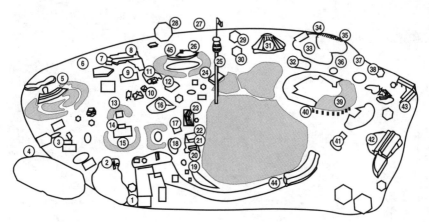

Part V
Dinner Shows and Character Meals

Chapter 20
Dinner Shows and Character Meals

If you're on vacation, why should the entertainment stop when you sit down to eat?

That's the thinking behind one of the fastest-growing industries in Orlando and the surrounding area—the dinner show. You can eat a Chinese meal while being entertained by Asian acrobats; you can pull apart a chicken with your bare hands while knights on horseback joust for your entertainment.

There are more than a dozen major dinner shows inside and outside Walt Disney World. Nearly every one of them has something to offer.

Prices for adults generally range from about $25 to $40 and usually include all courses and drinks; be aware that almost every show offers discounts from the listed price (you'll find some coupons in this book). You may be able to buy cut-rate tickets to dinner shows from ticket booths in hotels or on tourist roads; shop around a bit for the best deal.

One word of warning: most of the shows try to pad their nightly take with all sorts of appeals, including photos taken before you enter, photos taken at your table, souvenir booklets, flags, and other items. If you're not in the market for extra trinkets, just say no.

Call for hours of performance for any show; at the busiest seasons, some theaters will have two shows in a night.

Within Walt Disney World

The dinner shows at Walt Disney World resorts generally require advance reservations and purchase of tickets. Call (407) 934-7639 for reservations; most times of the year you'll need to do this weeks or even months before arrival. Guests at hotels within the park get a head start for reservations, too. Prices and times are subject to change.

Hoop-Dee-Doo Musical Revue. Pioneer Hall in Disney's Fort Wilderness Resort. (407) 939-3463, or (407) 824-2803 on the day of the show. Reservations are necessary most days; a walk-up waiting list is also begun at Pioneer Hall about 45 minutes before showtime.

A Western singing and dancing show, featuring all-you-can-eat chicken, ribs, corn, and strawberry shortcake. This is a hugely popular, raucous, thigh-slappin', hee-haw of a show; if that's the sort of entertainment you like, this is a fine example. Entertainment includes piano and banjo music, terrible jokes and gags, and an audience-participation washboard finale. Mixed in is a bit of improvisational humor as cast members sing songs about guests in the audience.

The large hall has two levels; the best seats are at the front of the balcony or a few rows back from the stage on the main level. Seats are assigned at the time of the reservation.

Veterans observe that although this is an all-you-can-eat adventure, the courses (including fried chicken, BBQ ribs, and strawberry shortcake) come and go pretty quickly and there is a show to watch, too. Disney also trimmed a half hour off the starting time of the late show by shortening the overall performance and turn-around times a bit. Seatings at 5, 7:15, and 9:30 P.M. Adults, $37 plus tax; children (3 to 11), $19.50.

If you're not already at Fort Wilderness as a guest and plan to use Disney transportation, you'll need to leave about an hour before your show time to make connections to the resort and walk to the Pioneer Hall, which is located near the beach on Bay Lake. There is also a parking lot at Fort Wilderness.

Hayrides at Pioneer Hall. Go for a horse-drawn tour of the Fort Wilderness area each evening at 7 or 9:30 P.M. Sign up at the booth outside Pioneer Hall. Adults $6, children $4.

Polynesian Luau. Disney's Polynesian Resort. (407) 939-3463.

An all-you-can-eat feast that features barbecue pork ribs, roasted chicken, mahimahi, fruit, and drinks, including frozen piña coladas, accompanied by island singers, hula dancers, fire acts, and other entertainment.

There's a partial roof over the dining room, with the stage open to the sky; mosquito repellent is worth adding to your preshow preparations in bug season. The show is much more dramatic when it is dark; the early show in summer is presented while it is still light. (By the way, it is possible to see portions of the show from the courtyard of the Polynesian Resort without paying for a seat and meal.)

Guests at park resorts can reserve seats when they reserve their rooms; others can make reservations within 30 days of the day of the show.

Seatings are at 6:45 and 9:30 P.M. Adults, $37, and children (3 to 11), $19.50.

Mickey's Tropical Luau. Disney's Polynesian Resort. (407) 824-4321. A Polynesian revue for the short set, featuring Disney characters dancing along with guys and girls in grass skirts. Presented at the Polynesian Resort daily at 4:30 P.M. A full dinner is included. Adults, $33, and children (3 to 11), $16.

Nearby Walt Disney World

Arabian Nights Dinner Attraction. 6225 West Irlo Bronson Highway (U.S. 192), east of the intersection with I-4 in Kissimmee. (407) 239-9223. (800) 553-6116. Beautiful horses, handsome caballeros, pretty young women, and a theatrical presentation in one of Orlando's largest and oldest dinner theaters.

This is first and foremost a horse show: more than 50 of them, including Arabians, Lippizans, Andalusians, Belgians, and Percherons, perform in the 1,200-seat Palace of Horses. Favorite stunts include "Airs Above the Ground" maneuvers, horse-drawn "water skiing," a chariot race, and an unusual square dance on horseback.

The arena itself was renovated in 1999 to bring the audience a bit closer to the show and create more of a palace-like atmosphere. And a spectacular new special effect brings "snow" to Central Florida every night.

The dinner features prime rib and salad; vegetarian lasagna is also available. The meal is accompanied by beer, wine, and soft drinks. The serving staff is extremely solicitous, and the audience is much less rowdy than at some of the other dinner shows in town.

Arabian Nights is also one of the only family-owned attractions in the area; it is the creation of Mark and Galen Miller, who previously owned an Arabian show farm near Gainesville, Florida. Shows are presented at 7:30 P.M. Adults, $36.95; children (3 to 11), $23.95. *Discount coupon in this book.*

Capone's Dinner & Show. 4740 West Irlo Bronson Highway (U.S. 192). (407) 397-2378. A musical comedy review with guns and an unlimited Italian buffet that offers items such as lasagna, baked ziti, sausage and peppers, baked chicken, pasta salad, plus beer, wine, sangria, and Rum Runners. Set in 1931 Gangland Chicago. Adults, $37; seniors, $19, children (12 and under), $24. *Discount coupon in this book.*

Medieval Times Dinner & Tournament. 4510 West Irlo Bronson Highway (U.S. 192), near Route 441 in Kissimmee. (407) 396-1518 or (800) 229-8300. Come to dinner as the guests of the royal family in the 11th century. The feast includes spectacular pageantry, dramatic horsemanship, swordplay, falconry, sorcery, and a jousting contest. The meal—which is served without silverware—includes a hearty vegetable soup, roasted chicken, spare ribs, potato, and dessert, plus beer, sangria, and soft drinks.

Medieval Times is one of the old-timers among dinner theaters, dating back 16 years in Florida, 30 years in Spain, and nearly 1,000 years in history. Twenty-five years ago, Jose De Montaner converted his farm in Majorca, Spain, into a barbecue dinner show and then a medieval-theme show for tourists. There are now Medieval Times dinner attractions in California (near Disneyland), New Jersey, Illinois, Texas, South Carolina, and Toronto, Canada.

The entertainment takes place in the 1,100-seat Great Ceremonial Hall; seats are not reserved—arrive early for the best seats (down low at midcourt). The show begins with some demonstration of horse training and riding skills, including the Carousel, a display of intricate horse maneuvers.

The tournament games begin with knights on horseback with lances galloping at full speed toward three-inch hoops suspended from posts; the next challenge is a javelin toss on horseback. The final confrontation pits knights against each other in jousting tournaments and hand-to-hand fighting.

Alongside the theater is the **Medieval Life** exhibit, an extraordinary collection of artifacts brought over from Europe; see the write-up in the attractions section of this book.

Adults, $38.95 plus tax; children (3 to 12), $23.95. Tickets include admission to Medieval Life. *Discount coupon in this book.*

MurderWatch Mystery Dinner Theatre. Grosvenor Resort at Walt Disney World Village. (800) 624-4109, or (407) 827-6534. A lively evening of food, song, and murder presented in the attractive restaurant, with above-average dinner buffet fare that includes prime rib. Baskerville's has a replica of Sherlock Holmes's 221B Baker Street office on display.

We enjoyed a campy, funny show involving an engagement party for the daughter of a mafia don; before we could begin the salad course, an FBI agent (who also played the piano) checked out our table for bombs, listening devices, and leftovers. Other characters, including detective Shirley Holmes, worked the tables during the show. Before the night was over, the dopey chanteuse was murdered, the marriage was off, and a good time was had by all. Tickets, including dinner, are $34.95; for $5 extra there's unlimited wine or beer. Children from ages 3 to 9 can attend for $18.95. Presented Saturday evenings with one or two shows per night. *Discount coupon in this book.*

Wild Bill's Wild West Dinner Show at Fort Liberty. 5260 U.S. 192 in Kissimmee. (407) 351-5151, (800) 883-8181. Step back into the Old West. The dinner show features can-can girls, western specialty acts, including a lariat master and marksmanship competitions, Native American dancing, and lively music of the period. Also featuring the **Brave Warrior Adventure Wax Museum** and a **Wild West Trading Post.** A typical meal includes platters of vegetable barley soup, fried chicken, sliced beef, corn-on-the-cob, baked potato, biscuits, tossed salad, and dessert plus unlimited beer, wine, sodas, coffee, and tea. Adults, $36.95; children (3 to 11), $23.95. *Discount coupon in this book.*

International Drive/Universal Studios Area

Aloha Polynesian Luau at SeaWorld. 7007 SeaWorld Drive. (407) 363-2559 or (800) 327-2424. Eat, drink, and be entertained by the Hawaiian Rhythms troupe. (Located at the perimeter of SeaWorld, you do not require a ticket to the park.) Adults, $35.95; juniors (8 to 12), $25.95; children (3 to 7), $15.95. Served from 6:30 to 8:45 P.M. nightly.

King Henry's Feast. 8984 International Drive, Orlando. (407) 351-5151, (800) 883-8181. Dine in the Great Hall and be entertained by dueling knights, magicians, and performers on stage. Your meal, which includes tankards of beer, wine, or soft drinks, is brought by singing serving wenches. Adults, $36.95; children, $23.95. *Discount coupon in this book.*

Mark Two Dinner Theater. 3376 Edgewater Drive. (407) 843-6275, (800) 726-6275. Live Broadway shows, preceded by buffet dinner featuring prime rib. Open Wednesdays through Sundays; some matinee performances. Tickets are priced from $34.50 to $42. Tables surround the stage on three sides; the closest tables are rows LA, LB, MB, MC, RA, and RB.

Pirate's Dinner Adventure. 6400 Carrier Drive. (407) 248-0590, (800) 866-2469. Ahoy, mateys. Just off International Drive near Wet 'n Wild and Universal Studios Escape, the impressive set includes a full-scale pirate ship afloat in a 300,000-gallon indoor lagoon. Pirates swing from ropes over your head, and battles rage all around. Presented nightly. After the show, guests can attend the Pirate's Buccaneer Bash to mingle with cast members and learn the latest dance steps. Adults, $37.95 plus tax; children (3–11), $22.95.

Sleuths Mystery Dinner Show. 7508 Republic Drive, off International Drive behind Wet 'n Wild. (407) 363-1985, (800) 393-1985. Step into the scene of the crime. Mix with the characters, search for clues, and help track down the culprit. The latest title in the troupe's repertoire is "Island for Sale." You'll also eat dinner along the way. One, two, or three shows per night. Adults, $36.95 plus tax; children (3 to 11), $22.95. *Discount coupon in this book.*

Disney Character Meals

For reservations at character meals at Walt Disney World properties, call (407) 939-7741.

Artist Point Character Breakfast. Disney's Wilderness Lodge. Tigger, Winnie the Pooh, and Eeyore. Breakfast 7:30 to 11:30 A.M. Adults, $14.50; children ages 3 to 11, $8.75.

Baskerville's Character Breakfast Buffet, Baskerville's Character Dinner. Grosvenor Resort. Call (407) 828-4444 for reservations and current information. Breakfast offered 8:30 A.M. to 10:30 A.M. on Tuesdays, Thursdays, and Saturdays; $8.95 for adults and $4.95 for children.

Cape May Café Breakfast. Admiral Goofy and crew at the Beach Club Resort, from 7:30 to 11 A.M. daily. Adults, $14.95; children 3 to 11, $8.50.

Chef Mickey's Buffet at Contemporary Resort. Starring Mickey and Minnie Mouse, Goofy, Chip 'n' Dale, and Pluto. Breakfast from 7:30 A.M. to 11 A.M. Adults, $13.95; children (3 to 11), $7.95. Dinner from 5 to 9:30 P.M. Adults, $19.95; children, $8.95.

Cinderella's Royal Table/Once Upon a Time Breakfast. King Stefan's Banquet Hall in Cinderella Castle, with Cinderella, Captain Hook, and friends. Daily from 8 to 10 A.M. Magic Kingdom ticket required. Resort guests can use early-morning entry for breakfast from 7:30 A.M. on Mondays, Thursdays, and Saturdays. Reservations required. Adults, $14.95; children ages 3 to 11, $7.95, plus theme park admission.

Country Fair Character Clubhouse Breakfast Café. Hilton. Call (800) 782-4414 for reservations and current information. Sundays from 8:30 to 10:30 A.M. Adults, $12.95; children, $9.95.

Crystal Palace in the Magic Kingdom. Winnie the Pooh and friends for breakfast on Main Street from 8 to 10:30 A.M. Adults, $13.95; children (3 to 11), $7.95. Lunch from 11:30 A.M. to 3 P.M. Adults, $14.95; children, $7.95. Dinner from 3:30 P.M. to closing. Adults, $19.95; children, $9.95.

Garden Grill Character Experience. Minnie, Mickey, and Chip 'n' Dale. Breakfast, lunch, and dinner at The Land pavilion of Epcot Center. Family-style breakfast from 8:40 to 11:10 A.M. Adults, $14.95; children, $8.25. Lunch from

11:30 A.M. to 4:20 P.M. Adults, $16.95; children, $9.95. Dinner from 4:40 to 8:10 P.M. Adults, $17.50; children, $9.95. Epcot admission ticket required.

Garden Grove Café Character Dinner. Rafiki and Timon appear Wednesdays and Saturdays, and Winnie the Pooh and Tigger visit on Thursdays. Order from menu.

Garden Grove Character Breakfast. Walt Disney World Swan. Wednesdays and Saturdays, 8 to 11 A.M. Buffet at $12.50 for adults and $6.95 for children; menu items also offered.

Harry's Safari Bar & Grille Character Brunch. Goofy, Pluto, and Chip 'n' Dale. Walt Disney World Dolphin. Sundays from 8:30 A.M. to 12:30 P.M. Adults, $15.95; children, $7.95.

Liberty Tree Tavern Character Dinner. Dinner from 4 P.M. to park closing with Mickey and Goofy. Lunch includes Colonial Chicken, pasta, turkey burgers, pot roast. Dinner includes chicken and flank steak entrees. Adults, $19.95; children ages 3 to 11, $9.95 plus theme park admission.

Mickey's Tropical Luau. Daily dinner at Luau Cove. Disney's Polynesian Resort at 4:30 P.M. Adults, $30; children (3 to 11), $14.

1900 Park Fare Character Breakfast Buffet with Mary Poppins and friends. Disney's Grand Floridian Beach Resort. Breakfast from 7:30 to 11:30 A.M. daily. Adults, $15.95; children, $9.95. Dinner with Mickey and Minnie, with prime rib, from 5:30 to 9 P.M. Adults, $21.95; children ages 3 to 11, $9.50.

'Ohana. Disney's Polynesian resort. Breakfast with Minnie from 7:30 to 11 A.M. Adults $14.95, children $8.95.

Olivia's Cafe Breakfast with Winnie the Pooh and Tigger. Disney Old Key West Resort. Sundays and Wednesdays from 7:30 to 10:15 A.M. $11.50 for adults and $7.50 for children.

Ristorante Carnevale Character Brunch. Walt Disney World Dolphin. Sundays only, from 8:30 A.M. to 12:30 P.M. Adults, $14.95; children, $7.95.

Watercress Café Character Breakfast. Buena Vista Palace, Hotel Plaza. Sundays from 8 to 10:30 A.M. Order from menu or buffet. Adults, $9.75; children, $4.95.

Part VI
Sports and Recreation Within Walt Disney World

Chapter 21
Disney's Wide World of Sports, Golf, Auto Racing, Marinas, Fishing, Tennis, and Health Clubs

Depending upon your point of view, Walt Disney World is either four theme parks surrounded by 99 holes of golf, or a country club so huge it includes four theme parks.

Or, the place is so big that it can park a baseball stadium, professional tennis complex, and track fieldhouse in one corner and an Indy-class auto racetrack in another without running out of popcorn and liniment.

If there was no Magic Kingdom, Epcot, Disney-MGM Studios, or Animal Kingdom, the Walt Disney World resort would deserve recognition just for its sports complexes.

Disney's Wide World of Sports

Lace up your sneakers, Mickey: Disney's Wide World of Sports burst onto the scene in 1997 with some of the most impressive all-around athletic facilities in the world.

It's a field of dreams for more than 30 sports. The 200 acres of facilities includes a handsome baseball stadium, a softball quadroplex, a fieldhouse that has six professional-quality basketball courts, 11 clay tennis courts, four soccer fields, and much more.

The site, which draws its name from the famous ABC sports television show—now part of the Disney corporate family—has become the Spring Training home of the Atlanta Braves, the training site for the Harlem Globetrotters, and the headquarters of the Amateur Athletic Union. The AAU plans as many as 100 annual championship events at Walt Disney World.

Visitors can purchase a day pass to the facilities for $8 for adults and $6.75 for children ages 3–9 (1999 prices) and observe training and many amateur tournament activities anywhere on the property. Parking is free. Some special events, such as Spring Training baseball games, will have an additional charge.

Major League Soccer schedules its spring training at the Disney facility, in mid-February.

The Globetrotters also began an annual holiday series at the complex.

The sports complex is located within the Walt Disney World complex, near I-192; it can also be reached on an internal bus via a transfer at the Blizzard Beach station.

Baseball Stadium. A field with major-league dimensions and 7,500 permanent seats. The Atlanta Braves will work out and play their home Spring Training games in February and March of each year. (Many of the players will be housed at the new Coronado Springs Resort.) The Braves also plan to use the facilities for their Gulf Coast Rookie League and Instructional League seasons for much of the rest of the year.

The handsome stadium is reminiscent of 1950s-style architecture; it includes a number of nice touches such as extra-wide seats and a pair of concession stands that face the field so fans won't miss a pitch if they're on an emergency safari for hot dogs.

Serious baseball fans and just about anyone else will appreciate how close you can get to the players and the game. Seats are mostly exposed to the rain or sun, except for rows P–U of the lower deck

The spring training home season includes about 16 games from late February through the end of March; there are also intrasquad games and practice sessions. For information on tickets, call (407) 939-1500. Prices range from about $8.50 to $15.50 and are available at the stadium or through Ticketmaster at (407) 839-3900.

The Doyle Baseball School conducts a school for young players in early January; the school is run by former major leaguers Brian, Blake, and Denny Doyle. And in late January, the World Series Baseball Camp offers adults a chance to play along with some of the game's greatest retired players. For information, call (407) 363-6600.

Fieldhouse. Six hardwood basketball courts with main-floor seating for 5,000 spectators. The Harlem Globetrotters will train here and play a series of holiday-season games each December. The fieldhouse is also expected to be used for gymnastics and special events.

Softball/Baseball Quadraplex. Four lighted softball fields with bleachers, three major league–sized fields with 500 seats each, and two youth baseball fields.

Track and Field Complex. A 400-meter polyurethane track, long jump and triple jump runway, and other facilities.

Tennis Complex. Eleven clay courts, nine of them lighted. 1,000 permanent seats at center-court stadium, with additional temporary bleachers available. The USTA Men's Clay Court Championship was held at the facility in 1998.

Beach Volleyball. Five sand courts.

Velodrome. The cycling facility from the 1996 Centennial Olympics in Atlanta was moved to Orlando for training and events.

All of the facilities are open to organized tournaments only.

Official All-Star Café. Just outside the main entrance to the baseball stadium, a spectacular outpost of the themed dining restaurant also features stages for special events and sports radio and television shows.

Nearby is a huge **Foot Locker Super Store**, stocked with the latest in athletic gear.

For information on events call (407) 363-6600.

Walt Disney World Golf Courses

Disney is one version of golfing heaven. Ever on the search for a cute phrase, Disney has taken to calling it "The Magic Linkdom." It's a way for mom and dad and even junior to come to Walt Disney World without having to spend all their time in the company of a bunch of cartoon mice.

There are five championship-level 18-hole golf courses within the World, plus the 9-hole Oak Trail practice course. Two of the courses are good enough to be stops on the PGA Tour. For information and reservations up to 60 days in advance, call (407) 939-4653 between 8 A.M. and 5 P.M. Guests at resorts in the park can reserve tee times 60 days ahead of time, while day visitors can request a starting time 30 days in advance. You may also be able to reserve a

More, you say? In addition to the Walt Disney World courses, there are dozens of municipal, public, and semi-private golf courses in and around the Disney area in Orange County. Here is a selection. All phone numbers are in the (407) area code.

Crystal Brook Golf Course. Kissimmee. 847-8721.
Cypress Creek Country Club. Orlando. Semi-private 18 holes. 351-2187.
Dubsdread Golf Course. Orlando. Municipal 18 holes. 246-2551.
Eastwood Golf & Country Club. Orlando. Semi-private 18 holes. 281-4653.
Falcon's Fire Golf Course. Kissimmee. 18 holes public. 239-5445.
Grand Cypress Resort. Orlando. Resort 45 holes. 239-4700.
The Greens. Orlando. Public 18 holes. 351-5121.
Hunter's Creek Golf Club. Orlando. Public 18 holes. 240-4653.
International Golf Club. Orlando. Resort 18 holes. 239-6909.
Kissimmee Golf Club. Kissimmee. Public 18 holes. 847-2816.
Marriott's Orlando World Center. Orlando. Resort 18 holes. 239-4200.
Meadow Woods Golf Club. Orlando. Semi-private 18 holes. 850-5600.
MetroWest Country Club. Orlando. Semi-private 18 holes. 299-1099.
Monastery Golf & Country Club. Orlando. Public 18 holes. 647-4067.
Orange Lake Country Club. Kissimmee. Semi-private. 239-1050.
Osceola Golf Club. Kissimmee. Public 18 holes. 348-4915.
Rosemont Golf & Country Club. Orlando. Semi-private. 298-1230.
Ventura Country Club. Orlando. Semi-private 18 holes. 277-2640.
Wedgefield Golf & Country Club. Orlando. Semi-private 18 holes. 568-2116.
Winter Park Municipal. Winter Park. Municipal 9 holes. 623-3339.
Winter Pines Golf Club. Winter Park. Public 18 holes. 671-3172.
Zellwood Station Country Club. Zellwood. Semi-private 18 holes. 886-3303.

Courses, rated.
According to the pros at the courses, here are the difficulty levels from most difficult to easiest:
  1. Osprey Ridge
  2. Palm
  3. Magnolia
  4. Eagle Pines
  5. Lake Buena Vista

starting time on the same day you want to play by calling the Pro Shop at each course directly.

Instruction is available through the **Walt Disney World Golf Studio** at the Magnolia driving range. The fee is $50 for a lesson, or $150 for a playing lesson. Call (407) 824-2270 for reservations.

The Walt Disney World Golf Classic, a stop on the PGA Tour, has been held in late October in recent years. Tickets are available through Golf Sales.

Golf Fees

Prices were in effect in 1999 and are subject to change. Carts included. Rates do not include tax. Guests at Disney resorts receive free transportation to the courses. Call (407) 824-2270 for reservations and to confirm seasonal rates.

Eagle Pines, Osprey Ridge	Day Visitor	Resort Guest	Twilight Rate
Late April to early Oct.	$100	$95	$55
Early Oct. to mid-January	$125	$120	$65
Mid-January to late April	$140	$135	$75

Lake Buena Vista, Magnolia, Palm	Day Visitor	Resort Guest	Twilight Rate
Late April to early Oct.	$90	$85	$50
Early Oct. to mid-January	$105	$100	$50
Mid-January to late April	$120	$115	$65

Oak Trail	9 holes
Age 18 and older	$32
Age 17 and under	$20

Rentals	
Clubs	$35
Graphite Clubs	$35–$45
Oak Trail Clubs	$15
Shoes	$6
Range balls	$5

Times for **Twilight** rates vary during the year; price allows play for as many holes as possible before nightfall. In recent years, the courses offered a **Summer Price Slice Special** from mid-May to early October, with reduced prices of $45 to $50 at any of the five championship courses after 10 A.M.

Magnolia. At the Shades of Green (formerly the Disney Inn). Named for the more than 1,500 magnolias on the course, this course plays to 6,642 yards from the middle tees and is the setting for the final round of the Walt Disney

World Golf Classic. There's water on 10 of the 18 holes. In 1993, the Magnolia received a complete facelift by course architect Joe Lee. The **Garden Gallery** offers breakfast, lunch, and dinner. The **Disney Golf Studio** offers lessons and videotape analysis. Pro Shop: (407) 824-2288.

No word on mouse ears. Disney enforces a dress code requiring golf attire that bans T-shirts and short shorts.

Course information: Par 72. Yardage: 5,232–7,190. Course/Slope Ratings: 70.5–73.9/123–133.

Palm. Considered the second most difficult course at Walt Disney World, it is included among *Golf Digest's* top 25 resort courses. It plays to a relatively short 6,461 yards from the middle tees, but water and sand seem to be almost everywhere. The 18th hole has been rated as the fourth toughest on the PGA Tour. Also located at Shades of Green, it shares the Garden Gallery and Pro Shop with the Magnolia course.

Course information: Par 72. Yardage: 5,311–6,957. Course/Slope Ratings: 70.4–73.0/124–133.

Lake Buena Vista. A wide open and heavily wooded course that reaches to 6,655 yards, extending from the Disney Village Clubhouse. Located at Disney's Village Resort near the Hotel Plaza resorts. The **Lake Buena Vista Restaurant** in the clubhouse serves breakfast, lunch, and dinner. The **Lake Buena Vista Golf Studio** offers lessons and analysis. Pro Shop: (407) 824-3741.

Course information: Par 72. Yardage: 5,194–6,819. Course/Slope Ratings: 69.4–72.7/120–128.

Osprey Ridge. By most accounts the most difficult course at Walt Disney World, it was designed by acclaimed golf course architect Tom Fazio. Osprey Ridge includes a circulating 18-hole routing with holes that play in every direction. The course extends 6,705 yards from the middle tees, including some remote tropical settings. Some of the tees, greens, and viewing areas are as much as 25 feet above grade; much of the earth was moved from the excavation at nearby Eagle Pines. The namesake "ridge" plays an important role in the course: you'll climb the ridge for the tee for Hole 3, the green for Hole 12 is built into its side, and the green for Hole 16 is atop it. Located at the Bonnet Creek Golf Club, it includes the **Sand Trap Bar & Grill**, a lunch spot with a view of the greens. The **Bonnet Creek Golf Studio** offers lessons and analysis. Pro Shop: (407) 824-2675.

Course information: Par 72. Yardage: 5,402–7,101. Course/Slope Ratings: 70.4–73.9/124–135.

Eagle Pines. Eight of designer Pete Dye's courses are included in *Golf* magazine's top 50. Unlike the high mounds and ridges of Osprey Ridge, this new course offers a low profile, although many balls will end up in the surrounding pines. Eagle Pines plays 6,224 yards from the middle tees and is considered a bit more forgiving than the other courses. Dye included a lip on the edge of fairways along water hazards to reduce the number of wet balls. The course shares the Bonnet Creek Golf Studio, pro shop, and Sand Trap restaurant with Osprey Ridge.

Course information: Par 72. Yardage: 4,838–6,772. Course/Slope Ratings: 67.5–72.3/116–131.

Oak Trail Executive Course. At the Shades of Green. A 9-hole, 2,913 yard, par 36 course with small rolling greens and elevated tees. It's no pushover, though, with some of the most difficult greens at Walt Disney World. No golf carts are allowed.

Course information: Par 36. Yardage: 2,532–2,913.

Winter Summerland Miniature Golf

In true Disney fashion, this pair of miniature golf courses is unlike any you will find in your neighborhood shopping mall. It seems late one Christmas Eve, Santa was flying back to the North Pole and glanced down to see an unbelievable sight: snow in Florida at Blizzard Beach. It was, Santa decided, the perfect place for a vacation getaway for his hard-working elves, a Winter Summerland.

The only thing the area lacked was a golf course; the elves took care of that, dividing the area into two camps, one that enjoyed the warm Florida sun and another that preferred the snow and cold of the North Pole. And so they built two courses: a "sand" course and a "snow" course.

On the summer course, Santa slumbers underneath a large mound of sand and innertubes litter the "beach." Nearby is parked a miniature aluminum "Elfstream" camper. The winter course includes Squirty the Snowman who stands in the way and sprays golfers with water if they get too close.

Whichever course you choose, you'll end up in an old log campground lodge for the final hole; you'll need to putt your ball between two model trains that circle below a decorated Christmas tree. When you put the ball in the cup, you'll travel through cyberspace for a special greeting direct from Santa.

The course is located off the parking lot of Blizzard Beach, to the right of the ticket plaza.

Both courses are open from 10 A.M. to 11 P.M. daily; greens fees for either course are adults $9.25, children $7.50. A second round of golf is offered for a 50 percent reduction. For information, call (407) 560-3000.

Fantasia Gardens Miniature Golf and Fantasia Fairways

Fantasia Gardens Miniature Golf offers two 18-hole courses near the Swan, Dolphin, and BoardWalk resorts. The garden settings of the courses draw their influence from various classic and classical sequences from the Disney movie, *Fantasia*. They include "The Pastoral Symphony," "The Nutcracker Suite," "The Dance of the Hours," and "The Sorcerer's Apprentice."

Alongside is Fantasia Fairways, a par 3 and 4 putting course with exaggerated contours, water hazards, and sand traps, with holes ranging from 40 to 75 feet.

Both courses are open from 10 A.M. to 11 P.M. daily; greens fees for either course are adults $9.25, children $7.50. For information, call (407) 560-8760.

The Walt Disney World Speedway

The Walt Disney World Speedway, a $6 million 1.1-mile course to the left of the access road to the parking lot for the Magic Kingdom, hosted the first Disney World Indy 200 in 1996, drawing tens of thousands of fans and creating a major slow-speed traffic jam.

The speedway, with 51,000 seats, is expected to be a regular stop each January in the new Indy Racing League and the Chevy Trucks Challenge, the opening race of the NASCAR Craftsman Truck Series calendar.

The Richard Petty Driving Experience moves motor sports fans out of the grandstands and into the driver's or passenger's seat of an authentic stock car capable of speeds of up to 145 mph. The program offers two levels of driving experience: "Rookie Experience" and "Experience of a Lifetime." The three-hour Rookie Experience includes eight laps of driving thrills. Participants in Experience of a Lifetime work on establishing a comfortable driving line and building speed in a series of three 10-lap sessions.

For those who'd rather leave the driving to a pro, Richard Petty Driving Experience also offers "Riding Experience." It includes three laps as a passenger in a stock car traveling at a top speed of 145 miles per hour.

Instructors put program participants through the paces in all sessions, beginning with on-track classroom instruction on safety and fundamentals. It continues with on-track technique concerning handling, passing, and drafting with the stock cars.

The sessions at Walt Disney World Speedway are planned for April 1 to September 30, with limited additional opportunities in March, October, and November.

For information on the program, call (407) 939-0130, or (800) 237-3889.

On the Water

Walt Disney World Marinas

Walt Disney World offers the country's largest fleet of pleasure boats, more than many navies of the world. There are three major areas: the Seven Seas Lagoon, which sits between the Magic Kingdom and the Ticket and Transportation Center and is surrounded by the monorail; Bay Lake, the largest body of water, which includes Discovery Island; and the Buena Vista Lagoon, a 35-acre body of water that fronts on Pleasure Island and Disney Village.

Marinas are located at the **Contemporary Resort, Fort Wilderness, Polynesian Resort, Grand Floridian, Caribbean Beach, Yacht Club,** and **Beach Club.** There is also a boat rental station at the **Disney Village,** where a variety of boats are available for rental to day visitors as well as guests at Disney resorts. In the summer, waiting lines for boats can be lengthy at midday.

Guests at some of the Disney resorts can purchase a pass that includes unlimited use of boats during their stay; if you're planning to make use of Disney's navy more than twice during a weeklong stay, the pass will save you money.

Boating away. The Kissimmee Waterway, a 50-mile-long series of lakes, connects Lake Tohopekaliga with Lake Okeechobee and, through that body of water, with both the Atlantic Ocean and the Gulf of Mexico. There are boat ramps at Granada (2605 Ridgeway Dr.) and Partin Triangle Park on Lake Tohopekaliga, and at Sexton on Fish Lake (2590 Irlo Bronson Memorial Hwy. [I-192]), all in Kissimmee.

Hunting and fishing licenses. Fishing (fresh and saltwater) and hunting licenses for persons 16 and older may be obtained from the Osceola County Tax Collector's office. More information is available from the Florida Game and Fresh Water Commission at (407) 846-5300 or the Florida Marine Patrol (saltwater fishing) at (800) 342-5367.

People-Power. One-person pedal boats, for about $8 an hour, are available at most marinas. Canoes for canal paddling can be rented at the Fort Wilderness Bike Barn for about $4 per hour, or $10 for the day.

Slow Boats. Pontoon Flote Boats putter around, very slowly, from Disney Village and other resort marinas. Rentals cost $22 per half hour. Also available are Canopy Boats, 16-foot V-hulls with an outboard, renting for $21 per half hour.

Sailboats. Wind-powered vessels, from little two-seater Sunfish and speedy Hobie Cat catamarans to heavier six-seater Capris are offered at Contemporary, Polynesian, Grand Floridian, Fort Wilderness, Yacht Club, and Beach Club marinas. Prices range from about $10 to $15 per hour.

Water Skiing. The marina at the Contemporary Resort offers a variety of water sports including water skiing, inner tubing, and kneeboards. The rate in 1999 was $130 per hour for up to five guests. For information, call (407) 824-2832.

Water Sprites. Small and low-powered, they're still zippy enough to be a lot of fun. They rent by the half hour for about $20; children under 12 are not allowed to drive. Available at Contemporary, Polynesian, Grand Floridian, Fort Wilderness, and Disney Village.

General information on many water activities is available by calling (407) 824-2832. You can also contact the Fort Wilderness Marina at (407) 824-2621.

Guided Pontoon Cruises

Nightly guided pontoon cruises, timed to coincide with nigthtime shows at Epcot and on Bay Lake are offered at several resorts.

Each night a pontoon boat, with a capacity of up to ten persons, departs any of the lakeside resorts for a circle of Bay Lake; the charge is $95 for a party of up to ten persons. A moonlight pontoon cruise on Bay Lake, including champagne and snacks, costs $150 for up to eight persons, and $200 for up to twelve guests.

Each evening a pontoon boat departs Disney's Yacht Club at 8:40 p.m. for a visit to Crescent Lake and the World Showcase with a view of the nightly Illuminations show at Epcot. The cost is $148.40. A similar cruise, at the same price, leaves the Boardwalk resort.

For information on pontoon cruises, call (407) 824-2832.

Fishing Within Walt Disney World

Though not quite a Florida wilderness experience, there's still some pretty good fishing to be had on Bay Lake, Lake Buena Vista, Crescent Lagoon, and other waterways within Walt Disney World.

Guests at Fort Wilderness or Disney Village can fish from the shore or on any of the canals. Equipment is available for rent at the Bike Barn (rods and reels) or at the Fort Wilderness trading posts (cane poles and lures).

Three times a day an escorted fishing expedition on Bay Lake and Seven Seas Lagoon leaves the Fort Wilderness Marina; the price is about $150 for two hours for a party of up to five persons and includes all gear. Call (407) 824-2621 for information and reservations.

Guided fishing expeditions on Lake Buena Vista are offered from Downtown Disney. Rates for up to five people are $137 for a two-hour excursion. Call (407) 828-2461 for reservations. An expedition on Bay Lake and the Seven Seas Lagoon costs $148.40, including waterside pickup from any of the resorts along Bay Lake. Another trip departs the Disney Yacht Club for Crescent Lagoon and the World Showcase Lagoon, for $148.40. And a shorter dawn expedition departs the Dixie and Port Orleans resorts at 6 a.m., at a cost of $50 per person. For information on any of these guided expeditions, call (407) 824-2832.

Finally, there is the **Fishin' Hole on Ol' Man Island** at Disney's Dixie Landings Resort hotel. The hole is stocked with bass, blue gill, and even catfish; they'll provide bamboo poles and bait. After all that, though, you'll have to return the fish to the pond after you catch them; this fishin' hole is just for sport. The cost is about $3.50 per hour, with a family rate of about $12.50 for up to six people. For information, call (407) 934-5409.

Pool and Beach Swimming

Guests at Disney resorts are surrounded by water, with swimming encouraged almost everywhere. There are more than five miles of white sand beach along the shores of **Bay Lake** and **Seven Seas Lagoon**. Both waterways were engineered by Disney; the sand was mined from beneath the lake muck during construction.

Water, water everywhere. Not to drink, but to swim in, boat and water-ski on, and parasail over. In addition to the offerings within Walt Disney World, there are numerous places for aquatic recreation in the Orlando area.

Turkey Lake Park offers sand beaches, swimming pool, and nature trails. For general information, call (407) 299-5594.

You can rent a houseboat for cruising on the St. John's River through **Hontoon Landing Marina** at (800) 248-2474.

Ski Holidays offers parasail thrill rides, jet-ski rentals, and water-ski charters on a private 400-acre lake adjoining Walt Disney World. Contact them at (407) 239-4444.

Experienced divers can explore the Atlantic or Gulf Coasts or inland springs with equipment rented from **The Dive Station.** Call them at (407) 843-3483.

Beaches can be found at Contemporary, Grand Floridian, Caribbean Beach, Fort Wilderness, Polynesian, Yacht Club, and Beach Club resorts. At certain times of the year, though, swimming may be restricted because of environmental or health concerns because of algae and natural bacteria growth; check with the resort for information.

All of the hotels within Walt Disney World offer swimming pools, some more exotic than others. For example, water slides can be found at the Polynesian and Caribbean Beach Resorts. Use of these pools is restricted to guests at Disney resorts. Day guests looking for cooling water are encouraged to visit River Country, Typhoon Lagoon, or Blizzard Beach.

Surfing

Never mind that Walt Disney World is 50 miles inland; you can still learn to hang ten. A daily class is offered at Typhoon Lagoon for any strong swimmer older than age eight; boards are provided. The 2½-hour lesson is conducted in the wave pool at the water park; surfboards are included. For information call (407) 824-2832.

Out and About

Tennis Courts Within the Park

For information on tennis clinics and instruction, call Disney's recreation information phone at (407) 824-2832. Instruction is presented at the Grand Floridian, Disney's Contemporary Resort, and the Disney Institute.

Disney's Contemporary Resort. The Racquet Club offers six lighted clay courts, open to all resort guests from 7 A.M. to 6 P.M. Rates are $15 per court per hour, or $50 per family for the duration of the stay. Racquets and ball machines are available for rent. Call (407) 824-3578.

Disney's Grand Floridian Beach Resort. Two clay courts are available to resort guests by reservation from 8 A.M. to 9 P.M. Rates are $15 per court per hour, $40 to play against the Pro, and $30 to $70 for lessons. Racquets and ball machines are available for rent. Call (407) 824-3000.

Disney's Yacht Club & Beach Club Resort. Two hard courts available to all resort guests from 7 A.M. to 10 P.M. for no charge; no reservations are taken. (407) 934-7000.

Disney's Fort Wilderness Homes/Campgrounds. Two hard courts are available to resort and day guests from 8 A.M. to 6 P.M. for no charge; no reservations are taken. Racquets available for rent. (407) 824-2742.

Horseback Riding

Trail rides depart from the Tri-Circle D Liverey at Fort Wilderness campground several times a day. Riders must be at least nine years old; the horses are very gentle, and experience is not required for the 45-minute guided tour. Only one rider per horse is permitted, and there is a weight limitation of 250 pounds. The rides cost $23. Call (407) 824-2832 between 8 A.M. and 3:30 P.M. for information and reservations.

Hayrides

A hay wagon leaves Pioneer Hall at Fort Wilderness every night at 7 and 9 p.m. for a 45-minute tour. Tickets are sold by the driver.

Biking Within Walt Disney World

More than eight miles of bicycle paths can be found at Fort Wilderness and at the Disney Village Resort; other places to bike include some of the spread-out resorts such as Caribbean Beach. In an unusual departure for Disney entertainment, use of the paths is free—that is, if you bring your own bike. You can pick up maps wherever bicycles are rented.

Rental bikes can be engaged at the Bike Barn at Fort Wilderness, the Villa Center at Disney Village or the marina at Caribbean Beach. Rates are about $5 per hour or $12 per day; tandems (bicycles built for two) can be rented at the Bike Barn. You must be at least 12 to rent a bike. Call (407) 824-2832 for information.

Port Orleans and **Dixie Landings.** A 2.5-mile tour around the Carriage Path and along the riverfront. Dixie Landings: rent single or tandem bikes at **Dixie Levee** near the marina. Port Orleans: single or tandem bikes at **Port Orleans Landing** near the marina.

Fort Wilderness Resort and Campground. More than eight miles of roads and trails in and among forests, beaches, trails, waterways, and boardwalks. Single and tandem bikes are available at the **Bike Barn.**

Disney's Village Resort and **Disney Vacation Club.** Easy riding along the golf course, waterways, and residential streets of the resort. You'll have to share the road with cars, buses, golf carts, and joggers. At this location, bicycles are available for rental only to guests at a resort within the park. Village Resort: rent single bikes at the **Reception Center.** Vacation Club: single and tandem bikes at **Hank's Rent 'n Return.**

Disney's Caribbean Beach Resort. A leisurely, flat circuit around Barefoot Bay Lake, including bridges to Parrot Cay Island and other interesting destinations. Rent single bicycles at the **Barefoot Boat Yard.**

Disney Health Clubs

Disney's BoardWalk Inn & Villas. Muscles and Bustles Health Club. Nautilus, circuit training, steam rooms, massage. Open daily 6 A.M. to 9 P.M.

Disney's Contemporary Resort. Olympiad Fitness Center. Nautilus, circuit training, cardiovascular, sauna, massage, tanning booths. Open daily 6:30 A.M. to 8 P.M.

Disney's Grand Floridian Beach Resort. Spa & Health Club. Saunas, steam rooms, whirlpools, couples treatment room, personal training, massage therapies, body treatments including facials, watery therapy and soaks, manicures, pedicures, and leg treatments. Open daily 6 A.M. to 9 P.M. For reservations call (407) 843-2332.

Disney's Yacht & Beach Club Resorts. Ship Shape Health Club. Nautilus, cardiovascular equipment, weight training, sauna, spa, steam room, massages. Open daily 6 A.M. to 9 P.M.

Disney's Old Key West Resort. Exercise Room. Nautilus, free weights, massages. Open 6:30 A.M. to midnight.

The Villas at the Disney Institute. Sports & Fitness Center. Cybex, cardiovascular equipment private treatment rooms, steam room, sauna, whirlpool. Open daily 8 A.M. to 8 P.M. Call (407) 827-4555 for reservations.

Chapter 22

Outside Walt Disney World: Participant and Spectator Sports

Major and Minor League Baseball

Spring Training is a dream fulfilled for the serious fan and an enjoyable sojourn for the casual observer. You are so close to the superstars of baseball, the young hopefuls trying for a one-in-a-million spot on a major league roster, as well as some of the greats of yesteryear soaking up the spring sunshine as coaches. Listen to the enthusiastic chatter of the ball players—talk of "taters" (home runs) and "hacks" (swings) and "beep" (batting practice).

There are two parts to Florida's Grapefruit League: the training and the not-quite-prime-time practice games. Pitchers and catchers arrive in Florida in mid-February to work themselves into shape with exercise and steadily lengthening throwing sessions. Their teammates usually arrive a week or two later. In general, the teams can be found at their practice fields each morning until early afternoon; check with the Spring Training sites before heading out. At most parks there is no admission charge for the workouts, and you will be able to wander in and among the superstars.

Most teams invite many of their upper-level minor league players as well as promising rookies to their camps; you'll see uniform numbers as high as 99.

Practice games begin about March 1, and most of the early games take place in the afternoon. Toward the end of the season, in early April, some games may be scheduled under the lights. Teams tend to concentrate on playing nearby neighbors to cut down on travel time; some of the games are "split squad," meaning that half of the large preseason roster may be playing elsewhere at the same time.

Ticket prices range from about $5 to $12. You can usually obtain tickets as late as the day of game, except for the more popular matchups, such as the Yankees vs. Mets or Mets vs. Red Sox.

If you're a golfer, you might want to check out a course near one or another of the training camps; many players and coaches share that sport and can be found on the links in the afternoon.

Once the big leaguers depart, many leave behind their minor league farm teams who play a full summer season in the Florida League.

As we know, of course, Disney wants it all, and so it came as little surprise to learn that Walt Disney Wold has snared a major-league team of its own—at least as a Spring Training tenant. The Atlanta Braves make their Florida base at Disney's Wide World of Sports. See Chapter 18 for more details.

Outside the boundaries of the theme park, other nearby training camps are those of the Houston Astros, Kansas City Royals, Florida Marlins, and Detroit Tigers.

Spring Training Camps

Tickets for many Spring Training events can be purchased through the TicketMaster web site, at www.ticketmaster.com

Atlanta Braves. The Braves train at Disney's Wide World of Sports within Walt Disney World. For information, call (407) 363-6600.

Houston Astros. Osceola County Stadium, 1000 Bill Beck Boulevard, Kissimmee. (407) 933-5400. Tickets $7 to $12. The **Osceola County Stadium and Sports Complex** is also the summer home of the Florida State League Osceola Astros at the Class A professional level. The complex includes a 5,120-seat stadium plus four other practice fields as well as clubhouse and training facilities.

Kansas City Royals. Baseball City Stadium, 300 Stadium Way, Davenport. (941) 424-2424. Tickets: $6 to $10.

Florida Marlins. Space Coast Stadium, 5800 Stadium Parkway, Melbourne. (407) 633-9200. Tickets: $5 to $12.

Detroit Tigers. Joker Marchant Stadium, Lakeland Hills Boulevard, Lakeland. (941) 688-7911. Tickets: $5 to $8.

Other Grapefruit League Teams

Baltimore Orioles. Fort Lauderdale Stadium, 5301 N.W. 12th Avenue, Fort Lauderdale. (954) 776-1921. Tickets: $6 to $9.

Boston Red Sox. City of Palms Park, 2201 Edison Avenue, Fort Myers. (941) 334-4700. Tickets: $6 to $11.

Cincinnati Reds. Ed Smith Stadium, 12th and Tuttle, Sarasota. (800) 829-5353. Tickets: $5 to $10.

Cleveland Indians. Chain O' Lakes Stadium, Winter Haven. Call (941) 293-3900 for information or (407) 839-3900 for tickets. Tickets: $5 to $10.

L.A. Dodgers. Holman Stadium, Dodgertown, 4101 26th Street, Vero Beach. (561) 569-6858. Tickets: $5 to $11.

Minnesota Twins. Lee County Sports Complex, 14100 Six Mile Cypress Parkway, Fort Myers. (800) 338-9467 or (612) 338-9467 in Minnesota. Tickets: $8 to $11.

Montreal Expos. Roger Dean Stadium, 4751 Main St., Jupiter. The Expos share their facility with the St. Louis Cardinals.

New York Mets. Thomas J. White Stadium, 525 N.W. Peacock Boulevard, Port St. Lucie. (561) 871-2115. Tickets: $9 or $12.

New York Yankees. Tampa's Yankee Stadium at Legends Field, 3802 Martin Luther King Blvd., Tampa. A new 10,000-seat home for the Yankees. Call (800) 969-2657 for ticket information. Tickets $8 or $10.

Philadelphia Phillies. Jack Russell Memorial Stadium, 800 Phillies Way, Clearwater. (813) 442-8496. Tickets: $9 to $12.

Pittsburgh Pirates. McKechnie Field, 1750 9th Street, West Bradenton. (941) 748-4610. Tickets: $6 to $9.

St. Louis Cardinals. Municipal Stadium. 715 Hank Aaron Drive, West Palm Beach. The Cardinals moved into a new facility shared with the Montreal Expos in 1998. (888) 447-4824. Tickets: $5 to $15.

Tampa Bay Devil Rays. Al Lang Stadium, 180 2nd Avenue S.E., St. Petersburg. (813) 825-3137. Tickets: about $6 to $12.

Texas Rangers. Charlotte County Stadium, 2300 El Jobean Road, Port Charlotte. (941) 625-9500. Tickets: $7 to $9.

Toronto Blue Jays. Dunedin Stadium at Grant Field, 311 Douglas Avenue, Dunedin. (813) 733-0429. Tickets: $8 to $10.

Major League Wanna-Bes

Chet Lemon's School of Baseball. (407) 333-3010. Lake Mary. A year-round instructional camp for ages 6 and up, taught by professional ball players.

NBA Basketball

The **Orlando Magic** of the National Basketball Association play at the Orlando Arena from October to April of each year.

The arena, which opened in 1989, seats 15,291 for basketball and includes a spectacular videoscreen used for replays and special encouragements to the fans. Tickets have been easier to obtain in recent years as the team's fortunes have waned. For ticket information, call (407) 916-2255. Seats may be available at the Orlando Arena or through TicketMaster for a fee by calling (407) 839-3900. www.magic.nba.com

And if you want to pick up a character T-shirt that doesn't have mouse ears, you might want to visit the **Orlando Magic FanAttic**, a store that sells official clothing and other items. It is located in Orlando at 715 North Garland, near the intersection of I-4 and Highway 50. Call (407) 649-2222 for details.

IHL Hockey

Professional hockey in Orlando? That's the concept, although time will tell if the Orlando Solar Bears can make a go of it as the southernmost member of the International Hockey League. The team plays its games in the Orlando Arena in a season that runs from late October through mid-April. For information, call (407) 872-7825.

Tickets are available at the Orlando Arena Box Office or through Ticketmaster for a service charge by calling (407) 839-3900. And the Solar Bears Ice

Den at the RDV Sportsplex is open to the public for ice skating. For information call (407) 916-2550.

Arena Football League

The Orlando Predators play a 14-game schedule at the Orlando Arena from mid-April through August. The league features eight-man "Ironman" football on a 50-yard indoor field; with the exception of the quarterback and an offensive specialist, players must play both offense and defense. Tickets are priced from $5 to $32. (407) 648-4444.

The Citrus Bowl

The Florida Citrus Bowl Classic college football game is held at the 70,000-seat stadium on New Year's Day. For information, call (407) 849-2500.

Greyhound Racing

Melbourne Greyhound Park. (407) 259-9800. Melbourne. Put your money on the dogs. Evening races Wednesday, Friday, and Saturday; matinees Monday, Wednesday, Thursday, Saturday, and Sunday.

Sanford-Orlando Kennel Club. (407) 831-1600. 301 Dog Track Road, Longwood. Racing from November 1 through May 2, nightly at 7:30 P.M. except Sunday, and matinees Monday, Wednesday, and Saturday at 12:30 P.M. General admission, $1; clubhouse, $2.

Seminole Greyhound Park. (407) 699-4510. Casselberry. Racing nightly at 7:30 P.M. except Sunday; matinees on Monday, Wednesday, and Saturday at 12:30 P.M. Clubhouse $2, grandstand free.

Roller and Ice Skating

Orlando Iceplex. (407) 352-0613. 7500 Canada Avenue, off International Drive near Sand Lake Boulevard. Spectacular lighting, sound, a DJ . . . and indoor ice skating.

Skate Reflections. (407) 846-8469. 1111 Dyer Boulevard. Roller skate to the latest music on 17,000 square feet of solid maple floor.

Fishing

Backcountry Charter Service. (407) 668-5516. Inshore saltwater trips on the Indian River near the Kennedy Space Center and on the St. John's River.

Bass America. (407) 281-0845.

Bass Anglers Guide Service. (407) 656-1052.

Bass Challenger Guide Service. (407) 273-8045, (800) 241-5314.

Cutting Loose Expeditions. (407) 629-4700, (800) 533-4746. Fresh and saltwater expeditions.

Florida Deep Sea Fishing. (813) 360-2082. St. Pete Beach.

J & B Central Florida Bass Guide. (407) 293-2791.

Horseback Riding

Grand Cypress Equestrian Center. (407) 239-1938, (800) 835-7377. Off Route 535, Orlando. $35 to $50 for trail rides, private lessons $50 half hour, $80 hour.

   Horse World Poinciana Riding Stables. (407) 847-4343. 3705 S. Poinciana Blvd., Kissimmee. Trail riding, hayrides, pony rides, and farm animals. Open daily from 9 A.M. to 5 P.M. Adults, $30 to $45; children (5 and younger riding double), $15. Pony rides for children 6 and younger, $6.

Rodeo

Kissimmee Rodeo. Kissimmee Sports Arena. (407) 933-0020. 958 South Hoagland Boulevard. Every Friday from 8 to 10 P.M. Adults, $10; children, $5.

   Silver Spurs Rodeo. (407) 847-5118 for tickets, (407) 847-4052 for information. Kissimmee. The largest rodeo east of the Mississippi, with bull and bronco riding, steer wrestling, and more, is held for one weekend in mid-February and early October only.

Bungee Jumping

The Orlando area features more bungee-jumping establishments than you could shake a tourist at; it's a very changeable industry, with cranes or towers moving from one open lot to another. If this is the sort of thing you're looking for, cruise Irlo Bronson Highway or International Drive, and take a look up.

Boating and Cruises

Airboat Rentals U-Drive. (407) 847-3672. 4266 West Vine Street, Kissimmee. Adults, $25 per airboat up to four adults; electric boats $20 for up to six adults. Airboats, electric boats, and canoes available for rental and use in a cypress swamp.

   Boggy Creek Airboats. (407) 344-9550. 3701 Big Bass Road, Kissimmee. Guided tours in Florida wilderness; night alligator hunts available in summer. Adults, $16; children (3-12), $10. *Discount coupon in this book.*

   Rivership *Romance*. (407) 321-5091. 433 North Palmetto Avenue, Sanford. Adults, $35; children, $25 for three-hour lunch cruise; Adults $45, children $35 for four-hour lunch trip. Cruises on 110-foot vessel on the St. John's River. Dinner cruises Friday and Saturday nights ($50 all tickets). *Discount coupon in this book.*

Blimps, Hot Air Balloons, and Sightseeing Flights

Kissimmee Aviation Services. (407) 847-9095. 3031 W. Patrick Street. Aerial tours of central Florida. All passengers $41 for one to three persons for half-hour flight; $82 for one-hour flight.

   Orange Blossom Balloons. (407) 239-7677. Lake Buena Vista. One-hour sunrise champagne flights over central Florida, followed by breakfast buffet. Adults, $160; children (10-16), $85 with adult.

Rise & Float Balloon Tours. (407) 352-8191. 5767 Major Boulevard, Orlando. Adults, $165; children, $85. $85 introductory offer.

Skyscapes Balloon Tours. (407) 856-4606. 5755 Cove Drive, Orlando. Sunrise champagne brunch flights. Adults, $175; children, $75.

Part VII
Attractions and Shopping In Kissimmee and Central Florida

Chapter 23
Church Street Station, Gatorland, Skull Kingdom, Splendid China, and Other Attractions

Orlando-Kissimmee Attractions

Major Attractions in Orlando and Kissimmee
Church Street Station
Gatorland
Green Meadows Farms
Kennedy Space Center Visitor Center
Space Shuttle Launch Viewing
Medieval Life
Movie Rider
Orlando Science Center
Ripley's Believe It or Not!
Skull Kingdom
Splendid China
Wet 'n Wild

Church Street Station. When you've maxxed out on rides and exhibits at Disney World, take a drive into Orlando for a visit to Church Street Station. This is a restored historical section of the city set up for live entertainment, shopping, and dining. The Station has been open for business for more than 25 years. In its typical fashion, the Walt Disney Company has "adopted" the concept for its own Pleasure Island complex within the park; Church Street is aimed at a slightly older crowd and has a more adventurous edge to it.

Church Street has been hard-pressed by competition from Disney's Downtown and Universal's Citywalk; after years of losses, the operation was sold to British developer Enric PLC in the spring of 1999 with future plans uncertain. Enric owns several soccer teams in Britain as well as the rights to develop restaurants themed on Warner Bros. characters.

Although attendance has dropped sharply in recent years, Church Street remains a lively place, particularly among locals and convention attendees staying in Orlando. Bus service links the area to International Drive, and developers hope for an eventual light rail link between the Universal Studios area and downtown Orlando.

Actually, **Church Street Station**—located in one block of Orlando's downtown Church Street—is two facilities at once. You'll see one Church Street Station if you go during the day and a completely different and exciting facility after the sun goes down and the lights come up. Admission is free for lunch; there's a cover charge after 5 P.M. ($17.95 for adults, $11.95 for children 4 to 12). Annual passes are $24.95 for one, and $44.95 for a two-person pass.

The mood is high-energy with musicians roaming through the dining areas or performing on stage. The rooms generally are crowded, noisy, active, and fun. This is one place where you don't have to choose one restaurant or bar, you can "hop" around all evening for food, drink, and entertainment.

Rosie O'Grady's Good Time Emporium is about 90 years behind the time, a rip-roarin' saloon with antique brass chandeliers, etched mirrors, and leaded glass that celebrates the Gay 1890s to the Roaring 1920s. It's a place of strumming banjos, Dixieland jazz, bartop cancan girls, Charleston dancers, and singing waiters and bartenders.

Apple Annie's Courtyard is a grand Victorian garden domed by arched pine and cypress trusses from the circa-1860 St. Michael's Church in New Orleans, ornamented with hand-carved Viennese mirrors and brass chandeliers.

Lili Marlene's Aviator's Pub and Restaurant memorializes the sweetheart of World War I in a room of classic wood paneling, fireplace, and a wine cabinet brought from the Rothschild house in Paris from about 1850. It is open for leisurely lunch, brunch, or dinner. There is a Sunday Brunch Buffet from 10:30 A.M. to 3 P.M., priced at $12.95 for adults and $6.95 for children from ages 4 to 12.

The **Cheyenne Saloon and Opera House** is a magnificent showroom constructed from lumber from a century-old Ohio barn; it took more than 50 craftsmen nearly two-and-a-half years to construct; no nails were used. The Cheyenne includes an eclectic collection of artifacts, including six 1895 chandeliers from the Philadelphia Mint and an 1885 solid rosewood pool table from San Francisco. The restaurant features beef, pork, and chicken barbecue as well as buffalo burgers with all the fixings.

Phineas Phogg's Dance Club celebrates great balloonists of the past and present with sounds from the latest Top 40 hits.

The **Crackers Seafood Restaurant** serves fresh Florida seafood and pasta specialties; **Rosie O'Grady's** offers deli sandwiches and red hots (hot dogs).

For lighter and quicker fast-food fare, try the **Exchange Food Pavilion**, a small covered mall with interesting shops and food. And there is also the **Wine Cellar**, with more than 5,000 bottles of fruits of the vine. The Exchange also includes an unusual collection of shops. There is no admission charge to the Exchange at any time. Church Street Station is open every day from 11 A.M. to 2 A.M., with nighttime entertainment beginning at 7:15 P.M.

There are "street parties" at Church Street Station on a regular basis; check with the attraction for exact dates: January, **Boola Bowl**, a post-Citrus Bowl party; February, **Valentine's Day Dinner, Salsa Rengue Street Party**; March, **St. Patrick's Day**; April, **Easter Brunch**; May, **IslandFest, Mother's Day Brunch**; June, **Father's Day Brunch**; September, **70s Street Party**; October,

Grand Reserve Dinner & Wine Tasting, Halloween Street Party; November, **Thanksgiving Day Brunch/Dinner**; December, **Christmas Tree Lighting, New Year's Eve Street Party.**

To get to Church Street Station, take I-4 toward Orlando. Exit on Anderson Street, and follow the signs to Church Street Station. Open parking is available under the I-4 roadway, but you must pay in advance and if you overstay your promised time, you will get ticketed. A better choice is to follow the parking garage signs to the covered parking. You'll walk a little farther, but you'll avoid a ticket. For information, call (407) 422-2434.

Church Street Station operates a shuttle bus service from International Drive, servicing eight hotels on Tuesday through Friday evenings. Call (407) 422-2434, ext. 400 for schedules. *Discount coupon in this book.*

Next door up Church Street is the Church Street Marketplace, a more modern dining and shopping area offering Pizzeria Uno, Olive Garden, Café Europa, B. Dalton, Brookstone's, Jungle Jim's, and more.

Gatorland. This is about as real a place and as un-Disney a theme park as you are likely to find in Central Florida, and it is one of our favorite places in the world. It is, quite simply, a shrine to the alligator, and when they say they have the world's largest collection of the fascinatingly creepy creatures, they're not exaggerating: there are thousands of them at every turn in this 50-acre park.

Gatorland is one of the older attractions in Central Florida, dating back to 1949. During the years, the park has grown from a handful of alligators with a few huts and pens into the Alligator Capital of the World and an active breeding station. You'll stroll along a boardwalk through a cypress swamp to see gators, herons, and dozens of other wild creatures. Other creatures on display include snakes, deer, goats, talking birds, and even a Florida bear. Semi-brave visitors can even "pet" an alligator—a baby with his mouth taped shut.

The park is also a mecca for birdwatchers, with thousands of native birds nesting in the area, making use of the alligators as protectors of their nests from natural predators such as racoons and opossums.

Gatorland opened the **Jungle Crocs of the World** display in mid-1998, featuring Nile, Cuban, American, and Australian saltwater crocodiles in a swamp-like setting. Visitors meander through the swamp on a raised walkway.

Each of the species of crocodiles has a slightly different stalking behavior, according to Gatorland experts. Cuban crocs tend to attack on land, while their saltwater cousins usually hide under the surface of the water and explode out to snap at any tempting target.

New exhibits include a walk-in aviary that is home to a flock of Australian Lories that may come to perch on your hand.

Florida "Crackers" (the term comes from the sound made by bullwhips cracking over the heads of cattle) were the first alligator wrestlers—of necessity. They would often have to fight gators that had grabbed calves for a snack. At Gatorland, you'll see an exhibition of stunt wrestling in the 800-seat **Wrestlin' Stadium**. Another highlight is the **Gator Jumparoo**, where giant alligators as big as 15 feet and 1,000 pounds jump out of the water to be hand fed.

The park also includes an alligator breeding marsh, a three-story observation tower, the **Gatorland Express Railroad**, and the **Snakes of Florida** show. A new water park for young kids, Lilly's Pad, opened in the summer of 1997. And plans are afoot for a major expansion of the park that could double its size, although it will retain its quirky character as the alligator kingdom.

Gatorland also offers a line of alligator boots, belts, wallets, and meat. Yes, meat: **Pearl's Smoke House** offers smoked alligator ribs, deep fried gator nuggets, and gator chowder. We tried the nuggets: they (of course) taste like chicken.

Open daily from 9 A.M. to dusk. Visitors should allow several hours; to catch the full cycle of shows, we'd suggest arriving early or at lunchtime. Tickets in 1999 were $16.93 for adults, $7.48 for children 3 to 12. Various combination tickets are available with other smaller attractions in the area. Located at 14501 South Orange Blossom Trail (S.R. 441) in Orlando, about a 20-minute drive from Walt Disney World. (407) 855-5496, or (800) 398-5297. *Discount coupon in this book.*

Green Meadows Farm. The ultimate petting farm for children of all ages, it includes a two-hour guided tour with introductions to more than 300 animals including pigs, cows, goats, sheep, donkeys, chickens, turkeys, ducks, and geese. Everyone gets to milk a cow, and children can go for pony rides, a tractor-pulled hayride, and a 10-minute train ride.

This is a lovely place for animal lovers of all ages to while away a warm afternoon; the farm setting could not be more different than a theme park with real oohs and aahs at every turn. On one of our visits, the tour came to a complete halt in front of a pen occupied by three-day-old Vietnamese pot-belly pigs. My children fell in love with some of the exotic chickens, including a variety named *mille fleurs* ("thousand flowers") because of the intricate pattern on their back.

The farm is one of eight similar operations around the country, the brainchild of Bob and Coni Keyes of Waterford, Wisconsin. It started in Wisconsin when that farm began to allow visitors to come and pick vegetables and raspberries. It expanded from that to allow urban youngsters to get up-close to farm animals. There are now Green Meadows Farms in Illinois, California, New Jersey, and New York.

Take I-192 east toward Kissimmee; turn right at Poinciana Boulevard; go five miles to the farm. Open every day but Thanksgiving and Christmas from 9:30 A.M. to 4 P.M. (407) 846-0770. Tickets $15; children under 2, free. *Discount coupon in this book.*

Kennedy Space Center Visitor Center. (407) 452-2121 or (800) 572-4636 in Florida. www.KennedySpaceCenter.com

The home base of America's Space Shuttle is the fifth most popular attraction in Florida, drawing nearly three million visitors each year; it's also one of the best tourist bargains anywhere.

The Space Center is about 55 miles from Orlando, and there's enough to occupy you for a full morning or afternoon. Parking and admission to all indoor and outdoor space exhibits is free. Here's your chance to climb aboard the *Explorer*, a full-scale replica of the Space Shuttle, accurate down to the switches in the cockpit. The **Gallery of Space Flight** includes a fabulous collection of spacecraft, moon rocks, and other items.

The entry to the center is themed after the International Space Station, complete with huge replicas of the station's solar panels. Robot Scouts is a walk-through exhibit that introduces NASA's most far-reaching space explorers, the robotic planetary probes. Highlights include the Viking Mars lander, Cassini Saturn probe, Lunar Prospector, and Hubble Space Telescope. The host robot for the display is the humorous "Starquester 2000."

The film "Quest for Life," presented in a new theater at the Visitor Complex, explores the mysterous spark of life that made our planet unique in the solar system. The film blends recent

The Space Shuttle departs Florida
Courtesy Kennedy Space Center Visitor Center

findings on Mars with theories from leading scientists. And it reveals how the process that lead to life on Earth may have been replicated on as many as two billion other planets that are believed to have the needed ingredients.

The International Space Station Center offers visitors the opportunity to look over the shoulders of workers assembling elements of the $30 billion orbiting research facility that will be jointly operated with the Russians.

The LC39 Observation Gantry gives an eagle's-eye view of the space shuttle as it is prepared for flight. It stands just half a mile from one launch pad and a mile from the other and also allows a peek into the massive Vehicle Assembly Building where the pieces of each spacecraft are brought together before flight.

At the space station center, visitors view a video about the program, narrated by one of the astronauts who will help assemble the craft in space. From there, guests can walk through mock-ups of the space station, including the crew quarters and labs.

Visitors can spend as much time as they want at each attraction; buses are available to transport guests from location to location on a frequent schedule.

In 1999, a "Maximum Access Pass" for a tour of the space center and two IMAX films sold for $26 for adults and $20 for children 3–11. A "Standard Access Badge" that include the bus tour and one IMAX film sold for $19 for adults and $15 for children ages 3-11.

The Kennedy Space Center tour offers views of **Space Shuttle Launch Pads A and B**, the massive **Vehicle Assembly Building**, and an authentic 365-foot-long *Saturn V* moon rocket—one of only three in existence—housed in the new *Apollo/Saturn V* center. The Firing Room Theater re-creates the atmosphere of the original firing room as it existed during the Apollo era. The Lunar Surface Theater restages the fateful moments of Apollo 11 when astronauts Neil Armstrong and Buzz Aldrin placed the first human footprints on the moon.

Also available is a tour of the **Cape Canaveral Air Force Station**, where the U.S. space program began in the 1960s. And an exhibit at the center explores the **Merritt Island National Wildlife Refuge**, which surrounds the spaceport. Visitors can explore recreations of the continental shelf, beach, grasslands, salt marshes, and lagoons and learn about some of the species that inhabit the area, including loggerhead turtles, manatees, black mice, scrub jays, and indigo snakes.

Spectacular IMAX movies are shown on the huge screen of the IMAX Theater. One of the most popular is the 37-minute *The Dream Is Alive*, which shows astronauts living and working in space.

Mission to Mir delves into the challenges of space exploration. A new 3-D space movie, *L5, First City in Space*, uses actual NASA footage and data to depict a space station.

The IMAX film format produces an image 10 times larger than conventional 35-mm film used in theaters. To share a view of Earth few humans have experienced, crews from five Space Shuttle missions operated the cameras.

The **Astronauts Memorial** honors the 15 American astronauts who gave their lives in the line of duty (including the crew of the *Challenger* and the *Apollo 1* spacecraft, as well as others killed in training accidents). The 42-foot-high Space Mirror is set by a quiet lagoon near the entrance.

The 140,000-acre space center itself is an interesting wildlife area with some 15 endangered species making their homes there. Watch for alligators in the many canals along the roadways; the cape is also home to numerous wild pigs.

A massive Saturn V moon rocket
Courtesy Kennedy Space Center Visitor Center

NASA's schedule hopes to have one Shuttle in space, one ready to go, and two in processing at any one time. If you are lucky, you may see one of the vehicles—mated to its external tank and rockets—moving down the 3½-mile road from the Vehicle Assembly Building to the launch pad on board a transporter. The entire assemblage weighs about 12 million pounds. Shuttles typically spend several weeks on the pad as they are prepared for launch. Most orbiters return for a landing on a special runway at the space center, making a signature double sonic boom as they cross over central Florida.

It is especially interesting to visit the center while a Shuttle is in orbit; the air crackles with radio transmissions to and from the orbiter and special displays track the progress of the current mission.

The park tends to be less busy on weekends than weekdays and is open every day of the year except for Christmas Day, from 9 A.M. to dusk. The visitor center may be off-limits on launch days, and bus tour routes may be altered or canceled when rockets are being prepared or launched.

The center is located off S.R. 405, NASA Parkway, seven miles east of U.S. 1. From Orlando, take S.R. 528 (the Beeline) to S.R. 407, about one hour total driving. From Atlantic Coast Florida, take Exit 78 off I-95. Follow signs for Kennedy Space Center.

Space Shuttle Launch Viewing. Current information on launches is available by calling NASA at (407) 867-4636, (407) 449-4444, or the Kennedy Space Center Visitor Center from within Florida at (800) 572-4636.

From outside the Space Center, the best places to watch a launch are along U.S. Highway 1 in the city of Titusville and along Highway A1A in the cities of Cape Canaveral and Cocoa Beach on the Atlantic Ocean.

A limited number of launch viewing passes that permit private cars to enter the Space Center and park at a site six miles from the pad are available for free by writing three months in advance to NASA Visitor Services, Mail Code: PA-Pass, Kennedy Space Center, FL 32899.

The visitor center at Kennedy Space Center sells about 1,500 tickets to board buses to a viewing site six miles from the launch pad. Come to the center within seven days in advance of a launch to purchase tickets, priced at $10, or $15 with admission to one IMAX film. Tickets sell out quickly for daylight launches. In addition, if there is an afternoon launch, you may be able to park at the Visitor Center and watch the blastoff from there.

Medieval Life. (407) 396-1518 or (800) 229-8300. 4510 West Irlo Bronson Highway, near Route 441 in Kissimmee. A little piece of ancient Spain, it includes a truly amazing collection of tools, personal items, and some of the darker elements of the Medieval times, including dungeons and torture chambers. This place is for real—an exhibit unlike most anything else in Central Florida or elsewhere in the United States.

Your visit will start at the architect's house, the home of one of the most respected members of the community; the craftsmen exhibits include authentically dressed tradesmen and artisans including potters, blacksmiths, millers, carpenters, and glassblowers.

Then—parents of young children be warned—it's into the dungeon where you'll see replicas and real instruments of torture that include the garrote, iron torture masks known as "branks," and the interrogation chair, a large wooden chair covered with sharp iron spikes used to "convince" a person charged with a crime to offer a confession. And be prepared to explain—or steer your kids around—a few real chastity belts.

Adults, $8; children (3 to 12), $6. Open between 4 P.M. and show time at Medieval Times. Free admission with the Medieval Times Dinner Show. *Discount coupon in this book.*

Movie Rider. (407) 352-0050. 8815 International Drive.

This is not your neighborhood cineplex; Movie Rider is a giant-screen, high-energy simulator theater wilder than most anything else in Florida. The 36-seat theaters are divided up into cars that move with the action on the 30-foot-high by 42-foot-wide screen. Its closest competition is "Back to the Future" at Universal Studios.

Your ticket buys you two features, each about three to five minutes long. In early 1999, the offerings were "Red Rock Run," a trip on a runaway mine cart within an active volcano, and "Super Speedway," a view of seven tracks in an Indy Car race.

Adult tickets are $8.95, children $6.95. Combination tickets with **Ripley's Believe It or Not!** are $15.95 for adults, and $13.95 for children ages 4 to 12. You can stay to watch the same pair of movies for a second showing for $2. Note children must be at least 42 inches tall to ride the movie. Open daily from 10 A.M. to midnight.

Orlando Science Center. (407) 514-2000 or (888) 672-4386. www. osc.org. 777 East Princeton Street. Orlando's newest museum is a hands-on exploration of our environment and the universe. You'll be greeted by live animals in an 8,000-gallon cypress swamp. You can become a Cosmic Tourist in an exploration of space, or travel through the human body as a piece of food in BodyZone. The Darden Adventure Theater features daily performances by the Einstein Players. The Dr. Phillips CineDome is the world's largest Iwerks domed theater and planetarium.

Adults, $8; children, $6.50. Double Adventure admission includes exhibits plus film or planetarium show: adults, $12.50; children (3-11), $9.25. Triple Adventure includes all three: adults, $14.25; children, $11. Senior tickets $1 off. Open Monday through Thursday from 9 A.M. to 5 P.M., Friday and Saturday from 9 A.M. to 9 P.M., and Sunday from noon to 5 P.M.

Ripley's Believe It or Not! (407) 363-4418 or (800) 998-4418. 8201 International Drive, one block south of Sand Lake Road. This is one strange place—something that will be immediately obvious when you look at the building; think of it as the leaning museum of Orlando and you'll get the idea. Among the oddities you'll find here are a replica of the Mona Lisa constructed out of toast, a 1907 Rolls Royce built from more than a million matchsticks, and extraordinary humans, including the world's tallest man and Liu Ch'ung, the man with two pupils in each eye.

The Orlando branch of the chain of museums also includes a portion of the Berlin Wall, a reproduction of Van Gogh's self-portrait created from 3,000 postcards, and a Disasters Gallery.

And the Orlando Ripley's even made it into the *Wall Street Journal* in late 1995 with a "believe it or not" of its own: eight of the 20 staffers at the museum became parents in a single year, each after touching an African fertility totem in the office lobby. The ninth was a delivery woman for an air express company.

This is a must-see for visitors who have a taste for the bizarre; it's even stranger than a theme park that celebrates a talking mouse. Allow about 90 minutes for a self-guided tour. Open daily from 9 A.M. to 11 P.M. Adults, $10.95; children (4 to 12), $7.95. Combination tickets with the nearby Movie Rider are $15.95 and $13.95. *Discount coupon in this book.*

Skull Kingdom. A haunted family attraction, this spectacular shrine to scarification stands at the top of International Drive, across from Wet 'n Wild. Enter, if you dare, through the Giant Skull Entrance. The theming never lets up, from the ticket booth within a giant winged dragon to a spiderweb chandelier in the entry chamber where groups of visitors are divided into small groups to walk through the sprawling building.

The concept is "fun and fright," and it is accomplished with some high-tech apparatus, including hydraulics, smoke machines, theatrical lighting, and robotics. Live actors pop out of the walls and respond to the actions of visitors—without touching them. One of the final sections of the adventure presents a fully animated alien that will knock your knees extraterrestrially.

The Skull Kingdom is open weekdays from 6 P.M. to 11 P.M. and weekends from noon to 11 P.M. In July and August the attraction is open every day from noon to 11 P.M.

Admission is $9.95; children 7 and under are admitted free. For information, call (407) 354-1564. *Discount coupon in this book.*

Splendid China. A journey of 10,000 miles and 5,000 years within a 76-acre theme park that includes miniature replicas of The Great Wall of China, The Lunan Stone Forest, and The Forbidden City. Performances and exhibits include Chinese acrobats, artists, Mongolian wrestlers, and martial artists.

The park, which opened at the end of 1993, is a near duplication of the original Splendid China, which is located in Shenzhen, China, near Hong Kong.

The "Mysterious Kingdom of the Orient" show features more than 70 acrobats; it is performed nightly at 6 P.M. Tuesday through Sunday. Admission is included in your Splendid China ticket; separate tickets can also be purchased for $14.95. If you visit the park on Monday, you can use your park admission ticket for a show later in the week.

A new cast of acrobats is rotated in every six months.

Splendid China also offers a dinner theater combination that includes a meal at the Suzhou Pearl Restaurant before or after the show.

Another show at the park is the Magical Snow Tiger Adventure, which features a 500-pound white snow tiger. It is presented every day but Wednesday.

Areas of the park include **Suzhou Gardens,** a life-sized replica of a commercial street in the "water city" of Suzhou in eastern China of 700 years ago; construction of the city included construction techniques utilized by the Chinese of the 12th and 13th centuries.

Near the entrance are some unusual **Tihu Stones,** rocks found in Tihu lake and other lakes in eastern China. The rock is much admired by the Chinese for its shou (slimness), lou (leaking), znou (folding), and tou (transparent) characteristics. The Chinese as a people greatly value mountain and water landscapes and go to a great deal of effort to create gardens to celebrate these themes; the Tihu stone is often used to re-create mountains in miniature.

The Great Wall of China, scaled down to a half-mile in length, includes six million replica bricks that were hand-laid by Chinese artisans. The Great Wall stretches 4,200 miles from east to west—wider than the entire continental United States. Beacon towers were built at regular intervals from which sentries could send smoke and fire signals if an enemy approached.

The grand 9,999-room **Imperial Palace** is the centerpiece of Beijing's **Forbidden City**. Built in 1420, it was the seat of power. The reproduction of the Forbidden City and Imperial Palace occupies a central location at the park.

The **Potala Palace** at the back of Splendid China is a reproduction of the Lhasa capital of the Tibet region, built in the 7th century by King Song Song Gombo for his bride. The 13-story palace atop a cliff has 1,000 rooms.

The spectacular **Leshan Buddha Statue** in Sichuan Province is located at a point where three rivers come together, creating turbulent waves and violent eddies that have caused many shipwrecks. More than a thousand years ago, a monk tried to end the disasters by carving a huge Buddha out of the hillside where the three rivers met. The 236-foot-tall statue was eventually completed. Two people can stand side-by-side in each of his ears, and more than 100 people can sit on each of his feet. When one of the Buddha's fingers was damaged, 5,000 bricks were used to mend it.

One of the most spectacular sights in the park is the re-creation of the **Stone Forest**. Some 300 million years ago limestone was deposited in thick layers on the ocean floor; about 30 million years ago the seabed rose above sea level to reveal the stone, and over the course of the following centuries, the wind and rain have sculpted the limestone into a strange forest of nearly 66,000 acres. Some of the stone forest peaks have been given vivid names such as "A Leisurely Stroller," "A Galloping Horse in the Sky," and "A Phoenix Combing Her Wings." Even in miniature, the reproduction towers over visitors.

The wonders of Splendid China also include the **Stone Sculptures of the Dazu Grottoes**, some 50,000 statues. Although they were completed as early as the 13th century, they remained hidden until 1939. Most of the statues are dedicated to Buddhism, but others represent Confucianism, Taoism, and the ordinary life of the times.

A now-vanished ethnic group created the **Cliffside Tombs of Eban** in southwestern China about 600 years ago; their beautifully preserved wooden coffins still hang on the cliffs, accompanied by paintings depicting horse racing, dancing, religious activities, and martial arts.

The **Dai Village** includes reproductions of the simple but efficient bamboo homes of the Dai people, which include advanced climate control. When the sun shines, the thatches of the roof curl upward and allow the sunlight in and the heat out; when it rains, the thatches absorb moisture and expand to seal the roof. Each April, the Dai celebrate a water festival in which every Dai man and woman takes a bucket of water and splashes each other in a joyous ceremony that is supposed to bestow good luck.

The **Guanyin Statue** is also known as "1,000 Eyes and 1,000 Hands." It celebrates the Bodhisattaba Buddha, a disciple of Buddha who was supposed to have sprouted all those eyes so he could see all human anguish and all the hands so he could appease the suffering.

The **Terra Cotta Warriors & Horses** display reproduces another wonder of China: the 1974 discovery of a hidden cave that had more than 8,000 life-sized and individually carved statues of soldiers and horses. The "army" was a guard of honor for the spirit of Quin Shihuang.

Restaurants at Splendid China include the **Hong Kong Seafood Restaurant**, offering Cantonese, Mandarin, Mongolian, Chiu Chow, Peking, Szechuan, and Hunan cuisine. Informal dining is also available at **The Seven Flavors** cafeteria in Suzhou Gardens, **The Great Wall Terrace**, **Wind and Rain Court**, and **Pagoda Garden**.

Busy times at the park include spring and fall, plus Christmas and Chinese New Year in January or February.

Splendid China is open daily from 9:30 A.M. to 7 P.M. in the off-season, and from 9:30 A.M. to 9:30 P.M. during the summer, the Chinese New Year's period, and other holiday periods. When the park is closed at 6 P.M., the Hong Kong restaurant remains open until 9 P.M.

At closing time, visitors will be admitted to the park to eat at one of the restaurants; during the day, you can purchase a ticket to go shopping and receive a refund for the ticket if you leave the park within a limited time.

The park throws itself a big two-week-long party for Chinese New Year's, which occurs near the end of January. Included are special athletic and musical entertainments and special dishes at the Suzhou Pearl.

At night the park takes on another dimension, with small white lights outlining the roof lines of the buildings in Suzhou Gardens, just as they do the buildings of the Forbidden City of Beijing.

Located at Splendid China Boulevard, two miles west of Disney World on U.S. 192. (407) 396-7111. http://www.floridasplendidchina.com. Adults, $28.88; seniors, $21.20; children, $18.88. A guided tour of the park by golf cart is available for $48 for up to five persons. You can also purchase an evening ticket to the "Mysterious Kingdom of the Orient" show for $16 for adults, or $10.65 for children. *Discount coupon in this book.*

Terror on Church Street. Boo! In mid-1999, the operators of this venerable freakfest on South Orange Avenue in Orlando near Church Street Station, pulled the plug because of financial difficulties. That's a frightful shame; I hope to see this place rise from the dead somewhere else.

Wet 'n Wild. (800) 992-9453, (407) 351-1800. 6200 International Drive, just off I-4. It's all in the name in this large water park; in 1998, nearby neighbor Universal Studios purchased the place. According to industry sources, Orlando's Wet 'n Wild is the busiest water park in the country, drawing about 1.3 million visitors in recent years, just a bit more than Walt Disney World's Blizzard Beach and Typhoon Lagoon.

Although it doesn't have the Disney "theme" magic, Wet 'n Wild does have some of the wildest—and most unusual—water rides anywhere around.

Attractions at the park include **The Surge**, a five-passenger bouncing tube that twists and turns its way down a 600-foot path, and the **Fuji Flyer** tower. Other attractions include **The Bomb Bay** and **Der Stuka**, claimed to be the highest, fastest water slides in the world; the **Black Hole**, a 500-foot twisting, turning journey through darkness, time, and space; the **Surf Lagoon** wave pool; and the **Kids' Playground**, with smaller versions of the park's most popular rides.

Last year the park added **Hydra Fighter**. Riders sit in back-to-back swings equipped with water cannons. By regulating water pressure, they'll be able to control how high and fast the swing goes. Serious players can send their gondola on swings that get them swinging 90 degrees or more from perpendicular. About once an hour, the area's lifeguards take to the ride to show amateurs how it's really done.

A new play area for kids ages 48 inches and under features mini slides, flumes, and games.

Our favorite here is **Knee Ski**. You'll snap on a life vest and a helmet and then plant your knees in a surfboard; then hold onto the handle for dear life as you are launched out onto the lake and towed by an overhead cable around a half-mile course. We've yet to see someone make it completely around on the first try, but after a few exciting tries, most visitors master the Knee Ski. My hotshot teenage daughter couldn't get enough of this unusual ride. I was perfectly happy to make it around once before retiring to a beach umbrella.

At **Wild One**, you and a friend ride on a pair of bouncy tubes pulled around the pond by a jet-ski. Open year-round, dependent on weather conditions. For most of the year, the park is open until 5 P.M.; from June until Labor Day, Wet 'n Wild is open until 9, 10, or 11 P.M.

During Summer Nights from mid-June to early August, the park is open from 9 A.M. to 11 P.M., with a concert stage on the deck of the Surf Lagoon Wave Pool for nightly music and entertainment.

Adults, $26.95; children (3 to 9), $21.95. Seniors (55 and older) are admitted for half-price. Half-price general admission is offered after 3 P.M. or 5 P.M., depending on closing time that day. *Discount coupon in this book.*

Other Attractions in Orlando, Kissimmee, and Nearby

Air Orlando Helicopter Service. (407) 352-1753. 8990 International Drive. Rides over Sea World, Universal Studios, Walt Disney World, and Orlando range from $20 to $395 per person with a minimum of two adult fares per flight.

A World of Orchids. (407) 396-1887. 2501 Old Lake Wilson Rd., Kissimmee. Botanical gardens that include an arboretum containing an ever-changing display of some 2,000 varieties of orchids, which bloom throughout the year. Open daily except Monday from 9:30 A.M. to 4:30 P.M. Tickets $9.58 with tax; children 15 and under, free; seniors $8.58. Half-price tickets in winter. *Discount coupon in this book.*

Congo River Golf & Exploration Co. Orlando: (407) 352-0042. 6312 International Drive, next to Wet 'n Wild. Kissimmee: (407) 396-6900. 4777 West Highway 192, three miles east of I-4. A miniature golf course and more, with exploration games, an arcade, and go-carts (International Drive) or paddle boats (Kissimmee). Golf fees, $6.50 for 18 holes, $9.50 for 36 holes; children younger than 4 years old, free. Open from 10 A.M.

Flying Tigers Warbird Air Museum. (407) 933-1942. At Kissimmee Airport, off I-192 on Hoagland Boulevard. An impressive collection of American warplanes in working condition or undergoing restoration by mechanics and artisans. The private collection features dozens of planes including a B-17 Flying Fortress bomber, P-51 Mustang fighter, and antique biplanes. Tour guides take you through the hangars. Open 9 A.M. until 5:30 P.M. daily, until 5 P.M. Sunday. Adults, $8; seniors (over 60), $6; children (6–12), $5. *Discount coupon in this book.*

Fun 'n Wheels. Orlando: (407) 351-5651. International Drive at Sand Lake Road. Kissimmee: (407) 870-2222. I-192 at Osceola Square Mall. The wheels include a Ferris wheel (in Orlando), bumper carts, boats, and small race cars; other fun includes miniature golf (in Orlando) and bumper cars (in Kissimmee). Free admission; purchase tickets for rides. Open from April to July noon to 11 P.M.; hours vary in off-season. *Discount coupon in this book.*

Haunted House at Old Town. (407) 397-2231. 5770 West Irlo Bronson Highway. Two floors of spooks and special effects. Adults, $5; children 10 and under, $3.50. Open noon to 11 P.M. daily.

Jungleland Zoo. (407) 396-1012. 4580 West Irlo Bronson Highway, Kissimmee. Primates, cats, birds, unusual animals from around the world, and indigenous animals of Florida are among the more than 500 animals displayed on seven acres. Open daily 9 A.M. to 6 P.M. Tickets $11.95 plus tax for adults; seniors $9.95, and $6.95 for children 3 to 11.

Kartworld Kissimmee. (407) 396-4800. Highway 192, four miles east of I-4. Indy-style and double-seater go-karts on a nearly mile-long track that goes over and under bridges. $4 per lap. Children must be at least 11 years old.

Katie's Wekiva River Landing. (407) 628-1482. 190 Katie's Cove, Sanford. Downstream canoe runs, with equipment rental and shuttle service. Open 7:45 A.M. to 6:30 P.M. Call for rates and runs. Runs range from 6 to 19 miles.

Malibu Grand Prix. (407) 351-4132. 5901 American Way, Orlando. Grand Prix-style fun in 3/4-scale models of racing cars. Open in season Monday through Thursday noon to 10 P.M., Friday noon to midnight, Saturday 10 A.M. to midnight, and Sunday 10 A.M. to 10 P.M. Call for hours in off-season.

Monument of States. Lakefront Park, downtown Kissimmee. Erected in 1943, the Monument of States is a 50-foot-tall solid concrete structure reinforced with 3½ tons of steel rails.

More than 1,500 stones represent every state in the nation and 21 foreign countries. Minerals and ores include gold and silver, plus chrome, cobalt, copper, iron, lead, platinum, and zinc. Stones include agate, alabaster, alva, coquina, coral, diamond-bearing rocks, feldspar, flint, Florida keystone, granite, limestone, marble, meteors, mica, petrified wood, petrified teeth and bones, quartz, sandstone, schist, slate, stalactites, stalagmites, and travatia.

Mystery Fun House/Starbase Omega. (407) 351-3356. Across from the main gate of Universal Studios at 5767 Major Boulevard in Orlando. A houseful of surprises, including the Forbidden Temple, an Egyptian tomb, a miniature golf course, a video arcade and the "Ultimate Lazer Game—Starbase Omega." Fun House tickets are $10.95 for all. Starbase Omega tickets are $9.95 for all. Miniature golf tickets are $4.95. Open from 10 A.M. to 9 P.M. daily; later in holiday periods.

Paintball World. (407) 396-4199. Behind Old Town, off Highway 192 East, Kissimmee. A 60-acre paintball preserve with trenches, forts, bases, spectator areas, concessions, and a pro shop (honest!). Open Wednesday, Saturday, and Sunday from 10 A.M. to 4 P.M. $25 per person plus cost of paintballs.

Pirate's Cove Adventure Golf. (407) 352-7378. 8601 International Drive in Orlando and (407) 827-1242. Exit 27 off I-4 at Lake Buena Vista. A clever pirate-theme golf course with two 18-hole challenges at each of its locations in the Orlando area. Adults, $7.50; children (12 and younger), $6.50. *Discount coupon in this book.*

Pirate's Island Adventure Golf. (407) 396-4660. 4330 West Irlo Bronson Highway, Kissimmee. Two 18-hole courses set in a tropical paradise. Adults, $5.50; children, $4. *Discount coupon in this book.*

Race Rock. (407) 248-9876. 8986 International Drive, Orlando. A restaurant packed with racing cars and memorabilia, including stock, funny, and Indy cars, plus monster trucks, hydroplanes, and dragsters. Open Monday-Thursday from 11:30 A.M. to 11:30 P.M., Friday and Saturday until midnight, and Sunday until 11 P.M.

Reptile World Serpentarium. (407) 892-6905. 5705 East Irlo Bronson Highway, St. Cloud. Cobras and other poisonous snakes. Open Tuesday through Sunday, 9 A.M. to 5:30 P.M. Adults, $4.25; students, $3.25; children 3 to 5, $2.25.

River Adventure Golf. (407) 396-4666. 4535 West Irlo Bronson Highway. All tickets $6.50; children under 4, free.

SAK Comedy Lab. (407) 648-0001. 380 W. Amelia St. in downtown Orlando. A small, informal storefront theater that features improvisational and scripted comedy shows. The young cast works without a net, and unlike the Comedy Warehouse at Pleasure Island, there are no Disney minders anywhere on the property. Three shows on Friday and Saturday nights at 7:30, 9:30, and 11:30 P.M. Adults, from $7 to $12.

Trainland. (407) 260-8500. Altamonte Mall, Altamonte Springs. Toy trains from the 1920s to the present, one of the largest indoor model train layouts in the country, and a gift shop for collectors. Adults, $8.95; seniors, $7.95; and children (3 to 12), $5.95. *Discount coupon in this book.*

Water Mania. (407) 396-2626 or (800) 527-3092. 6073 West Irlo Bronson Highway. Catch a wave at this water park right on I-192 in Kissimmee, in and among many of the off-site hotels. The slides are not as artfully decorated as those at Typhoon Lagoon, but still wet and fun. There's the Banana Peel two-person raft plunge, the Rain Forest children's water playground, and the Anaconda family raft ride. Heated pools in winter. Go-cart track. Open year-round. Summer hours from 9:30 A.M. to 7 P.M. daily; November to mid-March from 11 A.M. to 5 P.M. Adults, $25.95; children (3 to 9), $18.95.

WonderWorks. (407) 351-8800. Pointe*Orlando, International Drive, Orlando. It's hard to miss this place, even in the midst of the wall-to-wall, grab-your-eye tourist district: it's the place that looks like it has fallen from the sky and landed upside down on International Drive.

WonderWorks is a place where science has gone crazy—a sort of hands-on science museum for children of all ages.

Here's the cover story: since the end of World War II, the supersecret WonderWorks laboratory has been located on a remote, uncharted island off Florida—within the Bermuda Triangle—and has served as a haven for investigators of the unexplainable. But in 1997, something went awry in a top-secret experiment to harness the power of a tornado: the energy vortex lifted the research lab from its foundations and dropped it, upside-down, in Orlando.

Inside the building you'll find hands-on demonstrations of the forces of nature, including a hurricane chamber, an anti-gravity room, and the Earthquake Experience. In the Physical Challenge Lab, you can try out the Shocker Chair, test your coordination on a virtual balance beam, play virtual basketball, and arm wrestle a computer. In the UFO Lab you can split your image and distort your body, make music with a theramin or computer drums, and morph your voice.

Plan on a stay of at least two hours in the building; mom and dad may want to shop next door. Plans call for the installation of a large LaserWorlds laser tag facility on the upper floor of the building.

Adults $12.95, children (3–12) and seniors (55+) $9.95.

Other Attractions Outside Orlando

Bok Tower Gardens. (941) 676-1408. Located in Lake Wales, about 55 miles south of Orlando, off U.S. 27 to Alt. 27. Florida's historic bell tower, centerpiece of a magnificent garden, is at Florida's highest point—all of 295 feet. Bok Tower Gardens was dedicated to the American people by Dutch immigrant Edward Bok, Pulitzer Prize-winning editor of the *Ladies' Home Journal*. Some of the 57 bronze bells weigh as much as 12 tons. The 128 acres of gardens include thousands of azaleas, camellias, magnolias, and other flowering plants. The gardens are home to a colony of wood ducks and more than 100 other species of birds. A 45-minute carillon recital is presented daily at 3 P.M. Open daily 8 A.M. to 5 P.M. Adults, $4; children (5 to 12), $1.

Cypress Gardens. (941) 324-2111 or (800) 282-2123. http://www.cypress gardens.com. Florida's first theme park, established in 1936, Cypress Gardens is home of the famous water-ski team, Dixie Belles in hoop skirts, and thousands of varieties of plants, birds, and other creatures. There's also much more in this lush, green park off U.S. 27 near Winter Haven, Florida, about 45 minutes from Orlando.

The famed botanical gardens include more than 8,000 varieties of plants from 90 countries.

In 1999, Cypress Gardens introduced the **Southern Breeze,** a re-created Old South paddle wheel boat that cruises from Port Cypress on Lake Eloise. The 100-foot-long ship (with a draft of only 28 inches for the shallow lake) is a replica of a 19th century Mississippi riverboat. It can carry up to 200 passengers.

The ship takes passengers on half-hour excursions on the lake; tickets are $5 for adults, $4 for seniors, and $2 for children ages 6-17.

The *Southern Breeze* also offers two-hour dinner cruises, with prices ranging from $11 to $20 , and Sunday brunch cruises from $10 to $16.

Wings of Wonder at Cypress Gardens is a walk-through glass conservatory that is home to more than 1,000 free-flying butterflies from more than 50 species. Two glass-enclosed chrysalis houses contain unhatched butterflies imported from farms in Ecuador and El Salvador, a practice that helps protect species that come from the rain forests. The conservatory is also home to a flock of green and neon iguanas, mandarin ducks from Asia, ringed teal ducks from South America, and South African cape teals.

Guests are encouraged to snip and sniff a wide variety of herbs, including oregano, garlic, mint, lemongrass, rue, mallow, and safflower in the **Herb and Scene Garden**. The **Vegetable and Fruit Garden** bursts year-round with crops that include colorful burgundy queen cauliflower, tango onions, red Boston lettuce, sparkler radishes, and jade pagoda cabbage.

Nonedible but spectacular is the famed **Rose Garden**, which includes Europeana red, French Lace white, Summer Fashion yellow, and Angel Face lavender roses in appropriate seasons.

The park is perhaps best known for **The Greatest American Ski Show**, a water-ski extravaganza that showcases high-powered boat races and ski-jumping feats and a team of 56 skiers. Cypress Gardens' first water-ski show took place in 1943 when a group of local skiers gathered on Lake Eloise to entertain military troops on leave. Since then, skiers have recorded more than 50 world records, including the first four-tier human pyramid.

Variété Internationale has a changing selection of performers.

Other entertainment includes a magic show and an elaborate model railroad, **Cypress Junction**, which includes 20 high-speed model trains touring tiny replicas of U.S. landmarks on 1,100 feet of track. The **Eco Tour** is an electric boat ride through the man-made canals that wind through the 200-acre park; there is a $6 additional charge for the trip.

Island in the Sky is a 153-foot-high revolving platform that offers an aerial view of Cypress Gardens, the surrounding Chain of Lakes and countryside beyond.

And here's the chance (for some of us) to fulfill that dream to ski with the world-famous Cypress Gardens team. Each participant in the **Extreme Experience** program receives individual instruction from a professional, skiing time in the famed show circle, and an action photo taken during the session. Participation in the program costs $75 per person.

And finally, at certain times of the year Cypress Gardens almost outdoes itself with special festivals:

Spring Lights, early February to early May. The park is transformed into a bouquet of spring flowers set amid the twinkling of four million lights, including the Tree of Life with lighted blossoms, bees, and butterflies. Each evening features a Starlight Spectacular laser light show.

Spring Flower Festival, mid-March to mid-May. The park is decorated with several dozen stuffed topiary figures, many in bloom.

Mum Festival, early November to late November. More than three million brilliant blooms in magnificent arches, baskets, and other arrangements, with a 35-foot cascading waterfall as its centerpiece.

Poinsettia Festival,

The famous Cypress Gardens ski show
Photo courtesy of Cypress Gardens

late November to mid-January. More than 40,000 poinsettia blooms shape towering holiday trees, baskets, and beds. Other highlights include a miniature European village nestled among poinsettia alps.

Garden of Lights Holiday Festival, late November to mid-January. More than four million lights transform the park into a holiday fantasy land.

In 1999, admission was $31.95 for adults, $27.15 for seniors 55 and older, and $14.95 for youths from 6 to 17. *Discount coupon in this book.*

Fantasy of Flight. Near Polk City, off exit 21 of I-4, about 20 miles southwest of Walt Disney World. (941) 984-3500. A celebration of the wonders of flight, built around the personal collection and dream of founder Kermit Weeks.

The sprawling 300-acre facility includes indoor and outdoor displays of antique and unusual aircraft dating back to near the dawn of flight and featuring World War I and II fighting craft. There are also several multimedia exhibitions including a chilling re-creation of a World War I battlefield and a walk-through of a B-17 Flying Fortress. There's also a state-of-the-art flight simulation known as **Fightertown**, which puts visitors at the controls of a World

War II fighter on a Pacific mission; the eight planes are mounted a a full-motion simulator base that responds to your movements of the stick and rudder. As you fly your mission, you'll be in radio contact with a controller and the other flyers in your air group.

Visitors can also venture 500 feet above the central Florida countryside in **The Great Balloon Experience**, a 15-minute trip in a tethered balloon. On clear days, the view can extend as far as the Gulf of Mexico and downtown Orlando. The 115-foot-tall balloon is moored by 16 anchor points that can secure the balloon in wind speeds up to 80 knots.

Fantasy of Flight also offers introductory flights aboard ultralight aircraft with experienced FAA Certified Flight Instructors. During the ultralight introductory flights, conducted Tuesday through Sunday, guests as young as six years old can actually take over the controls of the aircraft.

Weeks, born into a wealthy oil family, put together his first home-built aircraft at the age of 17. A few years later he was flying in aerobatic competitions. He twice won the United States National Aerobatics Championship. Fantasy of Flight is open daily except Thanksgiving and Christmas Day from 9 A.M. to 5 P.M. Adults $18.95, children (5–12) $9.95, and seniors (60+) $16.95. Tickets include admission to exhibits, Fightertown Flight Simulators, and The Great Balloon Experience (weather permitting).

Lion Country Safari. (561) 793-1084. Located in West Palm Beach, off exit 99 of the Florida Turnpike, about 175 miles from Orlando. The nation's first drive-through zoo when it opened in 1967, the park includes more than 1,000 wild animals from all over the world, including giraffes, eland, bison, elephants, rhino, zebra, ostrich, and antelope, wandering free over hundreds of acres. Other areas include a petting zoo and an amusement area that includes paddleboats, a boat ride, and an old-time carrousel. A KOA campground is nearby. Open every day from 9:30 A.M. to 5:30 P.M.; convertibles must be exchanged for available rental cars to drive through the preserve. *Discount coupon in this book.*

Silver Springs. (352) 236-2121 or (800) 234-7458. www.silversprings.com Approximately 72 miles from Orlando; take exit 69 off I-75 to S.R. 40 East. Silver Springs has been drawing visitors to its natural beauties since the early 1800s. In the 1860s, steamboats explored the area. In 1878, Silver Springs became famous for the invention of glass-bottom boats for display of underwater wonders. Six of the original Tarzan movies were filmed at Silver Springs in the 1930s and 1940s; *The Yearling*, starring Gregory Peck and Jane Wyman, was filmed there in 1946. And more than 100 episodes of the *Sea Hunt* television series, starring Lloyd Bridges, were filmed at Silver Springs from 1958 to 1961.

Divers have mapped and explored what is said to be the largest spring system in the world, the source of up to 2 billion gallons of water daily. Discoveries at the site have included fossilized mastodon teeth dating back 10,000 years, a giant ground sloth claw, and a mammoth tooth from the Pleistocene period. In addition, several species of troglobitic life, including crayfish, have been found.

Silver Springs began a multimillion-dollar expansion in 1997, the largest in its history. New features include the World of Bears, Kids Ahoy! Playland, the Twin Oaks Mansion concert stage, Sprinkles Ice Cream Parlor, and Big Gator Lagoon.

In 1998, Silver Springs unveiled the new Panther Prowl attraction, featuring rare Florida panthers and their close relative, the eastern cougar, in an outdoor habitat of trees, caves, and ponds.

The World of Bears attraction is the only place in Florida where guests can see majestic grizzly and Kodiak bears, plus three other species. It was recently expanded with the addition of a pair of Asiatic black bears and two Sun bears from Southeast Asia.

And the Big Gator Lagoon added a half-acre cypress swamp habitat with more than two dozen of Florida's largest alligators, adding to the extensive collection at the park. Another exhibit showcases a white American alligator, one of only 17 known specimens in the world.

Visitors will cruise on glass-bottom boats on a tour that explores seven natural formations, including **Mammoth Spring**, the world's largest artesian limestone spring. Creatures in the nearly pure spring include alligators, turtles, garfish, and largemouth bass. Along the riverbanks are great blue heron, cormorants, ibis, egrets, raccoons, and river otters.

The **Jeep Safari** takes passengers on a four-wheel-drive vehicle into a jungle home to free-roaming wildlife, including two-toed sloth, Brazilian tapirs, African waterbuck, and four species of deer. The highlight of the safari is a trip through a three-foot-deep pit teeming with alligators.

The **Lost River Voyage** explores an untouched cypress jungle, a glimpse of wild Florida as it was thousands of years ago. At Cypress Point, you may be lucky enough to meet Sonek, believed to be the world's largest American alligator.

From about Thanksgiving to New Year's Eve, Silver Springs celebrates with a **Festival of Lights**, a central Florida version of a winter wonderland. Apropos of nothing else, the park is also the home of **A Touch of Garlits**, a museum of antique and race cars honoring famed drag racer Don "Big Daddy" Garlits.

Silver Springs is open every day from 9 A.M. to 5:30 P.M., with extended hours in the summer and on holidays. Adults, $30.95; children (3–10), $21.95. A combination ticket with Wild Waters, allowing one admission to each park within a week, was available for $1 more.

Adjacent to Silver Springs is the **Wild Waters** water park, which offers nine water flumes, including the Twister, a pair of 60-foot flumes for two-person inner tubes, the Tornado water ride, and a 450,000-gallon wave pool. The Lazy Bones River sends guests on a slow tour of an 800-foot jungle waterway, and Cool Kids Cove children's play area, an abstract replica of an 1800s riverboat with water cannons, net cage bridges, water slides, and more.

The water park is open spring through early fall. Call for operating schedules.

Prices in 1999 were adults, $21.95 plus tax, and children (3–10), $19.95. During the summer, the park offered a special price of $10 after 3 P.M. For information, call (352) 236-2121 or (800) 234-7458.

Valiant Air Command Warbird Air Museum. (407) 268-1941. Located near the Kennedy Space Center, on Tico Road in Titusville. Historic displays of aircraft and aviation memorabilia from World War I, World War II, Korea, and Vietnam. Adults, $6; children (4–12), $4. Open daily 10 A.M. to 6 P.M.

Weeki Wachee Spring. (352) 596-2062 or (800) 678-9335. North of Tampa on U.S. 19 at the intersection with S.R. 50. Mermaids abound at this water park on the Gulf Coast. Presentations include an underwater show, Little Pocahontas Meets the Little Mermaid, as well as a **Wilderness River Cruise,** a **Birds of Prey Show,** and a petting zoo. Adults, $16.95; seniors, 10 percent discount; children (3–10), $12.95.

Next to Weeki Wachee Spring lies the **Buccaneer Bay** water park, open from April to early September.

Chapter 24
Shopping

To heck with mice, sharks, and whales—for some folks, the ultimate Orlando recreational activity is . . . shopping. And the millions of visitors to the entertainment attractions of Orlando have proved to be a tremendous lure to retailers.

Bring an empty suitcase with you and leave time for some of the shopping adventures listed here.

192 Flea Market. (407) 396-4555. 4301 West Vine Street (I-192) in Kissimmee. A full-time, free admission market with as many as 400 dealer booths under one roof. Disney souvenirs, jewelry, crafts, clothing, and more. Open daily from 9 A.M. to 6 P.M.

Altamonte Mall. (407) 830-4400. North of Orlando, east of I-4 on S.R. 436 in Altamonte Springs. Burdine's, JC Penney, The Gap, Cache, The Limited, Sears, and more than 175 specialty shops. Open Monday-Saturday 10 A.M. to 9 P.M., and Sundays from 11 A.M. to 6 P.M.

Belz Factory Outlet World. (407) 352-9600. Located at the north end of International Drive, past Kirkman Road. A huge collection of factory outlet shops, with more than 180 companies represented in two enclosed malls and four shopping centers, all within walking distance of each other. Manufacturers include L'eggs/Hanes/Bali, Maidenform, Totes, Polly Flinders, Bally, Bass, Stride-Rite, Mikasa, Adolfo II, Anne Klein, Geoffrey Beene, Jordache, Leslie Fay, Levi Strauss, Van Heusen, Oshkosh B'Gosh, Capezio, Dexter, Corning, Burlington Brands, Guess Jeans, London Fog, Danskin, Londontown, Harvé Bernard, and Young Generations. Open Monday through Saturday 10 A.M. to 9 P.M. and Sunday from 10 A.M. to 6 P.M.

Dansk Outlet. (407) 351-2425. 5247 International Drive. Open Monday to Saturday 10 A.M. to 9 P.M., Sunday 11 A.M. to 6 P.M.

The Florida Mall. (407) 851-6255. Intersection of Sand Lake Road (S.R. 482) and South Orange Blossom Trail (Hwy. 441). Dillard's, Gayfers, JC Penney, Saks Fifth Avenue, Sears, and 200 specialty shops. Open daily from 10 A.M. to 9:30 P.M., and Sunday from 11 A.M. to 6 P.M.

International Designer Outlet. International Drive near Belz Factory Outlet. (407) 354-0300. A collection of upscale clothing and accessory stores, including Ann Taylor, Dansk, Saks Fifth Avenue, Anne Klein, Liz Claiborne, Jones NY, and Coach.

Kissimmee Manufacturer's Outlet Mall. (407) 396-8900. I-192 near Kissimmee. Shops include American Tourister, Casual's Unlimited, Fieldcrest Cannon, Geoffrey Beene Co., Nike Factory Store, Olde Times, Publishers Outlet, Tommy Hilfiger, Totes Factory Store, Van Heusen, and Westport Ltd. Open Monday to Saturday 10 A.M. to 9 P.M., Sunday 11 A.M. to 5 P.M. *Discount coupon in this book.*

Mercado. (407) 345-9337. 8445 International Drive. A small but interesting collection of shops and eateries. Just as Disney's creative roller coaster packaging makes Space Mountain an above-average ride, the Mercado "package" makes this mall a different sort of shopping experience.

Mercado includes more than 60 unusual specialty shops, including Kandlestix, Pet Palace, Krazy Kites, House of Ireland, Earth Matters (wildlife and marine-life clothing and accessories for the conservation-minded), and The Magic Shop.

Restaurants include Damon's—The Place for Ribs, Charlie's Lobster House, Bergamo's Italian Restaurant, The Butcher Shop Steakhouse, José O'Day's Mexican Restaurant, and the Blazing Pianos Red Hot Rock 'n' Roll Piano Bar. There's also Cricketers Arms, an English pub, and La Grille, a French eatery.

In the International Food Court, you'll also find The Greek Place, Wok 'n Roll, Sabor Latino, the All-American Grill, Gino's Pizza, Fiesta, The Sandwich Gallery, Chicken Magic, and Le Gelateria Molto.

At night, the grounds and shops are alight with twinkling lights, and free entertainment is presented in the courtyard.

Shops open from 10 A.M. to 10 P.M. daily, until 11 P.M. in season; restaurants and bars close later.

Titanic—Ship of Dreams. The *Titanic* lives again in this high-tech re-creation of some of the more interesting details of the great ship, at the Mercado.

The display includes more than 200 artifacts from private collections, many on public display for the first time. Among them are a deck chair recovered from the Atlantic following the sinking, first-class china and dinnerware; personal letters on *Titanic* stationery that survived the sinking, and a life jacket.

Actors in period costume share stories of those aboard.

Also on display is memorabilia from the movie "Titanic," including a costume worn by Leonardo DiCaprio, plus items from older classics, including "A Night to Remember," and "The Search for *Titanic*," hosted by Orson Welles.

The controversial letter of deceased Titanic survivor Nellie Walcroft, purchased at auction in England recently, will be on display. The letter sheds new light on the disaster and stirs up fresh controversy. Walcroft tells a chilling tale of the alleged shooting of steerage passengers who attempted to board one of Titanic's lifeboats.

Tickets for the display are $14.95 for adults, and $9.95 for children ages 6-11.

Pointe Orlando Entertainment Center. (407) 248-2838. International Drive at Universal Boulevard. www.pointeorlandofl.com

A sprawling retail and entertainment center that features more than 60 shops, a 20-screen movie multiplex, an IMAX theater, and seven restaurants, across International Drive from the Orange County Convention Center.

The two anchors of the mall are a huge FAO Schwarz retail toy store, designed to look like an upside-down toy box with toys scattered around the perimeter, and WonderWorks, designed to look like a three-story upside-down mansion that landed atop a brick warehouse. Do you get the point?

You'll also find the Muvico Pointe 21 Theaters with an IMAX 3-D theater, plus shops such as Gap and Gap Kids, Banana Republic, Abercrombie & Fitch, Victoria's Secret, B. Dalton Booksellers, Speedo, Bath & Body, Express, Biker's Image, and Image Leather.

You'll have to pay to park in the parking garage, although the ticket can be validated for free parking with purchase of a movie ticket or food and beverage at one of the participating restaurants.

Pointe Orlando shops are open every day from 10 a.m. to 10 p.m., and until 11 p.m. on Fridays and Saturdays. Many restaurants and bars stay open later. *Discount coupon in this book.*

Quality Outlet Center. (407) 352-6931. 5527 International Drive, one block east of Kirkman Road. A small outlet center, it features shops selling products from companies that include Bugle Boy, Corning-Revere, Disney Gifts, Divers Outlet, Florsheim, Laura Ashley, Le Creuset, Mikasa, Royal Doulton, Samsonite, and Yes Brasil. Open Monday through Saturday from 9:30 A.M. to 9 P.M.; Sunday from 11 A.M. to 6 P.M.

Part VIII
Busch Gardens Tampa Bay, Florida Aquarium, Museum of Science and Industry

Chapter 25
Busch Gardens Tampa Bay and Adventure Island

Busch Gardens Tampa Bay opened as a hospitality center for the Anheuser-Busch brewery in Tampa in 1959, showcasing a collection of exotic birds and some of the Busch family's collection of African animals. In 1971, when the era of Florida as theme park began, the company began a massive expansion of Busch Gardens.

Today, the park is like stepping onto the African veldt—albeit a veldt with a monorail circling above and some of the most outrageous modern roller coasters and other rides on the horizon. In June of 1999, Busch Gardens unveiled Gwazi, a mammoth double-track wooden roller coaster. It joins recent expansions, including The Edge of Africa up-close animal safari and the spectacular Montu coaster in the Egypt area of the park.

Busch Gardens is a welcome getaway from the concrete of Walt Disney World and environs, drawing 3 million visitors a year to its 355 acres, home to more than 2,800 animals representing nearly 320 species. The brewery that was the original reason for Busch Gardens Tampa was closed at the end of 1995; part of that land at the heart of the park was used for the new Gwazi coaster.

The Montu and Kumba occupy the third and fourth slots on *Amusement Today's* 1998 Top 25 list of steel coasters around the world.

The map of Florida looks so huge to many visitors that the thought of a drive from Orlando to Tampa seems like an all day drive; it's not. Measured from the intersection of I-4 and I-192, Tampa Bay is an easy 70 miles at 65 mph to the gates of Sea World, about 75 minutes.

Although it is only about 70 miles away, it is on the other coast of Florida and sometimes in a different weather pattern than Orlando. One March day, we left Orlando in the rain and arrived to find the sun blazing in Tampa.

The busiest times of the year are similar to those of the Orlando attractions: June to Labor Day and Spring and Easter Breaks. Other times of the year bring large crowds of foreign visitors, including planeloads from South America and

MUST-SEES

The Edge of Africa

Gwazi
(new double-trouble wooden roller coaster)

Montu
(the latest and greatest steel roller coaster)

Moroccan Palace Theater
(ice show fans)

Myombe Reserve: The Great Ape Domain

Akbar's Adventure Tours
(the ride is simulated, the fun is real)

The Monorail

Kumba
(ever so slightly less intense than Montu)

The Scorpion
(a steel coaster ever so slightly less intense than Kumba)

The Python

Congo River Rapids

Claw Island

Stanley Falls Log Flume

Tanganyika Tidal Wave

Brazil. Lines, though, rarely approach anything like those at Walt Disney World or Universal Studios Florida.

Operating hours are 9:30 A.M. until 6 P.M. Extended hours into the evening are offered in summer and over selected holiday periods.

Busch Entertainment Corp. operates entertainment parks, including Busch Gardens in Tampa and Williamsburg, Virginia; Sea World parks in Orlando, San Antonio, San Diego, and Aurora, Ohio; Adventure Island in Tampa; and Sesame Place in Langhorne, Pennsylvania.

From Orlando: Take I-4 West about 60 miles to Tampa. Exit to I-75 North and then take the Fowler Avenue off-ramp (Exit 54) and follow signs to the park.

Power Trip for Summer and Holiday Periods

Begin your Busch Gardens tour by studying the schedule of entertainment you will be handed at the gate; some shows like the ice extravaganza at the **Moroccan Palace Theater** and **The Dolphins of the Deep Show** are put on numerous times during the day. Other presentations may be scheduled only once or twice. Adjust your Power Trip to include any must-see shows.

The leading attraction for many guests will be the new **Gwazi** double track roller coaster. If you've got the heart and stomach for it, head there first. Or, you can go against the flow and go to Egypt to ride **Montu**. Lines are sure to be lengthy at both rides in the heart of the day, so visit early or late. Serious coaster fans will also want to move on to the Congo to ride **Kumba**, yet another thriller.

While you're in Kumba's neighborhood, check out **The Congo River Rapids**. We like all three of the major water rides at Busch Gardens; you might want to leave a dry sweatshirt in a locker for the occasional chilly day. Now

Busch Gardens Tampa Bay
Ticket Prices (not including 7 percent tax). Prices were in effect in mid-1999 and are subject to change.

	Adults	Children
Single-Day Ticket	$43.70	$34.70 (3–9)
Busch Gardens Tampa Bay/SeaWorld Florida Value Ticket One day each at Busch Gardens Tampa Bay and SeaWorld Florida in Orlando	$79.00	$64.00
5-Park Orlando FlexTicket	$196.95	$157.95
Unlimited admission to Universal Studios Florida, Universal Studios Islands of Adventure, SeaWorld Florida, Wet 'n Wild, Busch Gardens Tampa Bay. Valid 10 days.		
Busch Gardens 12-Month Pass	$94.95	$74.95
Adventure Island 12-Month Pass	$69.95	$69.95
Busch Gardens/Adventure Island Combination Ticket One day each at Busch Gardens Tampa and Adventure Island water park	$58.42	$51.22
Wild Card Annual Pass	$119.95	$104.95
Unlimited admission to Busch Gardens Tampa Bay and SeaWorld Florida for one year		
Wild Card Plus 3-Park	$149.95	$134.95
Unlimited admission to Busch Gardens Tampa Bay, SeaWorld Florida, and Adventure Island for one year		
Surf 'n Safari Pass	$109.95	$109.95
Unlimited admission to Busch Gardens Tampa Bay and Adventure Island water park for one year		

try the awesome **Python** roller-twister-coaster. When you're through, the majestic tigers on **Claw Island** will probably seem tame, but they're certainly worth a visit.

Of the two remaining water rides, **Stanley Falls** may be more fun but the **Tanganyika Tidal Wave** is more dramatic. What the heck: ride 'em both.

Go early to The Edge of Africa to experience a close-up encounter with hippos, lions, giraffes, and more.

For a different type of thrill, consider heading very early for the sign-up for the **Serengeti Safari** tour into the animal preserve. This extra-charge trip sells out early; tickets are sold at the booth near the animal nursery.

If you are not in the mood for an immediate upside down rattle and roll, you can instead start your day by bearing right from the entrance toward Crown Colony to visit the wack new **Akbar's Adventure Tours** simulator

Serious shoppers only. Busch Gardens offers a plan for visitors who want a quick shopping spree at one of the shops just inside its gates. Buy your ticket, go forth and shop, and be back at the Guest Relations booth within 30 minutes and you will be given a refund of your ticket. (You'll have to pay for parking, though.) We're told that some visitors make a mad dash from the gate to the Smokehouse restaurant for take-out ribs or chicken.

adventure. Once you return to earth, backtrack to the Skyride and Monorail station. We'd recommend a trip on the **Monorail** to explore the Serengeti Plain; come back later in the day for a Skyride if you have the time.

At busy times of the year, we'd advise you to now press on through Nairobi without stopping and head for the thrill ride areas, stopping in Timbuktu. If you've got the stomach for it you've got to ride **The Scorpion**; it'll set you up for even more of a wild ride later on. If a show is planned that matches your schedule, visit the **Dolphin Theater** now.

At this point, you will have ridden on all of the major rides. Now take a second, more leisurely circuit of the park and visit the animal exhibits and shows and finish with the **Skyride** and **Trans-Veldt Railroad**.

Busch Gardens Attractions

WOW Gwazi. In African legend, or at least African theme park legend, Gwazi is a fierce creature with with a lion's body and a tiger's head.

At Busch Gardens Tampa, the Lion and Tiger chase each other for a mile and a half, heading right at each other on six "fly-by" maneuvers in which they come within feet of each other at crossing speeds approaching 100 mph. We're talking about a roller coaster, of course, and quite a ride this is: Gwazi opened in June of 1999 in the center of the park on part of the land formerly occupied by the brewery.

The mammoth double track wooden coaster has two different tracks. Gwazi Tiger includes a section of slalom track, more like a bobsled than a wooden coaster. Gwazi Lion's highlight is a nearly continuous series of spirals.

As the two trains crest at the top of the 90-foot lift hills, both drops are on a precise "stingline," allowing riders to see the opposite train charging straight at them. At the last moment, the trains veer to the side. In the fourth of six fly-bys, each coaster arcs at a 51-degree angle; the fifth fly-by delivers a weightless stretch on a parabola of track.

Top speed for the coaster is a zippy 50 mph; when the two trains head at each other, engineers consider them moving at a "crossing" or "closing" speed of 100 mph. Though the wooden coaster follows an old concept, constructed out of more than 1.25 million board feet of lumber and more than two million bolted connections, modern technology is also applied. Computer sensors attached to both tracks monitor Gwazi's trains, regulating their spacing along nearly 7,000 feet of track. The computer also manages the braking systems, a far cry from the days when an operator had to physically pull a hige hand brake to slow down a train at the station.

Morocco

A re-creation of the exotic city of Marrakesh, featuring unusual architecture and a wide range of demonstrations of Moroccan crafts, snake charmers, the Mystic Sheiks of Morocco marching band, and the Sounds of Steel, a five-man steel drum band.

Marrakesh Theater. Two 20-minute shows alternate daily.

Sultan's Tent. A snake charmer performs daily.

WOW Moroccan Palace Theater. In late 1999, "World Rhythms on Ice" took to the ice in this 1,200-seat arena.

The show includes skaters displaying the costumes and cultures of many parts of the world, including Germany, England, Brazil, and the United States.

Midday performances fill up within 20 minutes of show time. The 35-minute show features 14 skaters and two vocalists.

Serious shoppers may enjoy a visit to the brass store just past the ticket booths; an artisan/importer from Morocco offers an impressive display. And, if you like to pay to carry someone else's corporate slogan or ad campaign, check out the **Rabat Label** store, where you can buy just about any article of clothing or sporting equipment with one or another Anheuser-Busch logo on it.

Egypt

WOW Akbar's Adventure Tours. Hold on to your hats—and your wallets—when you embark upon the wacky journey led by comedian Martin Short, starring as a shady Egyptian tour guide hanging on to a shoestring travel business. His newest product is a simulated journey across Egypt, which he desperately hopes will save his business from reposession by Stanford "Don't call me Stan" Wharton (played by comedian Eugene Levy).

Equipped with his brother Omar's home movies, Akbar embarks on his greatest venture ever.

Visitors waiting to board the simulator will see posters depicting some of the awesome attractions of the tour . . . and they won't be able to avoid noticing the very humble means by which Akbar proposes to take them there. Before boarding, you'll meet Akbar himself, the "world's greatest tour guide." In a preshow film, Akbar will take you into his workshop, where his possessions are being removed by Stanford Wharton. After a bit of friendly persuasion by his "baby" brothers Corky and Chip, Stanford reluctantly agrees to give Akbar one more chance at success with his homemade simulator.

And then you'll be face-to-face with the simulator: homemade may be too kind a description. Perhaps "nouveau dump" would be better. But Akbar promises that no misfortune could possibly befall anyone on the maiden voyage. You believe him, right?

The journey begins on camelback, jostling through a bustling marketplace as merchants and pedestrians dive for safety. Weaving and banking just above the desert surface, the simulator, now a biplane, struggles up into the sky to reveal a perilously close encounter with the ancient pyramids. From there it is on to the Sphinx, and this time it's not a near-collision: let's just say that the big cat receives a long-over-due face lift.

Once the simulator regains control, it's on to the excavation of the forbidden tomb, riding on an out-of-control mine train. Surprise: the train somehow gets on the wrong track and ends up in a spooky, skull-filled chamber. The monstrous guardian of the chamber expresses its displeasure with Akbar's intrusion by sending the visitors hurtling through a vortex and out of control . . .

Did you expect anything less?

Akbar's Adventure is located just outside the gates to Egypt, the former home of the Questor simulator. There are two simulator cabins, each seating 59 guests. The total length of the show is about six minutes, which gives an hourly capacity of about 1,416 passengers.

All kidding aside, the simulators themselves are very high-tech, with each cabin hydraulically powered to move in six directions—pitch, roll, yaw, heave, surge, and sway. The audiovisual system is based on an eight-channel laser video disc surround system.

WOW Montu. The world's largest inverted steel roller coaster, soars across nearly 4,000 feet of track and includes four first-of-a-kind elements:

Upside-down on Montu
Photo courtesy of Busch Gardens Tampa Bay

- The "Immelman," an inverse loop named after a famed German stunt pilot;
- The world's largest vertical loop on an inverted coaster, at 104 feet; and
- Two vertical loops slanted at 45-degree angles, known as a "batwing." Coaster experts say these are the wildest stretches of track.

As the trains leave the loading station, they drop toward a pond that is home to several live crocodiles.

Other elements include a camelback maneuver that delivers three seconds of weightlessness, sweeping arcs crossing over and under the tracks of the Transveldt Railway, and a corkscrew finale.

There are three trains comprised of eight cars, each of which holds four passengers across for a total of 32 riders per train. The cars hang from the top and swing out from side to side; the foot platforms drop out when the train departs, leaving feet dangling below the car; at one point the swooping cars dive as close as 18 inches above the ground. The tracks dive into three Egyptian-theme tunnels below ground.

Peaking at speeds in excess of 60 miles per hour, Montu reaches a maximum G-force of 3.85 at certain points during the three-minute trip. Riders must be at least 52 inches tall.

The approach to the loading area for the ride is through a portal in a spectacular 55-foot-tall wall decorated with hand-carved hieroglyphs.

Montu is named after a hawk-like Sun God worshiped by ancient Egyptians at Thebes. The ride is the centerpiece of Egypt, Busch Gardens' largest expansion and ninth themed area.

Visitors to Egypt will be able to tour a six-room replica of King Tutankhamen's tomb as it looked when it was first discovered by archeologist Howard Carter in the early 1920s. Young visitors will be able to dig through a sand pit with buried artifacts of the ancient culture. The area also includes shopping bazaars for the older visitors. Items for sale at the **Golden Scarab** and **Treasures of the Nile** shops include hand-blown glass and cartouche painting on scrolls.

Transveldt Railroad. The train offers some of the best close-up views of the animals on the Serengeti Plain between the Nairobi and Congo stations. Other portions of the track offer a tourist's eye view of the back sides of the Python and Scorpion roller coasters. The train is a ¾-scale replica of an actual African steam engine and cars; the engine is an unusual combination of energy sources, using propane gas to boil water for steam that powers an electric generator for the wheels.

Nairobi

WOW! Myombe Reserve: The Great Ape Domain. Busch Gardens' newest animal habitat, featuring six lowland gorillas and eight common chimpanzees in a tropical forest setting. Gorillas include Lash, a 15-year-old, 330-pound silverback male who was hand-raised by surrogates at the Cincinnati Zoo after his mother died. Also resident is a social group of five gorillas on a

Vanishing gorillas.
Gorillas, the largest living primates, are seriously endangered or in some cases on the brink of extinction in the tropical forests, woodlands, and mountain regions of Africa. Most threatened is the mountain gorilla subspecies; perhaps fewer than 450 remain.

long-term breeding loan from Emory University in Atlanta, Georgia.

Visitors enter the three-acre habitat through dense foliage to a clearing that has a glass wall where they can observe the chimps; passing through a bamboo thicket, guests will come upon the gorillas at the base of a mountain between waterfalls in a simulated tropical rain forest. (On cool days, boulders near the viewing areas are heated to draw animals.) There are chimp nests scattered in the trees, as much as 70 feet off the ground.

Animal hospital. The veterinary clinic includes operating rooms, X-ray, laboratory, and recovery areas, as well as brooder rooms for birds.

At each turn in the reserve, you will see educational displays that tell you about the lives of the gorillas, and how humans are threatening their natural environment. Some other things you'll learn: a young female uses blades of grass and stems to extract termites, a chimp delicacy; chimps, who eat mostly fruit, also use plants for medicinal purposes to kill parasites, fungi, and viruses; before chimps were observed using tools it was assumed that humans were the only ones to do so.

Aldabra Tortoise Habitat. Opposite the train station, you'll find a collection of gigantic tortoises, including the Aldabra tortoise, often found on Aldabra Island in the Indian Ocean. Brought back from near extinction, Aldabras often weigh as much as 600 pounds when mature, and are now seen in large groups wallowing in mud or shallow lagoons.

In the same area, you may also see an African Spurred Tortoise, Africa's largest land tortoises. They span the continent along the southern fringe of the Sahara desert to the Red Sea.

Serengeti Safari. I enjoy roller coasters well enough, but for me the real thrill at Busch Gardens is a very special tour available to only a handful of visitors each day: the Serengeti Safari.

Several times a day, as many as 20 visitors clamber on board an open flatbed truck for a one-hour visit behind the fences of the 60-acre **Serengeti Plain**, with close-up views of giraffes, zebras, hippopotamuses, and other animals. A park guide accompanies visitors on the truck.

It's a fabulous opportunity for camera buffs and animal lovers of all ages. On one memorable trip, a herd of giraffes ambled over to our truck to snack on apples, with a few friendly nips at hats and jackets; into the middle of the giraffes came a group of nearsighted ostriches that pecked at anything within reach. A good time was had by all, including the animals; several of the giraffes loped along behind the truck to bid us goodbye.

Only four to six truck tours are conducted each day; there is a charge of $12.50 per person. Check early in the day at the entrance for availability.

Animals. As close as you can get to some of the animals, and some special treats for the children. You'll find an unusually attractive **Petting Zoo**, but don't overlook the fascinating **Nairobi Station Animal Nursery**, home to Busch Gardens' newest and littlest arrivals including tiny birds, alligators, and snakes, set in a replica of a yesteryear African hospital.

The **Elephant Wash** is just what it sounds like: ponderous pachyderms stand still for showers several times a day; nearby is a small enclosure where guests can climb onto a seat on the back of an elephant for a short ride.

Crown Colony

The Skyride. An open cable car ride from the Crown Colony to the Congo and back, passing above the Serengeti Plain and then deep into deepest, darkest amusement park–land with good views of the Scorpion and the Congo River Rapids. A lovely way to see the park on a lovely day; when it is not lovely, the ride can be a bit chilly, and it is shut down in high winds and inclement weather.

WOW The Monorail. An ultra-modern train that hangs from an overhead single rail for a nearly silent 10-minute cruise in and among the zebras, rhinos, ostriches, and other animals of the Serengeti Plain. The track drops down low for close-up views of some of the residents.

The driver of the train, which can carry about 72 persons in its six air-conditioned cabins, will fill you in on all sorts of things you always wanted to know—like the fact that more people are killed each year by river hippos than by crocodiles.

Animals. Some of Anheuser-Busch's famous corporate symbols can be visited in their stables at the **Clydesdale Hamlet**. The largest adults can be as large as six feet at the shoulder and weigh about a ton.

Serengeti Plain

The largest open area of the park, an 80-acre natural setting that features more than 800 animals in free-roaming herds of camels, elephants, zebra, giraffes, chimpanzees, rhino, Cape buffalo, gazelles, greater kudus, and hippos. Ride the Monorail for the closest views; the Transveldt Railroad also circles the Plain, while the Skyride passes overhead.

WOW The Edge of Africa

In the largest animal expansion in the park's history, guests to The Edge of Africa venture forth on a safari in search of hippopotamuses, giraffes, lions, baboons, meerkats, crocodiles, hyenas, and more. The area makes use of moats and other hidden barriers to preserve the appearance of the wild. Busch Gardens' monorail has been rerouted to go through the middle of the area.

The trek into the 15-acre compound begins with an exploration of the remains of an old fishing village, a riverine habitat where hippos, baboons, and various species of fish coexist. A glass window allows up-close observations of hippos from above and below the surface of a pool; hippos, which are born underwater, ordinarily stay underwater for three to five minutes but can remain submerged for as long as 30 minutes.

Respect the animals. Please don't throw anything into the animal preserves. Human food disrupts the animals' natural diets, and plastic objects—such as straws or drink lids—could be lethal playthings.

As the excursion continues, you'll come to a Masai village, where members of the nomadic African tribe have vacated one of their many temporary homes; the reason for the hasty exit becomes apparent when you discover the lions and hyenas that have taken over the village.

Among rock outcroppings and giant termite mounds, expeditioners will also discover species such as vultures and meerkats in areas offering distant views of the Serengeti Plain.

Roaming safari guides and naturalists offer guests educational facts about the various animals and regions.

Look for the visitor's information center posting the day's animal sightings and diets. As you move into the area, watch for sleeping lions in one of the abandoned safari vehicles parked in the compound; lions spend as much as 18 hours a day relaxing. In the wild they would spend their waking time hunting; at Busch Gardens they receive catered meals of about seven pounds of raw meat several times per week. (The much smaller hyena, along with the lion, one of the most feared hunters in the jungle, eats as much as 100 pounds of food—including animal bones—per week.)

Timbuktu

WOW **The Scorpion.** It goes up to the top of its tower, then down and to the left at 55 mph before entering a full 360-degree loop into a series of corkscrew descents that put you on your side. The Scorpion is by most accounts in the middle between Python and Kumba on the wildness meter.

Parental Guidance: The exit to the ride is in a different area from the entrance. You must be at least 42 inches tall to ride.

Carousel Caravan. A most unusual merry-go-round, featuring desert camels and Arabian horses.

The Phoenix. A dry boat ride that gives new meaning to the term "rock 'n' roll." The platform moves forward and then backward with increasing power until riders make a complete pass up and over the top a few times. This is a bigger and wilder version of the amusement park pirate ship ride.

Other rides here include the **Sandstorm**, an aerial whip; the **Crazy Camel**, a collection of children's rides, an electronic arcade, and a group of carnival games of skill.

Dolphins of the Deep Show. Bud and Mich (sounds vaguely commercial, doesn't it?), with their sea lion sidekick and their trainers, demonstrate their speed and agility in an entertaining show at the Dolphin Theater.

In front of Dolphins of the Deep Theater, be sure to locate the Floss Silked Tree. Native to South America, in late fall the leaves shed and large showy flowers appear. At the peak of color, the canopy is a mass of pink orchid blossoms. When flowering is over, pear-shaped fruits appear that explode when they are ripe, sending a silky cotton material floating to the ground.

Congo

WOW Kumba. Kumba means "roar" in a dialect of the African Congo. It might have been better to call it "aiyeeeee!" or some other such scream. Kumba is one of the largest and fastest steel roller coasters in the country, reaching speeds in excess of 60 mph and putting as much as 3.75 Gs on the bodies of its lucky riders.

The coaster includes several unusual elements, including a diving loop, which plunges riders into a loop from a height of 110 feet; a camel-back, a maneuver that creates three seconds of weightlessness while spiraling 360 degrees; a 108-foot vertical loop, the world's largest; a cobra roll that turns passengers upside down as they twist around a spectator bridge; and more ordinary super-coaster thrills, including an oblique loop, a vertical spiral, and a double corkscrew-shaped twist.

> **Kumba-yah!** Here are the vital specs for Kumba, one of the largest and fastest steel roller coasters in the country.
> **Track length:** 3,978 feet
> **Maximum speed:** 60 mph
> **Maximum G-force:** 3.75
> **Maximum drop:** 135 feet
> **Length of ride:** 2:54
> **Capacity:** about 1,700 riders per hour.

But the ride itself is even wilder than its description—longer and with more twists and turns than three or four ordinary coasters put together. Riders are securely locked into place with an overhead harness and are seated four across. The outside seats give the best view—that is, if you are able or willing to turn your head while moving.

But before I scare you off, consider the fact that Kumba's roar is much worse than its bite. You are moving so fast that you hardly realize that you are on your head or your side or your back. And if it makes you feel any better, know that my then-nine-year-old daughter led the family onto the ride one morning; she rode it once with me and her big brother, a second time with her brother, and a third time by herself when we all insisted on a rest.

The ride is very nicely integrated into the bushes and trees of the park, with many of the dips and turns in the bushes. You can walk beneath much of the track, too, which offers a great view for spectators and bragging rights to successful riders.

You must be at least 52 inches tall to ride and in good physical condition. Did I mention that I started that day with two Dramamine tablets?

WOW The Python. Only at a park like Busch Gardens would a roller coaster like the Python have to settle for second-class status behind Montu and Kumba. The Python includes wicked twists and turns and a 360-degree *double* spiral, and cars reach speeds of more than 50 mph as they travel some 1,200 feet. All that said, the Python is a very short ride; you'll be back at the loading station before your heart has returned from your throat.

If you're a little uncertain about your roller coaster credentials, you may want to try your stomach at Python, then move on to Scorpion, and then make it all the way to Kumba and finally to Montu.

You must be at least 48 inches tall to ride.

WOW Congo River Rapids. Riders sit in a 12-passenger circular air raft and are let loose on a churning whitewater trip in an artificial river with rapids, logs, and other boats in the way. We'd tell you to sit at the back of the boat to avoid getting soaked, but the darned thing keeps turning around. The ride won't get your heart pounding quite as fast as one of the flume trips, but it's still a lot of fun. Riders must be at least 38 inches tall, or at least two years old and accompanied by an adult.

By the way, on the footbridge overlooking the rapids beneath the Kumba track there is a coin-operated water cannon aimed at the rafts below. Put a quarter into the **Congo Water Blasters** and add a little extra water to the passengers below.

Other rides in this area include the **Ubanga-Banga Bumper Cars,** the **Monstrous Mamba** octopus ride, and more kiddie rides.

WOW Claw Island. Here's your chance to get as close as you may ever want to a rare white Bengal tiger.

Stanleyville

WOW Stanley Falls Log Flume. Over the edge of a 43-foot plastic cliff in a hollowed-out log. Lines build at midday; visit early or late in the day to avoid long waits.

Congo River Rapids, Busch Gardens Tampa Bay
© *Busch Entertainment Corp.*

WOW Tanganyika Tidal Wave. Go for a pleasant little cruise through lush, tropical foliage. Sounds relaxing . . . that is, until your 20-passenger boat plunges over the edge to fall 55 feet into a splash pool. The result is a huge wave—really huge—that wets the passengers but can really *soak* observers standing in the wrong place on the walkway below.

For a great view of the tidal wave, climb the bridge and stand within the glass-walled tunnel. If you are riding, the back of the boat gets wet the least. You must be at least 42 inches tall to ride.

In 1999, the park added a new habitat for a white rhino by the name of Timmy. His home can only be seen by guests while in the air on the Tanganyika Tidal Wave.

Animals. Orangutans.

Stanleyville Theater. Daily variety shows in season.

Zambezi Theater. Improvisational comedy presented several times daily in season. Resident zanies are the **Congo Comedy Corps.**

Land of the Dragons

Busch Garden's children's play area is built around a shaded three-story tree house. The Land of the Dragons is home to Dumphrey, a whimsical and friendly beast. Kids are invited to explore the winding stairways and mysterious towers of the treehouse. The area also includes a children's theater, slides, a rope climb, a ball crawl, and a gentle waterfall. The rides area includes a mini-sized Ferris wheel, flume ride, and a dragon carrousel.

Bird Gardens

Bird Gardens. The oldest area of the park, built in the shadow of the brewery in 1959; the brewery is now closed. The lush foliage includes nearly 2,000 exotic birds and birds of prey, representing 218 species and including one of the largest managed flocks of Caribbean flamingos.

Lory Landing. Birdwatching soars to new heights at Busch Gardens' aviary, featuring more than 75 colorful and unusual tropical birds from around the world.

The lush environment is designed to look like a deserted island with waterfalls, floral landscapes, vine-covered trellises, and ponds. It is the home to lorikeets, hornbills, parrots, avocets, touracos, and other brilliantly colored species.

In a large free-flight area, visitors become human perches as lorikeets land on arms, shoulders, and heads to feed on nectar (sold for a nominal fee).

Closer to the aviary's entrance, separate enclosures offer views of several types of endangered parrots, including thick-bills, red-tailed black cockatoos, hyacinth macaws, and hawk-headed parrots.

Amateur bird watchers will find educational feathered facts and artifacts such as eggs tucked into surrounding trees, as well as species identification signs and notes describing threats to the species' native habitats.

Busch Gardens Bird Show. Several performances each day of a show that includes macaws, cockatoos, and birds of prey in free-flight demonstrations.

Lizard Habitat. A showcase for Asian water monitors, crocodile monitors, rhinoceros iguanas, and green iguanas from regions that include Indonesia, South America, and the Caribbean.

Hospitality House. The patio nearby fronts on a small pond, patrolled by a flock of geese; it's one of our favorite places for a break from the sun and crowds. Free samples of Anheuser-Busch beer are offered, along with a simple sandwich-and-pizza menu. A musical variety show including ragtime jazz piano is presented on a small stage.

Animals. Some of the park's most famous species are on display here, at **Flamingo Island, Eagle Canyon**, and the **Koala Display.** Eagles on display alongside the brewery include golden and American bald eagles. The koala habitat also includes Dama wallabies and rose-breasted cockatoos.

The park's Chilean Flamingos ordinarily live in large colonies on brackish lagoons in South America. Their bent bills are fringed at the edges and when held upside down in the water filter out mud and retain shrimp and algae.

Koala Display. A series of educational exhibits leads up to the home of the park's koalas, among the most unusual animals at Busch Gardens. You'll glide past the glassed-in cages on a moving sidewalk; at the end, you can also climb up some stairs to a stationary viewing area. Koalas are marsupials, unique mammals with a pouch that covers the mammary glands on the abdomen. In the Americas, the only current species of marsupial is the opossum.

Special Programs

Busch Gardens offers a variety of educational programs; check with the park for a schedule. Among the offerings is **Zoo Camp**, five different weeklong summer camp programs for children from kindergarten through ninth grade.

Coming Attraction: A Place to Lay Your Head

Sometime in the next millennium, you may have a chance to bed down with the lions, giraffe, and hippos. Before you go too far with visions of bedrolls in the veldt, think instead of a four-star luxury hotel. Busch Gardens hopes to build a $100 million, 800-room animal theme convention hotel overlooking the Serengeti Plain Area. The project, if completed, would be the largest hotel in the Tampa Bay area.

Eating Your Way Through Busch Gardens Tampa Bay

Morocco

⊞ **Boujad Bakery.** An exotic place to grab breakfast or a sweet at any time of the day. Check out the gigantic blueberry and other types of muffins; also sold are impressive turnovers and pastries for $2 to $3 each.

⊞ **Zagora Cafe.** An exotic outdoor bazaar setting for unexotic burgers ($5.50), onion rings, and turkey sandwich platters ($6.25).

Congo

⊞ **Vivi Storehouse.** Near the Python coaster, this restaurant is open in season only from 11:45 A.M. to 4 P.M. Offerings include sandwich platters for about $5.59, and chicken fajitas.

Crown Colony

▲ **Crown Colony House.** A lovely 240-seat restaurant with spectacular views of the Serengeti Plain from its glass-walled Veldt Room. Another interesting location is the Library, stocked with antique books and a collection of photographs from Colonial days in Africa. A piano player entertains during meals.

Featured is Crown Colony's Famous Family-Style Chicken Dinner: platters of batter-dipped chicken, cole slaw, soft yeast rolls, dressing, mashed potatoes and gravy, garden vegetables, and cranberry relish. $8.95 per person; diners

12 and younger are billed a reasonable $3.95. The same platter can be ordered with batter-fried fish instead of chicken. Other offerings include a broiled Florida grouper sandwich for $7.95 or a chicken breast filet for $6.95.

KEY:

⏏ = Fast food

🍸 = Pub

🏠 = Full-service restaurant

There are only 12 tables next to the windows in the Veldt Room, and they go fast. No reservations are accepted. The least crowded times are before noon, and from 4 to 5:30 P.M.; each day a throng heads for the restaurant about 12:15 P.M. when the midday ice show lets out.

Timbuktu

⏏ **Das Festhaus.** The ceiling is an attractive blue-and-white striped tent. In the center of the large 1,200-seat hall is an elevated bandstand, home of the **Bavarian Colony Band and Dancers** who present the **International Show.** The show harks back to the early German settlers in Africa who made their home in Timbuktu. Also seen on the stage is the **Festival of Nations Show,** which features music and performances from around the world.

Offerings include the Alpine Platter (corned beef, potato salad, cabbage or sauerkraut, and drink), the German Sampler Platter (two sausages and side orders), or a turkey sandwich, each for about $6. There is also a spaghetti platter for $4.95, canneloni for $5.49, and a Safari kids spaghetti meal for $2.99. A range of Anheuser-Busch beers is offered.

Stanleyville

⏏ **Stanleyville Smokehouse.** Slow-smoked chicken, beef brisket, and pork ribs, served with french fries and cole slaw. Prices range from $5 to $7.95; a good deal is the $7.95 combo platter. Grab a bunch of napkins and prepare for a tasty mess.

⏏ **Bazaar Cafe.** Barbecue beef sandwich platters at $5 and salads for $2.

Bird Gardens

⏏ **Hospitality House.** Pepperoni and Chef's Combo pizzas, at $3 to $4 per slice. Tampa sandwiches—salami, turkey, cheese, and salad on a roll—sell for about $5.50. Free samples of Anheuser-Busch beers for adults.

Adventure Island

Although the tidal wave and rafting expeditions at Busch Gardens are guaranteed to dampen your hairdo, if you want to get really wet, you may want to head around the corner to Adventure Island.

The 22-acre water park, also owned by Busch Entertainment Corp., offers giant speed slides, body flumes, diving platforms, inner tube slides, a wave pool, water games, a white sand beach, and volleyball courts. Splash Attack is a huge water playground that offers squirt guns, waterfalls, slides, and a huge bucket that dumps water.

Aruba Tuba is a "tubular" slide that twists in and around and below Calypso Coaster; the ride can be enjoyed by solo riders or two at a time.

Calypso Coaster is a spiraling snake-like ride down an open flume in an inner tube or raft for two; **Rambling Bayou** is a slow float along a rambling river around bends, under bridges, and through a man-made rain forest; the **Caribbean Corkscrew** takes riders from a four-story tower down a fully enclosed, twisting translucent tube; **Water Moccasin** is a triple-tube water slide that cascades riders downward through a spiral before dumping them in a pool; **Tampa Typhoon** is a free-fall body slide that drops from a height of 76 feet before it levels out in a slick trough; and **Gulf Scream** is a speed slide in which riders can go as fast as 25 mph down a 210-foot slide.

**Adventure Island
1999 Ticket Prices**
Prices are subject to change and do not include tax

Adult 1-day	$23.95
Child (3–9) 1-day	$21.95

**Busch Gardens/
Adventure Island
Combo (1 day at
each park)**

Adult	$58.42
Child (3–9)	$51.22
Parking	$4.00

Everglides takes riders down a steep 72-foot double slide on water sleds that hydroplane up to 100 feet over a splash pool; a lift system carries the sleds back to the top of the slide platform. **Runaway Rapids** is a 34-foot-high artificial mountain that features five separate curving and twisting water flumes as long as 300 feet.

Paradise Lagoon is a 9,000-square-foot swimming pool fed by waterfalls; built into the surrounding cliffs are 20-foot-high diving platforms, a cable drop, a cannonball slide, and tube slides. Stretching overhead across the pool is a hand-over-hand rope walk. The **Endless Surf** is a 17,000-square-foot pool that mechanically produces three- to five-foot waves for body and rubber raft surfing.

The addition of heating for the outdoor pools now permits the park to be open from Valentine's Day through October; at the beginning and end of the season the park is open on weekends only.

🟥 The Florida Aquarium

Florida was here long before the Mouse, and one of the most spectacular collections of creatures that have an aquatic link can be found at the Florida Aquarium along downtown Tampa's waterfront.

Alligator hatchlings, roseate spoonbills, river otters, mangrove forests, coral reefs, and thousands of fish are among the exhibits awaiting visitors.

The Florida water story begins at the **Florida Wetlands Gallery**, which includes nearly 50 juvenile American alligators, river otters, and great horned owls. The **Florida Bays and Beaches Gallery** offers a diverse display that includes bonnethead sharks, Southern stingrays, flounder, and bighead sea robins; at the **Florida Bay Bottoms** gallery creatures include spiny lobsters.

The heart of the Florida Aquarium is its **Coral Reefs Gallery**, an unusual glimpse into a habitat ordinarily only explored by divers. The design simulates a 60-foot dive from shallow water reefs to deeper, darker waters. At the top of a walking tour, visitors discover a variety of corals populated by grouper, moray eel, and parrotfish. From there is a descent through the reef face into an underwater coral cave with windows that offer peeks into the fascinating denizens of the dark caverns.

And finally there is an underwater theater facing a 43-foot-wide, 14-foot-tall panoramic window. There you'll see coral colonies silhouetted by beams of sunlight from the surface, with brightly colored fishes and wandering sharks. Several times a day, divers descend into the tank, sometimes conducting question-and-answer sessions with viewers on the other side of the window.

Tickets in 1999 were $10.95 for adults, $5.95 for children (ages 3–12), and $9.95 for seniors (50+). For information, call (813) 273-4000. www.sptimes.com/Aquarium

⭐WOW⭐ MOSI: The Museum of Science and Industry

The amazing, expanding Museum of Science and Industry in Tampa has tripled in size to become the largest science center in the Southeast. Permanent exhibits include **The Amazing You** where you can tour the human body in all its complexity from DNA to cells to organs to individuals; the **Challenger Learning Center**, a living memorial to the crew of the shuttle orbiter *Challenger,* with a replica of a space vehicle and mission control; the **BioWorks Butterfly Garden**; and a flight simulator.

A new permanent exhibit showcases a pair of 75-foot-long diplodocus skeletons guarding the lobby. The skeletons were from remains found in Wyoming.

The dinosaurs were believed to weigh about 20 tons when they flourished in the western United States during the Jurassic period. Diplodocus carnegii were named in honor of industrialist Andrew Carnegie who funded the expedition that recovered the first specimens in 1901. Diplodocus means "double beam", referring to the chevron-shaped vertebrae in the creature's tail.

The **IMAX** Dome Theater includes a giant domed screen.

MOSI is located at 4801 East Fowler Avenue, one mile north of Busch Gardens Tampa. For information, call (800) 995-6674, (813) 987-6000, or consult a web page at www.mosi.org

Admission prices to the museum in 1999 were: $12 for adults, $8 for childrens (2-13), and $10 for seniors (50 and older).

BUSCH GARDENS

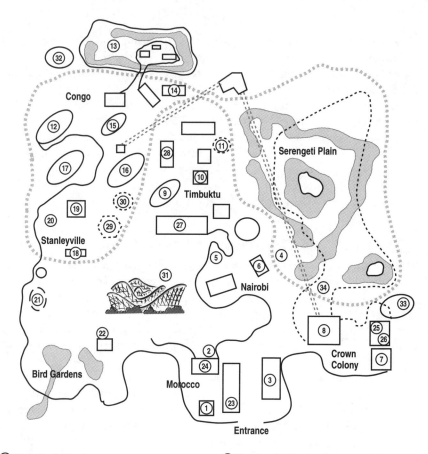

1. Marrakesh Theater
2. Sultan's Tent
3. Moroccan Palace Theater
4. Aldabra Tortoise Habitat
5. Myombe Reserve: The Great Ape Domain
6. Train Station
7. Akbar's Adventure Tours
8. Skyride and Monorail Station
9. The Scorpion
10. Carousel Caravan
11. The Phoenix
12. The Python
13. Congo River Rapids
14. Congo Station Transveldt Railroad
15. Claw Island
16. Stanley Falls Log Flume
17. Tanganyika Tidal Wave
18. Stanleyville Station Transveldt Railroad
19. Stanleyville Theater
20. Zambezi Theater
21. Land of the Dragons
22. Hospitality House
23. Boujad Bakery
24. Zangora Cafe
25. Crown Colony House
26. Anheuser Busch Hospitality Center
27. Das Festhaus
28. Oasis
29. Stanleyville Smokehouse
30. Bazaar Cafe
31. Gwazi
32. Kumba
33. Montu
34. The Edge of Africa

Redeem this coupon at any Universal Studios Florida® admission window for $2.00 OFF up to six one-day Studios Passes.

Present this coupon at any Universal Studios Florida® admission window to receive your discount. Discount valid for up to six people toward the purchase of a one-day adult or child Studio Pass through December 31, 2000. This coupon has no cash value. Not valid with any other specials or discounts. Offer subject to change without notice. Parking fee not included. Coupon must be presented at time of transaction. Not valid for special events requiring a separate admission charge.

Universal Studios Florida ® Universal Studios. Live the Movies SM & © 1999 Universal Studios. UNIVERSAL STUDIOS ESCAPE, a Universal Studios/Rank Group Joint Venture. All Rights Reserved.

For more information, call (407) 363-8000.
Take I-4 Exits 29B (westbound) or 30A (eastbound) and follow the signs to Universal.
Expires 12/31/00.

6136986001990

ECONOGUIDE TRAVEL BOOK A1 C1 A2 C2 A3 C3

Redeem this coupon at any UNIVERSAL STUDIOS ESCAPE℠ admission window for $3.00 OFF up to six 2-Day Escape Passes℠.

Present this coupon at any UNIVERSAL STUDIOS ESCAPE℠ admission window to receive your discount. Discount valid for up to six people toward the purchase of a 2-Day Escape Pass℠ through December 31, 2000. This coupon has no cash value. Not valid with any other specials or discounts. Offer subject to change without notice. Parking fee not included. Coupon must be presented at time of transaction.

Universal Studios Florida ® Universal Studios. UNIVERSAL STUDIOS ESCAPE, Universal Studios Islands of Adventure, Universal Studios CityWalk and Orlando Will Never Be The Same SM & © 1999 Universal Studios. UNIVERSAL STUDIOS ESCAPE, a Universal Studios/Rank Group Joint Venture. All Rights Reserved.

For more information, call (407) 363-8000.
Take I-4 Exits 29B (westbound) or 30A (eastbound) and follow the signs to Universal.
Expires 12/31/00.

6136986001990

ECONOGUIDE TRAVEL BOOK A1 C1 A2 C2 A3 C3

Redeem this coupon at the CityWalk® ticket window for $3.00 OFF up to six CityWalk Party Passes℠.

*Valid any night through 12/30/00 except New Year's Eve. Not valid with any other discount or for special ticketed events. No cash value. Some venues require 21 years of age or older for entrance. Valid photo ID required: valid passport, U.S. foreign or international driver's license; active U.S. military ID. Prices and entertainment subject to change. Individual cover charges and CityWalk Party Pass not valid for separate special ticketed events and concerts. Subject to availability. Restrictions apply.

CityWalk ® Universal Studios. UNIVERSAL STUDIOS ESCAPE, Universal Studios CityWalk, CityWalk Party Pass SM & © 1999 Universal Studios. UNIVERSAL STUDIOS ESCAPE, a Universal Studios/Rank Group Joint Venture. All Rights Reserved.

For more information, call (407) 363-8000.
Take I-4 Exits 29B (westbound) or 30A (eastbound) and follow the signs to Universal.
Expires 12/31/00.

6136986001990

ECONOGUIDE TRAVEL BOOK A1 C1 A2 C2 A3 C3

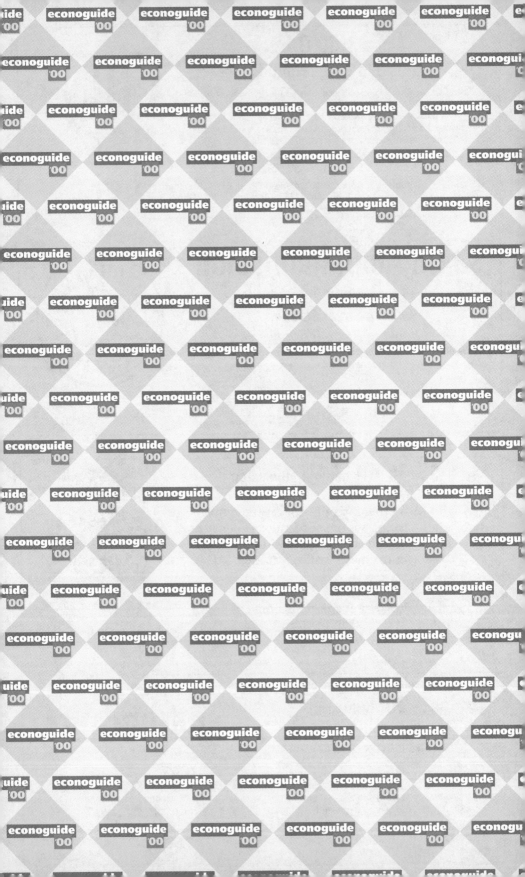

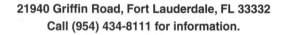

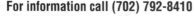

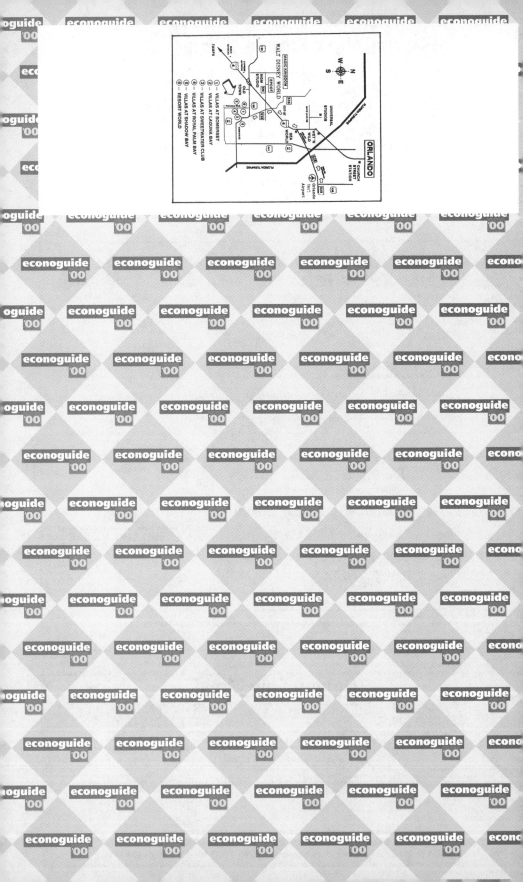

Orbit One Vacation Villas

2 bedroom/ 2 bath condo, $85.00 + tax

$139.00 + tax, Jan. 30–Feb. 12, Feb. 22–April 3, April 19–April 25, June 13–Aug. 29, Nov. 20, Nov. 28

$159.00 + tax, Feb. 13–21, April 4–18, Dec. 19–Dec. 22

Located 2 miles West of Walt Disney World®
Enjoy fully equipped kitchen, washer/dryer and full amenities

*Rates are subject to availability and do not include taxes.
Blackout dates: Dec. 23, 1999–Jan. 4, 2000

FL00-26

ISLAND ONE
R E S O R T S

(800) 634-3119
2345 Sand Lake Rd.
Orlando, FL 32809

Expires 9/1/2000

Bryan's Spanish Cove

2 bedroom/ 2 bath condo, $85.00 + tax

$139.00 + tax, Jan. 30–Feb. 12, Feb. 22–April 3, April 19–April 25, June 13–Aug. 29, Nov. 20, Nov. 28

$159.00 + tax, Feb. 13–21, April 4–18, Dec. 19–Dec. 22

Located 2 miles West of Walt Disney World®
Enjoy fully equipped kitchen, washer/dryer and full amenities

*Rates are subject to availability and do not include taxes.
Blackout dates: Dec. 23, 1999–Jan. 4, 2000

FL00-28

ISLAND ONE
R E S O R T S

(800) 634-3119
2345 Sand Lake Rd.
Orlando, FL 32809

Expires 9/1/2000

Parkway International Resort

2 bedroom/ 2 bath condo, $85.00 + tax

$139.00 + tax, Jan. 30–Feb. 12, Feb. 22–April 3, April 19–April 25, June 13–Aug. 29, Nov. 20, Nov. 28

$159.00 + tax, Feb. 13–21, April 4–18, Dec. 19–Dec. 22

Located 2 miles West of Walt Disney World®
Enjoy fully equipped kitchen, washer/dryer and full amenities

*Rates are subject to availability and do not include taxes.
Blackout dates: Dec. 23, 1999–Jan. 4, 2000

FL00-27

ISLAND ONE
R E S O R T S

(800) 634-3119
2345 Sand Lake Rd.
Orlando, FL 32809

Expires 9/1/2000

Isle of Bali

25% Off Room Rates Year-Round

1, 2, & 3 bedroom villas, minutes from the magic of
Walt Disney World®
Villas include full kitchens, washer/dryer & full amenities
Guests can also enjoy our very own on-site water park

Liki Tiki Lagoon

FL00-29

ISLAND ONE
R E S O R T S

(800) 634-3119
2345 Sand Lake Rd.
Orlando, FL 32809

Expires 9/1/2000

Savings are subject to certain restrictions, holiday blackouts, and availability.
Good for domestic and international travel that originates in the U.S.
Valid for flights on most airlines worldwide. Service fees apply.

Minimum Ticket Price	Save
$200	$25
$250	$50
$350	$75
$450	$100

HRN REBATE COUPON

Coupon Rules:

1. Must return this coupon to receive rebate.
2. Coupon expires 12/31/00.
3. Rebate mailed after check-out.
4. Coupons non-combinable.
5. Not retroactive.
6. After check-out, send this coupon with self-addressed stamped envelope to:
   HRN 8140 Walnut Hill Lane, Suite 203, Dallas, TX 75231.
7. Rebate check mailed within 2–3 weeks.
8. One rebate per customer.

1-800-USA-HOTELS.com

Where cost-savings, peace of mind and superior service are guaranteed
For All Your Hotel Needs Worldwide

Visit Us at Our Web Site:
www.1800usahotels.com
(800) 872-4683

VACATION TRAVEL SPECIALISTS

A DIVISION OF VTS TRAVEL ENTERPRISES, INC.

We realize that every vacation you take is a major personal investment and that you require value for your vacation dollar. Our vacation experts will offer exceptional service with no exceptions. Proficiency and knowledge of private villas, resorts, cruise lines, worldwide destinations and willingness to assist with every vacation need with one-on-one, personalized attention.

Visit Us at Our Web Site:
www.vtstravel.com/vacation.htm

Quick-Find Index to Attractions
(See also the detailed Contents)